Self and Society

Tenth Edition

Self and Society

A Symbolic Interactionist Social Psychology

John P. Hewitt
University of Massachusetts at Amherst

Boston   New York   San Francisco
Mexico City   Montreal   Toronto   London   Madrid   Munich   Paris
Hong Kong   Singapore   Tokyo   Cape Town   Sydney

Senior Series Editor: Jeff Lasser
Editorial Assistant: Erikka Adams
Senior Marketing Manager: Kelly May
Production Editor: Roberta Sherman
Editorial-Production and Electronic Composition Services: Progressive Publishing Alternatives
Composition Buyer: Linda Cox
Manufacturing Buyer: JoAnne Sweeney
Cover Administrator: Kristina Mose-Libon

For related titles and support materials, visit our online catalog at www.ablongman.com

Library of Congress Cataloging-in-Publication Data

Hewitt, John P.
    Self and society : a symbolic interactionist social psychology / John P. Hewitt.—10th ed.
      p. cm.
    Includes bibliographical references and index.
    ISBN 0-205-45961-7
      1. Social psychology.   2. Symbolic interactionism.   I. Title.
    HM1033.H49 2007
    302—dc22

                                                  2006046021

Printed in the United States of America
10 9 8 7 6 5 4 3 2 1   10 09 08 07 06

Contents

Preface

When this book was first published in 1976, I could not have imagined that three decades later I would be preparing its tenth edition. Nonetheless, thanks to continuing support from students and their professors, it has endured and thrived, as have I.

In addition to my usual efforts to update examples and polish the writing, I have concentrated my work for this edition in three areas. First, several parts of Chapter 3, The Self in its Social Setting, have again been extensively rewritten for the sake of clarity, and the section on self-esteem has been completely redone. Second, I have streamlined Chapter 5, Social Psychology and Social Order, removing what I believe were outdated discussions of collective behavior and crowds and emphasizing the creation and joining of social movements as one of the major ways in which social activities are coordinated. And third, I have drastically revised Chapter 6, Deviance and Social Order, moving away from an argument with classic theories of deviance in order to define the interactionist approach more clearly and to show better its connection to issues of social order.

Thanks are due to many people: To reviewers Jennifer Dunn, Southern Illinois University; Clark Hudspeth, Jacksonville State University; David Marple, Loyola Marymount University; John Mitrano, Central Connecticut State University; and Steve Worden, University of Arkansas, who made suggestions for improvement; to Jeffrey Lasser, Sociology Editor and Erikka Adams, Editorial Assistant, at Allyn and Bacon, Inc.; to Heather Meledin and her team at Progressive Publishing Alternatives; to students at the University of Massachusetts and to readers elsewhere who have communicated with me about it; and to faculty who have honored me by adopting it.

Most of all, I owe thanks to my best friend and wife Myrna Livingston Hewitt; my daughter, Professor Elizabeth A. Hewitt and her husband, Professor Jared Gardner; my son Gary L. Hewitt and his wife, Madère Olivar; and my wonderful grandchildren Elijah, Gideon, Margaret, and John. This edition is dedicated to the memory of my late parents, John H. Hewitt and Anna D. Hewitt.

Chapter 1

Social Psychology and Symbolic Interactionism

What's in a name? That which we call a rose
By any other name would smell as sweet.

These lines—spoken from her balcony by Juliet to Romeo in William Shakespeare's *Romeo and Juliet*—crystallize a major dilemma of human life. The names we use to categorize ourselves and others may seem to be merely labels, but they have profound consequences for what we can, may, must, or must not do. Juliet, a member of the Capulet family, and Romeo, a Montague, are barred from loving one another by the feud between their two families. "O be some other name," Juliet urges Romeo, and then poses the famous question. If he were not a Montague and she were not a Capulet, Juliet believes, they would be the same individuals but could marry.

Two names—*social psychology* and *symbolic interactionism*—categorize the subject matter and author of this book. *Social psychology* locates the book's content within a diverse body of research and theory that spans the disciplines of sociology and psychology. *Symbolic interactionism* locates the author within a particular tradition of sociological theory and research that is itself understood in varied ways both by those who subscribe to it and by those who do not. Hence, the first task in developing a symbolic interactionist social psychology is to explore these names, their origins, and their implications. Later in this chapter, I will compare symbolic interactionism with other perspectives in social psychology and develop a systematic statement of its major tenets.

What Is Social Psychology?

The term *social psychology* has been used for nearly a century by both psychologists and sociologists to designate a field of specialization within their respective disciplines. They began to share custody of the term in 1908, when two books were published, each with *social psychology* in its title. One, written by the psychologist William McDougall, argued that in order to understand how human beings are affected by society, it is necessary to study what he called the "native basis of the mind."[1] Like other scholars of that era, McDougall relied on the concept of *instinct*. He believed that it was necessary to discover the "innate tendencies of thought and action" that characterize human beings in order to explain the influences of society on them. The other book, by sociologist Edward A. Ross, placed more emphasis on social forces, arguing that certain processes come into existence because human beings associate with one another. Ross felt that the spread of fads and fashions, for example, cannot be explained simply by the nature and structure of the individual mind. The very fact of human association creates processes that cannot be reduced to the study of individuals.[2]

McDougall and Ross sounded themes that can still be heard in the work of social psychologists, for the members of each discipline are still oriented to their own traditions of theory, ways of doing research, and basic images of human behavior. Psychologists do not deny that social and cultural forces shape the environment within which such basic psychological processes as learning, cognition, or emotion take place. But their main interest is in the processes themselves rather than in their social setting. As a result, psychological social psychologists make the *individual* their main unit of analysis. Sociologists, on the other hand, seek to describe and explain patterns of conduct among larger aggregates of people—groups, communities, social classes, and even whole societies. Without denying the importance of the mind or of processes that operate at the individual level, sociological social psychologists give priority to human association and make *society* the beginning point of their analysis.

Psychologist Gordon Allport defined *social psychology* as the "attempt to understand and explain how the thought, feeling, and behavior of individuals are influenced by the actual, imagined, or implied presence of others."[3] Although the theoretical and research interests of psychologists have changed over time, his classic definition still captures the essence of their approach to social psychology. Studies of conformity, for example, have explored how the group shapes the thoughts and actions of individuals. In the historic experiments of Solomon Asch, subjects were induced to misjudge the relative lengths of lines (a task that should lead each subject to the same conclusion) by pressures to agree with the erroneous judgments of confederates of the experimenter. Confederates intentionally judged longer lines to be shorter in an effort to get subjects to conform to their opinions.[4] Likewise, in his studies of obedience, Stanley Milgram found that he could readily induce individuals to obey directions that required them to inflict apparent harm on others. Milgram showed that he could create laboratory conditions in which subjects would administer what they believed were electric shocks to other subjects, even over their strong protests and expressions of pain. The shocks were not real, of course, but the experiment was carefully staged to create the impression that they were.[5]

More recently, psychological social psychologists have paid considerable attention to the cognitive processes that shape individual behavior in social settings.[6] In order to act, they theorize, human beings must have considerable organized knowledge of themselves and of the social world. To explain what they do, therefore, social psychologists must study how people acquire, store, retrieve, and utilize this knowledge. As I note later in this chapter, the concept of the *schema*—an organized set of cognitions about a person, role, or situation—helps in this task. We humans do not meticulously catalog bits and pieces of information about the others with whom we interact, about ourselves, or about the situations we encounter. Rather, we form schemas—composite pictures—that shape what we see and experience, as well as what we remember. Professors are apt to see students, for example, not as individuals in all their variety, but as representatives of a type—"student"—and to act toward them as if they had the characteristics and motives typical of this type. Such schemas—in everyday language we call them *stereotypes*—crucially shape our actions. In a sense, they suggest Juliet's assertion may be erroneous; a rose by any other name may *not* smell as sweet.

Sociologists approach social psychology differently.[7] Their efforts are driven not by an effort to explain what individuals do and why they do it but by an effort to understand how organized social life is possible, how it works, and how it changes over time. Hence, they tend to focus on the social world itself rather than on the individual, treating social structure, culture, social roles, groups, organizations, and collective behavior not simply as environments within which individuals behave but rather as crucial levels of reality in their own right. They often use concepts similar to those developed by psychologists—what cognitive social psychologists call a "schema" the sociologist is apt to call a "typification"—but with a different purpose. For example, the psychologist is interested in how individual professors use a "student" schema to organize their understanding of and actions toward students, whereas the sociologist may be more interested in how the "student" typification came about and how it functions to organize relationships between students and professors.

Where a single term is used in differing ways by two disciplines, there is nothing to be gained by arguing about which approach is better or who has a prior claim on using the term. Psychologists and sociologists are not Capulets and Montagues, and their respective offspring are free to marry or not in accordance with their desires. The two disciplines are nonetheless two separate families, each with its own ideas about how to pursue the task of studying and explaining human conduct.

My goal in this book is to present and develop a symbolic interactionist approach to social psychology. *Symbolic interactionism* is a general sociological perspective, and its theories and research are not limited to the realm of social psychology. Indeed, the basic concepts and theoretical insights of symbolic interactionism developed here can serve as a foundation for sociology as a whole and not only social psychology. But symbolic interactionism is centrally concerned with the questions that have preoccupied sociological social psychologists. It is those questions—chief among them the matter of how the individual and the society are linked—that are central to this book.

Sociologists take a distinctive view of the relationship between the person and the social world. On one hand, they say, society is the source of human knowledge, language, skills, orientations, and motives. Individuals are born into and shaped by a society that will persist long after they are dead. They are products of that society and its culture. On the other hand, that same society owes its existence and continuity to the conduct of its members. Neither "society" nor "culture" actually does anything, for both are abstractions. Only people act, and by acting, they create and perpetuate their society and its culture.[8]

This paradoxical relationship between individual and society leads to some difficult questions: How does the individual acquire from society the capacity to be an active, functioning member? Indeed, *what* does the individual acquire—what skills, knowledge, ideas, and beliefs? How do the individual and the cooperative acts of its socialized members create and sustain a society? How can society shape the very individuals on whose actions its existence depends, and how can it live on when its members die? How can we say that people create society if they are created by it?

Questions such as these are particularly important because learning has replaced biologically programmed instincts or drives as the most important factor underlying human behavior. The human world is primarily cultural, and human conduct is shaped by the knowledge, skills, values, beliefs, and ways of living held in common by the members of society. Thus, an orderly and persisting society is not guaranteed by our biological programming but by what we have learned. And, by the same token, individuals are not guided by instinct but must themselves rely on society and culture for their own survival.

The assertion that behavior is shaped primarily by culture begs the question of how its influence works. Human sexuality, for example, is profoundly influenced by culture. Human beings find a great variety of things—female breasts, the size of genitalia, feet, spanking, leather clothing—sexually arousing. They engage in sexual activity in a variety of places—bedrooms, beaches, public restrooms, before cameras. They have phone sex, virtual sex, and sex that utilizes the Internet to control mechanical sexual toys remotely, a practice known as "teledildonics." They enjoy sex with others of the same sex, the opposite sex, both sexes, animals, and themselves. This variety is brought about by culture, not human nature. But how does culture shape human sexual preferences and conduct? Indeed, how does it govern anything that human beings do?

Sociologists have adopted varied attitudes toward the problem of linking society and culture to actual conduct. Some have argued that our attention should be focused on *culture* and *social structure* rather than on conduct itself. In their view, patterns of conduct are so profoundly determined by culture and social structure that the question of *how* these forces actually shape behavior can safely be ignored. After all, they assert, much of social life is quite routine: People perform the same tasks over and over, the situations and social relationships in which they find themselves are pretty much the same from one day to the next, and their culture essentially provides ready-made ways of behaving. As a result, explaining how culture and society actually shape conduct is less interesting and important than explaining the origins and persistence of cultural patterns and social structures.

Sociologists who adopt this point of view have developed numerous concepts designed to describe and help explain social phenomena. For example, the concept of *social class* refers to the fact that societies are typically divided into segments whose members have a similar position in the division of labor, comparable education and incomes, and similar views of themselves and their places in the world. One social class, for example, might consist of small business owners, another of service workers, and another of corporate managers. In each case, the similarities are likely to be greater among the members of the class than between the members of that class and those of another. Class is a structural concept; its focus is on the patterned and repetitive conduct and social relationships that can be observed within and between various groups in a society at any given point in history.

A structural perspective has many attractive features. Human social life is highly repetitive, and it is necessary to look beyond the details of individual behavior and its formation in order to see patterns and regularities. Moreover, although society ultimately depends on the conduct of individuals, their actions and interactions typically have conse- quences they do not foresee and frequently do not recognize. The everyday actions of peo- ple as they work, eat and drink, play, make love, socialize, vote, take walks, and attend meetings *do* seem powerfully influenced by social class. Their actions not only maintain familiar patterns of behavior but pass them on to their children, who, in enacting these pat- terns, re-create the structures of social class.

Although it is crucial to study social and cultural patterns, confining attention to this level of analysis has serious drawbacks. First, even though social life is highly repetitive, it is not completely so, for patterns change over time, sometimes slowly and other times quite dramatically and quickly. Contemporary men and women in Canada or the United States, for example, inherit social roles and images of one another that were created during the nineteenth century but that have been periodically modified since then. Although some still believe women lack the political or intellectual skills for public life and that their tal- ents and moral obligations should confine them to home and family, the majority now rejects those beliefs. Challenged both by feminism and by the economic facts of contem- porary life, practices that once seemed rooted in human nature now seem antiquated, and patterns that once seemed entrenched have changed.

A second limitation of focusing strictly on patterns and regularities is that social arrangements are as often matters of conflict and controversy as matters of widespread agree- ment. The contemporary United States, for example, is rife with conflict between a substantial minority who considers itself religiously very conservative and a majority whose orientation is more secular. Whether the issue is abortion, the place of religion in public life, homosexuality, or the roles of men and women, there are fundamental disagreements. To grasp how the soci- ety works and to understand the place of the individual within it, we cannot only study the dominant secular pattern but also must look at the tension between it and the socially and reli- giously conservative resistance to it. Or, to take a different example, the culture of the United States is often described as "individualistic," meaning individuals are encouraged to think of themselves before others, to believe that they are the authors of their own destinies, and to resist the demands of family or community when they think it necessary or desirable. At the same time, however, members of this society give generously to charities, belong to churches and other organizations in large numbers, and often seem to crave the intimate connections of family and friendship. Does the social pattern consist of "individualism" or "communitarian- ism," or does it lie in an ongoing tension between the two?

The facts of social change and of cultural patterns in conflict make it difficult to explain conduct as simply determined by existing forms of society and culture. We must look at it as shaped not only by these external forces but also by the efforts of people who work within, and sometimes *against,* an inherited culture and existing social arrangements. People are not thoroughly and passively socialized to accept and reproduce culture and society, for under many circumstances they resist and rebel, finding ways to escape from the patterns of conduct that are urged upon them. They are not merely agents of an existing social order but are also active agents who create and change that order.

A great many sociologists, therefore, do not believe that they can concentrate on social structure and culture and ignore conduct. They recognize that they must have a basic *theory of action*—that is, an account of how people actually form their conduct in everyday life that can be related to the society and culture that both sustains and modifies.

The main task of sociological social psychology is to create such a theory of action. Its job is to examine the details of action and interaction, to show how people are influenced by society and culture, but also to show how their everyday actions both sustain and change these larger realities. To do so, the social psychologist must concentrate on such topics as socialization, the nature of the person, and the actual formation of conduct in everyday life. At the same time, however, culture and social structure cannot be ignored: The person is created and transformed, and everyday life takes place, within a framework provided by society and culture.

A theory of action can be based on a great variety of theoretical perspectives. The theory to be developed here—symbolic interactionism—has been influential within sociology. My next task is to show in a general way how symbolic interactionists approach a theory of action that can account for the influence of society and culture on the person but also to explain how action and interaction both reproduce and change society and culture.

What Is Symbolic Interactionism?

Symbolic interactionism is a distinctively American sociological perspective whose roots lie in the philosophy of pragmatism.[9] This philosophical tradition, identified with such scholars as Charles S. Peirce, William James, John Dewey, and George Herbert Mead, contains an important clue to its outlook in its name, *pragmatism,* the commonplace meaning of which is "practical." Proponents of this approach to philosophy view living things as attempting to make practical adjustments to their surroundings. As philosophers, they are interested in the fundamental questions of philosophy: What is truth? What is good? What is knowledge? How do we acquire knowledge? How do we know that we know the truth? In seeking answers to these questions, they argue that the truth of an idea or the meaning of a statement is dependent on its practical consequences. An idea, they say, is true if it works. Pragmatists see all living creatures as attempting to meet the demands of their environments in practical ways. They view knowledge as continually confronting practical tests of its usefulness. The lens through which they view truth thus emphasizes the consequences of ideas rather than their logical elegance or internal consistency.

Pragmatists see living things as probing and testing their environment. Truth is, therefore, not absolute, but is always relative to the needs and interests of organisms. An idea—for example, the idea that the sun rises in the east—is "true" if it leads to empirical predictions that help people adjust to the requirements and circumstances of their world. Questions of how members of a species know and interact with their environment are, for pragmatists, matters of great moment, not merely peripheral concerns. Knowing and acting, in the pragmatist view, are intimately linked: We act on the basis of our ideas about the world. The reality of the world is not merely something that is "out there" waiting to be discovered by us, but is actively created as we act in, and toward, the world.

What is the relationship between philosophical pragmatism and symbolic interactionism? A brief overview of the work of George Herbert Mead can provide an important part of the answer to this question. Contemporary symbolic interactionism reflects the influence of Mead, Dewey, Peirce, and James, and various symbolic interactionists trace their ideas to one or another of these figures. But if there is a single intellectual ancestor honored by all interactionists, it is Mead. He was not nearly as well known as Dewey and James, who were important public intellectuals in their time, nor thought by philosophers to be as important as Peirce. Nonetheless, Mead's theory of mind, directly or indirectly, profoundly shaped the work of symbolic interactionists. His work comes to us primarily through his students at the University of Chicago, who assembled their notes on his courses in social psychology into a book, *Mind, Self, and Society,* after his death in 1931.[10]

Mead's theory of mind attempts to account for the origins and development of human intelligence by linking it to the process of evolution by viewing mind and conduct as inescapably linked and by showing that the origins of human mind lie in human society. Mead felt that human intelligence emerged from a process of evolutionary change. Moreover, he was convinced that the mind is not a separate, disembodied entity but an integral aspect of the *behavior* of the species. He rejected the *dualistic* view of mind and body that had plagued philosophy, a view that led people to separate the physical organism from intelligence and to imagine the latter as existing within some ethereal realm of ideas. For Mead, mind, body, and conduct are inseparable aspects of a process of evolution that has produced a uniquely human life form.

All organisms come into existence and persist (or fail to persist) in interaction with their environments. Their physical structures and their capacities to act do not exist in a vacuum but are created under specific environmental conditions. Nor are organisms merely the passive receptors of stimuli that emanate from their surroundings. Each organism has a set of capacities to respond to its world; bees, for example, are sensitive to the angle of light coming from the sun and use this knowledge in locating and returning to food sources. Humans are sensitive to the nuances of language and employ this capacity in everything they do. Such capacities have evolved over long periods of time as environmental conditions have changed, mutations have appeared, and new structures have developed. An organism's capacities to respond to the environment help to make the environment what it is. The sun is an important part of the bee's environment, for example, because the bee has the capacity to respond to the sun's position. And to be able to respond to the environment is also to be able to act on it. The human child who learns how to react to the parental "no" is acting on his or her parents, obeying their demands in order to influence their acts and thus secure personal needs for nurture or praise, every bit as much as he or she is being acted on by the parents.

In Mead's time, many social scientists explained human mind and conduct as the result of instincts. If people cared for their children, resisted change, or sought novel experiences, it was believed they did so because they were programmed with particular maternal, conservative, or novelty-seeking instincts. Mead argued that human conduct was far too complex to be explained by instincts. Although the complex individual conduct and social coordination of the insect society—the beehive, for example—might be explained by genetically programmed (and therefore largely unlearned) forms of behavior, there is too much cultural diversity, novelty, and complexity for instincts to be a satisfactory explanation of human conduct. Thus, Mead rejected the instinctivist sociological and psychological theories of the time.

Mead also found much to criticize in *behaviorism,* whose foremost exponent was the psychologist John Watson. The behaviorists insisted that the true path to the explanation of human behavior (or any animal behavior) lay in paying strict attention only to what the scientists could *directly* observe—both behavior and environmental events (stimuli) associated with the behavior. They emphasized that behavior was learned, and they sought to uncover the laws that governed the learning of behavioral responses to environmental stimuli. The behaviorists eschewed any concept of mind, saying that what is essential in conduct is not what people think they are doing but what they observably do and how they are rewarded for doing it. Mental events—thoughts, ideas, images—are for them mostly irrelevant because, they believed, such events cannot be observed.

Mead felt that the behaviorists' emphasis on behavior was correct, but he thought that internal, mental events were crucial to the explanation of conduct. Contrary to Watson, Mead argued that mental events are a form of behavior that can be observed. Human beings talk about inner experiences and in so doing make them observable. Moreover, behaviorism had far too individual a focus for Mead's taste. Although it is true that it is the individual who behaves, individual behavior is rarely disconnected from the acts of others. Human behavior is socially coordinated, often in very complex ways over extended periods of time, and an explanation of behavior that fails to take this fact into account is doomed from the start. Most individual acts are a part of more complex, socially coordinated activities involving several people. Shaking hands, for example, is not merely a bit of behavior in which one person extends a hand in response to the stimulus of the extended hand of another, but it is also a socially coordinated act in which the past experiences and future hopes of two individuals, as well as established social conventions, are important. Shaking hands to seal a business agreement differs from shaking hands in a situation where one of the individuals was hoping for a kiss. To abstract the individual's part of an act from a more extensive social act is to attempt to explain far less than what we can and must explain.

It was Mead's genius to provide an explanation of the nature and origins of human intelligence—the mind—that could deal with inner experience and at the same time take into account the social nature of human life. Although a full account of his theory and its application in contemporary symbolic interactionism will have to await Chapter 2 of this book, the outlines of Mead's contribution are sketched here.

Many living things other than humans exist in association with others of their own kind and are profoundly affected by this. Other mammals vary in their gregariousness, for example, but all have at least some forms of association with one another, whether as members of a herd or of a small band of primates whose social organization and interdependence are more complex. Mead argued, however, that the basis for human interaction differs substantially from that of other animals, including our primate cousins. Among other animals, interaction takes a form that Mead called the "conversation of gestures." Each individual, in beginning an act, engages in overt and visible actions that can be detected by others and serve as stimuli to their responses. A dog, beginning a fight with another dog, bares its teeth and assumes an aggressive stance; its physical gestures are stimuli that key an aggressive response from the other. Interaction thus proceeds between the animals, with the control of each dog's behavior effectively in the hands of the other.

It is quite otherwise for humans, as Mead so incisively saw and explained. First, the most important gestures for people are *linguistic*. Humans are animals who possess language and whose conduct occurs in a world of words. We are attuned not just to the overt bodily movements of others but also to a complex set of vocalizations that precede and accompany their acts and our own. Second, these vocal gestures—acts of speech—have the unique property of arousing in the one using them nearly the same response as they arouse in the others to whom they are directed. They are, in Mead's words, "significant symbols." Shouting the word "Fire!" in a public place, for example, does not merely elicit a flight response from those present. The word creates, both in the crowd and in the one who shouts it, a certain attitude—a readiness to act in a particular way, an image of the conduct appropriate to the situation, a plan of action. It is this creation of a common *attitude* in both symbol user and symbol hearer that makes possible the individual's control of his or her own conduct. People who, by anticipating what others will do in response to their acts, are able to plan their own subsequent acts have attained *control* over their own conduct. For example, anticipating the possibility of panic flight if I hastily alert a crowd to the presence of fire, I may decide instead to attempt a more subdued, quieter warning that will improve the chances for safe evacuation. When I do this, I exert control over my behavior.

The significant symbol not only affords humans a form of control over their own conduct that other animals do not possess but also gives them a form of consciousness not found elsewhere: consciousness of *self*. Our capacity to employ symbols in imagining the responses of others to our own acts also gives us the capacity to be conscious of ourselves. To use a term to be developed in greater detail later, we are able to become *objects* to ourselves; that is, we become able to act toward ourselves as we act toward others, to be one of the many things, ideas, persons, or experiences of which we are conscious and toward which our activity is directed. We can name ourselves, think about ourselves, talk to ourselves, imagine ourselves acting in various ways, love or hate ourselves, and feel proud or ashamed of ourselves; in short, we can act toward ourselves in all the ways we can act toward others.

Mead's account of human behavior, mind, and self is a significant milestone in human self-understanding. His theory stresses the explanation of human conduct in scientific terms on the basis of scientific observation. At the same time, it admits inner experiences as capable of observation, for we are able to report and communicate to others about our private experiences and feelings by using significant symbols. His theory recognizes the sociability of human beings as a primary fact of their evolution and existence and uses this fact to explain how human beings mind their environment in distinctive ways. His theory puts the human experience of self on center stage. Human beings are conceived as creatures whose evolution has yielded a capacity for self-control.

Chapter 2 of this book builds on these basic ideas, developing a conceptual framework for a symbolic interactionist social psychology. As a preface to this task, the remainder of this chapter will develop a general overview of contemporary symbolic interactionism, first by showing its major points of similarity to and difference from other theoretical perspectives and then by stating its major tenets.

Other Theoretical Approaches

Contemporary sociologists have looked to a variety of theoretical sources, past and present, for answers to the questions Mead addressed in his social psychology. By examining a few of these alternative theoretical perspectives, we can better grasp the interactionist perspective. The goal is not to demonstrate the superiority of symbolic interactionism, for such an effort is inimical to the spirit of pragmatism, which regards all knowledge as tentative and probing and never complete. Rather, the purpose is to illuminate both symbolic interactionism and the social world by showing how a variety of theories conceive and approach their subject matter. Learning theory, psychoanalytic theory, exchange theory, phenomenology and ethnomethodology, social cognition, social constructionism, and postmodern theory are the approaches we will consider. All play a role in the contemporary understanding of social psychology, and all have had an impact on contemporary symbolic interactionism.

Learning Theory

The behaviorism of John Watson, which was already mentioned in discussing the ideas of Mead, provided the foundations for a school of psychological thought that dominated much of twentieth-century psychology. This approach is variously known as *behaviorism, learning theory,* or, in its more explicitly social psychological form, *social learning theory.*[11] Behaviorism has historically refused to consider unobservable, "mental," and "subjective" phenomena, choosing instead to emphasize directly observable behavior and environmental events. Among contemporary psychological social psychologists, strict behaviorism has by and large given way to an interest in cognitive phenomena of the very sort Watson ruled out of consideration. Nonetheless, it will be helpful to our understanding of symbolic interactionism to contrast it with the strict behaviorist approach.

The basic ideas of behaviorism are familiar to students who have studied psychology and know something of classical (or respondent) conditioning and operant conditioning. *Classical conditioning* is typified in the work of the Russian psychologist Ivan Pavlov, who demonstrated that a response, such as a dog's salivating in the presence of food, could also be elicited by an unrelated stimulus, such as the sound of a bell, if the bell were rung each time the food was presented to a hungry dog. After a certain number of trials in which food and a bell are simultaneously presented, the bell alone will produce the salivation response. This response is involuntary (the dog has no control over it), but it can be associated by the dog with a stimulus other than the one (food) that usually elicits it. *Operant conditioning* focuses on more voluntary behavior—that behavior over which the organism has some control and that it can produce in order to yield a certain effect. In this form of conditioning, for which the psychologist B. F. Skinner is the chief architect of ideas, the stimulus *follows* the response. That is, some behavior (such as a pigeon pecking on a certain spot on its cage) is followed by a specific event (such as a kernel of corn being released into the cage). If the event (stimulus) is positively valued by the organism, the behavior is more likely to be repeated in the future. Under these conditions we would say that the behavior has been positively reinforced.

How do the principles of classical and operant conditioning provide a basis for social psychology? The governing idea is that the individual's environment, including the other human beings with whom interaction occurs, is the source of stimuli—both those that trigger classical, involuntary responses and those that serve as positive and negative reinforcement or as punishment for voluntary activities. Thus, one might say that the child learns a repertoire of behavior from his or her parents, who provide reinforcements or punishments for the child's behaviors. The child learns to brush his or her teeth or say "Thank you," for example, because he or she is positively reinforced for doing so and perhaps punished for not doing so. An important extension of learning theory is the observation that learning in social contexts is frequently vicarious: By *observing* the behavior of others and the rewards their actions earn, we are able to learn what they are learning without making any actual trials ourselves. The child can learn that he or she will get praise for being polite to adults by observing other children experience this reinforcement. The child can then enact this behavior, get the reinforcement, and thus experience *model learning*. This theory of *social learning* expands the basic ideas of learning theory and adapts them to the realities of social life as we observe it: People learn by observation and imitation and not simply by blind trial and error.

Symbolic interactionists find much that is appealing in this perspective. Behaviorists, like symbolic interactionists, emphasize the study of actual and observable behavior. Their perspective makes learning an important process, and symbolic interactionists agree that people learn their repertory of conduct. Moreover, there is much in the behaviorists' ideas about operant conditioning that symbolic interactionists like. The idea that a future stimulus (namely, the reward associated with an activity) can control a behavior is an important one, for it is a way of conceiving behavior as being goal oriented. Much of what we do seems designed to produce some desired future effect.

But in the eyes of symbolic interactionists, classical behaviorism also has some serious flaws. Although both classical and operant conditioning can be found in human behavior, the symbolic interactionist also finds evidence of processes that are not observed in other animals. The interactionist would say, for example, that we can become *aware* of our conditioned responses, whether they are respondent or operant. We can and typically do become aware of the relationship of present conduct to future events. Indeed, much of what we do is intended to influence what will happen to us in the future—whether in the next moment or the next year. *Self*-awareness is crucial to intentional behavior, for it is the person's capacity to be conscious of his or her own present and future actions that makes it possible for these actions to be controlled. Becoming *aware* of the relationship between what I do at this moment and some future event is the first step in acquiring the capacity to control that response. And my ability to govern my behavior so as to secure some goal depends on my capacity to imagine myself acting in alternative ways so that one particular act can be chosen.

Moreover, although contemporary behaviorism conceives the social environment as an important source of stimuli, it still tends toward a microscopic view of behavior in which the complexities and real significance of that environment are ignored. Think of our earlier example of a child learning that politeness and obedience produce such rewards as praise and affection. To apply behaviorism in a very strict manner, one has to assume that the child, whether gradually on a trial-and-error basis or more quickly and vicariously, learns to behave in ways that produce the desired results. Symbolic interactionists argue that there is more to the process of learning than the reinforcement of specific acts. People seem to be guided not merely by rewards but also by more general ideas of how their own conduct is expected to be fitted to the conduct of others. Although in the earliest stages of our experience these ideas may be fairly concrete ("If I eat all my food, my mother will be happy with me"), they become gradually more complex and abstract as the person grows older. Our conduct comes to be guided more by general principles than by discrete reactions to concrete situations.

For the symbolic interactionist, it is the individual's conception of self in relation to the social group of which he or she is a part that underlies the capacity to be aware of his or her own responses, to control these responses, and to formulate hypotheses about the expectations and responses of others. One develops an awareness not just of the specific behavior that will produce a particular result in a given situation but more generally of one's place in the life of the group as a whole. One knows that one will be called on to play various roles, that the roles one enacts must somehow mesh with the roles of others, and that one must control one's own acts so that they fit with the acts of other people. Thus, the interactionist conception of how conduct is learned is more global, more complex, more social, and more dynamic than that posed by a simple learning model.

Psychoanalytic Theory

Few social psychologists work explicitly from a psychoanalytic perspective, but the influence of Sigmund Freud and his intellectual followers on the social sciences as a whole and on our everyday, commonsense ideas about psychology has been considerable.[12] We must, therefore, make some effort to convey the essence of this perspective. There is much more to Freud's theory than the ideas presented here, of course, but these are the ideas of most immediate interest to sociologists.

Freudian theory has a view of both the nature of society and of the development and vicissitudes of the individual personality. Freud regarded the individual and society as in conflict with one another and argued that we can grasp the dynamics of society and culture, as well as the place of the individual in society, only by understanding the dynamics of personality.

Freud's conception of personality divides it into three components. The *id* is the source of the individual's drives, instincts, and behavioral energy. The forces that move behavior—such as sexuality or aggression—are biological and universal, are exceedingly powerful, and are the central fact with which the individual as well as the society must contend. The id is the source of motivation and supplies the person with images of those objects that will meet its needs. It is, for example, the source of both the sexual drive and images of sexual activities or partners that will satisfy that drive. The second component of personality is the *ego,* which is a kind of operating mechanism that searches in the external world for opportunities to meet the organism's needs. The ego lives in the real world; that is, it confronts the external world and attempts to secure objects that will actually satisfy the person's drives. In a sense, the ego is driven by the id, for it attempts to accomplish what the id wants. In doing so, it must also cope with the third component of personality, the *superego,* which is the internalization of society and culture in the individual. The superego represents what society stands for, as opposed to what the id wants, and it is as powerful and demanding a force as the latter. It represents morality, perfection, and the socially necessary as against the unremitting biological imperatives of the id. The ego can thus be thought of as the negotiator or manager that is caught between these two powerful forces. The ego has the difficult tasks of trying to satisfy both the id and the superego simultaneously, and in doing so it relies on many defensive techniques (defense mechanisms) whose objectives are to deceive the id and superego into thinking that their imperatives are being met. One of the more common mechanisms is repression, whereby potentially dangerous ideas or wishes are pushed out of the conscious part of the mind and into the unconscious. For example, if the values of the society view sexuality negatively, the ego may deal with the insistent sexuality of the person by repressing it, pushing sexuality out of consciousness.

Symbolic interactionists, like other sociological social psychologists, have generally either ignored psychoanalysis or rejected it because of its weakest features instead of attempting to grapple with the problems it poses for social theory. In particular, most social psychologists reject Freud's biological and instinctual theory of motivation—his image of human beings as seething pots of impulses barely contained by a thin veneer of civilization. Symbolic interactionists have felt that the relationship between society and the person is more cooperative and that culture does not invariably battle biology. In their view, humans are animals without instincts; culture replaces the biological guidance that the human species has lost in the course of its evolution. As a result, culture guides human beings rather than restrains their antisocial impulses. If this is so, much of the force of Freud's theory seems to be lost.

It is possible, however, to reject a theory of instincts and a theory of culture and biology as hopelessly pitted against one another without also rejecting some more important and valid insights of psychoanalysis. Donald Carveth argued that the instinctual basis of motivation can be rejected without discarding other aspects of Freud's theory. Indeed, according to Carveth, the theory of instincts *must* be rejected in order to get to the really important insights of psychoanalysis.[13] In a general sense, Freud's theories strongly caution against an oversocialized conception of human beings. Although culture does take the place of instinct, it does not automatically or mechanically dictate conduct. There is no lack of conflict between people or between the person and society, and what people do often seems unpredictable and inexplicable.

Moreover, it is not necessary to posit antisocial biological drives in order to explain how society and the individual come into conflict. In both psychoanalysis and symbolic interactionism, there is a basis for viewing the individual and society as in a natural state of tension with one another, although not in a constant state of war. Like Freud, symbolic interactionists say that acts have their beginnings beneath the level of consciousness. Psychoanalysis posits an unconscious with a life of which the individual is unaware and does not control. Symbolic interactionists have been reluctant to adopt this conception but do acknowledge that people only become aware of the nature and directions of their acts after they have begun, thus acknowledging that some part of mental life is unconscious. Symbolic interactionists also imbue the person with the capacity to inhibit and redirect incipient acts—to say "no" to the impulses that arise within them, impulses that are derived from culture as well as from individual plans and purposes. The result is that the individual is no puppet of society but an active creature struggling for self-control and sometimes developing plans and purposes that run counter to what culture demands or encourages.

Exchange Theory

A third influential approach to sociological social psychology is the broad tradition known as exchange theory.[14] Drawing on intellectual sources as diverse as behavioral psychology and microeconomics, this perspective focuses on exchanges of goods or benefits between people. It begins with a key social fact: People must obtain much of what they want or need from others. Not only material things, such as food or shelter, but also such social goods as status or approval can be obtained only if the individual interacts with others. The resources and skills people need frequently lie in the hands of others who must be induced to give them up. People are, in other words, interdependent, and the nature, extent, and consequences of this interdependence are the focus of exchange theory.

Although there are several varieties of exchange theory, underlying most approaches is a common set of ideas about the nature of human conduct and the relationships that build up among people as they exchange benefits. Linda Molm and Karen Cook[15] have described four core assumptions of exchange theory, here paraphrased as follows:

- Exchange relations develop among people within "structures of mutual dependence."
- People act in ways that tend to increase outcomes they value or desire and to decrease outcomes they dislike.
- Over time, social relationships develop and are sustained as people develop mutually beneficial exchanges.
- A valued outcome becomes less valued the more it is provided.

Taken as a whole, these core assumptions portray a social world of interdependence based on the exchange of those things people need or want.

Exchange theory argues that interdependence is socially structured. Exchange relationships develop where social arrangements dictate that actors must secure the things they value from one another. Exchange relationships develop between factory owners and workers, for example, because the owners need the labor of the workers and the workers need the money their labor earns in order to purchase the necessities of life for their families. The interdependence need not be equal, for one participant may be more dependent on the development of a relationship than the other. If there is a large unemployed or underemployed work force from which to hire workers, then the owners are less dependent on any particular worker than is the worker on the owners. If there are many places to work and few workers to fill the jobs, the opposite is true. Nor must participants in an exchange be mutually dependent for everything. Workers, for example, may be dependent on owners for an income, but they will seek other gratifications—confirmation of their worth, emotional support, and informal social contacts—from other sources.

Exchange relationships develop in an established social world that shapes the way people depend on one another and exchange benefits. Some people have resources—money, land, tools, knowledge—that others need, and the unequal distribution of these resources determines social exchange. Established cultural definitions and expectations also structure relationships of dependence. In the nineteenth-century United States, for example, a popular ideal held that men should work outside the home to earn an income for their families and women should stay home to maintain the house, raise children, and nourish the family's emotional life. Women's rights to own and control property were restricted; men were expected to display strength and to keep their emotions in check. These cultural definitions—the gender order—shaped patterns of dependence between men and women and thus also the character of exchange between them. Men's labor at work provided the income needed to purchase the material necessities of life, and women's emotional labor provided for their men a "haven in a heartless world" of occupational striving.

The basic motivational premise of exchange theory is that people act in ways that tend to increase outcomes they value and decrease those they do not. In other words, over time, individuals will tend to do that which earns them benefits they want or need and to avoid doing those things that result in excessive costs. Over time, children will behave in ways that earn parental approval and avoid punishment, students will do what gets good grades and prevents criticism, and politicians will do what gets them votes and escapes their constituents' ire. People will do these things, of course, only if they value them and if they have the resources or opportunity to do so. The proposition that students will do what earns them good grades is true if they value good grades and have what it takes to earn them. Politicians will act so as to get votes if they value votes more than other goods—such as personal integrity or honesty—and if they can figure out what will get them elected.

Exchange theory says nothing about *what* people are likely to value. In other words, the theory predicts that if people value something, they will strive to achieve it and will tend, over time, to behave in ways that secure it. But the theory does not attempt to explain what people value. Thus, the theory is somewhat less individualistic or egocentric than it seems, for individuals may value that which benefits particular others or the community as a whole and not just themselves. A child's values may favor hugs, candy bars, or a bigger allowance for himself or herself, but they may also favor a happy or contented pair of parents. Or, in a worse case, the child may value parental actions that confirm the child's image of himself or herself, even if that image is negative and the confirming actions of parents are disapproving and punishing.

Do people consciously or unconsciously select behavior that increases valued outcomes and decreases undesirable ones? Contemporary exchange theorists argue that the process may range from largely unconscious to very conscious. Exchange theory is based partly on the precepts of learning theory. That is, over time, action and reward become linked, even if the individual is not consciously aware of the connection. The more an action is rewarded, the more it tends to be repeated. Exchange theorists, however, are generally willing to consider what behavioral psychologists are not—namely, that people may consciously and rationally calculate what will get them the things they value. Thus, a child may not consciously construct actions that earn parental disapproval and thus confirm a negative view of self. However, the student who always agrees with the professor's opinions may do so in a calculated effort to earn the professor's favor and thus improve the chances of a good grade. Likewise, a person may turn to the same people for help with his or her problems without being conscious of doing so. But he or she may also calculate rationally that some people will give help whereas others will deny it.

Taken together, these first two key precepts of exchange theory—socially structured interdependence and the tendency to repeat successful actions—imply a third basic idea: Over time, social relationships between specific partners will tend to stabilize. That is, as people find dependable sources of the things they value, they will tend to return to these sources over and over again. If two people meet and begin to provide each other with companionship, approval, and aid, their relationship as friends will gradually stabilize. Each will find the other a reliable source of those valued goods; the behavior of each will, in effect, reward the behavior of the other.

The development of a stable relationship depends on the fact that exchanges are contingent, both within a particular transaction and across time. A neighbor who borrows a tool receives the benefit of using the tool. In that particular transaction, the neighbor's repayment to the lender may well take the form of expressions of gratitude. "I really appreciate your letting me use your tile saw," she might say. "Thank you!" is a form of repayment because it confirms the self-image of the lender as a generous and helpful person. This particular transaction also establishes expectations for the future: The lender will feel comfortable borrowing a tool from the neighbor in the future, and the neighbor is apt to expect this to occur. In other words, an exchange conducted in the present has implications for exchanges to be conducted in the future.

Social relationships endure so long as benefits continue to be exchanged. A neighbor who borrows a tool but expresses no gratitude casts a slight shadow on the relationship—a shadow that grows and becomes darker if the pattern continues. A borrower who refuses to be a lender casts an even darker shadow. To refuse to do a favor for one who has done a favor is to interfere with the expected pattern of exchange. If a person cannot receive a benefit from someone on whom he or she has bestowed benefits, that person is apt to feel cheated, to turn to other people to supply future needs, and to refuse to provide benefits to the person who has refused to provide them. Over time, if benefits are not reciprocated, social relationships cease to exist. In their everyday lives, people regularly extend one another interpersonal credit. That is, they bestow benefits without expectation of immediate return. But when interpersonal credit limits are exceeded, people tend to act very much like Visa, MasterCard, or American Express: The card is revoked and no more purchases are allowed.

Whatever the valued outcomes of behavior, they become less valued the more they are provided. Just as water is more valuable to a thirsty person than to one who has just drunk his or her fill, so it is with other wants and needs. People can become satiated with advice, tools, approval, or money, and find each increment to their supply of less use. As Molm and Cook point out, both psychological and economic principles are involved here. One of the key findings of behavioral psychology is that the more a given reward is obtained, the less valuable (i.e., the less "rewarding") each subsequent unit of that reward becomes. When the pigeon becomes satiated with corn, the behavioral outcome of pecking is less valuable and the pigeon is less likely to peck. Likewise, *diminishing marginal utility* is a key precept of economics. The more of a good the actor possesses, the less useful each additional unit of that good becomes, and so the less worthwhile it is to expend resources obtaining additional units.

Valued things do not diminish in value at the same rate. One can only consume so much food or drink at a time, and the average person's need for tools is likewise presumably finite. These valued things have rather particular and finite *use value,* and when the actor can no longer use additional quantities of them, their value diminishes. In contrast, money tends not to lose its value so quickly. The reason is that money has *exchange value.* That is, money is a valued thing that can always be exchanged for other valued things. The actor can exchange money for food, but when needs for food are met, he or she can exchange money for other things as well: housing, transportation, entertainment, and almost anything else in a society in which practically everything is for sale. Prestige also has exchange value. If association with someone of high social standing is valued, then prestige can be exchanged readily for the things a person desires from others. The admiration, respect, or adulation paid to Hollywood celebrities by politicians, for example, may be explained on this basis. The movie star gets adulation in exchange for conferring prestige-by-association on the political candidate.

Symbolic interactionists tend to be quite wary of the assumptions about motivation on which exchange theory is built. Rather than positing such a universal motivation as the inclination to mazimize gains and minimize losses, symbolic interactionists look at what people say about their motives and at the real contexts of social interaction in which people actually form their conduct. Instead of assuming that conduct is propelled by a single set of meanings, symbolic interactionists study the meanings people actually produce. Exchange theory may capture the meanings that people create within contemporary capitalist society, but this does not mean that people do or must produce such meanings at all times and in all places.

Phenomenology and Ethnomethodology

Two perspectives closely related to one another—phenomenology and ethnomethodology[16]—deal more directly and explicitly with the meaning of human conduct than either learning theory or exchange theory. Phenomenology is a philosophical perspective whose founder was the German philosopher Edmund Husserl. As an approach to sociology and social psychology, its ideas have been adapted in the work of Alfred Schutz as well as in that of Peter Berger and Thomas Luckmann. Phenomenological sociology makes the subjective standpoint of individual actors its central focus of attention. Unlike a more objectivist approach, which views the social world as a reality that exists independently of any individual's perception of it, phenomenology sees that reality as constituted by our view of it. There is, therefore, not a single, objective social reality that can be analyzed in the same manner that a scientist might analyze physical reality. Rather, there are multiple realities; indeed, pushed to an extreme, one might say that there are as many social realities as there are perspectives from which to view them. A phenomenological approach asserts that it is impossible to say that there is some objective reality called "American society" or "John Smith's family" whose existence is so clear and straightforward that it can be literally described and explained. "John Smith's family" is a different reality to each of its members, as it is to a variety of outsiders who come into contact with it and perceive it. To John Smith it may be a source of pride and satisfaction; to his wife it may be a chafing set of restrictions; to his child it may be a haven from a cruel world of teachers and peers. It is a different reality to each. The phenomenologist accounts for human conduct by attempting to "get within" and to describe the subjective perspectives of people, on the premise that one can only understand and account for what people do by understanding the reality they perceive and act toward.

Ethnomethodology is a variant of phenomenology. Like phenomenologists, ethnomethodologists are interested in the perspectives of actors, in how they view and act in their world as they see it. The main concern of ethnomethodologists is with the methods people use to produce meaning. Ethnomethodologists assert that meaning lies in the accounts people give of their experiences and interactions with others. These accounts are verbalizations, and they attempt to introduce order, sense, rationality, and predictability into the social world. For example, an ethnomethodologist might study the way in which people are diagnosed as schizophrenic. The ethnomethodologist does not assume that there is some real disease called schizophrenia, nor that its diagnosis is merely a matter of applying medical knowledge so as to ferret out the category of illness into which a given patient belongs. Instead, the ethnomethodologist suspends judgment on such questions and focuses on how the psychiatrist *explains* the diagnosis—the behavior he or she says is important, the rules he or she invokes to justify calling that behavior schizophrenic, and the like.

Underlying this approach is the belief that people are constantly engaged in a process of creating sense, making it appear that their behavior is correct or appropriate, that they are being sensible and normal human beings doing things in the usual way. The perspective argues that culture does not provide a specific set of rules that guide people in their everyday behavior but that it provides the resources—including rules—that people can make use of in creating the illusion of normality and meaning in their everyday lives. Pursued to an extreme, ethnomethodology appears to take no interest at all in what people do, nor in explaining why people do what they do, but concerns itself only with how people make sense of what they do.

Ethnomethodologists place considerable emphasis on the detailed analysis of conversation. Given their perspective on the creation of social order, *talk* is of great importance. As people engage in conversations, they bring various resources to bear on their task of creating order. Moreover, they do so in very structured, regular ways. Conversations exhibit regular patterns of turn taking, for example, and frequently involve paired utterances, such as questions and answers or requests and refusals. Moreover, it is in mundane, everyday conversations that important social categories and distinctions are brought to life. If gender and social class are important ways in which people categorize one another, for example, they must be employed and reproduced in people's talk.[17]

Symbolic interactionists find some features of phenomenology and ethnomethodology to be interesting and useful additions to its approach (we will discuss some of these later in this book) but do not consider these perspectives to be an adequate basis for a comprehensive social psychology. Although symbolic interactionism, like phenomenology, views a person's perspective and perceptions as very important, the former avoids the extreme subjectivity into which the latter is prone to fall. Symbolic interactionists argue that people act on the basis of meanings, so that one's actions in a particular situation depend on the way that situation is perceived. If I believe the world is a hostile and dangerous place, I will interpret the actions of others in accordance with my belief and act accordingly. Yet the world external to the individual does not simply become what the individual thinks it is—there are limits to the person's capacity to imagine that the world is what it is not. My view may be that of a paranoid, and my actions may even cause other people to dislike me and to act in ways that confirm my paranoia, but their perceptions do not necessarily accord with mine. The world, as they see it, is different, and their actions have different meaning for them than I attribute to them. There is an external world that confronts and constrains the individual regardless of how he or she perceives it.

The major contribution of ethnomethodology is the insight that people construct meaning and sensibility through their conversations. Although symbolic interactionists emphasize the meanings that people share as they interact with one another, it is easy to overemphasize the extent to which meanings are fully and genuinely shared. Ethnomethodology emphasizes that shared meaning is often an illusion and not an actuality, that people have ways to convince themselves that they agree with one another or that they share the same motives when, in fact, they do not. Beyond this insight, which will be incorporated in this book, ethnomethodology is too limited in its scope to constitute an adequate foundation for social psychology as a whole. By reducing everything to the question of *how* people create meaning, it ignores such important matters as how people actually decide to act in particular ways, how interaction influences conduct, and how selves are formed. By paying attention only to what people say, ethnomethodology ignores the great variety of actions other than speech actions. Social psychology is necessarily concerned with all forms of conduct, not just talk.

Social Cognition

Social cognition has been developed mainly by psychologists and is currently the leading approach to social psychology in their discipline. Nevertheless, this approach addresses questions of importance to sociology and some of its basic ideas are strikingly similar to, or at least compatible with, those of symbolic interactionism.

As its name implies, social cognition focuses on knowledge—its content, organization, creation, and processing. What do people know about themselves and the social world? How is this knowledge organized? How does it get created? How is it processed or manipulated in order to solve problems or achieve other individual objectives? The theory of social cognition is not very much concerned with behavior; "what people do and why they do it" is not the central question. Nor do practitioners of social cognition focus much on emotions or on how people feel about themselves or others. In the social science trinity of thoughts, feelings, and actions, the emphasis in social cognition is almost exclusively on thoughts.

Although social cognition resists easy summary, its major ideas can be stated as follows:[18]

- People are "cognitive misers" who develop cognitive structures that enable them to process efficiently the vast amounts of incoming information about themselves and others.
- These structures assist cognitive processes, such as paying attention, remembering, and making social inferences.
- These structures and processes are socially formed and socially consequential.

These ideas reveal a theoretical perspective that is not much concerned with an overall portrayal of the nature of the social world but that instead prefers to focus on the ways its members process information about it.

Social cognition theory postulates that the individual in the social world is constantly receiving far more information about others (and about the self) than he or she can process. Visual inspection may inform the person about the age, gender, race, occupation, social class, or other characteristics of other people. People have wrinkles or gray hair, dress as men or women, have light or dark skin, and wear the uniforms of physicians or telephone workers. Likewise, their words and deeds are sources of information about them, their intentions, their interpretations of a situation, and their attitudes toward one another. People speak in the measured words of a college professor or in the slang of the street; they act toward others with sympathy, hostility, or indifference; they seem calm or anxious; they offer praise or criticism.

This potentially confusing welter of information, according to social cognition theory, must somehow be structured if the individual is to know how to respond to it. In organizing information, human beings are miserly. That is, they attempt to be economical in their efforts to grasp and process information. They take shortcuts, assuming, for example, that someone with white hair is old (as opposed to prematurely gray) or that a person wearing a dress is female (and is not cross-dressing). They must take shortcuts because the alternative—inspecting the many details of the other's behavior or appearance—would make it impossible to act. Imagine how difficult it would be even to say hello to another person if one had to sift through the mass of information that the person presents in order to decide on the appropriate thing to say and how to say it.

The major concept invoked by social cognition theorists to explain how people organize or structure cognitions is the concept of the schema. *Schemas,* according to sociologist Judith Howard,[19] "are abstract cognitive structures that represent organized knowledge about a given concept or type of stimulus." The schemas that individuals develop and hold contain information about an object, ideas about the relationships among various cognitions of the object, and examples of the object. Schemas can focus on specific other people, situations, types of people, social roles, social groups, specific events, and even the self. Thus, for instance, a given individual might have schemas about a spouse, disciplining the children, office parties, workaholics, supervisors, fellow nurses, the war against terrorism, and self.

A schema is a kind of "picture" of any of these things. Parts of this picture are quite abstract: An individual's schema for a supervisor might include such abstract traits as superior knowledge and wisdom, willingness to listen, and capacity to make quick decisions. It may include negative as well as positive traits—for instance, insufficient knowledge, stubbornness, and indecisiveness. Other parts of a schema are far more concrete, involving images of physical appearance, strength, clothing, or other material things. Thus, for example, the schema for a corporate lawyer might include an expensive pin-striped suit, well-tailored shirts, and costly shoes, as well as such traits as intelligence, self-confidence, and the ability to articulate a strong position on behalf of a client.

A schema functions as a loosely organized theory that people use to make sense of their world, predict the behavior of others, and decide on their own course of action. People use person schemas to make sense of the behavior of specific other people, such as friends or spouses. They use role schemas to accomplish the same ends with respect to others whom they do not know personally but with whose role they are familiar. They use event schemas to grasp expected series of events in such routine situations as sitting in a college classroom or attending a wedding or funeral. They use self-schemas to make sense of and predict their own behavior, attributing traits, strengths, and weaknesses to themselves much in the same way they do to others. Particularly with respect to role schemas, people maintain the schema and make it more concrete by keeping in mind one or more *exemplars* of that schema. Thus, a favorite professor might be the exemplar of one's professor role schema, providing a concrete illustration of the more abstract traits that make up one's schema.

How do these cognitive structures aid in the processing of information about self and others? They do so first by shaping the individual's attention to stimuli, helping to determine what will be salient and thus receive attention and what will be ignored. Second, schemas are critical in the organization and functioning of memory. And third, schemas influence the way people make inferences about themselves and the social world.

The various schemas that people carry with them provide the background against which particular stimuli are perceived. A person schema for a friend, for example, shapes one's responses to the friend's behavior because it defines what is normal or expected from that friend. If the schema constructs the friend as caring, gentle, and even-tempered, then conduct that violates the schema will be quite noticeable. If the friend acts in a way that seems indifferent, rude, or angry, those stimuli will be attended to. Similarly, if an event schema for a family dinner contains expectations of silence while eating, conversation will be perceived as an unwanted intrusion. Schemas thus provide the ground against which the figure of behavior is perceived.

The selection of stimuli as salient and therefore needing attention and response is not done consciously. That is, individuals are not engaged in a process of consciously selecting a schema and then consciously selecting the stimuli to which they will attend. Indeed, the "cognitive miser" view of cognition rests in part on the assumption that people could not act if they had to select schemas and stimuli in a conscious way. Rather, schemas operate in the background and the selection of stimuli is done preconsciously. The individual is not consciously aware, in other words, of the processes that cause him or her to notice that the other's behavior is out of keeping with a person or event schema. The individual is aware that something is unusual about the other's behavior but is not aware of the cognitive processing that leads to that awareness.

Behavior is highly dependent on memory—on the retrieval and activation of information previously secured and stored. People know how to interact with their friends—what to say and do—because they have stored memories of their friends. They know their food preferences, the music they cannot stand to hear, and the others with whom they like to spend time. People know how to behave at a wedding or a Bar Mitzvah because they have information, stored in a schema for those events, that they can retrieve and use as a basis for acting appropriately in the situation.

Cognitive schemas are also crucial to the retrieval of information. Memories of particular events are shaped by the schemas that organized the perception of those events. In other words, what an individual remembers about an event he or she has witnessed depends in part on the schema the person applied to it. Imagine that a person witnesses a crime—say, a mugging on a dark street—and organizes his or her perception of the event as a crime committed by an African American. In doing so, the individual may invoke social group schemas about African Americans as well as more particular schemas about Black criminals. It is quite likely that the person's subsequent memories of the event will emphasize those aspects related to these schemas. He or she might remember the race of the mugger but not the victim, for example, or remember the victim as White when he or she was actually Black. Group and event schemas might even supply remembered details that were not actually observed. The person might remember the perpetrator's clothing—say, for example, a black ski mask and leather gloves—not because those objects were observed, but because they are part of the person's schema for crimes committed by African Americans. What a witness to a crime scene remembers about it is in part a function of what he or she thought was occurring and not necessarily of what actually took place.

The structures and processes of social cognition are intensely social. Although they are possessed and used by individuals, their origins typically lie in the social world as well as in individual experience. Individuals form schemas, but they do so out of materials provided by a social world and not exclusively on the basis of their own cognitive efforts. And schemas, which enable the individual to function in the social world, do so in part because they are shared and thus used collectively or in situations of social interaction and not only individually.

The foregoing points are especially significant to sociologists who have worked within and favor the social cognition approach. For the sociologist, an important question to be asked is where schemas come from and how they are applied in social situations. Clearly, the locus of the schema is within the individual mind—where else could it be? But it seems clear that people build their schemas on the basis of experience with others, knowledge gained from others, and using ideas that are widely shared. Thus, for example, an event schema that views street crime as predominantly involving Black perpetrators assaulting or robbing White victims is both factually wrong and widely shared. In spite of the fact that Black-on-Black crimes far outnumber Black-on-White crimes, event schemas that emphasize the latter persist. How and why is this so? Efforts to answer questions such as this take us beyond the fairly narrow limits of social cognition as psychologists have conceived it.

Many of the ideas developed within this approach fit well with an interactionist perspective. Indeed, for several concepts in social cognition—role schemas and event schemas, for example—there are parallel or equivalent concepts developed by symbolic interactionists. Indeed, students of social cognition seem to have independently (though belatedly) discovered ideas interactionists have used for decades.

At the same time, there are important differences. Symbolic interactionists are interested in actions and feelings and not only in cognitive processes. That is, they study what people actually do and how their emotions enter into their actions. And symbolic interactionists much more commonly study thoughts, feelings, and actions in the real situations of everyday life rather than in the laboratory.

Social Constructionism

After the publication of Peter Berger and Thomas Luckmann's *The Social Construction of Reality* in 1967 (see Note 8), a new phrase, *social construction,* came into widespread use and exerted a strong influence on the social sciences. The social constructionism their book helped spawn, however, is less an organized theoretical perspective on the human world and more a set of questions that researchers ask about the phenomena in which they are interested. As the philosopher Ian Hacking has argued,[20] the constructionist perspective rests on a characteristic attitude toward the social world. Social constructionists look at existing social patterns or forms of behavior and try to show how they might have developed differently. Whether the phenomenon in question is juvenile delinquency, depression, child abuse, or even the concepts of physics, constructionists argue that the "reality" people see when they look at such phenomena is socially constructed. That is, they argue, the phenomenon is not an inevitable product of the laws of nature but is a human creation. Whereas common sense tells us that depression and quarks are simply facts of nature, constructionists argue that they are human products, and often they also argue that we would be better off had they never been created. Social scientists do social constructionist analyses because they want to reveal the social origins of what is commonly seen as "natural" rather than "social," a part of a given "reality" rather than a human creation.

What does a constructionist analysis look like? Depression provides a useful illustration. From a constructionist perspective, people generally take for granted that this mental illness is a medical problem to be treated by specialists in behavioral health (a term now often used in place of *mental health*). In other words, depression is the province of psychologists and psychiatrists, who may use a variety of treatments, all founded on the notion that depression is an illness. The constructionist argues that the contemporary conception of depression as an illness is widely assumed to be true because it has captured "reality." Therefore, the social origins of the idea of depression should be brought to light because they are not obvious to most people, including the diagnosed, their healers, and various relevant social circles and communities. Depression is *not* an inevitable fact of human biology or psychology, they argue. There are alternative ways of defining or conceiving the phenomenon— that is, the behavioral or mental experiences, or symptoms, of depression—and some of them may be better than our existing conceptions. Moreover, the multitude of folk beliefs, medical practices, scientific findings, diagnostic categories, and the like that comprise "depression" have bad consequences. They expose people to antidepressant drugs whose long-term effects are unknown. Drugs make it cheaper for the managed-care system to prescribe pills rather than explore the psychological and especially the social origins of human problems. Psychotherapists treat patients at arm's length and pharmaceutical companies are enriched.

A variety of fields and topics have attracted the attention of social constructionists: quarks, madness, child abuse, weapons research, geology, and anthropology. Andrew Pickering[21] takes a strong constructionist stance in his book *Constructing Quarks,* arguing that even the discoveries of physicists are not inevitable products of the nature of things but reflect the state of scientific knowledge and the questions scientists ask and can answer at particular times. Not surprisingly, physicists reacted with outrage to the idea that their theories and research could have led them to any other conclusions than the ones they reached. Sociological studies of child abuse have showed how this phenomenon emerged as a social problem around 1961 and examined how the activities and claims of particular groups shaped its social definition.[22] Child abuse activists, again not surprisingly, likewise have reacted with some anger to suggestions that their conceptions of child abuse and the "facts" they propound may not be as real as they claim.

Whether a particular phemomenon is or is not "real" frequently becomes an issue in debates about the social constructionist approach. Natural scientists, not to mention most ordinary people, believe there is a "real world" and that science can discover solid and immutable facts about it. Quarks exist, and with the right ideas and techniques, they can be discovered. Constructionists say no, quarks come into being as answers to the questions we raise about the physical world, as do phenomena such as depression or child abuse. As questions change or as the means of answering them become exhausted or new ones are invented, "reality" changes. Physics (and everything else), say constructionists, could have come out otherwise, had it asked different questions, developed other techniques, or been influenced by other historical circumstances. Indeed, periodically it does come out otherwise.

How does the constructionist view of things relate to symbolic interactionism? From an interactionist perspective, human acts sculpt "reality" from "materials"—ideas, things, methods, knowledge—that people find as they seek to solve problems that confront them. Some of these materials people have already created, though they may not recognize their authorship when they find them. Other materials are not humanly created and lie beyond our control—or at least are out of our control at certain times. We respond to them on the basis of our ideas about them, but they do not respond to us on the basis of our ideas about them. What we sculpt this "reality" to be is probing and tentative, partial and incomplete, useful for some purposes but not others. Human beings doggedly pursue "reality," which refuses to sit or stay on command.

To go back to the example of depression, a symbolic interactionist might say—in partial agreement with constructionists—that a still-evolving body of ideas and practices has created something we now call "depression." The "materials" out of which past and contemporary people have sculpted the phenomenon of depression come to us from many sources: religious beliefs and concepts, the theories and practices of psychiatry and psychopharmacology, popular ideas about why people are sad and why they have the right to be happy. A variety of individuals and social groups—sufferers, healers, insurance companies, do-gooders, and government regulators—have created the concept of depression. Some symbolic interactionists would go further and argue that the sculpting and the sculptors encounter not just materials other humans have earlier created and foisted on the present, for now and then they strike a hard place that does not so readily yield to ideas about it. Psychological bootstrapping is urged but frequently does not work. Therapists and their patients talk and talk and talk to no avail, but a few weeks of Prozac alters the serotonin reuptake process in ways not well understood but that make earlier therapy suddenly effective. Individuals know how happy they ought to be and know they are not, and discover they never can be no matter what therapy they are given.[23]

Social constructionists and symbolic interactionists alike argue that it makes no sense to say that depression is "real" or "not real." It does makes sense to say that people have carved out the idea of depression as they have sought to cope with what appears to be a widespread human affliction. Human actions have created a set of ideas and practices, and some of these practices work some of the time, some work at other times, and some never do but persist nonetheless. The "reality" that psychopharmacology is beginning to carve out has been gaining favor over that inherited from religion or psychiatry, for a host of reasons: Pills work as well as or better than talk, pills are cheaper, and taking pills and getting well is a major cultural script for illness and recovery. But it also makes sense to say that the "reality" carved out by those who treat depression with medication is itself incomplete and will remain so, however much they take umbrage at the idea. Theories of how serotonin and other neurotransmitters affect what we call "depression" also encounter obstacles, in part because the socially constructed category of "depression" may combine a number of different problems in the brain. This is why, in fact, many students of so-called depression have concluded that it is not one disease but several, and that treating depression is the wrong way to conceive of and treat the affliction. Perhaps the most useful illness categories might be derived from various drugs and their effects. By this light, one would not be depressed, but rather one would have the disease that Prozac treats.[24]

Postmodernism

An influential perspective that has recently shaped the scholarly environment, not only for symbolic interactionism and social psychology but also for most other perspectives and disciplines, is *postmodernism*.[25] This diverse and sometimes elusive set of ideas emerged from European philosophy and social theory starting in the 1960s. Its view of what the human world is like is accompanied by a strong critique of social science (including symbolic interactionism) as a way of producing knowledge. Difficult to summarize, some account of this perspective is nevertheless necessary to an understanding of contemporary symbolic interactionism.

Postmodernism is not a single theory but rather a broad effort to challenge the assumptions, theories, and methods that the social sciences take for granted. Its critique rests partly on the belief that the human world has been drastically transformed, particularly after World War II. Mass communications and the development of a culture of consumption, for example, have transformed everyday life. People are overwhelmed by such modern technologies as the computer, the fax machine, and the cellular telephone. They have become obsessed with consumption, not (as they think) because they really want or need or will use the things they crave, but in order to assure themselves of their own reality and social worth. They live, according to French philosopher Jean Baudrillard, amidst a "hyperreality," having lost the capacity to distinguish between what is real and what is an illusion. Symbols, Baudrillard says, no longer stand for things, but only for other symbols. Postmodernists assert that the world changed so greatly by the late twentieth century that social science became incapable of understanding it or communicating its understanding in ways that would make sense to contemporary people.

Moreover, postmodernists hold that the self, which is an object of great importance to symbolic interactionists, to other social psychologists, and to the modern culture that produced these disciplines, has disappeared—if, indeed, it ever really existed. Symbolic interactionism postulates a self-conscious individual who perceives situations, makes choices, and acts. In contrast, postmodernism views the active, deciding individual not as a reality that any theory must contend with, but rather as an illusion. It is a product of ideology—of our ideas about the social world and our belief in the individual. In other words, we—meaning symbolic interactionists and other social scientists as well as ordinary people—believe in the deciding and acting individual not because such a thing exists, but because our systems of ideas force us to believe in this kind of being. To put this another way, the postmodern critique accepts the proposition, discussed earlier, that the individual is a social product but not the corresponding idea that society is a human product. In the contemporary world, this illusion is not only untrue but irrelevant. That is, the idea of an autonomous and independent self—the term postmodernists often use is *the subject*—just cannot account for the way people live and experience themselves in the contemporary world.

One of the changes that most preoccupies postmodernists—and they view it positively—is the decline of what they call grand narratives. A *grand narrative* is any overarching account or story that seeks to explain the nature of the world or of human experience in sweeping and singular terms. A belief in progress—the idea that human history moves inexorably toward greater knowledge and power and better living conditions—constitutes a grand narrative. The theology of Judaism that sees the scope of human history leading to the advent of a messiah and the theology of Christianity that the messiah has already come and we are awaiting his return are examples of grand narratives. Science itself—the conviction that human beings can know their world and assemble a comprehensive and true picture of it—is likewise a grand or master narrative. Such narratives direct us to perceive and believe in certain "facts"—that contemporary people live longer and better lives, for example, or that salvation requires the acceptance of Jesus Christ. But these so-called facts are significant—indeed, we only see them as facts—because we already believe in the truth of the theory on which they are based. Believing in progress leads us to see certain "facts"—such as people leading longer, healthier lives—and we then take those "facts" as evidence for the theory that has produced them.

For postmodernists, all narratives are essentially equal. That is, there is no basis for deciding that one narrative is true and the others are false. In their words, one narrative should not be "privileged" over any other. This attitude applies as much to scientific knowledge as it does to other forms. Hence, the grand narrative of evolution should be accorded no special place, nor should that of any particular religious tradition. Each claim to "truth," postmodernists argue, reflects what the German philosopher Nietzsche called the "will to power." Knowledge is not neutral, in this view, but always a source of power over others. To claim to speak "the truth" is to assert power, and typically claims by one group or another to know "the truth" conceal the goals and interests of such groups. The "truth" of religion or the "truth" of science, in other words, represent not just a desire for power in society but also the concealment of the interests of religion or science in holding power.

Claims to possess the truth conceal the interests of their claimants because they are embedded in what postmodernists call discourse. Broadly speaking, the concept of *discourse* refers to characteristic ways of conceiving, speaking, and writing about things. We can think of science—or, for that matter, symbolic interactionism—as a discourse that entails a set of terms and concepts, ways of seeing and thinking about the world, propositions and ideas, and, perhaps most important, texts. The discourse of symbolic interactionism, for example, has produced such texts as George Herbert Mead's *Mind, Self, and Society* and Herbert Blumer's *Symbolic Interactionism*. These texts embody the interactionist way of seeing, speaking, and writing about the social world. Such texts always conceal an ideology, a set of beliefs that are not based on any empirical evidence, but only on the interests and preferences of those who hold them.

Symbolic interactionists share some suppositions with postmodernists, including the conviction that knowledge is relative; the belief that to understand narratives, we must "situate" them in the social contexts that produce them; and the understanding that discourses shape our views of reality and are not merely reflections of reality. Based on pragmatism, symbolic interactionism conceives of knowledge not as fixed and final but as always evolving and changing, a response to the need to solve problems and overcome obstacles rather than a socially neutral quest for objective truth. Moreover, the postmodernist view that the self is an artifact of our ways of thinking about the social world to some extent mirrors the symbolic interactionist view of the self as an ongoing, mutable product of social interaction rather than a fixed entity. For interactionists, the self is not a structure located solely within the individual person but arises and exists in a social space that person shares with others. It is, in a basic sense, always something in the process of being created rather than something that gets created and then simply exists as an unchanging entity.

But there are also major points of difference between postmodernism and symbolic interactionism. First, interactionists argue that the self is an *acting* subject as well as a product of discourse. Postmodernism inclines toward a view of the person as nothing more or less than an artifact of modern discourses, whether those of religion or social science or consumer capitalism. If we see the individual person as making decisions or resisting social constraints, it is because our discourse—our ideologies—force us to see things this way. In truth, they say, people do not create discourses; rather, discourses create people. Interactionists say, no, the person is not merely a fiction constructed by discourse but an active and creative constructor of that discourse. People confront obstacles and problems, they survey their circumstances, they consider alternatives, and they act to overcome these obstacles and solve problems. In doing so, they exercise creativity and do not merely speak the lines that discourse hands them.

Second, interactionists believe there is an empirical world that resists human actions. Interactionists grant that human ideas about the reality of this empirical world are inevitably imperfect and incomplete. In that sense, as social constructionists argue, "reality" is socially constructed, and there will never be a full or final knowledge of that reality, because as human interests and problems change, the "reality" they construct will change. Nonetheless, the empirical world is not merely a social construction founded on discourse. Problems do not disappear when we try to think them away. Religions that promise a better life in the hereafter nonetheless have followers in this world who have to be fed, clothed, and housed. Indeed, religions that seek to hasten the hereafter by encouraging their members to martyrdom or suicide end up with dead members but with no evidence that the hereafter exists. There is, in other words, an obdurate, resisting empirical world that does not roll over and play dead in the face of human constructions of it.

Symbolic interactionists do not claim to possess the absolute truth, nor do they think such a thing exists. Indeed, symbolic interactionists often argue that the postmodernist critique of the modern quest for absolute truth and morality represents a rather belated discovery of something pragmatists discovered a century ago. At the same time, many interactionists grant that postmodernism has developed some useful ideas and that its critique is worth attending to even if it goes several steps too far.

Major Tenets of Symbolic Interactionism

What, then, is the essence of symbolic interactionism? Although there is more than one version of symbolic interactionism, most symbolic interactionists would subscribe to the following general principles.[26]

- The task of social psychology is to develop a theory of action.

Like all sociologists, interactionists are interested in the patterned regularities of human social life. Human conduct is social and cannot be explained merely as the result of idiosyncratic individual efforts. The fact is that our conduct does have a great deal of regularity; it is, as sociologists say, socially structured. But symbolic interactionists also believe that patterns and regularities cannot be fully grasped without understanding the social processes in which they are created. The regularities of social class or gender, for example, do not persist of their own accord or through sheer inertia but because human beings actively construct their conduct in particular ways.

- Human conduct depends on the creation and maintenance of meaning.

Unlike the behavioral psychologists, who see meaning as either nonexistent or irrelevant, symbolic interactionists say that conduct is predicated on meaning. Unlike many sociologists who believe that culture and society dictate meanings to people, interactionists see meaning as variable and emergent. Meaning arises and is transformed as people define and act in situations; it is not merely handed down unchanged by culture. This emphasis on meaning "means" several things.

First, it means that people act with plans and purposes—that when they get in the car or speak words of love to someone, they do so with purposes in mind. Human conduct is directed toward objects, which is to say that it always looks toward some goal or purpose. People do not always pursue their purposes single-mindedly once they set their conduct in motion, for they are often deflected from their intended paths by obstacles or by more appealing objects. Nor are people conscious of their purposes or of how they will attain them at every moment, for much of what they do depends on habit. When I get in the car to go to the store, I do not have to think constantly of the store or of the techniques of automobile driving I have learned. Habit takes over many tasks. I may sometimes speak words of love out of habit, not really intending what I am saying.

Second, the interactionist approach emphasizes that "meaning" and "intention" are two sides of the same coin. For symbolic interactionists, meaning lies in intentions and actions, and not in some ethereal realm of pure meanings or interpretations. Meaning is found in conduct, both in conduct that is overt and therefore visible to others and in plans and purposes that are formulated and verbalized only silently and are thus not observed by others. Our conduct is meaningful because it is fundamentally purposeful; it can be purposeful because it rests on meaning.

Third, symbolic interactionists stress the possibility of meaning being transformed, and they recognize individual as well as shared meanings. Clearly, human beings are restricted to certain kinds of meaning by the words they learn, for words represent the objects they can imagine. People cannot act toward that which they cannot name. But symbolic interactionists say not only that humans live in a named world but also that naming is an activity that is central to the way they approach the world. People have the capacity to think of new ways to act by inventing new objects—new names. Although they may not do so frequently, they have the capacity to do so, and this guarantees that sometimes they will do so. Faced with novel situations or obstacles to conduct under way, human beings think of alternative goals and alternative methods. Thus, the meanings on the basis of which we act are never fixed or final, but emerge and change as we go about our affairs. These meanings—the objects of our actions—are personal as well as social, for human beings rather easily learn to pursue goals that are inimical to the goals pursued by others.

- Human conduct is self-referential.

The individual human being is both an acting subject and an object in his or her own experience. Unlike other animals, who regard the world from the center of their own being, but can never themselves be fully a part of the picture, human beings have self-consciousness. They act toward themselves with purpose much as they act toward the external world with purpose. They take themselves—their feelings, their interests, their images of self—into account as they act.

The self is a valued and crucial human object, a major source of the purposes that people bring to their environment. Human beings do not merely wish to act in concert with others to secure the things they are taught by culture to value, but they wish to find a sense of security and place—a sense of social identity—by participation in group life. They do not merely take themselves into account as they act, but seem to want to develop and sustain coherent images of themselves. They also want to attach a positive value to the self, to regard themselves favorably, to maintain and enhance their self-esteem.

Consciousness of self thus confers not only the capacity to exert control over conduct, but also to make the self an important focus of conduct. Human beings are capable of very precise social coordination, for they are able to consider their own acts from the vantage point of the group as a whole and thus to imagine the consequences of their acts for others. But they are also capable of considerable self-absorption and of putting their own interests before those of others. One can attain a coherent self and maintain self-esteem by cheerful cooperation with the organized life of a community, but one can also obtain these ends through more individualistic means.

• People form conduct as they interact with one another.

Psychologists, particularly the learning theorists, have typically emphasized the individual's history of rewards and reinforcements as a way of explaining individual conduct. Many sociologists have emphasized the determining effects of roles, norms, social class, and other aspects of our membership in society. The former often seem to depict a human being imprisoned within his or her own previous patterns of action and reward, the latter an individual fully shaped and determined by society and culture. Without denying the importance of either individual histories of reward or of social and cultural variables, symbolic interactionists emphasize that conduct is formed in real time as people form plans and purposes, take themselves into account, and interact with one another.

Most human acts, interactionists think, are not individual acts but social acts, requiring the coordinated efforts of several individuals. Although individual capabilities affect the capacity of individuals to perform their parts in social life, the actual performance of such actions as shaking hands or delivering a lecture is sustained not just by individual skills but also by their maintenance in a social setting. The audience is as important to the lecturer as his or her own speaking skills—a disinterested audience can flatten even the liveliest speaker. And although the social acts we perform are handed down to us by our society, they do not persist by themselves, but only because interacting people use their understandings of these acts as templates to reproduce them. A handshake exists not only in a name or an idea but also in the actual pressing of one sweaty palm to another.

Symbolic interactionists thus regard the actual outcomes of any given episode of social interaction as potentially novel. Most of the time, we human beings shake one another's hands or deliver or hear lectures in a routine fashion. It is unusual for a social encounter to follow a truly novel course, but not impossible. Human beings do encounter situations they have not faced before; they find their paths are blocked by one obstacle or another; they misunderstand one another, failing to define situations as others do. In these and a variety of other ways, routine situations can become novel. People must find new meanings—new purposes and new methods—and they must reach into their stock of individual skills and socially acquired knowledge for general principles that can help them deal with novel situations. Thus, skills learned in other contexts are generalized as people encounter problematic situations; roles that cannot be performed in the routine way are performed in new ways.

• Society and culture shape and constrain conduct, but they are also the products of conduct.

In common with other sociologists, symbolic interactionists emphasize the prior existence and impact of society and culture. We humans are born into an already existing society and culture, and we are quickly swept into its flow. We are surrounded by others who define reality for us, showing us the objects in their world and in some ways requiring us to make them our own. The child, for example, learns that there is a god, or that there are many gods, and that one must tread carefully in his, or her, or their presence.

Yet we human beings do not have to reproduce the society and culture we inherit, and sometimes we do not. Regardless of what is at issue—belief in the powers of the gods or that it is important to drink beer cold or to be faithful to a spouse—the persistence of a belief or social practice rests on individual and collective action. Society is not a self-perpetuating, autonomous system of roles or social relationships. Rather, as Herbert Blumer said, society consists of people interacting with one another. Culture is not an invariant set of lessons from the past but the environment in which we all live, an environment composed of objects whose persistence depends on our continuing to take them into account, even as our survival depends on coming to terms with them.

Keywords

This and subsequent chapters will conclude with a review and discussion of *keywords*—important terms introduced or significantly developed in each chapter. The entries are arranged alphabetically, for quick reference, and each begins with a succinct definition. Their purpose is to provide you with a ready source of definitions, to review and extend your understanding of the chapter's content, and to provide an additional resource for studying and understanding the material in the chapter. Terms in boldface have their own entry in the chapter's keywords. In some cases, entries refer to keywords in other chapters.

Conditioning Conditioning is a process in which animals learn to respond to substitute stimuli, which become associated with other stimuli to which they have previously learned to respond (or to which they have natural responses). For example, Pavlov's dog learned to respond (by salivating) to a new stimulus, the sound of a bell, that substituted for the stimulus of food. Although symbolic interactionists think that human behavior cannot be explained simply on the basis of conditioning, it is nonetheless important to our behavior. Human beings respond selfconsciously to **significant symbols** (later defined), but we also respond unreflectively to various stimuli to which we have been conditioned to respond.

Culture Culture is defined in a multitude of ways in the social sciences, but its definition almost invariably involves the idea that culture is a source of meaning. The ideas, norms, expectations, values, and knowledge that make up culture are sources of meaning for

individuals who participate in that culture. Culture thus defines what is important (success, honor, sex, education, etc.), how people are to strive to achieve valued things (through hard work, for instance), what they need to know in order to achieve their goals, what will happen to them when they die, and so forth. Culture is thus a very encompassing term, for it covers all that human beings learn as participants in a social world. Symbolic interactionists do not make extensive use of the concept, although it can be readily defined as the field of **objects** (see Keywords in Chapter 2) that the members of a society or community recognize and toward which they act. In other words, as we will see, culture is another word for the complex, symbolic human environment.

Pragmatism Pragmatism is a predominantly American school of philosophy that views human beings, like all living things, as problem-solving creatures who create knowledge as they seek to live in the world. This approach to philosophy has several consequences. First, it views the world—social and physical—as an environment that presents both opportunities and obstacles to the organisms that live in it. Second, it emphasizes the active, goal-oriented, knowledge-seeking qualities of animals, including human beings, who must learn in order to adapt to the world. Third, it views knowledge as relative rather than absolute; that is, human beings do not discover "the truth" about the world, but rather construct "truths" of limited scope and duration. These so-called truths are true relative to the purposes for which they are sought, rather than in some absolute sense. In other words, pragmatists believe that we see and know reality through the lens of our collective needs and purposes.

Pragmatism is the philosophical approach most closely associated with symbolic interactionism. Mead, James, Dewey, and Peirce, on whom interactionists rely for philosophical insights, were pragmatists. The interactionist image of the world and its human inhabitants is a pragmatist image. Human beings are seen as striving to live in a physical and social world that presents them with opportunities but also imposes limitations and creates problems for them. Collectively, they strive to utilize the opportunities they see and to overcome problems of various kinds. Human beings are thus conceived as naturally active, using whatever practical means they can find and knowledge they can create to select and achieve their individual and collective goals.

Significant Symbol   In Mead's theory, the significant symbol is a gesture that arouses a similar response both in the one *employing* the gesture and in the others who *perceive* it. A gesture is anything to which an organism can respond. In gestural communication, it is the beginning portion of the act of another that serves as the stimulus to which one responds. Significant symbols may involve such behavioral gestures, but for human beings it is the system of symbols we call language on which we mostly rely. Human beings arouse responses in themselves and others by using words—by naming things and thus signaling their intentions or plans of action to one another.

The key to understanding Mead's concept of the significant symbol is the fact that significant symbols arouse the same or a very similar response in the one using the symbol and the others who perceive it. In the conversation of gestures, one animal's gesture arouses a response in the other animal. In the significant symbol, the symbol user stimulates himself or herself at the same time he or she stimulates others. It is the significant symbol, in other words, that is the basis for shared meanings in human life. When I say to another that I am sad, I (hopefully) arouse in that person an attitude of sympathy toward me; but I also stimulate myself to feel sympathetic toward myself.

By thus arousing the same or a very similar response in self and other, I cause us to see things in the same way—I cause both me and the other to take a certain attitude toward things. Naming, which is a primary way we human beings use our capacity for significant symbols, thus creates a shared view of reality, one that affects the namer as much as it does others.

Social Structure   Sociologists frequently use the term *social structure*, but what they mean is not always clear and it is not always the same. In general, to describe something in the social world in "structural" terms or as an aspect of "social structure" is to regard it as both external to the individual and constraining individual and collective activities. To describe "social class" as an element of social structure, for example, is to say that the division of a society into more or less distinctive groupings on the basis of occupation, income, wealth, education, social origins, and other characteristics is external and constraining. People experience social class as external—that is, as a given and inevitable part of the social world; and they find that membership in a social class constrains their life chances. It affects how much education they can receive, what sort of medical care they can get, how vulnerable they are to economic downturns, and the like.

Social structure is sometimes used in contrast with **culture** (previously defined). *Structure* refers to the external and constraining facts with which a society confronts its members (social class, for example, or male domination in the workplace), whereas *culture* refers to the norms, knowledge, and beliefs that members of a society hold in common and that help sustain its structure. Thus, a structural explanation of occupational success would emphasize the barriers to success erected by unequal access to educational opportunity. A cultural explanation would show how beliefs (in the importance of education, for example) can inhibit or encourage the pursuit of more years of education.

Endnotes

1. William McDougall, *Introduction to Social Psychology* (London: Methuen, 1908).

2. Edward A. Ross, *Social Psychology* (New York: Macmillan, 1908).

3. See Gordon W. Allport, "The Historical Background of Modern Social Psychology," in the *Handbook of Social Psychology*, vol. I, eds. Gardner Lindzey and Elliot Aronson (Reading, MA: Addison-Wesley, 1968), pp. 1–80.

4. Solomon Asch, "Effects of Group Pressure upon the Modification and Distortion of Judgments," in *Groups, Leadership, and Men*, ed. H. Guetzkow (Pittsburgh: Carnegie Press, 1951), pp. 177–190.

5. Stanley Milgram, *Obedience to Authority* (New York: Harper & Row, 1974).

6. See Susan J. Fiske and Shelley E. Taylor, *Social Cognition*, 2nd ed. (New York: McGraw Hill, 1991).

7. For a survey of sociological social psychology, see *Sociological Perspectives on Social Psychology*, eds. Karen S. Cook, Gary Alan Fine, and James S. House (Boston: Allyn & Bacon, 1995). This book is the successor to an earlier book with similar goals; see *Social Psychology: Sociological Perspectives*, eds. Morris Rosenberg and Ralph H. Turner (New York: Basic Books, 1981).

8. Peter Berger and Thomas Luckmann discuss this issue as the dialectic of individual and society: "Society is a human product. Society is an objective reality. Man is a social product." See their *Social Construction of Reality* (New York: Doubleday Anchor, 1967).

9. The literature on pragmatism and symbolic interactionism is vast. For a review and analysis, see Dmitri N. Shalin, "Pragmatism and Social Interactionism," *American Sociological Review* 51 (February 1986): 9–29. For a discussion of Mead as a social reformer in the political context of his time, see Shalin, "G. H. Mead, Socialism, and the Progressive Agenda," *The American Journal of Sociology* 93 (January 1988): 913–951. For other views of Mead and his ideas, see the commemorative issue on Mead in *Symbolic Interaction* 4 (Fall 1981) and another issue of *Symbolic Interaction* 12 (Spring 1989). Those interested in the relationship between pragmatism and critical theory should see "Special Feature: Habermas, Pragmatism, and Critical Theory" in *Symbolic Interaction* 15 (Fall 1992). For a historical review of Chicago sociology,

see Berenice M. Fisher and Anselm L. Strauss, " Interactionism," in *A History of Sociological Analysis*, eds. Tom Bottomore and Robert A. Nisbet (New York: Basic, 1978), Chapter 12. For an excellent discussion of pragmatism and sociological theory, see Hans Joas, *Pragmatism and Social Theory* (Chicago: University of Chicago Press, 1993). See also by Joas, *The Creativity of Action* (Chicago: University of Chicago Press, 1996). For a review of developments in symbolic interaction, see Gary Alan Fine, "The Sad Demise, Mysterious Disappearance, and Glorious Triumph of Symbolic Interactionism," *Annual Review of Sociology* 19(1993): 61–87; for a discussion of the emergence of a new "Chicago School," see *A Second Chicago School: The Development of a Postwar American Sociology*, ed. Gary Alan Fine (Chicago: University of Chicago Press, 1995). Also see David R. Maines, *The Faultline of Consciousness: A View of Interactionism in Sociology* (New York: Aldine de Gruyter, 2001). For reviews of antecedents of symbolic interactionism, see Robert Prus, "Ancient Forerunners" and Larry T. Reynolds, "Intellectual Precursors," in *Handbook of Symbolic Interactionism*, eds. Larry T. Reynolds and Nancy J. Herman-Kinney (Walnut Creek, CA: AltaMira Press, 2003), pp. 19–58.

10. See George Herbert Mead, *Mind, Self, and Society* (Chicago: University of Chicago Press, 1934) and *The Philosophy of the Act* (Chicago: University of Chicago Press, 1938). Also see *George Herbert Mead: On Social Psychology*, ed. Anselm L. Strauss (Chicago: University of Chicago Press, 1964); Gary A. Cook, *George Herbert Mead: The Making of a Social Pragmatist* (Urbana: University of Illinois Press, 1993); David L. Miller, *George Herbert Mead* (Austin: University of Texas Press, 1973); John D. Baldwin, *George Herbert Mead: A Unifying Theory for Sociology* (Beverly Hills, CA: Sage, 1986); *Women and Symbolic Interaction*, ed. Mary Jo Deegan (Boston: Allen and Unwin, 1987); Hans Joas, *G. H. Mead: A Contemporary Reexamination of His Thought* (Cambridge, MA: MIT Press, 1985).

11. The major statement of social learning theory is that of Albert Bandura. See his *Social Learning Theory* (Englewood Cliffs, NJ: Prentice-Hall, 1977).

12. General discussions of Freudian theory and social psychology can be found in C. S. Hall and G. Lindzey, "The Relevance of Freudian Psychology

and Related Viewpoints for the Social Sciences," *The Handbook of Social Psychology*, 2nd ed. eds. G. Lindzey and E. Aronson (Reading, MA: Addison-Wesley, 1968), pp. 245–319.

13. Donald L. Carveth, "Psychoanalysis and Social Theory: The Hobbesian Problem Revisited," *Psychoanalysis and Contemporary Thought* 7 (1984): 43–98.

14. For presentations of exchange theory, see George C. Homans, *Social Behavior: Its Elementary Forms*, rev. ed. (New York: Harcourt Brace Jovanovich, 1974); Peter M. Blau, *Exchange and Power in Social Life* (New York: Wiley, 1964); Richard M. Emerson, "Social Exchange Theory," in Rosenberg and Turner, *Social Psychology*, pp. 30–65 (Note 7); and Linda D. Molm and Karen S. Cook, "Social Exchange and Exchange Networks," in Cook, Fine, and House, *Sociological Perspectives on Social Psychology*, pp. 209–235 (Note 7). For essays discussing rational choice theory, see *Rational Choice Theory: Advocacy and Critique*, eds. James S. Coleman and Thomas J. Fararo (Newbury Park, CA: Sage, 1992).

15. Molm and Cook, "Social Exchange and Exchange Networks" (Note 14).

16. In *Social Construction of Reality*, Berger and Luckmann (Note 8) present an essentially phenomenological perspective. For the work of Schutz, see *Alfred Schutz: On Phenomenology and Social Relations*, ed. Helmut Wagner (Chicago: University of Chicago Press, 1970). For a symbolic interactionist view of ethnomethodology, see Mary J. Gallant and Sheryll Kleinman, "Symbolic Interactionism versus Ethnomethodology," *Symbolic Interaction* 6 (1) (1983): 1–18. See also John Heritage, *Garfinkel and Ethnomethodology* (London: Blackwell, 1984); Douglas W. Maynard and Steven F. Clayman, "Ethnomethodology and Conversation Analysis," in Reynolds and Herman-Kinney, pp. 173–202 (Note 9).

17. For a discussion of conversational analysis and its relationship to symbolic interactionism, see Deirdre Boden, "People Are Talking: Conversation Analysis and Symbolic Interaction," in *Symbolic Interaction and Cultural Studies*, eds. Howard S. Becker and Michal M. McCall (Chicago: University of Chicago Press, 1990), pp. 244–274. For an analysis of conversational style and the self, see Susan E. Chase, *Ambiguous Empowerment: The Work Narratives of Women School Superintendents* (Amherst: University of Massachusetts Press, 1995). Also see Douglas W. Maynard and Marilyn R.

Whalen, "Language, Action, and Social Interaction," in Cook, Fine, and House, *Sociological Perspectives on Social Psychology*, pp. 149–175 (Note 7).

18. See Judith A. Howard, "Social Cognition," in Cook, Fine, and House, *Sociological Perspectives on Social Psychology*, pp. 90–117 (Note 7).

19. Howard, "Social Cognition," p. 93 (Note 18).

20. Ian Hacking, *The Social Construction of What?* (Cambridge, MA: Harvard University Press, 1999). See also a review of this book by John P. Hewitt, "The Social Construction of Social Construction," *Qualitative Sociology* 24 (Fall 2001): 417–423.

21. Andrew Pickering, *Constructing Quarks: A Sociological History of Particle Physics* (Chicago: University of Chicago Press, 1984).

22. See Richard J. Gelles, "The Social Construction of Child Abuse," *American Journal of Orthopsychiatry* (1975) 45: 363–371. Also see John M. Johnson, "Horror Stories and the Construction of Child Abuse," in *Images of Issues: Typifying Contemporary Social Problems*, ed. Joel Best (New York: Aldine de Gruyter, 1995), pp. 17–31.

23. See John P. Hewitt, Michael Fraser, and L. B. Berger, "Is it Me or Is it Prozac? Antidepressants and the Construction of Self," in *Pathology and the Postmodern*, ed. Dwight Fee (London: Sage, 2000), pp. 163–185; Hewitt, "The Social Construction of Self-Esteem," in *Handbook of Positive Psychology*, eds. C. R. Snyder and S. J. Lopez (New York: Cambridge University Press, 2001), pp. 135–147.

24. Peter D. Kramer, *Listening to Prozac* (New York: Viking, 1993).

25. For a variety of views and arguments on postmodernism and symbolic interactionism, see Patricia. T. Clough, "A Response to Farberman's Distinguished Lecture: A Closer Encounter with Postmodernism," *Symbolic Interaction* 15 (3): 359–366; Harvey A. Farberman, "Symbolic Interactionism and Postmodernism: Close Encounters of a Dubious Kind," *Symbolic Interaction* 14 (1991): 471–488; Norman K. Denzin, "Postmodern Social Theory," *Sociological Theory* 4 (1986): 194–204; Michael A. Katovich and W. A. Reese, "Postmodern Thought in Symbolic Interaction: Reconstructing Social Inquiry in Light of Late-Modern Concerns," *Sociological Quarterly* 34 (3): 391–411; David R. Maines, "On Postmodernism, Pragmatism, and Plasterers: Some Interactionist Thoughts and Queries," *Symbolic Interaction* 19 (4): 323–340; Ken Plummer, "Staying in the Empirical

World: Symbolic Interactionism and Postmodernism," *Symbolic Interaction* 13 (2): 155–160; and Dmitri N. Shalin, "Modernity, Postmodernism, and Pragmatist Inquiry: An Introduction," *Symbolic Interaction* 16 (4): 303–332.

26. For a statement of an avowedly more social structural version of symbolic interactionism, see Sheldon Stryker, *Symbolic Interactionism: A Social Structural Version* (Menlo Park, CA: Benjamin/Cummings, 1980); Sheldon Stryker and Anne Statham, "Symbolic Interactionism and Role Theory," in *The Handbook of Social Psychology*, 3rd ed, eds. Gardner Lindzey and Elliot Aronson (New York: Random House, 1985); and Sheldon Stryker, "The Vitalization of Symbolic Interactionism," *Social Psychology Quarterly* (1987) 50 (1): 83–94.

Chapter 2

Basic Concepts of Symbolic Interactionism

In their efforts to study the relationship between self and society, symbolic interactionists have developed an array of concepts. Just as carpenters employ saws and hammers to convert wood and nails into structures, interactionists employ their conceptual tools to transform their observations of the social world into descriptions and analyses of human life. In this chapter we examine the basic concepts of symbolic interactionism. They derive from the work of George H. Mead, Herbert Blumer, and several subsequent generations of symbolic interactionists. Taken together, they form not only a set of tools for studying the phenomena in which social psychologists are interested but also a set of images of the nature of social reality.[1]

These basic concepts form an interlocking and interdependent set of tools, but we must present them one by one. At first they may seem to be bits and pieces of ideas disconnected from one another. Gradually, however, they will begin to "hang together," to form a coherent set of tools, each functioning in relation to the others. Likewise, the image of social life they convey will begin to appear in progressively higher resolution. At the end of this chapter you will have a good grasp of the bedrock of symbolic interactionist ideas on which subsequent chapters will build.

We begin with the concept of the symbol, upon which all other aspects of the symbolic interactionalist view of human beings and their behavior rest. Utilizing symbols, we will see, people can act purposefully in and toward a world of objects rather than merely responding to stimuli. They can define and redefine the situations they encounter as they engage in social interaction, make roles that accomplish individual and collective goals, and put themselves imaginatively into the perspectives of others through role taking.

Symbols

The most important conceptual building block on which symbolic interactionists have based their analysis of human conduct is the concept of the *symbol,* or, as Mead called it, the *significant symbol.* As we saw in Chapter 1, a significant symbol is a vocal or other kind of gesture that arouses in the one using it the same response as it arouses in those to whom it is directed. Because they can use significant symbols, human beings interact with one another on the basis of meanings. Their responses to one another depend on the interpretation of symbols rather than merely on the enactment of responses they have been conditioned to make. They engage in symbolic interaction. Our first task in this chapter, then, is to explain the nature of symbols and the implications of using them.

The Nature of Symbols

We can begin the task of defining and explaining symbols by considering the concept of a *sign* and the idea that signs influence behavior.[2] A sign is something that stands for something else—that is, an event or thing that takes the place of or signifies some other event or thing. Smoke, for example, is a sign of fire: When we see smoke on the horizon we assume that there is an accompanying fire that has produced it. To my dog Spenser, my opening the container in which his food is stored is a sign of food: When Spenser sees me open the container, he begins to salivate in anticipation of my filling his dish with food. In both examples, one thing or event is important because it signifies some other thing or event.

A sign can exist only if there is an organism capable of perceiving and responding to it. Smoke is a sign of fire because various animals can perceive it, somehow relate it to fire, and respond to it in some way. A forest animal seeing or smelling the smoke of a forest fire, for example, might move away from the source of the smoke, just as it would avoid an actual fire. A human being might call the fire department or the forest service, on the theory that where there is smoke there is fire. Spenser responds to my opening of the food container by salivating, just as he would do if he came upon the dish already filled with his food. In these examples, experience has somehow convinced an organism that one event is accompanied by another regularly enough that the one may be taken as a reliable sign of the other.

How do signs influence behavior? It appears that Spenser, for example, has *learned* to *associate* my actions with the imminent presence of food in his dish. A hungry dog presented with food will salivate in preparation for digesting the food; this salivation is a *direct* response to food. The salivation response is direct in the sense that it occurs immediately and inevitably in the presence of food. Presented with food it can see or smell, the hungry dog salivates, and it does so right away, without having to learn to do so, and without being able to prevent itself from doing so. Spenser's salivation in response to my actions, however, constitutes a *learned* response. Indeed, Spenser has become conditioned to my movements in the same way that Pavlov's laboratory dogs became conditioned to the sound of a buzzer. Just as the repetitive sounding of a buzzer followed by the presentation of food conditioned the dogs in his classical experiments to salivate whenever the buzzer was sounded, so my movements have conditioned Spenser to salivate. Responses to signs are thus conditioned responses. One stimulus, or sign, gradually acquires the power to elicit behavior that formerly required another stimulus. Even if the sign is intrinsically of no importance to the animal, it acquires importance when the animal learns that it is associated with an important stimulus.

Conditioned responses are important in the behavioral repertory of any animal, including human beings. The signs we learn to respond to often occur before or at a distance from the important events with which they become associated. The forest animal may smell smoke at a considerable distance from a fire, and thus well before the fire is an immediate threat. Likewise, Spenser prepares to digest his food even before it is on his plate; he is able to anticipate the food and thus get his digestive system going. Signs thus enable the organisms that learn them to act in ways that may well be more effective than if they relied only on direct responses. Signs of danger give animals a head start on their adaptive responses to the situations they face. Even though we often think of conditioning as a way of controlling the behavior of an animal, it confers a certain degree of freedom or mastery of the environment. The external environment is still in the driver's seat, since it has determined what events will be associated with what other events, and has thus constrained what signs the animal can learn. But the animal's responses are somewhat less directly and immediately tied to important environmental events.

Animals differ in the ways they can respond to signs. In some cases they are tied almost as immediately to the sign of an event as they are to the event itself. A dog, for example, can learn to salivate in response to a buzzer or to its master's behavior, but it cannot control the salivation, which is a wired-in biological response. In other instances, however, animals seem to have greater freedom or mastery in relation to signs. A chicken will pace back and forth in frustration alongside a fence that separates it from food; a dog in the same situation will see a break in the fence a few feet away, run along the fence, through the break, and back to the food. The chicken seems able to respond only to one element of the situation—namely, the food itself or, perhaps more probably, the presence of a container in which the food is kept (the container would then be the sign of the food). Seeing the food or the sign of it, its response is to move toward it immediately and in the most direct way it can. Since it cannot get through the fence, the chicken becomes frustrated.

The dog, in contrast, seems to respond to several elements, or signs, in the situation. It sees not only the food or the sign of it but also the break in the fence, and somehow responds to these signs in a relatively complex way. For the dog who sees a break in the fence—as well as the chimpanzee that uses a stick to knock down a bunch of bananas—there is a delay between the sign or signs of something of importance or interest and the initiation of action. Instead of responding immediately, such animals seem able to inhibit an immediate response and to use the time to process more information or more complex associations between signs and the things they signify. This capacity to inhibit or delay a response while the animal formulates a more complex response is important. It enables the animal that possesses it to respond more precisely to its surroundings by taking more information into account; it thickens or expands the temporal dimension of life. We could say that the capacity for simple conditioning introduces the time dimension because it enables the animal to *anticipate* events by responding to advance signs of them. The capacity for more complex forms of conditioning not only adds to what the animal can anticipate but also stretches out the period of time during which it does the anticipating.

The signs we have discussed thus far are *natural* signs. That is, these signs have a relationship to that which they signify that is effectively "given" in nature. Smoke regularly occurs when there is a fire, and I regularly open the food container before I fill Spenser's dish. From the perspective of the forest animal or of Spenser, the signs are just "naturally" there. Each animal must, of course, *learn* to make the connection and respond to the sign, but neither has any influence on the existence or appearance of the sign. The association of smoke and fire is a matter of physics and chemistry, and the way I feed Spenser is something I decide on. Moreover, each animal must learn for itself the connection between the sign and what it signifies. Neither the deer in the forest nor Spenser in my kitchen has the capacity to pass on this accumulated wisdom to other deer or dogs or to acquire it from them. Each animal must make the connection for itself as it encounters its environment and the particular combination of events and potential signs that environment presents.

Imagine, however, an animal capable of *creating* signs—that is, of producing things or events that it can associate with other things or events. Further, imagine that the animal can learn to respond to the signs that it has created in the same way that it has previously responded to the actual things or events for which they stand. And imagine that these signs are *shared* by a group of animals and learned in a group context, rather than simply on the basis of individual learning. What would such signs look like? How would they differ from natural signs? Of what consequence would they be?

Such invented signs—which are more properly termed *conventional signs*—are what symbolic interactionists mean when they talk about *symbols*. A symbol is a conventional sign. That is, a symbol is a thing or event associated with some other thing or event, but it is one that is produced and controlled by the very animals that have learned to respond to it. The symbol has no natural connection with that for which it stands—it does not occur "in nature," nor is it a fixed part of the environment over which the animal has no control. Rather, it has an entirely arbitrary relationship to what it represents, a relationship that has been created by and is shared among a group of animals.

Human *language* constitutes the most important and powerful set of symbols we can identify. Words that *name* various things, relationships, and events have no inherent connection with the things whose place they take. "House," for example, is a symbol that names a particular kind of structure that humans inhabit, but the sound of the word has nothing whatever to do with the structure. One might just as well call the house a "maison," or a "casa," or a "haus," which is, of course, precisely what speakers of languages other than English do. The particular word that denotes this structure has its meaning only within a community of speakers of a particular language, who are in agreement with one another as to the significance of the word.

Symbols are like other signs in several respects. Whoever would use the symbol must learn its connection with that which it signifies, for a word has significance—or meaning—only if the individual speaker can learn to associate the word with the same things or events as do other speakers of the language. Moreover, we respond to symbols as

TABLE 2.1   Natural Signs and Conventional Signs (Symbols)

	Natural Signs	Conventional Signs (Symbols)
What do signs stand for?	Natural signs stand for (or signal) the presence of important things and events.	Symbols stand for (or signal) the presence of important things and events, but symbols also help create things and events because they refer to abstract objects as well as tangible ones.
How are signs learned?	Natural signs are learned through experience—the animal learns to associate the sign with that for which it stands.	Symbols are learned through experience, but humans learn a system of symbols when they learn language and often learn the symbols before they experience the things and events for which they stand.
Are signs private or public?	Natural signs are private—they are learned anew, through experience, by each individual animal.	Symbols are public—the meaning of a symbol may be communicated intentionally by one person to another, and the response the symbol creates in the user is like the response it creates in the hearer.
When do signs appear?	Natural signs appear at the whim of the environment—they appear only when the things for which they stand appear and are thus beyond the animal's control.	Symbols are used when the user wants to use them, and the things for which they stand need not be present in order for the user to use them.
How are signs connected to what they stand for?	Natural signs have an inherent connection with the things for which they stand.	The connection between symbol and that for which it stands is entirely arbitrary.
What establishes the meaning of the sign?	The meaning of the natural sign is embedded in the ways the individual organism has learned to respond to a particular thing or event that signals the presence of something important to the organism.	The meaning of the symbol rests on the agreement of a community of users to apply the symbol consistently to certain things and events and to respond in similar ways to it.

we do to signs, by responding to the symbol in much the same way as we would to that which it symbolizes (see Table 2.1). If the sight of my house evokes a feeling of comfort or security, the words *my house* are capable of having the same effect on me. As is the case with all signs, symbols elicit responses from those who have learned to respond to them. Just as natural signs introduce an element of anticipation and delay into the temporal framework, so do symbols. That is, symbol-using animals respond to symbols in advance of and at a distance from the things they signify, and just as more complex forms of conditioning entail response to multiple signs, so do symbols entail such more complicated responses.

Not all symbols take the form of spoken or written words, although for all practical purposes language provides the key set of symbols. Things—such as flags—may be symbols, since they stand for nations or causes and they evoke common responses (patriotic feelings, for example, or hatred) from those who share the symbols. Likewise, hand gestures and facial expressions have symbolic import: An extended middle finger has a particular vulgar or obscene meaning in the Western world and is generally taken as an insult by the person to whom it is directed. Likewise, facial expressions indicate anger, fear, joy, and other emotions. Although there may well be a considerable degree of uniformity across cultures in such basic facial expressions as fear or anger—thus suggesting an innate basis for these expressions—many facial expressions are not universal.

Symbols have two additional characteristics that make them a particularly important form of sign. First, symbols are public. Each animal must learn for itself the connection between the natural sign "smoke" and the fire that it signifies. Moreover, the mental process in which each animal constructs its response is hidden from other animals. Only when the deer in the forest responds to smoke by running away does it do anything that its fellow deer can see and respond to. They may individually respond to the smoke itself, or to the deer's actual behavior, but they cannot respond to what is taking place within the deer's brain. Symbols, in contrast, have public meaning. That is, when a word is uttered, it is heard by the one using it as well as by others who participate in its meaning. Hence, uttering a word in response to an environmental event has the effect of taking the individual's private response to the event and making it a public response.

A second key aspect of symbols is that they can be employed even in the absence of the things they signify. Natural signs occur only when the things they stand for are present or occur. It takes a fire to produce smoke, for example. In contrast, symbols are not tied to their referents. We can use words—*fire, house, baseball*—even when the objects or events they designate are nowhere in sight. It is the environment that controls the appearance of a natural sign, whereas it is the user who controls the appearance of a symbol. Thus, we can invoke symbols well in advance of the appearance of what they designate as well as after the objects or events have disappeared.

The Consequences of Symbols

The development of the capacity to use symbols, however it came about, is perhaps the single-most important development in the evolution of the human species.[3] Although some scholars would argue that our primate cousins, the great apes, can be taught to employ rudimentary symbols, human beings are nevertheless the only species in which the development of symbols has gone so far that our very evolution as a species centers on this fact.[4] Our existence as a species depends on our ability to organize our responses to the environment using symbols. To understand how and why this is the case, we need to look in greater detail at the consequences of symbols for human conduct and the relationship of human beings to their environment.

Three facts are key to the impact of symbol using on human beings:

1. Symbols transform the very nature of the environment in which the human species lives.
2. Symbols make it possible for the behavioral dispositions, or attitudes, of one individual to be reproduced in another person.
3. Symbols make it possible for the individual to be a part of the very environment to which he or she responds.

Symbols transform the human environment, first, because they expand its scope both spatially and temporally. Animals that can respond only to conventional signs are, for all practical purposes, confined to an environment that is defined by how far and fast they can travel and by the nature and acuteness of their senses. To say this is not to downplay the intelligence or capabilities of other species, for many animal species are, in fact, capable of considerable learning and rather complex behavior. Their world is, however, by and large a rather confining one, because they can respond only to what they can sense. Thus, even though my dog Spenser is acutely sensitive to my movements, the sound of my voice, and even my facial expressions, he must have me in sight or within hearing in order to respond to these signs.

It is quite otherwise for human beings, who can use symbols as a means of imagining what is not present but might be or what was once present and may be present again at some point in the future. Because symbols are not tied to the actual presence of the things for which they stand, we can invoke them even when those things may be at quite a distance in space or time. I can utter my children's names and thus evoke mental images of them and the feelings of affection they arouse in me, even though they live quite a few miles away. I can likewise remember scenes from my childhood and anticipate events that have not yet occurred but which will. In other words, human beings can respond to things that are spatially and temporally distant because they can invoke the symbols for these things. In doing so, they quite literally expand their world so that it encompasses whatever they can imagine.

Symbols also transform the human environment by making it a *named* environment. In the simplest sense, *names* substitute for *things,* and thus enable us to bring the external world inside our minds and manipulate it there in fairly complex but also economical ways. Although symbols do not entirely displace concrete images of things in our minds, nonetheless a great deal of our thinking about the external world is done by manipulating words rather than those images. Symbolic creatures do not need to picture the world literally in order to think about it, but can instead mentally process things and events through the efficient shorthand that symbols provide. For example, a student can tell himself or herself to study, then set the alarm, then awaken on time to get to the social psychology exam in symbolic shorthand without having to picture these various activities.

There is more to naming than economy of effort, however, for names also transform the environment from a relatively concrete and particular world into a relatively abstract and general one. The animal capable of natural sign behavior experiences each sign and the event for which it stands as a unique and separate event. There is, to be sure, some rudimentary generalization entailed in learning how to respond to a sign, for the animal does recognize a similarity between one event and another. Naming things, however, makes the environment considerably more general and abstract. To attach a name to a thing—to call a particular structure a "house," for example—is not only to label the thing but also to create a category into which similar things can be placed. "House" designates not merely a particular house, unique in all the world, but also a category of things that share a set of attributes in common. The symbolic attitude, in other words, is a generalizing, abstracting attitude.

Symbols also transform the nature of the environment because they make it possible not only to name things but also to create things by creating names. The human environment does not consist of a finite set of tangible things to which language attaches names. Rather, the environment in which humans live and to which they must adapt includes a great many abstract and imaginary objects that have no tangible existence. "Love," "liberty," "responsibility," and "respect," for example, are names used by speakers of English. But to what tangible things do they refer? We may take hugs and kisses as an indication of love, or meeting a deadline as an indication of responsibility, but clearly "love" and "responsibility" name something more abstract and far less tangible than these particulars. We speak of these things, and we are convinced they have a reality, but they do not have the same kind of existence as, say, a "dog" or a "house." The former are abstract, the latter concrete. The abstracting and generalizing quality of symbols, together with the fact that symbols are not tied closely or intrinsically to things, means that we can invent things by inventing names. The environment is thus, to a considerable extent, a product of our names for it.

The same properties of symbols also make it possible to attach more than one symbol to the same tangible thing. "Book" is a name we attach to a particular kind of thing with pages filled with words between covers. But we can call this same physical thing by other names: When I write about it in this context, I can call it an "example"; when I use the same thing to prop open my door, I can call it a "doorstop." Thus, it would seem, names are not merely tags for the tangible things in the world, for the name of a thing seems to have implications for what we do with it. I use a "book" in a different way than I use a "doorstop," even though in either case I may be using the same tangible thing. We will explore this property of names in greater detail later when we examine the concept of the *object*.

A second major consequence of symbols is their capacity to reproduce the behavioral dispositions or attitudes of one individual in one or more other individuals. As we pointed out, natural signs are inherently private. Each animal can learn to respond to the sign, but since the sign is tied to the thing it signifies and is not under the animal's control, the relationship between sign and signified remains locked within the individual animal's experience. Symbols, however, are by their nature public; they have meaning only because they are shared by a community of speakers. Moreover, because symbols can be invoked at will and even in the absence of the things they stand for, a symbol user may invoke a symbol, either as a way of imagining the presence of the signified or as a way of signaling its presence. As Mead pointed out, a significant symbol arouses in the person using it the same response as it does in the one to whom it is directed. When one person speaks a name and others hear it, they share a response to the symbol. The mental attitude of the symbol user has thus been recreated in those who hear it.

A concrete illustration will help make this idea clear. Suppose that the members of a family are having dinner at home and one of them says, "I smell something burning."

In saying this, the individual symbolically designates or names some fact or condition in the environment to which he or she is inclined to respond in a certain way. In fact, the sentence itself strengthens and focuses the speaker's own response to the situation, for it is probably not until it is uttered that the person forms a clear inclination to act. But at the same time, the sentence arouses a similar inclination or range of inclinations in the others. They, like the speaker, feel that there is a need to take some action, that the source of the smell ought to be discovered and something done to eliminate it.

As this example suggests, symbolic communication consists of the arousal of shared responses among two or more individuals by the use of a symbol. It is important to understand that not all communication is symbolic. Two dogs, growling and baring their teeth at one another, are engaged in a form of communication, for the behavior of each influences or shapes the behavior of the other. At bottom, communication exists when one animal influences the conduct of another through its behavior. Dogs and other nonsymbolic animals, however, engage in communication through what Mead called the "conversation of gestures." Each act, or even the beginning portion of each act, of an animal serves as a *sign* to which the other has learned to respond; its response, in turn, is a sign to the other dog.

This form of communication is called a conversation of gestures because the beginning part of the act of one individual is a gesture—a sign—that indicates or signifies the impending act and keys an appropriate response in the other. Interaction at this level depends on responses to signs, where each sign is actually a small, initial fragment of an entire act that is to follow. Given a growl, the dog is conditioned to respond by attacking, because the growl is a sign of an attack on it. There is no reflection, however, no "choice" on the part of the dog as to which response it will undertake. Given the gesture, the response is fixed, whether by conditioning or genetics.

In symbolic communication, the essentially involuntary sequence of responses of one animal to another is replaced by the voluntary use of symbols to arouse shared responses in a group of symbol users. Instead of merely responding to one another's acts, symbol users can respond jointly to a situation because the response of one can be recreated easily in another. Hearing someone say that something seems to be burning, I can adopt the same attitude of concern or urgency as the speaker adopted when he or she spoke the sentence. By adopting the name the speaker has used, I adopt his or her disposition to act.

It is important to understand that the attitude of the other that is implied by his or her use of a symbol is itself something I may designate with another symbol. I may readily share the attitude of another who alerts me to the possibility of danger by using the word *fire,* but I may also designate that person's response to the situation as a "mistake" or as a "joke." In other words, symbols make shared responses possible but do not guarantee them. Precisely because symbols may be invoked without the presence of the things or events they stand for, human beings sometimes have to apply symbols to symbols, distinguishing between truth and falsity, sincerity and deception, reality and illusion. Human beings participate in a world of shared meanings, but it is a potentially tricky, deceptive world that often calls on them to interpret the symbols others use.

One consequence of the use of symbols remains to be explored. The distinction between the organism and its environment is fairly straightforward for animals that do not use symbols. The two are clearly separate from one another; the environment is what lies outside the individual animal, and the line of demarcation between the two is clear.

The symbolic capacity introduces a strikingly new element into the relationship between organism and its environment. If organisms can create and use symbols to designate their external environment, they can also use them to designate (to name) one another as entities in their environment. Their propensity to do so leads to another tendency— namely, for individual symbol users to use their own names as designations for themselves. In this way, the symbolic capacity makes the organism itself a part of its own environment. Because it can name itself, it can respond to and act toward itself.

It is not surprising that animals who have learned to use symbols to deal with their environment would use them on one another. Since they are social animals (recall that symbols are inherently social since they require consensus for their meaning), the coordination of their activities would be improved if they could *name* one another. However, implicit in the practice of naming is the possibility that a given member might himself or herself use the designation others have applied to him or her. If a given member is called XYZ, that is a name he or she can pronounce as well as hear. To use a name for oneself is to acquire a *self,* to become one of the objects in the environment toward which the individual can act and, indeed, must act.

Such a development, the full implications of which we will explore later in this chapter, is as revolutionary as the symbol itself. By participating in a community of symbol users in which a person is designated symbolically, and in which he or she can use the symbol for self, the individual takes on a completely new relationship to his or her own existence. No longer just an organism acting in relation to an external environment, the person acts toward an environment of which he or she is part. Indeed, it is when the capacity to respond to oneself as a part of the world develops that we can speak of a dawning of self-consciousness, for it is only then that we can think of organisms as being aware of their own actions. The organism that minds itself is aware of itself as a part of the world, and has gained an important capacity for control over its own acts. For just as it can anticipate the behavior of others of its species, it anticipates (imagines) its own acts as well.

To grasp fully the implications of symbol use for the nature of the human environment and the way human beings relate to it and to one another, we need to introduce a new concept, the *object*. The foregoing analysis helps to make clear the nature of symbolic meaning. The concept of the object helps us link symbols and the actions people take on the basis of them.

Objects

Symbolic interactionists rely on George Herbert Mead's concept of the *object* to portray the way in which people perceive and act on their environment. Human beings live in a world of objects—of symbolically designated things, ideas, people, activities, and purposes. The environment they experience and toward which they act is neither an undifferentiated blob of sensory experience nor a microscopically perceived stream of stimuli. It does not consist solely of the material world that we can see and touch. Instead, people live in, pay attention to, and act toward a world of objects.

What Is an Object?

The term *object* is not easy to grasp, perhaps because symbolic interactionists use it in a way that differs from its everyday meaning. Ordinarily, when we talk about an object we mean something that has material existence—such as a table, a rock, or a screwdriver—and that we can see or touch. Indeed, the first definition of *object* found in *The Random House Dictionary* says that it is "anything that is visible or tangible and is stable in form." Symbolic interactionists use the word more broadly and in a way that reflects a more subtle conception of how things and events in the environment become visible or tangible as well as stable in form.

After defining an *object* as something tangible, the dictionary lists four additional meanings:

> 2. *anything that may be apprehended intellectually; objects of thought. 3. a person or thing with reference to the impression made on the mind or the feeling or emotion elicited in an observer:* an object of curiosity and pity. *4. a thing, person or matter to which thought or action is directed:* an object of medical investigation. *5. the end toward which effort is directed; goal; purpose.*

These definitions convey two basic meanings that are superficially different but actually very closely linked to one another. These meanings help convey an essential symbolic interactionist (and pragmatist) idea, which is that the very nature of the human environment is shaped by the activities and intentions of acting human beings.

The first of these two meanings emphasizes the process of indicating, referring to, or acting toward whatever is in some sense "out there" in the environment and that can be symbolically designated. The cup of coffee an author picks up and drinks from as he or she writes is an example of an object in this sense; it is something external toward which attention can be directed, that can be designated by a symbol, "coffee," and in this case something he or she can also act toward by making it an example in a book on social psychology. The cup is a material thing, to be sure, but it becomes an object when it is symbolically designated and acted toward. Moreover, the "cup of coffee" is really more than one object. As the thing I act toward by drinking, it is one object, something to quench my thirst or keep me awake; as something I act toward by writing about it, it is quite a different object, something I use to illustrate a point. An "example" can assume a variety of tangible shapes and forms, for I could just as easily have used a "pencil" or a "computer" as an "example" in order to make my point. Nonetheless, the "example" is something we designate and act toward when we try to explain something, just as "a cup of coffee" is something we act toward when we try to stay awake.

The second meaning conveyed in the dictionary definitions conveys a sense of an object as a goal or purpose of activity. In this sense of the term *object,* a cup of coffee or an example is not merely something toward which one can act by picking it up and drinking it or by writing about it. It is also something the person picks up or writes about *in order to* "have a cup of coffee" or "give an example." This meaning of the word *object* is closely related to the preceding one. An object is not only something given shape and significance because the person designates and acts toward it but it arises out of goal-directed conduct and is itself frequently a *goal* of the person's action. Human beings live in a world of objects that they constantly create and recreate by symbolically designating and acting toward them. And their orientation to the objects that constitute the environment at any given time is purposive and goal oriented. Human beings fashion a world of things and stimuli into a world of objects because they act with purpose toward it. In this sense, cups of coffee and examples exist as objects in the human world because people act with intent, with the purpose of having a cup of coffee or giving an example.

This view of objects as both created by human activity and as the goals of that activity has two important implications:

- Human beings live in a world of objects, not of things or stimuli.
- Human conduct is oriented to goals and purposes.

Because their conduct depends on symbols and language, people act toward objects they designate and do not merely respond to stimuli that impinge on them. In Herbert Blumer's words, from the standpoint of people acting at any given moment, "the environment consists *only* of the objects that the given human beings recognize and know."[5] As this book is being read, the reader's environment consists of what he or she is immediately designating and acting toward, primarily these words—unless, say, it is a spring day and the reader is distracted or bored. Things are abundant, but at any given moment only a few of them are transformed into objects by the attention given them by people who act purposefully toward them.

The concept of an object becomes clearer (and more powerful) when we realize that physical things are only one category of object that people designate and toward which they act. Symbols, we said, make it possible to designate things that are not present and even things that do not physically exist. A child, for example, can designate the shadows that play on the bedroom wall as ghosts and act toward them as if they were real—jumping under the covers or into the parents' bed for protection. This is an example of the creation of an object by symbolic designation. No "thing" exists (apart from shadows on the wall) that is made into the object "ghost." Yet the child acts toward the ghost as if it were as real as any physical thing.

The concept of an object becomes even more significant when we move from an individual to a social level of analysis. The child who treats shadows as ghosts has designated an imaginary object that is nonetheless treated much as any physical object. When the child acts toward the ghost by seeking parents' company and reassurance, the child and parents jointly create a new object.

This new object—let us call it "reassurance"—is a *social object* created by a *social act*. The object comes into existence because parent and child act toward one another for the purpose of giving and receiving reassurance. The act is social because its object is social; that is, the parent and child are able to coordinate their separate individual acts because each can keep the social object of "reassurance" in mind to represent the purpose of their conduct.

It may seem strange to think of something so abstract as "reassurance" as an object. Reassuring and being reassured that ghosts will do no harm seems to be of a different order from action toward other objects, particularly physical objects. Reassurance cannot be tasted, touched, or painted. Yet we indicate and act toward many such social objects in our daily lives, and we do so as if they were as real as any material thing. Jobs, marriages, political philosophies, love affairs, deadlines, responsibilities, projects—the list could be extended indefinitely—are not material or tangible. Yet each exists and is made real in the coordinated actions of individuals toward it. A "deadline" is not a thing, but it exists because a newspaper editor and reporters coordinate their activities by attending to it and acting as if it must be met. "Responsibility" shapes our behavior, as when we work hard to fulfill an occupational obligation, even though no one can touch or taste responsibility.

This view of objects also shapes the way symbolic interactionists view human *motives* and *purposes*. Both individually and socially, human action is typically oriented toward goals. More precisely, whether we speak of the individual as acting alone or in concert with others, actions typically "look toward" an end state or object. The child seeking parents' company on a windy night when the moon is full anticipates the completion of a joint action with them—namely, being reassured that the ghosts will not get him or her. Action generally moves toward an end state—toward the completion of an object. Bernard Meltzer, summarizing Mead's view of the object, wrote:

> *An object represents a plan of action. That is, an object doesn't exist for the individual in some pre-established form. Perception of any object has telescoped in it a series of experiences which one would have if he carried out the plan of action toward the object.*[6]

Thus, the world of objects that surrounds the human being at every moment is not an inert set of things, but is intimately linked to and, in fact, represents and reminds us of the variety of experiences we have had with that world and of the motives and goals we have in relation to it. The objects that make up the human world embody the purposes and experiences human beings have in that world, and they invite us to act toward them in familiar ways.

Objects and Language

The world of objects in and toward which we act is not created anew each time people encounter and interact with one another. Instead, each of us is born into a world of objects that already exists in the conversations and actions of others. Snow, automobiles, happiness, toothaches, beer, liberation, and thousands of other words that are known by, or at least capable of being known by, a speaker of English are not made out of fresh interpretations each time individuals act. Rather, each person is born into a community of individuals who speak a particular language and who—by using this language to designate and act toward the world—also enclose us within it. When we learn the names of the things around us, we take it on faith that things exist, that they are what they are called, and that they are important. This may not seem obvious in the case of concrete things, for many of our words seem simply to name the material things we can see and touch around us. But the world of objects contains more than concrete things such as rivers, snow, and tomatoes. It also contains more abstract objects, such as love and liberty, whose existence we must infer and believe in because they are words used by other people.

Moreover, even the array of material objects that are present can be labeled in different ways. Vocabulary is related to culture in the simple sense that there are likely to be more names for things that are important in the life of a people than for those that are less significant. If camels are used for transportation, food, and other purposes, there are likely to be several words for naming and talking about camels. If a group lives in the Arctic, there will probably be fine distinctions among various kinds of snow, as there will be also among cross-country skiers, who must wax their skis differently depending on the temperature and moisture content of snow. It is reasonable to say that camels are different objects for the Bedouin than for the Israelis of Tel Aviv, and that the snow that rarely falls in the southern United States is a different object from that which falls on the Inuit. Language is a repository of the objects that have proved important in the life of particular peoples.

Despite the fact that individuals are born into a world of preexisting objects, embodied in language and conversations, they are not imprisoned within this world. Objects are provided for us by language, but we can also create objects as we use language. Speech and written language give us the capacity to relate objects in the world to one another in ways that are familiar, but also in new and different ways. Thus, we can say things that make no literal sense but carry metaphorical meaning. "I felt like my whole world was caving in," for example, is a meaningful expression when used by someone who has suffered a major setback in his or her life. Its meaning arises from the human capacity to use familiar words in new ways and to recognize such expressions as indicative of a type of human experience or relationship rather than descriptive of reality.

Language is creative of reality and not merely reproductive also because new words can be coined and defined. The words that make up a language constitute a system; each word can be talked about, if not fully defined, by using other words. Hence, it is possible for us to agree to use old words in new ways or to coin new words and agree on how we will use them. In either case, language helps create new objects just as much as it embalms a world of objects created by others before us. The "digital age" has spawned a great many new words: DVD, iPod, MP3, megapixel, downloading, peer-to-peer file transfer, and many others. These words denote objects that did not exist even a few years ago.

Finally, although we are born into a community of speakers of a particular language, the continuity of that language and the world of objects depends on us as much as on them. Speech exists in acts of speech; the objects designated by speech continue to exist only so long as they are talked about. Thus, if language is a prison that confines us and shapes our view of the world and its objects, we, its inmates, must constantly construct and reconstruct its walls and bars.

Acts and Social Acts

Our discussion of objects and social objects referred to acts and social acts without defining these terms precisely. Now we must turn our attention to these concepts, for they represent the symbolic interactionists' view of how individuals organize their conduct in relation to objects in the environment. The *act* is an elementary unit of conduct that represents the smallest meaningful unit we can abstract from the stream of human behavior. For behaviorists, as we pointed out in Chapter 1, the stimulus-response linkage is the basis for defining the basic unit of conduct. We suggested that this unit is too small, and our task now is to specify a larger and more useful unit—the act.

If we were to attempt to describe an individual's behavior during the course of a day, we would need to make some decision about how to organize the description. The person's behavior might well seem to involve constant activity, a stream of conduct without visible seams or joints, but we would be hard put to describe it that way. Instead, we would make some effort to describe the various "things" a person did. The same is true if we attempt to describe our own individual behavior: When I got up this morning, for example, I first "went to the bathroom," then "washed and shaved," then "ate breakfast," then "read the morning newspaper," then had a "second cup of coffee," and then "went to my office" to write these words. In providing this description, I break my stream of activity into a number of discrete parts and label each on the basis of some major purpose or object in relation to which I was acting.

An act is such a discrete unit of behavior. It has a more or less definite beginning point and usually an identifiable end point. It is related to one or more objects. "Eating breakfast" is an act, so conceived. It begins at a particular point when I sit down at the table, and it ends when the eggs are finished, the toast is gone, the coffee cup is empty, and I get up from the table in order to begin some other act. Its object is "breakfast." It is a functional unit of conduct in that it seems to have some relation to my purposes. It has a coherent, identifiable relationship to what I must do to stay alive and healthy, to accomplish other goals, or to satisfy the expectations of other people.

We may define an act as a functional unit of conduct with an identifiable beginning and end that is related to the organism's purposes and that is oriented toward one or more objects. As we shall see, it is not always easy to determine when a given act begins or ends, and sometimes it appears that acts are contained within acts in the manner of boxes within boxes. But, in general, it is a useful definition that enables us to identify a slice of conduct upon which we can focus and whose structure we can describe.

Phases of the Act

Acts have beginnings and endings, and so our task is to examine what makes them begin, what moves them along, and what brings them to a conclusion. To do so we turn once again to the work of George Herbert Mead, whose analysis of the act provides a major foundation of symbolic interactionism. Mead found the beginnings of the act in what he termed *impulse,* and he examined the act as it proceeds through the stages of *perception* and *manipulation* toward the final stage of *consummation.*[7] An act starts with an impulse, which occurs when our existing adjustment or line of activity is disturbed. It proceeds quickly to a stage of perception in which we begin to name or designate objects and thus give our acts direction. It then moves through a stage of manipulation, when we take concrete steps to reach our goal. The act ends with consummation, when our original adjustment or line of activity is restored.

The nature of an impulse can be seen most clearly with an example. Imagine yourself in a social situation with a small group of people—perhaps a set of friends or acquaintances having pizza together or watching a football game on television. Everything seems to be going pretty much normally until you notice that the behavior of a member of the group toward you seems unusual. Perhaps your eyes meet for a moment and a smile forms on the other's lips, or you detect what may be a glimmer of attraction in the other's eyes, or a touch lingers a bit longer than necessary. When this happens, something is strikingly altered in your attitude toward the situation. Where you were previously focused on the game, or on your slice of pizza, or on the conversation, your interest has now shifted to the possible significance of the other's act.

As you notice the other's smile or lingering touch, you experience an impulse to act. The other's act disturbed the situation for you—that is, it made uncertain or problematic a situation that was previously routine. You thus feel an urge to act—to respond in some way to the other's smile or touch. You want to do something, and you are ready to do it—to return the smile, to figure out what it might mean for your relationship with that person, perhaps even to ignore it.

This view of conduct does not imply that the person is merely a responder to outside stimuli, remaining motionless and inactive unless and until something impinges and sets an act in motion. It is more accurate to think of people, and indeed all animals, as constantly and naturally active in some way. At any given moment, we are engaged in a particular line of conduct, but we have within us the capacity to respond to a great variety of stimuli, for there are many impulses "striving" to be released. The balance among our internal sensitivities changes from time to time; we may be very receptive to winks at one point but more interested in food at another. Sometimes we are interested in sex, whereas at other times erotic stimuli are less important than our wish to create a favorable impression in another person, or merely to get a few hours of sleep. Some of the internal changes that affect our sensitivity to stimuli are more or less periodic—such as those associated with food and hunger—and are not under our conscious control, whereas others reflect conscious developments as well as our ongoing interactions with our surroundings. In any case, we should not think of living things as simply aroused by external stimuli, but also as seeking such stimuli as a result of events going on within them.

Given that a person becomes ready to act in response to a stimulus, what happens next? How will you respond to the other's smile or touch? Asking this question jumps the gun a bit, for we cannot talk about the results of impulse until we examine how the stimulus is perceived. What object will you designate in response to the other's act? What will be the goal of your own act, if any, toward the other? A stimulus alerts and sensitizes one to the need to act, but it does not itself define the object of the act.

In order to act, you must interpret or designate the other's smile or touch in a meaningful way. You must attach a name to it and in so doing establish a goal for yourself. But doing so is at least potentially problematic. Does the smile have any meaning at all? Were you the intended object of the smile? Was the lingering touch merely accidental? Was it a meaningful caress, or was the other just steadying herself or himself by grasping your shoulder?

How you respond to the other depends on your relationship to that person as well as to your internal condition. Suppose, for example, that you have a previously unspoken and unacknowledged romantic interest in the other. If so, you may be likely to interpret the touch as somehow indicative of the other's interest in you—and therefore as an act to which you should respond in like manner. More generally, we can say that *impulse* and *perception,* as successive phases of the individual's act, are inextricably linked: The perception of and designation of objects and stimuli are strongly influenced by the condition of the individual, so that the actions it initiates stem from its own internal condition as well as from the occurrence of external events or stimuli. Indeed, it is the internal condition—in this instance your interest in the other—that makes an external event a stimulus.

Assume, for example, that you are romantically or sexually interested in the other and that you interpret the touch as an indication that the other is interested in you. The next phase of the act, which Mead labeled *manipulation,* requires an overt action. Suppose that you return the other's gaze, holding eye contact for longer than the usual time, or that you respond to a touch by grasping and holding the other's hand or arm. This is the overt portion of the act—the external manifestation of a process that, until now, has gone on internally.

What happens next? It is certainly possible—and from your perspective quite desirable—that the other responds positively to *your* look and touch. Smiles deepen, the mutual gaze lengthens, and the two of you move closer together, or go off by yourselves, or hold hands, or do any of the countless things people do to confirm romantic interest. If this is the outcome, then the act has reached *consummation*. That is, your adjustment to the situation, which was disturbed by the other's look or touch, has been restored, and you can turn your attention back to the pizza or the game, albeit with a new hope for what might be in store later for the two of you. Or the two of you leave the situation and begin a new round of activity.

But suppose your response to the other's look or touch meets another reaction. You lock eyes with the other only to find a quizzical or, worse, disgusted look in return. Or you meet the other's hand on your shoulder with your own hand, only to find the other wrenches away from your grasp. Horrors! Your adjustment to the situation has not been restored but made even more problematic and thus put you on the track of another act whose object will be to get you out of this difficult situation. You turn your eyes quickly away, realizing you have misinterpreted the other's gaze; or you quickly remove your hand, mutter something in apology, and look for a rock to crawl under.

Mead's approach to the act neatly solves the problem of the "meaning of meaning." For the person in this hypothetical situation, the other's look or touch is an object—something he or she must indicate to self and then act toward. The meaning of this object at first lies in the individual's initial readiness to act toward it in a certain way. The meaning of the look or touch is not inherent, however, for it can be interpreted and acted toward in a variety of ways. Nor is one's understanding of another's look or touch merely a matter of remembering past occasions on which that person, or other persons, have looked at or touched one. We know from experience that looks and touches may have a variety of meanings. The other in this example *intends* the look or touch in a certain way, anticipating a certain response to this act; but intent does not control interpretations.

For symbolic interactionists, then, meaning is anchored in behavior. The meaning of an act is neither fixed nor unchanging, but is determined in conduct as individuals act toward objects. As acts proceed, meaning may be transformed. Initial readiness to act toward an object in a given way does not mean that action will necessarily follow that course. One may change one's mind, redesignate the object, and act in a different way, or one may find that the act gets one nowhere, that one must adjust by getting ready to act in a different way. As the individual's actual conduct toward an object changes, the meaning of the object likewise changes.

In analyzing the individual's act in this way, Mead meant to call our attention to the necessity of seeing human behavior in terms of both its external manifestations and its internal processes. The individual's act does not consist merely of what may be observed by others, but also entails an internal process of control in which the individual directs conduct toward some goal or object.

In the preceding example, there are both individual and social objects, as well as individual acts and social acts. By attending to and acting toward another's look or touch, one constitutes it as an object—it becomes something one's behavior must take into account. At the same time, one participates with others in the creation of a *social object,* which is an object created and sustained by coordinated or social acts. A conversation is such a social object—it is something toward which the attention of participants is jointly directed in a social act. They begin it, try to keep it going, and perhaps feel badly if it is interrupted. Likewise, in this example, two people may begin to "flirt"—that is, to engage in a set of actions both recognize as contributing to the object of "flirting."

People are themselves social objects to one another as they interact. When you have to decide whether to treat someone who has touched you as signaling a romantic interest, or merely flirting, or just steadying himself or herself on your shoulder, you are really deciding what object that person will be. The reality of the other, at that moment, depends on how you constitute him or her as an object. What or who people are is a function of the way we jointly designate them as we interact.

Social objects are created as people engage in *social acts*. In Mead's words, a social act is one that involves "the cooperation of more than one individual, and whose object as defined by the act . . . is a social object."[8] Social acts depend on social interaction and interpretation; that is, in order for individuals to cooperate with one another in the creation of social objects, they must orient their conduct to one another. Each must take into account the possible response of the other to his or her own impending act and assume that the other will do the same. Such a process of mutual orientation in completing social acts is what we mean by social interaction—whether the social act in question has as its object a conversation, as in the preceding example, or something very different, such as a baseball game or a debate.

In order for people to engage in social interaction, and thus complete the social object of a social act, they must be able to interpret one another's acts (see Table 2.2). The individual engaged in interaction with another must be able to assign meaning to the acts of the other in such a way that he or she can act appropriately. An individual engaged in a conversation must be able to interpret—assign meaning to—what the other says so that he or she can make an appropriate reply. In a baseball game, the pitcher must be able to assign meaning to the catcher's signals, so that he or she can throw the appropriate pitch.

The interpretation of others' acts generally focuses on their intent. We ask ourselves what someone intended by what she said, and the pitcher asks himself what pitch the catcher intended to call for. There is nothing mysterious about the close association of meaning with intention. "Meaning" really consists of answers to the question of what we are going to do, what others will do in return, and what we will do in response. In this sense, meaning is *triadic*, to use Mead's term: When an individual acts (by making a statement or command, shaking a fist or turning away, or even by means of a facial expression), she indicates to the other what she plans to do, what the other is expected to do in return, and what social object is being created by them. The catcher who signals for a given pitch is indicating what the pitcher is to do, what the catcher is prepared for, and what he expects will happen as a result—a curve, a fast ball, a change of pace, or an intentional walk.

One additional fact about the symbolic interactionist approach to conduct needs to be stressed: It is the *problematic* event or situation that makes it necessary for people to orient themselves self-consciously to objects and to try to interpret the meaning of one another's acts. Much of what we do in our everyday lives is routine—we awake and dress, make coffee, drive to school or work, and conduct a variety of activities in much the same way from one day to the next. Accordingly, a great deal of what we do can be explained in

TABLE 2.2   Individual Acts and Social Acts

When does an act begin?	A new act begins when something occurs that disrupts the individual's ongoing act. *Example*: A student about to leave his apartment in order to drive to class for a scheduled examination discovers his car won't start.	A new social act begins when something interferes with an ongoing individual or social act: *Example*: The student fears he may miss the exam and contacts the professor to explain that he will try to find alternative transportation and may be late or may not be able to get there.
How is the object defined?	The individual imagines what must be done and then thinks of alternative ways of doing it. *Example*: The student tries to decide whether it would be better to take a bus to class or to borrow his roommate's car.	Several individuals cooperate to achieve a definition of the situation and thus an agreement on what social act is called for. *Example*: The student talks to his roommate, who offers the use of the car provided he can bring it back immediately after the exam.
Who does the acting?	The individual manipulates various objects in order to move toward the goal of the act. *Example*: The student gets his roommate's car keys, transfers his backpack to the car, and heads for class.	Individuals act cooperatively to achieve a social object—that is, each contributes individual acts that are coordinated in such a way that they move jointly toward the social object. *Example*: The roommate lends the keys, explains how to work a door that sticks, and wishes the student well on the exam.
When is the act complete?	The act is complete when its goal has been reached and the individual can return to the act that was interrupted. *Example*: The student gets to class and takes the exam for which he had studied very hard.	The act is complete when its goal has been reached, which requires the explicit or tacit acknowledgment of all participants that this has been done. *Example*: The professor thanks the student for letting her know he would be late and assures him it isn't a problem, and he thanks her for her understanding. After taking the exam, the student returns the car to his roommate.

terms of *habit,* and we need not invoke more complex conceptions such as those we have just been considering. Some of these habitual forms of conduct involve basic skills, such as standing erect and walking, that are so ingrained and repetitively exercised that we never have to think about them unless disease or disability interfere with our capacity. Other habitual forms of activity, such as driving an automobile, are more complex and involve response to the acts of others as well as the exercise of basic skills.

However simple or complex the habit, it is when something interferes with the progress of an act toward its usual object that we become more keenly aware of the object itself and of the most appropriate ways of designating and responding to the acts of others. For a person responding to another's gaze, it is the ambiguity of the look that makes it necessary self-consciously to designate its meaning. For the driver of an automobile, it is when the vehicle refuses to start or when other drivers do not act in accordance with expectations that habit becomes an insufficient basis for conduct, and the environment and the individual's plan of action toward it must be more self-consciously designated. "What is going on?" we are apt to ask. "Why did the other person do that? What should I do?"

It is thus true, in a limited sense, to say that we human beings sometimes act as if we were merely responding to stimulation from the external world. When we encounter red lights at intersections, we do not have to engage in a conscious process in which we designate the meaning of a red light. We more or less automatically and habitually respond by putting on the brakes. Yet at some point in the past when we were learning to drive we did have to designate the meaning of a red light and learn explicitly and consciously how to respond to it. Moreover, there are many occasions, even in such simple activities as driving an automobile, when our habitual responses are not adequate and we must actively designate the objects toward which we are acting. Other cars fail to stop as they should for red lights, traffic signals break down, and we sometimes fail to see a red light in time and have to decide what to do. It is in the face of such problematic occurrences that our capacity to designate and interpret is crucial to the success of our actions.

Self and the Control of Behavior

The human capacity to exert control over conduct—to coordinate our behavior with that of others and create complex social acts and social objects—is linked to a uniquely human phenomenon, the possession of *self*. Symbolic interactionists use this familiar word in a distinctive way to designate both an object that is created as we interact with others and the process through which this object is created. Both as a process and as an object, the self is a crucial part of the way humans regulate what they do.

Self as Object

The essence of the symbolic interactionist concept of self lies in the idea that human beings can be objects to themselves. Each person can be an object in his or her own experience—that is, an object that he or she can name, imagine, visualize, talk about, and act toward. One can like or dislike oneself, feel pride or shame in real or imagined activity, and, in general, act toward oneself within the same range of motives and emotions that shape actions toward others. This, for symbolic interactionists, is a fundamental fact of human existence.

How is it possible for people to constitute themselves as objects? How can individuals become conscious of themselves and so become a part of their own experience, of the very environment in which they live and act? And what does this capability imply about the nature of human conduct?

Answers to these questions turn on the special nature of the act when it is symbolically organized. The characteristic human response to situations is the inhibition of an immediate response until an act can be constructed that seems to "fit" the situation. Noticing another's prolonged gaze or seemingly gentle touch, one feels impelled to act, but generally one holds a response in check until one can decide what to do, considering several possible objects, selecting one, and then acting.

In the evolution of the human species, such inhibition of the individual's act naturally occurred in social situations, since human beings were social animals before they were symbolic. In the course of becoming human, our ancestors were doubtless faced with many circumstances in which individuals had to check their own acts in order to consider the possible results of those acts—not only in terms of what the natural environment might next do but also in terms of what their fellows might next do. Indeed, to function effectively in a group setting, say in the pursuit of food, individuals would have to imagine not merely the possible actions of the prey and of their fellows but also their own actions in response to alternative possible events.

But how could individuals anticipate their own acts? From the perspective of an individual organism, the world is outside itself, and the organism is not a part of that world at all—it merely responds to and acts on it. Thus, in saying that individuals would have to anticipate their own actions and see them in relation to the actions of others, we seem to be imposing an impossible requirement.

But not really, because individuals do have a way of anticipating their own conduct, for visualizing themselves as a part of their environment, and for seeing their own acts in relation to those of their fellows—namely, *the symbolic designation of others and self*. Members of a species that can name objects can name one another. And since one hears one's own name, and not only the names of others, one can *use* one's own name. To hear and speak one's own name—to designate oneself as an object just as others designate one—is to alter not only one's relationship to the social world but also the very nature of that social world.

However it first happened, the individual who first used the group's name for himself or herself managed to internalize the whole group of which he or she was a part. By naming self as well as the others, the individual could internally represent not only others and their behavior but also his or her own responses and their responses in turn. Without a symbol for self, the individual can represent others and their acts; with a symbol, a name, the individual can represent self as implicated in their acts, and thus imagine and depict the activities of the group as a whole.

By naming group members and themselves, human beings import the social process within the individual mind. As individuals participate in group life, each can represent the activities of the group within his or her own mind and act according to how he or she thinks others will act. Indeed, not only does one represent the activities of the group as a whole and imagine various scenarios taking place but one also interacts with oneself. This can be accomplished because the act of giving oneself the name that others give one makes one an object in one's own world. One does not merely symbolically represent a world of social objects—people—of which one is a part, but one acts toward (and interacts with) those objects, including oneself.

The evolutionary significance of naming the self was that the coordination of group activities could become more precise and flexible if each individual could imagine alternative scenarios of action. By taking self into account as a factor in the situation, the individual is better able to control his or her own acts and better able to anticipate the outcomes of alternative acts. And, as precision of control over self and of coordination with others increased, the competitive position of a group using such procedures must have been significantly improved.

However self-designation and self-interaction arose in evolution, we see the operation of these processes in our everyday lives. "Talking to oneself" is an everyday experience. It is also a necessary activity, for "thought"—which is the name we give to such internalized conversation—cannot take place unless individuals treat themselves as social objects with whom they can conduct a conversation. In conceiving of thinking as an internalized conversation, we are in effect saying that what we call the human "mind" or "consciousness" is really the incorporation of social process within the organism. People have "minds" because they are able to act toward themselves, talk to themselves, and take themselves into account as they act. "Mind," therefore, is not some mysterious entity that is distinct and separate from the "body." What we call "mind" is a form of behavior like any other kind of human behavior, for it is inherently a social behavior that depends on the human symbolic capacity.

When humans mind themselves, they constitute the self as an object. Each time we imagine ourselves doing something—whether saying "no" to a party invitation, achieving a promotion on the job, or getting a grade of A in a social psychology course—we are acting toward ourselves as objects. When I say to myself, "I'm going to work hard to earn an A in this course," I am creating and acting toward an object—myself. This object, me, is a crucial object in my life, for it is implicated in my every act. Although it may be transformed, modified, or revised as I interact with different people and find myself in different situations, it is always an object that figures in my conduct.

The self as object does not refer to the body. People have corporeal existence, of course, but also, and more importantly, a great many intangible attributes and characteristics. People are mothers or farmers or criminals. They are moody or kind or capable or strong. They are self-confident or insecure, anxious or relaxed. They are, in short, whatever kind of objects their own acts (and, we will see, the acts of others) indicate them to be. When we constitute others or ourselves as objects with such attributes and characteristics, we are dealing in abstractions. We are talking about objects and not simply about the material thing that is the body.

This is an important point to grasp, particularly since some of the terms we use to discuss the self—the very word *self* as well as two other terms, *I* and *Me,* to be discussed shortly—incline us to think of the self as something tangible. To some degree our language forces us into such a misconception. Since objects are designated in English by nouns, we are led by our linguistic habits to think of them as things. As generations of English teachers have pounded into our heads, nouns are the names of persons, places, and things. Very well, we are inclined to think, the self is a thing, a structure in the mind. It is not; it is an object we create and re-create as we act toward it.

Self as Process

The preceding discussion has hinted at the nature of the process in which the self is objectified. These ideas can be made more precise, however, by turning once again to Mead's ideas about the self, and particularly to his distinction between the "I" and the "Me."

Mead (as well as William James) used the personal pronouns *I* and *Me* to describe what we can think of as two phases of the process whereby the self is created and recreated. *I* designates the "subject" phase of the process, in which people respond as acting subjects to objects or to the particular or generalized others in their situations. *Me* labels the "object" phase of the process, in which people imagine themselves as objects in their situation.

The significance of the "I" and the "Me" can be grasped by putting these terms within the general framework of the act as Mead described it. An act begins when the individual's adjustment to a situation is disturbed. The initial, impulsive tendency is to react to a disturbance in some way; if the telephone rings, if the significance of a glance is unclear, or if what someone says is not understood, the individual is spontaneously moved to respond. Typically, conduct already under way is interrupted, and attention is turned toward the new stimulus. If one is reading a book and the telephone rings, the impulse to react to the sound occurs because one is distracted from the activity of reading.

Mead intended the concept of the *I* to capture this immediate, spontaneous, and impulsive aspect of conduct.[9] The initial part of any act, whatever the source of impulse, involves an acting "subject" who is becoming aware of the environment and the objects within it toward which action must be directed. Action always is initially unorganized and undirected, so far as the conscious awareness of the person is concerned, for it represents a response to something, and the person cannot become aware of that response until it gets under way. The person cannot designate an object and begin an act toward it until he or she has become aware of the initial, impulsive response to a stimulus.

The individual's awareness of his or her own initial response to a stimulus signals the beginning of the "Me" phase of the self. Consider a mother disciplining her child: Deemed guilty of misconduct, the child is told she is banished to her room until dinner. She begins to protest her exile, but checks herself and goes off quietly. The child has begun to protest, has imagined her mother's likely response, and has realized that biting her tongue and keeping quiet is the best way to avoid further difficulty. In such occurrences, we see the emergence of the "Me." The child in this example has responded to the imagined attitudes of the other (her mother) toward her own possible response to a situation. We call this the "object" phase of the self because the individual takes herself into account as an object. In taking the point of view of her mother, the little girl becomes a "Me." Indeed, it is at such a moment that she may use the objective case of the personal pronoun, saying to herself, "She'll only be more angry with *me* if I object!"

The "I" and the "Me" continually alternate in ongoing conduct. At one moment, the individual responds as an "I," responding to a particular situation and to the objects it contains; at the next moment, that response becomes a part of the past and so is part of the "Me." Because the response has passed into recent memory, it is now available as an object of reflection. The person further responds as an "I" to this image of self—this "Me"— which was itself a moment ago an "I." A parent sometimes shows anger toward his or her children, beginning to speak harshly to them; in so doing, the parent is acting as an "I." A moment later, becoming aware of this harshness by imagining how he or she looks from the perspective of the children, the parent becomes a "Me," and then may respond to this "Me" by apologizing or by speaking less harshly. In doing so, the parent again becomes an "I," this time responding to an image of self rather than to something outside of the self. And so the alternation between "I" and "Me" continues. (Again, it is important to stress that the "I" and "Me" are states of consciousness, not entities, in spite of the fact that our language leads us to speak of them as if they were things or parts of the self.)

This constant alternation of "I" and "Me," of impulse and reflection, is the way human beings achieve control over their conduct. The "I"—or impulse—phase of conduct is not under the person's control, for human beings do not really know what they are going to do until they begin to act. Our impulses to respond harshly or angrily to another's act, for example, can be brought under control only after they have started; one cannot really control one's temper until one has started to lose it. Impulses are governed by the state of the organism itself—that is, by its sensitivities to its surroundings, and these are not themselves directly accessible to consciousness. Physiological states such as hunger, conditioned responses to a variety of stimuli ranging from reactions to a red light to facial expressions, and perhaps many other matters affect how the individual selects and impulsively responds to a given stimulus. As the person responds, of course, his or her conduct usually can be brought under control, and we can think of the alternations between "I" and "Me" as successive approximations to an act desired by the individual and the others present. As the father checks his temper and responds evenly to his son, the son relaxes, and the father, in turn, responds to this relaxation with fatherly advice rather than punishment.

We see this process of self-formation also at work in the internal conversation that takes place when, for example, we feel caught between what we want to do and what others want us to do. Suppose a person has been invited to a party, but would really prefer to spend a quiet evening at home. "If I go," she might say to herself, "I won't have a good time, because I'm tired and I don't feel like partying. But if I don't go, I'll hurt his feelings. Well, maybe he'll understand if I explain that I'm tired. No, he'll remember I also refused an invitation last week. Perhaps I can go but not stay long. But that might also hurt his feelings or make him angry." In this internal dialogue, we also see the alternation of "I" and "Me." The person imagines how she will feel if she goes to the party, then imagines herself refusing to go, and then imagines various alternative responses and the way in which her inviter might respond to them.

This is the essence of the self as process. There is an impulse to act, imagined responses to such an act, imagined alternative actions, and some eventual resolution of the inner dialogue into some overt course of action. The dialogue may not always be as verbal and explicit as we have portrayed it here, for we do not always formulate precise verbal descriptions of our conduct and others' responses. Instead, we can also carry on this dialogue in swiftly formed and dissolved images, in fleeting glimpses of ourselves and others. Nor is our attitude necessarily a coldly disinterested, rational one. Typically, we do not merely imagine how another will react to us, but actually feel the sensations and emotions we attribute to them. The "Me" is constituted by emotional as well as cognitive responses.

The successive "Me's" that enable the individual to gain a measure of control over conduct are possible because the individual is able to imagine the perspective of another. In the moment-to-moment alternation between "I" and "Me," the person successively imagines his or her appearance in the eyes of the other and is able to control the direction of the act by responding to that imagined appearance. This may seem to be simply a way of showing how the individual is able to conform to social expectations, because with each successive "Me" the person appears to come closer to an act that the other expects and wants. However, matters are more complicated than this. Although it is true that the "Me" in a sense guides the person toward acts that are more or less in conformity with the expectations of others, human beings are not simply conforming creatures, for they are also capable of considerable novelty, creativity, and sheer self-interest. There is tension as well as cooperation between "I" and "Me."

This is so, first, because the capacity of the person to exert control over conduct depends on the inhibition of the initial, impulsive response to a situation. The father who begins to respond in anger must be able to prevent the angry impulse from turning into an overt angry word or deed. Clearly, this is not always possible, for impulses are sometimes so powerful that they carry forward into overt conduct before we can get hold of them and check them. To lose one's temper is, in effect, momentarily to fail to exercise control, to permit an impulse to issue unchecked into conduct. Thus, people are forever doing things they do not wish to do and that others do not like simply because the capacity to control conduct is not perfect.

Moreover, people make mistakes in their efforts to control their acts. They do so, for example, by misperceiving the expectations of others or of society as a whole. Each "Me" is the result of an effort to imagine how we appear from the perspective of the other, and is thus susceptible to failures or errors of imagination. The father may fail to control his anger simply because he does not see himself as harsh; that is, he imagines himself as just in the eyes of his misbehaving child, and so feels no need to check his impulse to respond angrily. And, some mistakes in control are simply the result of simple errors of perception or of muscular control. The outfielder in a baseball game may realize quite well that he is supposed to catch a fly ball but fails to do so because he misjudges its location or path. Similarly, a person may fail to see the flicker of doubt or hurt in another's face and thus misses a cue that would assist in the imagination of that person's response and the formation of an appropriate "Me."

Finally, the capacity to control conduct confers an ability to choose an act other than that which is socially expected and approved. Because human beings can inhibit their responses, form images of themselves, and then choose an act, they can refuse to act as they are expected, choosing inappropriate acts instead. To put this another way, because they have the capacity for the self-conscious control of conduct, human beings also have the capacity to act in self-interested ways and to choose alternative and even socially disapproved ways of doing so.

Roles and the Definition of Situations

Our discussion of basic concepts up to this point has equipped the person with the capacity to act, to coordinate acts with those of others, and to anticipate acts and thereby bring them under control. The analysis has glossed over some of the most important details of social coordination and self-control, however. We have not shown how it is possible for acts to be socially coordinated, for several individuals to act in such a way that each fits his or her own line of conduct to that of others. This is the next task of this chapter.

Since social coordination rests on the capacity for self-control, which depends on our ability to become objects to ourselves, we can begin to fill in the details of social coordination by looking more closely at self-objectification. Earlier, it was suggested that the person, by having a name for self as well as for others, can "get outside" the self and include the self in calculations about the group and its activities. But this is a vague formulation. What does it mean to "get outside oneself"? Where does one go and where does one stand in order to have a vantage point from which to look at oneself?

These questions are not meant literally, to be sure, for the experience of self does not rest on "out of body" experiences! It does, however, rest on the capacity to have some perspective other than one's own from which to view self as well as the situation one is in. We do not experience ourselves directly and intuitively, nor is our grasp of the circumstances that confront us limited to our own point of view. Instead, we see ourselves from the vantage point of others. We know ourselves indirectly and socially by imagining the responses of others to us. Likewise, we are able to grasp the situation of which we are a part by temporarily adopting the perspectives of others.

How are we able to do this? We say, for example, that a child anticipates the response of her parents to her actions and takes this into account in her relations with them. A daughter wants to stay out until two in the morning for a big dance, but a father is reluctant to give her permission to do so. Although her impulse may be to argue with him or to stalk angrily from the room when she is denied permission, she imagines her father will not respond positively to that behavior and that it might even make him intransigent. Thus, imagining herself acting in a way that might destroy all hope of getting what she wants, she elects to try some other approach, perhaps engaging her father in a calm and reasoned conversation about his reluctance to allow her to stay out so late. But the questions remain: How can she anticipate her father's responses to her possible acts? How can she predict that he will respond more favorably to reason than to anger?

Part of the answer—but really only a small part—lies in the fact that the daughter has had other such experiences with her father. She has learned how to ask permission to do things he will only reluctantly allow her to do, and she knows which of her actions will make him angry and which will appeal to his sense of reason and fairness. Although experience helps explain the daughter's behavior, it is not a good general explanation of how people are able to anticipate one another's acts. Much human interaction occurs among people who do not know one another, who have not established a fund of experience on the basis of which they can predict one another's behavior. We interact successfully with store clerks, lawyers, students, and many others whom we have never met. Moreover, we interact with familiar others in novel situations, where we must rely on something more than past experience to enable us to anticipate their actions.

People are able more or less successfully to anticipate one another's actions for two main reasons:

- First, at nearly every moment of our activity we know the *situation* of which we are a part. We know what we are doing, what is expected and forbidden, what is typical and what is atypical, what others are doing, and what we are doing with them because we have a *definition of the situation*.
- Second, we know *who* the others are with whom we are interacting. We know not only what is happening but who is making it happen because we have knowledge of the *roles* contained in the situation in which we find ourselves, and because we know which role is ours and which are the roles of others.

Situations

Conduct does not occur in a vacuum, but in specific, concrete, and usually well-known situations that present us with a familiar configuration of acts and objects. This configuration is termed the *definition of the situation,* which may be thought of as an overall grasp of the nature of a particular setting, the activities that have taken place there and are seen as likely to occur again, the objects to be sought or taken into account, and the others who are present. More formally, a definition of the situation is an organization of perception in which people assemble objects, meanings, and others, and act toward them in a coherent, organized way.

People act on the basis of their definitions of situations. Where a situation is familiar and its configuration of meaning is known, people organize their own conduct and their expectations of others in relation to its definition. Students and professors in a classroom, for example, usually act on the basis of a familiar definition of a situation. They know that the situation contains professors and students who will act toward such objects as questions, explanations, lectures, exams, and grades. Where there is no definition of a situation to start with—where people find themselves without confident knowledge of who is present or what is going on—they must first focus on establishing a definition. If while driving along a highway one encounters stopped vehicles and people standing around, one attempts to define the situation—to decide, for example, whether there has been an accident and, if so, how recently it has occurred—so that one can know what to do.

The concept of the definition of the situation stresses the fact that acts do not occur in an abstract, rootless, or mechanical way. Human conduct is always situated. Our acts, along with the expectations and interpretations on which they are based, are rooted in our cognition of the situations of which we are a part. To return to an earlier example, people do not interpret even such bodily gestures as glances or touches in an abstract way, but rather within particular situations, such as cocktail parties where they know who is present and they know some things are likely to occur and others are not. People know, for example, that there are limits on what constitutes a proper topic of conversation at a party—although their sense of what is proper will vary along such lines as social class or religion. It is permissible in many circles to tell off-color jokes, for example, but the revelation of intimate facts about one's own sex life would not be easily tolerated. Knowledge of what others will find tolerable or desirable is an important part of the definition of the situation. Similarly, the definition of the situation encompasses a sense of who is present and what they will do together. We know, for example, that a cocktail party will contain others who are more or less our social equals, that it will involve drinking alcoholic beverages, and that we will be expected to carry on polite conversations. Knowing in advance what a cocktail party is and who will be there, we are able to make more-or-less correct interpretations of others' acts and to construct acts they will find acceptable.

The definition of the situation not only allows us to anticipate or understand the actions of others but it also provides an important basis for our capacity to see ourselves. Because we have a definition of the situation, we can see ourselves as a part of it. That is, because we know what is going on and who is making it happen, we have a basis for seeing not only who others are and what they are doing but also who we are and what we are supposed to be doing. The "Me" that arises as we grasp the meaning and direction of our own acts is always a situated "Me." That is, we do not generally have a global image of ourselves, but a specific image that arises in a specific situation. We see ourselves in classrooms, at cocktail parties, driving our cars, and in countless other concrete, defined situations in everyday life.

When we see ourselves in these situations, we are in essence using the definition of the situation as the platform on which we stand to have a view of ourselves. Or, to shift to a different metaphor, the definition of the situation can be thought of as a map with "You are here" prominently marked at the place where we are supposed to be standing. When one holds a map in hand and visualizes one's place on it, one does so in order to determine how to get where one wants to go. When one contemplates a definition of the situation and visualizes one's place in it, one does so in order to decide what one can or should do. In both cases, we rely on an abstract representation of the world as a device to locate our position in it.

Situations contain a great many elements, and their definitions convey a great deal of knowledge about them and about ourselves. Most important for the analysis at present is what the definition of the situation conveys about who is present—about the roles that the situation contains.

No matter what the situation in which we find ourselves, we have a grasp of the way in which its activities will be socially organized. We know, more or less, who will be responsible for doing what, who is allowed to do what, who must do what, and who cannot do what. For example, if we are playing baseball, we know that the catcher crouches behind the plate and is responsible for catching pitched balls (as well as having a few other responsibilities). If we are going to a cocktail party, we know that there are different categories of persons there, called hosts and guests, and we know that each has certain responsibilities for the success of the party as a whole. Guests must circulate, talk, consume food and drink, and yet not drink too much or allow their conversations to become heated arguments.

Another way of putting this is to say that we approach each situation with a sense of how it will be organized, and that this sense of its organization is expressed in terms of *roles*. For symbolic interactionists, the concept of role provides a key link between the perspective and behavior of individuals and the social situations in which they find themselves. Moreover, just as the definition of the situation provides one platform from which we can achieve glimpses of ourselves, the roles contained within the situation provide another crucially important platform.

Role

Role is among the most widely used concepts in social science. Unfortunately, it is also among the more difficult to grasp, for its use by many sociologists differs sharply from the way symbolic interactionists use it. Because of this fact, it seems reasonable to explain the conventional usage first, and then show how the interactionist approach to role is different.[10]

In the conventional sociological view, a role is defined as a cluster of duties, rights, and obligations associated with a particular social position (or, as it may be called, status). This approach emphasizes the normative requirements of a particular role. That is, a position such as *professor* obligates one to do certain things—to show up in class to teach students, to assign them work and grade it promptly, and to keep up-to-date in one's specialty. These normative requirements constitute the professor role. Just as there is a professor role, there is a reciprocal student role, with its own set of normative requirements—to come to class, to take notes, to participate in discussions, and to show up for examinations.

The conventional sociological approach to role sees these normative requirements as providing guidance for individuals as they try to construct their conduct. That is, one knows what to do—how to "play" one's role—because the norms that define the role provide a script for any given situation in which one is called on to play the role. A role requires one to read the lines it provides, doing and saying what one must in order to live up to the normative requirements of the role.

This is a very misleading portrayal of the way people actually form their conduct and of the significance of roles in this process. It is so, first, because it exaggerates the importance of conformity to social norms in the construction of conduct. Human beings follow and make use of norms, to be sure, but for the most part, our moment-to-moment conduct as we "play" roles does not depend on efforts to conform to norms, and our attention is not focused on obligations or rights. Our attention is ordinarily focused on objects and social objects and on our individual and collective efforts to reach them. Only occasionally— when we are uncertain of what to do or when someone challenges our conduct—do we focus explicitly on norms. And often, when we do think of what we ought to do in the performance of a role, it is after the fact rather than before; we act and then consider whether we have done what we should, rather than starting with a norm and proceeding to construct our act. Moreover, a normative approach to a social role is unrealistic because even the simplest roles human beings enact would be difficult to describe or summarize with any list of duties, rights, and responsibilities.

The symbolic interactionist approach to role does not emphasize a position to which a fixed list of duties is attached. Instead, interactionists emphasize three related ideas. These ideas stress the pragmatic and creative capacities of human beings rather than their tendencies to adhere to rigid schedules of conduct.

1. Participants cognitively structure situations into roles.
2. A role is a configuration of ideas and principles about what to do in a situation.
3. People use roles as a resource for interaction in social situations.

First, they emphasize that the participants in any social situation have a sense of its *structure*. That is, when a situation is defined, so that the participants know who is present and what will occur, they can cognitively structure the situation in terms of roles. If one knows one is in a social psychology course, for example, one knows there will be students and a professor. When a situation is defined (and thus also named), its participants are also known and named, and the names we use are the names of roles—student, professor, host, guest, physician, patient, and the like.

The second idea is that a role is a configuration or gestalt—not a list of duties, but rather an organized set of ideas or principles that people employ in order to know how to behave. The role of a professor does not consist of a list of things a professor must do, but rather of a set of more general ideas about how professors and students are related to one another in various situations in which they interact. This sense of role as a whole thing rather than a set of parts is closely linked to the sense of role structure people have in defined situations. That is, to have a grasp of the situation as a whole and of the way its joint activities are parceled out to various participants (identified by their role names) is to have a grasp of several configurations or gestalts, those of others as well as of oneself. The catcher in a baseball game has a sense of the overall role structure of the game (as played by batters, pitchers, infielders, outfielders, catchers, and so forth), of his or her own location in that structure and its implications for what he or she will be expected to do, and of the locations and operating principles of others in the game.

Third, a role can be thought of as a *resource* that participants in a situation employ in order to carry on their activities. People *use* roles—that is, they bring into play their knowledge of roles in order to achieve their individual and joint goals. A pitcher uses his or her own role as a basis for acting in the situation; that pitcher also uses his or her knowledge of the roles of others in order to understand their actions. A situation provides a "container" for roles and makes it possible for participants to bring them to life, and in this sense roles are a property of the situation. But it is the participants who use the roles to bring the situation to life, and so roles are also the property of those who use them.[11]

We can sum up the interactionist conception of role by suggesting that a role be defined as a *perspective* from which conduct is constructed. A role is not a concrete list of behavior, but a more abstract perspective from which the individual participates in a social situation and contributes to its social acts and social objects. A role is thus a place to stand as one participates in social acts. It provides the perspective from which one acts—just as the roles of others, through our acts of imagination, provide perspectives from which we view both their conduct and our own. The catcher acts by grasping the baseball game as a whole through the eyes of a catcher, but also by occasionally transporting himself into the perspectives (roles) of the pitcher or batter in order to anticipate or make sense of their acts.

This approach to role recognizes that roles constrain conduct and also that the more fundamental human tendency is not merely to accept the guidance of a role but also cognitively to structure situations into roles. Our attitude toward social situations of all kinds is to organize or structure them in our minds. In other words, we look for order or meaning in the situations in which we find ourselves, and where we cannot easily find it by assigning the name of a familiar situation, we work hard to create order. Thus, if we encounter a situation in which it is not clear who occupies what positions and who enacts what roles, we turn our attention to figuring out these matters. We are role-using and situation-defining creatures. We decide who around us has authority over us, to whom we are supposed to address a question, and who we are or seem to be in the eyes of the others who are present. And if we find ourselves in a situation that is so ambiguous that there is no structure, we create one. A newly formed group, for example, may be quite undifferentiated, but before it has been in existence very long, some people will be leaders and others followers, some will be active and some will not, some will take on this task and others that one. In short, we look for structure, and where we do not find it, we create it.

For symbolic interactionists, it is the fact that our knowledge of roles provides us with a grasp of structure and organization that is important, not the particular structure provided by a given set of roles. People, we will see, act within their roles, but in a manner that permits them far more latitude and flexibility than that provided by an actor's assigned role in a play. Although roles provide them with a sense of the structure of social situations, people are capable of altering the structure when it seems necessary or desirable to do so. We are not locked within particular role structures, but have the capacity to create new ones.

Definitions of situations, together with the role structures associated with them, provide human beings with two important capacities:

- We gain the capacity to anticipate or predict the actions of the others with whom we are interacting.
- We gain the capacity to make sense of the actions of others, even those actions we did not anticipate.

Our knowledge of who is doing what permits us to make reasonably accurate predictions about the actual behavior of others. We enter a physician's examining room, for example, knowing who is the patient, who is the physician, and who is the nurse. We know that medical talk and activity will occur, and that we may be asked to disrobe or to sit on a table or to take deep breaths as the physician listens to our chest with a stethoscope. We can anticipate what the physician may ask us to do, what questions will be asked, and what his or her manner will be. This is not to say, of course, that we routinely catalog all possible happenings in our minds before entering such situations, so that we are prepared for anything and everything. We do not, in fact, imagine everything that will take place, nor do we attempt to do so, nor could we do so. But we do entertain at least some ideas about what may occur—we imagine what is going to happen—and we get our ideas about what may happen from our knowledge of the perspectives provided by roles and situations.

Our capacity for sense making is as important as our capacity to predict. Although much that actually transpires during a situation could have been anticipated had we taken the time to do so, we do not anticipate everything. Yet, there is little that does occur that does not make sense in terms of the definition of the situation and its associated roles. Knowledge of situations and roles gives us a sense making as well as a predictive capacity. To put this another way, we can make retrospective "predictions" so that, whatever does happen in a defined situation, we can make sense of it in terms of the definition of that situation and its roles. When we enter a physician's office, we assume the physician is acting within his or her role as physician and that we will act within our role as patient. This is a very powerful set of assumptions, for it disposes us to interpret whatever the physician does as an instance of his or her role. The physician's behavior—the things he or she asks us to do, the questions he or she asks, the comments he or she makes—makes sense to us (even though we may not have anticipated it) because we treat that behavior as an instance of appropriate physician role behavior. We can interpret it as behavior that makes sense from the perspective of a physician. Obviously, we cannot treat everything the physician does in these terms, for it is always possible for people to fail in their roles—that is, to act in ways regarded as inappropriate and as not interpretable as an expression of a role. As a rule, however, our expectation that people will do what is appropriate for their roles is powerful, and it stretches to cover a considerable amount of variation in what they actually do. To put this another way, behavior sometimes has to get quite far out of alignment with its role before we challenge its propriety.

The predictive and sense-making capacities roles are crucially important when it comes to our grasp of *our own behavior* in the situation. The same sense of organization and structure that enables us to predict and make sense of the behavior of others also enables us to do the same thing with respect to our own. We can get outside ourselves and anticipate and make sense of our own conduct by putting ourselves imaginatively in the shoes of others in the situation. The roles contained within a situation as well as the definition of the situation as a whole give us a place to stand and provide us with a perspective from which to view *ourselves*.

Consider again the example of going to see a physician. The same knowledge of roles that lets us imagine what the physician might do and that gives us reason to interpret the physician's behavior as plausible also allows us to imagine our own possible responses. A male, for example, who goes to a female physician for a routine physical examination will likely anticipate various parts of the examination, including the need to disrobe and submit to some intimate probing. He will perhaps wonder if he will be embarrassed or uncomfortable during the experience. He will also probably imagine the physician's disapproval were he to show much discomfort or embarrassment. After all, he might imagine her saying, women routinely submit to internal examinations by male gynecologists.

It is our hypothetical male's organization of the situation into the roles of patient and physician, as well as the roles of males and females, that leads to such imagined events and his own imagined response to them. By anticipating the possible actions of the physician, and by looking at his own reaction to the situation from her vantage point, he is able to get control of his own conduct. It is by standing in the role of the physician that this man is able to see both his own possible behavior and her possible reactions to it. Only when these possibilities are known is the person able to choose which line of conduct to pursue—whether to disregard the physician's gender or to be embarrassed because he is a male and she is a female.

As the foregoing example suggests, individuals sometimes must act within or in relation to more than one role in a situation. This is often the case with respect to gender, for no matter what other specific roles individuals have, they are almost always visibly male or female. As a result, gender is always available as a perspective on which to base one's own conduct or to interpret the conduct of others. Where occupants of a particular role—such as an occupational role—are predominantly or overwhelmingly of one sex, a special problem arises when we interact with someone whose gender is not typical of that role. In U.S. society, physicians are still predominantly men, and so the female physician presents the male patient with an atypical situation where he must, so to speak, stand naked before a female adult in a nonsexual situation. For women, accustomed to male physicians, it is more likely to be defined as "normal" to expose the body in this situation. The female physician faces a different and more serious problem, for she is apt to be treated differently than are male physicians—perhaps with less respect—and sometimes may have difficulty even convincing others to regard her as a physician. Hospital patients, for example, may assume that she is a nurse, not a physician, since nurses are predominantly female.

Role Making and Role Taking

Two concepts capture the essence of social interaction and conduct formation as they are shaped by social roles.[12]

- *Role making* is the process wherein the person constructs activity in a situation so that it fits the definition of the situation, is consonant with the person's own role, and meshes with the activity of others.
- *Role taking* is the process wherein the person imaginatively occupies the role of another and looks at self and situation from that vantage point in order to engage in role making.

These two processes are intimately linked. There can be no role making without role taking, for one cannot construct a role without at some point occupying the perspective of the other and viewing self and situation from that vantage point. And there can be no role taking without role making. As interaction proceeds, the acts of oneself and of others *document* the roles that are being made. That is, each act observed in self and in others serves as evidence that the roles we think are being made are actually being made. Only to the extent that we feel confident that we know the role of the other can we momentarily adopt their perspective in order to see ourselves as they are seeing us.

Symbolic interactionists speak of role *making,* rather than role playing or role enactment, in order to stress two important aspects of the process. First, behavior "in role" is not a matter of the routine enactment of lines in a script, where each action is well known in advance and where there is little latitude in what we can say and do. Roles are not packages or lists of mandatory behavior, but perspectives from which people construct lines of conduct that fit the situation and the lines of conduct of others.

In other words, roles provide us with an organizing framework that we can use to *make* a performance that will meet the needs of a particular situation. Each performance of a role has to be oriented to the particular demands of the situation and to the social acts that are being constructed there. It has to be tailored to meet particular conditions. Thus, for example, a physician encountering an automobile accident along the highway has to face a different situation than he or she does when examining a recalcitrant patient in his or her office. On both occasions, the individual is engaged in making his or her role as a physician, but the way he or she does so must fit the situation and its demands. No single script provides all the required directions for action. Role making thus becomes a self-conscious activity in which the person is creatively engaged in making an appropriate role performance, not a blind activity in which a script is routinely enacted.

Second, role making is a self-conscious activity. In order to make an adequate role performance—one that others will interpret as appropriate and that will also be acceptable to the one making it—there must be consciousness of self. The person must be aware of his or her own role performance in the making so that it can be adjusted to suit personal goals, the demands of the situation, and the expectations of others. This is where role taking enters the picture. To be conscious of one's own role performance, one must have a way of conceiving it, and this is attained by assuming the perspective of the others. To know where to throw the ball so that he or she can get the runner out, the catcher must know where the second baseman expects the ball to be thrown. If the catcher fails to grasp the infielder's expectations, he or she may throw the ball past the second baseman into the outfield, allowing a runner to advance and perhaps to score a run. The catcher knows what the second baseman expects by taking the infielder's perspective and by looking at the play from his or her perspective. Thus, seeing a runner on first making a move to steal, the catcher signals the second baseman, then gauges the latter's movement so that he or she can aim the ball appropriately. The catcher has used his or her grasp of the other's impending role behavior to control his or her own action.

Role taking always involves cognitively grasping the perspective of the other whose role is taken, and sometimes it also involves identification. The catcher in the foregoing example uses the perspective of the second baseman to control his or her own conduct, but this is essentially a matter of cognition. The second baseman's role is the source of a factual prediction about what he or she is likely to do. In contrast, the child who responds to parental discipline—as in the case where the child apologizes and resolves to try to do better in the future after having been called to account for some transgression—engages in role taking in which affect and evaluation are significant and identification is clearly evident. The child not only makes a factual prediction that the parent will be pleased with an apology and a resolution to do better in the future, but may also identify with the parent's perspective. That is, the child both grasps and accepts the parent's point of view, viewing what he or she did as inappropriate and viewing the parent's imposition of punishment as just. His or her subsequent conduct is thus an effort to rebuild and maintain a favorable conception of himself or herself as someone the parent will like. This constitutes role taking just as much as the more neutral, factual conduct of the catcher in relation to the second baseman.

Role Taking as a Generalized Skill

The central idea of role taking is that the individual can imagine a situation from a perspective other than that afforded by his or her role in the situation. A role provides the person with a vantage point from which to view the situation and from which to construct one's own action. As we have seen, to make one's own role performance, one must be able to grasp the situation and oneself from the vantage points provided by the roles of others. This ability to see the world through a perspective other than one's own is a generalized skill: Human beings not only see things from the vantage points of others' roles, but also from perspectives provided by the situation itself, by specific acts in the situation, and by what Mead called the *generalized other*.

Earlier, it was suggested that the situation itself offers us a place to stand and view the situation as a whole. When we assert that a definition of a situation gives us a sense of how roles structure its activities, we are in essence saying that the definition is a "platform" on which we stand to view the whole scene. If we encounter a situation and do not know at first what is happening and then assign a label to the situation—for example, by saying "This is an automobile accident in which there are injured people"—this is what we do: We "take the role of the situation," as it were, surveying the events taking place before our eyes from the "perspective" of the situation as a whole.

Moreover, specific social acts or sequences of social acts also provide us with a platform from which to view and assess what is taking place. Consider two children constructing a scenario by means of which they hope to persuade their parents not to get rid of a kitten that has been destroying the household's plants and furniture with its claws. "When Mom says they're going to give the kitten away," one might say, "I'll start to cry, and then you come into the room with the scratching post and explain how you made it so the cat will leave the furniture alone, and then Mom will say that we can try it for a few days." The child constructing the scenario is taking the role of the mother, to be sure, anticipating how she is likely to respond to a tearful child and to the other child's act of building a scratching post. But the child is also adopting the "perspective" of a social act, looking at what should or must occur in the behavior of each participant in order for that act to be carried out successfully. Here, it is the child's conception of the social act itself that provides the perspective from which the situation can be viewed.

Finally, we are afforded a place to stand and a perspective on our own and others' conduct by the generalized perspectives of the groups to which we belong or to which we aspire to belong. Our behavior is always situated, shaped by the perspective of our role in a particular social situation, whether we are playing baseball, eating dinner with our family, or attending a lecture. Situations and roles are anchored, however, in a larger context of organized group life. Baseball games occur within such larger organizational contexts as Little League Baseball or Major League Baseball. Eating a family dinner presupposes the existence of a durable group called the family. Lectures are given and attended in such larger organizational settings as colleges and universities. Furthermore, these groups and organizations themselves exist within the still larger context of community and society.

Not only do situations, roles, and social acts provide us with perspectives, then, but so do groups, organizations, communities, and societies. The physician examining a patient, for example, adopts the perspective not only of the patient and of the specific situation in which the examination occurs but also of the profession of medicine itself. That is, he or she takes into account not only the patient's definition of the situation but also the views of other physicians, who have expectations as to how an examination should be conducted—of how the patient should be treated, what tests ought to be ordered, and what forms of behavior are inappropriate.

Similarly, the child who has done something of which he knows his parents will disapprove may feel impelled to try to escape punishment by denying that he did it, and yet ultimately decide to tell the truth about his actions. To some extent, the child tells the truth because he has taken the role of his parents, identified with their expectation that he will tell the truth, and thus modified his conduct to meet this expectation and earn their approval. A more generalized process of role taking is at work here, however, for "telling the truth" is not an expectation specific to this child in relation to his parents, but is a more generalized expectation of the community or society in which the child lives. Thus, in addition to taking the role of his parents, the child also takes the role of what Mead called the *generalized other,* by which he meant the generalized perspective of the group, community, or society as a whole.

The generalized other is, like a role, a perspective that the person must imaginatively adopt in order to take it into account in forming his or her own conduct. It is made up of standards, expectations, principles, norms, and ideas that are held in common by the members of a particular social group. In a complex society, there is not one generalized other, of course, but many. Although some very general ideas about conduct seem to be held in common by all members of the society and thus represent the perspective of the society as a whole, others are confined to specific religions, ethnic groups, social classes, or even regions of a country. Thus, in their everyday lives people may at various times take different generalized others into account in constructing their behavior. Each generalized other represents the unique perspective of some community, organization, group, occupation, religion, social class, or ethnic group.

The generalized others whose perspectives the individual assumes need not be confined to groups of which one is a member. *Reference groups,*[13] defined as those social groups that provide generalized others to whom the individual refers his or her conduct and against whose standards that conduct is evaluated, may include groups of which one is not an actual member as well as groups to which one belongs. Thus, for example, a higher social class than the one of which an individual is a member may serve as a reference group for that individual and provide him or her with a generalized other whose views must be taken into account. Persons with aspirations for upward social mobility typically take higher occupational or status groups as their reference groups, using them to establish patterns of behavior appropriate to the kind of persons they hope to become.

The Place of Emotions

Thus far, our discussion has emphasized the *cognitive* aspects of the self, defining the situation, role making, and role taking. But human behavior entails more than the cognitive activity in which people calculate and coordinate their conduct, for people also respond affectively to one another and to social situations. Social life creates *feelings* of diverse kinds—fear, hate, love, empathy, embarrassment—and these emotions play an important part in shaping conduct.[14] They are as essential a part of the self as is the social world on which it rests.

What is emotion? In everyday speech, people use the term to refer to a number of feelings—such as love, hate, or anger—that they think of as being naturally or spontaneously aroused under particular conditions. Thus, they say that they "love" or "hate" certain individuals, or that in certain situations they are "afraid." The commonsense view of emotions often treats them as antithetical to rationality. When people are being emotional, people say, they are being irrational, not in full command of themselves and their actions. Although emotions are seen as a normal part of life, they are often defined as feelings that should be brought under control. Thus, an individual who is frightened may be urged to conquer his or her fear; a bereaved person may be encouraged to stop grieving after a certain period of time. There are also occasions when it is felt people *should* give vent to their feelings, when they are reassured by others that it is acceptable to cry or to shout in anger. In any case, the emotion is thought to be a natural individual response to the situation in question.

The sociological conception of emotions differs from the commonsense view. Emotions are an important element of behavior, but not because they stand in opposition to more "rational" conduct. Instead, emotions typically accompany and support cognition. People do not just make roles or define situations; they do so with accompanying feelings, such as passion or dedication, that may well enhance the effectiveness of their actions. Similarly, when human beings engage in role taking and thus form attitudes toward themselves, their attitudes are affective as well as cognitive. The self is as much an experience of feelings aroused by this object as it is a mere image of the object. People do not merely see themselves; they love or hate, cherish or despise themselves. Moreover, in the sociological view, emotions are not merely individual responses to particular individuals or situations. Instead, emotions are imbedded in the fabric of social life: They are meaningful experiences as much as any other form of behavior, and their origins and effects are likewise social and not merely individual.

Emotions have two major components:

• First, emotions are associated with physical sensations; they are physiological responses to situations.

Fear, for example, entails an increased rate of respiration and pulse, as do several other emotions, such as anger, anticipation, or excitement. Similarly, sadness appears to be associated with a depressed psychological and physiological state—tiredness, lack of interest or animation, and the inability to concentrate or sleep. Whether characterized by elevated or depressed physiological activity, however, emotions are grounded in noticeable physical states.

- Second, emotions are named, and their names shape and sometimes determine how we experience them.

"Fear" and "sadness" are not only experienced as physical sensations but also named and talked about, both by those who experience them and by others who witness people experiencing them. One can have the physical sensation associated with a particular emotion without naming it, but in doing so one experiences only a fragment of the emotion. Emotional experience requires self-objectification as much as any other form of human experience. Thus, to experience fear, one must not only have the sensations associated with fear, but also label those sensations as "fear." In doing so, the person experiences fear in a self-conscious way, seeing himself or herself as "afraid" by taking the perspectives of others. One is afraid when one is being followed on a dark street in unfamiliar territory, for example, not only because fear is a natural reaction to the situation but also because one takes the role of the person following one (and of the generalized other) and recognizes fear as an appropriate response and as an appropriate label for what one feels.

The fact that emotions are both physiological and meaningful responses to situations has led to some controversy about the relative importance of each component. Some argue that there is an identifiable physiological state that corresponds to each named emotion; others argue that the same physiological states underlie all emotions, and that the only thing that differentiates one emotion from another is the label and its implied expectations of behavior and feeling. The extreme physiological view ignores similarities in physical sensation between differing emotions, such as fear and guilt, and it ignores variations from one culture to another in the labels attached to emotions. The extreme social constructionist view tends to ignore differences in sensations between such emotions as fear and anger.

Theodore Kemper has advocated a compromise position.[15] According to Kemper, it is possible to identify four *primary* emotions, each of which has evolutionary significance, is grounded in a different and identifiable physiological state, appears relatively early in the development of the individual, and appears in every culture. *Fear, anger, depression, and satisfaction* are the four primary emotions. Fear, for example, can be seen as an evolutionary adaptation that energizes the animal in the face of danger; it is associated with the action of a specific neurochemical, epinephrine, on the sympathetic nervous system; it can be identified quite early in infancy; and it appears in every culture. In contrast to these primary emotions, Kemper says, there are more numerous and varied *secondary* emotions, such as pride, shame, guilt, love, and gratitude. These emotions are grounded in the primary emotions, but the specific experience of them depends on a set of shared social expectations. These expectations, as well as their names, are a product of culture and are therefore quite variable from one society to another. Guilt, for example, is based on the physiological responses of fear, but the nature and experience of guilt depends on our having learned to respond to certain social situations by labeling our physiological responses as "guilt."

Whether there are four primary emotions, or two, or six, emotions have their origins in social life; we experience emotion because of our participation in social interaction. The physiological states associated with various emotions can be induced by chemical means: Pulse and respiration can be increased, for example, by administering epinephrine, and various antidepressant drugs, such as Prozac or Wellbutrin, have the effect of brightening or elevating mood. But these same states are also—and more significantly—induced by our normal involvement in social situations. And just as emotions originate in social inter-action, they are regulated as people interact, and by the same general processes that regu-late our conduct in general. Three facts are especially important in this regard.

First, emotions naturally arise in our efforts to complete individual and social acts. When an act runs successfully to its conclusion, it is apt to engender feelings of satisfac-tion or even elation in those who have been involved in completing it. The football player who runs 50 yards to a touchdown does not ordinarily respond neutrally to this accom-plishment but is excited by it. The parent who has just successfully taught a child to ride a bicycle feels proud or satisfied as a result of this success. Likewise, when individual and social acts meet obstacles and are thus blocked, people respond with feelings as well as thought. A car that fails to start on a cold winter morning and thus prevents a student from taking an important examination produces a feeling of anger or frustration as well as a cal-culation of how to get to school and how to convince the professor to provide an opportu-nity for a makeup.

Second, our experience of emotions is an experience of *self.* Although bodily sensa-tions—trembling, tightening of muscles, rapid breathing, or a feeling of supreme well-being—are an important part of emotions, it is the attribution of meaning to these sensations that permits emotional experience. This attribution of meaning requires the objectification of self through role taking. We see ourselves—as happy, sad, afraid, or angry—as we imagine others see us in the social situation. The football player who feels elated when he scores a touchdown does so in a social context in which he shares the imag-ined judgment of others that his touchdown merits this feeling of elation. The student who misses an examination because her car won't start is angry with herself because she imagines and shares the views of others that she ought to have checked the condition of her battery.[16]

Third, emotions are a regular part of the role-making process. When people con-struct performances that they think will make sense to others, mesh with the others' roles, and meet the requirements of the situation, they take emotional expectations into account. We are somber at funerals and happy at weddings because we grasp the fact that appropri-ate emotional expressions are a part of our role performances. We will discuss the ways in which people are able to construct either the appearance or the real experience of emotions appropriate to situations in Chapter 4.

Keywords

Act   An act is a functional unit of conduct, with an identifiable beginning and end, that is related to the organism's purposes and that is oriented toward one or more objects. The full meaning of this definition can best be grasped by examining the words that make it up.

What does it mean to say that an act is a "functional unit of conduct"? Interactionists argue that conduct is best understood not as a series of responses to particular stimuli, but as an ongoing process in which people are trying to adapt to or master their

surroundings, to accomplish tasks, and to reach goals. Human beings want to care for their children, make a living, or get good grades in college. Acts are made up of a number of responses to stimuli—and sometimes a great many such responses over a long period of time—that move the person toward the accomplish-ment of such goals. A professor interrupting a lecture to answer a student's question has produced such a "functional unit of conduct." That is, his or her conduct from the time the student's raised hand is first noticed until the lecture is resumed constitutes a unit of activity that advances the professor's overall goal of communicating information and understanding to the students.

When does an act begin and when does it end? The previous example offers a good way to grasp what is happening. A student question during a lecture "interrupts" the lecture (as a professor who likes questions, I hasten to add that such "interruptions" are very welcome). The professor has an act—a lecture—underway. A student's raised hand is an interruption in the sense that it prevents the professor from continuing the lecture as if nothing had happened (or at least it makes it difficult for the professor to do so). Rather, the professor must suspend the lecture and turn his or her attention to the question, even if only to tell the student to wait a few minutes for the answer.

An act begins, then, typically when some other act meets an obstacle of some kind and is interrupted in its course. Likewise, the act ends when the obstacle has been removed and the original act can be resumed. This analysis portrays people as constantly engaged in activity, faced with a variety of obstacles or interruptions, and attempting to get activity back on track and keep it there. Professors interrupt their lectures to answer questions and then strive to return to where they were and continue with the lecture. Carpenters interrupt their work to consult with homeowners when difficulties or questions arise, and then return to the task of getting the job done. Students interrupt their studying to have a cup of coffee or to chat with a roommate, and return to their books.

Acts are directed toward and make use of **objects** (later defined), a word that can be confusing because of its dual meaning. For professor and students in a classroom, "understanding" is an important object; when a student asks a question, an "answer" temporarily becomes the object of their attention and effort, until it is achieved and "understanding" can once more occupy center stage. For the carpenter, "installing the door" is the main object, until the point where a difficulty arises, when the object then becomes a "decision" or an "agreement" with the homeowner as to how to overcome the difficulty. An object is both a tangible or intangible thing indicated by one or more people and used by them to grasp their circumstances and it is a goal of their conduct.

An act ends when its object is attained. The professor's act of answering a question ends when he or she has produced what both the students and the professor can regard as a satisfactory "answer." The carpenter's act of consulting with the homeowner ends

when the latter makes a decision as to what to do. When one act of this kind ends, the act that was interrupted resumes, and presumably it also ends at some point. The professor completes the lecture; the carpenter installs the door.

Communication Communication is often—but misleadingly—defined as the transfer of information from a sender to a receiver. A newspaper informs its readers that the day's weather will be cloudy and rainy; a sociology professor informs students that the middle class is shrinking and that the disparity of wealth between the richest and poorest segments of the society is growing. This approach to communication, although not completely wrong, ignores the most fundamental part of the phenomenon: influence. The essence of communication is not the transfer of information but rather the influence that the behavior of one person (or animal) has on another.

Symbolic interactionists argue that communication is a pervasive phenomenon—indeed, that it is the most important social phenomenon there is. Every act is communicative, for it is either intended to influence the other or it actually influences the other even if not consciously intended to do so. A student raising a hand in class intends to influence the professor—that is, to change his or her conduct by interrupting the lecture and securing an answer to a question. A student whose unintentionally outstretched arm is interpreted by the professor as a hand raised to ask a question also influences the professor, even though he or she was only stretching an arm. In both cases, communication occurs because the act of one influences the act of the other.

Human communication is symbolic, which is to say that people base their responses on the interpretation of one another's acts and gestures. Not all communication is symbolic, however. Animals influence one another's conduct and therefore communicate. However, there is no interpretive process in their conversation of gestures. In symbolic communication, responses are predicated on the designation of another's act as meaningful or purposive. Such interpretations can be wrong—as in the case of the professor who interprets a stretch as a raised hand—but it is nonetheless on interpretations that responses are based.

Definition of the Situation A definition of a situation is an organization of perception in which people assemble objects, meanings, and others, and act toward them in a coherent, organized way. A definition of the situation, in other words, organizes meanings in such a way that people can act individually and jointly. It tells people *who* is present in a situation, *what* conduct to expect from others and what to do themselves, *how* events are likely to unfold over the course of the situation, *where* the situation is located in relation to other situations, and what *goals* are to be pursued by self and others. A definition of a situation as a "college class," for example, establishes that there will be students and a professor, that lectures and discussions will occur, that the class will begin and end at a fixed time, that the class is one of a series of other classes taken by students and taught by the professor, and that the situation's goals include such things as "understanding" and "answers."

Two aspects of this important interactionist concept are especially worth remembering. First, a definition of the situation is necessary for organized and successful conduct to occur. Without a shared definition of the situation, people are confused or paralyzed because they have no basis on which to anticipate the actions of others or to know what they are expected to do. For example, drivers at an intersection where traffic signals have ceased to work will be confused and uncertain until they define the situation as "broken signals" or a "power outage." Only then will they be able to improvise an orderly flow of traffic by taking turns, acting as if the intersection were controlled by a four-way stop sign.

Second, definitions of situations are external and constraining. Even though definitions are "carried" in the minds of individuals, their reality is collective rather than an individual. This is because each person's definition of the situation is a hypothesis about what is taking place and what he or she should do in response to the acts of others. The hypothesis can only be confirmed by observing the acts of others and seeing how one's own acts fit with theirs. Moreover, once it is established, the definition of the situation is constraining because it is taken as *reality* by those who have created or accepted it. Even those who doubt the accuracy of the definition are constrained by it, for they are apt to feel there is something wrong with them if they do not see what others see.

Emotion   Emotion is one of three general ways—cognitive, conative, and affective—in which human beings orient themselves to their world and to themselves. *Cognition* refers to our perception and interpretation of objects and events in our surroundings, as, for example, when a professor sees an eraser on the tray of the chalkboard. *Conation* is the experience of will or purposefulness, as when the professor uses the eraser to remove his earlier scribblings from the board so that he or she can write something new. *Affect* refers to emotions and sentiments, to the feelings of satisfaction, anger, frustration, jealousy, and the like, as when the professor feels proud of a new idea he or she has just explained.

Everyday experience blends these three elements together, and some scholars would argue that it is impossible to separate them. A craftsperson hard at work making a piece of pottery or furniture, for example, may simultaneously experience feelings of pride (affect), have a sense of purpose (conation) as he or she manipulates tools to shape a pot or smooth a surface, and engage in perceiving and interpreting the shape of a pot or the grain of a board (cognition). Even so, it is worth separating them at least analytically in order to call attention to their differing importance for social life.

The study of emotion calls attention to several important facets of human conduct. First, it reminds us that people have bodies and that they are behaving entities, not disembodied selves or role takers and role makers. Mead emphasized that mind and body should not be separated—that the study of mind is really the study of behavior. Contemporary students of emotion emphasize that emotions are an integral component of social life and of the self—that the very same emotions that are aroused in us in relationships with others are also aroused as we perceive and act toward ourselves. We may be angry with ourselves, in love with ourselves, or feel detached from ourselves.

Second, emotions are part and parcel of every individual and social act. Some emotions arise when acts are thwarted or blocked—we are apt to feel frustrated or upset when we cannot do what we want to do because of some obstacle, as when a car will not start and we cannot get to class on time or when a loved one dies and our whole life pattern is for a time disrupted. Emotions also arise during the course of our acts. For example, a baseball pitcher at the height of his or her game is likely to have strong feelings of confidence while striking out a series of batters. In fact, emotions that arise during the course of an act are important parts of the motivation to continue in those acts. Confidence is not just a product of the pitcher's activity, but it also *enables* his or her strong performance. Additionally, emotions accompany the consummation of acts, as when one feels pride in a task successfully accomplished. For instance, the pride a student feels on completing an assignment may come from his or her own appraisal of the work or from the praise of the professor, but in either case, it is a result of the completed act.

Generalized Other   The generalized other is best thought of as the imagined perspective of an imagined other, whether this other is the whole society, the community to which the individual belongs, or some smaller category or grouping of people. The generalized other may thus represent the imagined perspectives of people as diverse as all members of U.S. society, one's fellow students or professors, all human beings, other African Americans or Jews, or all men or all women. The crucial point about this concept is that when human beings interact, they frequently, if not invariably, do so not only with concrete other human beings but also with a generalized idea of the expectations, values, beliefs, and standards of some category of human beings.

Another and perhaps more vivid way of portraying the generalized other is by thinking of each situation of human interaction as containing a set of imaginary others present in the mind of each interactant. A professor in the classroom, for example, is very cognizant of the expectations of a particular set of students. The professor is aware of the content of the lecture he or she is giving, can see the looks of understanding or confusion on student faces, and thus gears his or her conduct toward the imagined meaning of their responses and gestures. But there is an invisible presence in the classroom, for the professor also responds to the imagined expectations and standards of other professors. An off-color joke that might illustrate a point and that students might think funny might not be told because, standing behind the professor there is an imagined other, representing professors as a whole, expressing disapproval.

"I" and "Me"   The *I* and the *Me* are names for the alternating phases of consciousness that human beings experience in the course of their acts. The crucial fact to remember about these words is that they stand for the perspective the acting individual takes toward self and others. One can either be an acting subject, an "I," whose attention is focused on events outside oneself; or one can be an object of one's own action, a "Me," with attention focused on one's own real or imagined actions. One cannot be both simultaneously, and so interactionists, following Mead, argue that there is an alternation between these two phases of consciousness. At one moment, the person begins to respond to a stimulus, and in doing so begins to form an object and develop a plan of action toward it. At the next moment, the individual becomes aware of his or her response and does so by taking the perspective of another toward it. And at the next moment, the individual responds to this awareness of self.

Another example may help illustrate the concepts. I was carrying my young grandson, a toddler, in my arms and he was looking with interest at a nearby saguaro cactus, a rather small one that I thought he might enjoy seeing up close. So I carried him closer to the cactus, but as I did so I noticed that he was squirming a bit in my arms and acting decidedly uncomfortable. I remembered that he had been taught not to go near or touch cacti, and that often he would say, "Cactus, ouch!" when he saw one. I thought to myself that he was feeling afraid as we grew closer to the plant, and so I moved away from it. At one moment I was in the "I" phase, moving toward the cactus; at the next moment, I was in the "Me" phase, imagining my action from the vantage point of my grandson; and in the next moment, I was again in the "I" phase, responding to my own action by changing direction.

Object   An object is anything to which attention can be paid and toward which action can be directed. There are several key points to keep in mind about objects. First, in symbolic interactionist usage, objects may be both tangible and intangible. That is, an object may be a thing that can be named and acted toward, such as a cup of coffee or a computer, but it can also be an abstraction, such as "love" or "truth," that cannot be directly grasped but that nonetheless is named and acted toward. Second, objects do not exist except insofar as they are named and acted toward. The thing we call a cup of coffee obviously has a physical existence that does not depend on our naming it or drinking it—the cup does not disappear from the earth when we turn away from it. But it is an object only by virtue of the way we pay attention to it and act toward it, and its physical characteristics do not determine its nature as an object. The "cup of coffee" can become another object, an "example," if someone uses it in that way, such as in a book on social psychology. Third, objects are linked to the goals of acts. Every act has an object in the sense that participants move toward some desired state of affairs—an object—such as "an agreement" or a "new house." As people engage in acts, they also make use of objects—we construct agreements with contracts and new houses with hammers and saws.

Phases of the Act   The phases of the act describe a process through which every act proceeds from start to finish (though not without interruption). *Impulse* is the initial phase in which the person feels a readiness or a need to act because some stimulus has occurred. The telephone rings, a friend smiles, a student sees a low grade written on his or her examination, and in each instance, the individual is ready or mobilized to act in some way. *Perception* is the next phase, in which the person grasps the nature of the stimulus that has led to the impulse. One hears the telephone, begins to interpret the smile, realizes the significance of the grade. During this phase, human beings engage in a process of reflection, in which they gradually and often very self-consciously move from the initial perception of the stimulus to the formation of a plan of action—an object. The person sees himself or herself answering the phone, smiling in return, or asking the professor for an appointment to discuss the examination grade. *Manipulation* is the phase in which the person takes steps to move toward the object—answering the phone, creating a smiling face, or consulting the professor after class. *Consummation* is the phase in which the object is attained—a phone answered, a smile returned, an appointment made.

Role   A role is a perspective from which the person acts in a defined situation. It is not a list of desired or expected behaviors, nor is it a firmly written script that the everyday actor merely memorizes and repeats. Rather, it is one among several interlocked perspectives that the individual knows about and from which he or she can act or imagine others acting in the situation. A player in a baseball game knows the rules of the game as a whole and the part to be played by each player, as well as the part he or she is called on to play, such as pitcher or outfielder. To know the role of pitcher or outfielder is to understand the perspective from which such a player approaches the game, and to be able to use that understanding to construct one's own behavior or to anticipate the behavior of others.

Role Making   Role making is the construction of a performance that is relevant to the situation and appropriate to one's perspective within it. The image of role making emphasizes the fact that people must often think hard in order to know what to do and that they must often invent new ways of acting in order to create a successful performance. Even though a student knows how to sit in a college classroom and act like an interested student, he or she must be able to respond to less familiar or less common events, such as being asked a question by the professor. Role making is often very routine, but sometimes it is not. It is the nonroutine instances of role making that remind us that people engaged in social interaction must be attentive to the situations in which they interact and have a grasp of the perspective—the role—from which others expect them to act.

Role Taking   Role taking is the imaginative placing of oneself in the shoes of the other in a situation, so that one can grasp his or her perspective (role) and understand the other's conduct *and one's own* from that point of view. To take the role of the other is not to enact, play, or make the other's role, but rather to *imagine* that role, how the situation looks from its vantage point, how one looks to the other, and what the other expects of one. Role taking is essential to role making, since the construction of an adequate performance in a social situation requires the person to know how others in the situation view him or her. That knowledge does not generally come from questions directed to the other or from long-term acquaintance with them, but rather from a knowledge of the situation as a whole and the perspectives (roles) of others within it.

Self   The self is a social object. That is, the reality of the self lies in the actions that are taken toward it by the person and the others with whom he or she is interacting or imagines himself or herself interacting. The self is not a thing, nor is it equivalent to the body, nor is it mysteriously located somewhere inside the person. Rather, like any other object, the self is something named, to which attention is paid and toward which actions are directed.

The importance of the self lies in its role in the formation and control of human conduct. Because human beings can name and thus objectify themselves, they have the capacity to take themselves into account when they act. That is, they can imagine themselves acting in a particular way, they can imagine others acting toward them, and they can consider the effect of alternative ways of acting on themselves, on others, and on the situation as a whole. Thus, the self is a key object people make use of in their efforts to achieve control over their conduct, for it is because we can imagine ourselves that we can guide our own conduct in a direction that will suit the situation as a whole and make sense to others. In other words, the self is both a product of **role taking** (previously defined) (because we see ourselves when we imagine the perspectives of others) and a key object in **role making** (previously defined) (because we have to see ourselves in order to make an acceptable performance).

Sign A sign is something that stands for something else. In animal (and human) behavior there are many instances where an animal learns to respond to a sign of a stimulus instead of or in addition to the stimulus for which it stands. The classic illustration is Pavlov's dog learning to salivate at the sound of a buzzer, a sign that it learned to associate with the stimulus food. Signs are either natural or conventional. A *natural sign* is one that comes to stand for something else because an animal has learned that the sign and the stimulus it stands for are regularly associated in its world. A *conventional sign* is one whose meaning is established by some kind of agreement among those who use it and whose significance can be communicated from one to another. Another word for conventional sign is **symbol** (later defined).

Social Act A social act is the coordinated activity of several individuals jointly focused on and moving toward the completion of a social object. In a business contract, the various activities of people engaged in doing business constitute the social act: meetings, proposals, negotiations, offers, and counteroffers are undertaken in an effort to create "the contract" whereby they will do business together in the future. Just as an act is completed when its object is reached, a social act is completed when the social object is attained.

Social Object A social object is an object created by the attention and action of several individuals coordinating their conduct toward it. Just as an **object** (previously defined) is anything that can be the object of attention and toward which action can be directed, so a social object requires attention and action. But in the case of the social object, it is the coordinated behavior of interacting individuals that pays the object its attention and directs action toward it. A business contract is a social object, by this definition, because several people jointly negotiate the terms of a business arrangement and strive to bring a document—"the contract"—into existence.

Symbol A symbol is a conventional sign. That is, a symbol is something—a gesture, a picture, and most often, a word—that stands for something else. Like any sign, a symbol stands in place of that which it signifies, and thus enables people to respond to it in place of what it signifies. Unlike natural signs, however, symbols have properties that give their users greater mastery over their worlds. Symbols are public rather than private, and this makes it possible for a symbol user to reproduce his or her reaction to a particular situation in the mind of another. Moreover, because their meaning can be communicated, they do not have to be learned by trial and error by the individual but can be taught to others. Symbols have no natural connection with the things they signify, and so can be invoked even in the absence of that for which they stand. Indeed, symbols can be invented that do not stand for anything concrete—thus, symbols give rise to abstract objects. Symbols also make it possible for users to refer to themselves as a part of their environment, thus giving rise to the phenomenon we call self.

Endnotes

1. Symbolic interactionists, as much because of their own pragmatism as because of the critiques of postmodern theory and social constructionism, use the word *reality* with caution. For a recent effort to reclaim the word *reality* (as well as *objectivity* and *truth*) for sociology, see Stephen Lyng and David D. Franks, *Sociology and the Real World* (Lanham, MD: Rowman & Littlefield, 2002).

2. This discussion is influenced by the classic work of Ernest Becker and Leslie A. White. See Ernest Becker, *The Birth and Death of Meaning* (New York: Free Press, 1952), especially Chapters 2 and 3; and Leslie A. White, "Four Stages in the Evolution of Minding," in *The Evolution of Man*, ed. Sol Tax, vol. 2 of *Evolution After Darwin* (Chicago: University of Chicago Press, 1959). See also John P. Hewitt, "Symbols, Objects, and Meanings," in *Handbook of Symbolic Interactionism*, eds. Larry T. Reynolds and Nancy J. Herman-Kinney (Walnut Creek, CA: AltaMira Press, 2003), Chapter 12.

3. A classic portrayal of language evolution can be found in Charles F. Hockett and Robert Ascher, "The Human Revolution," *Current Anthropology* 5 (1964): 135–168. For another view, see Gordon Hewes, "Primate Communication and the Gestural Origin of Language," *Current Anthropology* 14 (1973): 5–24. A more recent theory of language can be found in Terrence W. Deacon, *The Symbolic Species: The Co-evolution of Language and the Brain* (New York: Norton, 1997).

4. In addition to Deacon, *The Symbolic Species* (Note 3), Part One, see Davydd J. Greenwood and William A. Stini, *Nature, Culture, and Human History* (New York: Harper & Row, 1977).

5. Herbert Blumer, *Symbolic Interactionism: Perspective and Method* (Englewood Cliffs, NJ: Prentice Hall, 1969), p. 11.

6. Bernard N. Meltzer, "Mead's Social Psychology," in *Symbolic Interaction: A Reader in Social Psychology,* eds. Jerome Manis and Bernard Meltzer (Boston: Allyn & Bacon, 1972), p. 15.

7. See George Herbert Mead, *The Philosophy of the Act,* edited and with an introduction by Charles W. Morris (Chicago: University of Chicago Press, 1938), pp. 3–25.

8. George Herbert Mead, *Mind, Self, and Society* (Chicago: University of Chicago Press, 1934), p. 7.

9. Ibid., pp. 173–226 and 273–281.

10. The conventional sociological view finds its classic expression in the work of Robert K. Merton and William J. Goode. See Merton, "Sociological Ambivalence," in his *Sociological Ambivalence and Other Essays* (New York: Free Press, 1976), pp. 3–31; and Goode, "A Theory of Role Strain," in his *Explorations in Social Theory* (New York: Oxford, 1973). Others have argued that the conventional and interactionist approaches to role are more alike than they seem. See Warren Handel, "Normative Expectations and the Emergence of Meaning as Solutions to Problems: Convergence of Interactionist and Structural Views," *American Journal of Sociology* 84 (1979): 855–881; and Jerold Heiss, "Social Roles," in *Social Psychology: Sociological Perspectives,* eds. Morris Rosenberg and Ralph H. Turner (New York: Basic Books, 1981), pp. 94–129. Ralph H. Turner effectively rebuts their arguments. See his "Unanswered Questions in the Convergence Between Structuralist and Interactionist Role Theory," in *Micro-Sociological Theory,* vol. 2, eds. H. J. Helle and S. N. Eisenstadt (London: Sage, 1985), pp. 23–36. For a recent review of role theory and research, see Norman A. Dolch, "Role," in *Handbook of Symbolic Interactionism,* Chapter 6 (Note 2).

11. See Wayne E. Baker and Robert R. Faulkner, "Role as Resource in the Hollywood Film Industry," *American Journal of Sociology* 97 (September 1991): 279–309.

12. The classic symbolic interactionist statement on role is by Ralph H. Turner, "Role-Taking: Process versus Conformity," in *Human Behavior and Social Process,* ed. Arnold M. Rose (Boston: Houghton-Mifflin, 1962), pp. 20–40. For another excellent statement, see also Peter L. Callero, "Toward a Meadian Conceptualization of Role," *Sociological Quarterly* 27 (Fall 1986): 343–358.

13. See Tamotsu Shibutani, "Reference Groups as Perspectives," *American Journal of Sociology* 60 (1955): 562–569; Shibutani, "Reference Groups and Social Control," pp. 128–147 in Rose, *Human Behavior* (Note 12); and Ralph H. Turner, "Role-Taking, Role-Standpoint, and Reference Group Behavior," *American Journal of Sociology* 61 (1956): 316–328.

14. For background on the sociology of emotions, see Steven L. Gordon, "The Sociology of Sentiments and Emotion," in Rosenberg and Turner, *Social Psychology* (Note 10), pp. 562–592; and Lyn Smith-Lovin, "The Sociology of Affect and Emotion," pp. 118–148 in Karen S. Cook, Gary Alan Fine, and James S. House, *Sociological Perspectives on Social Psychology* (Boston: Allyn & Bacon, 1995). A more recent and very useful statement of the interactionist approach can be found in David D. Franks, "Emotion," in *Handbook of Symbolic Interactionism,* Chapter 32 (Note 2).

15. Theodore Kemper, "How Many Emotions Are There? Wedding the Social and Autonomic Components," *American Journal of Sociology* (September 1987): 263–289.

16. Cathyrn Johnson extends Mead's theory of the self by including an emotional dimension. See her "The Emergence of the Emotional Self: A Developmental Theory," *Symbolic Interaction* 15 (Summer 1992): 183–202.

Chapter *3*

The Self and Its Social Setting

The conceptual tool of symbolic interactionism most closely associated with the perspective and most central to its view of human beings and their conduct is the concept of *self*. In the preceding chapter we sketched the outlines of this concept, pointing to its dual nature as a social process and a social object. In this chapter we develop these ideas in greater detail, beginning with an account of the origins of self.

The Acquisition of Self

There is no self at birth. The newborn has the capacity to acquire a self, but since it has not yet learned to speak, it lacks the developed symbolic capacity necessary for self-designation. Indeed, at the beginning of life it is scarcely aware of any distinction between itself and its environment. It will, in the early weeks and months, learn to distinguish its own body from the surrounding world, and in so doing it builds a necessary foundation for a self. But in the beginning the infant does not act toward itself as an object, and its behavior is not regulated by a dialogue between "I" and "Me." These capacities lie in the future.

Obviously, babies are not inert, for they respond to events in various ways, nursing at their mothers' breasts, crying when they are uncomfortable, and responding to the sound, smell, and touch of other humans. They are capable of and engage in immense amounts of learning in their early months. But neither their learning nor their behavior is at first characterized by self-consciousness. Whether their needs are satisfied depends largely on the inclinations of their parents or other caregivers. Others act toward the infant in a symbolic way, for they interpret its cries and coos as expressions of its needs or of its pleasurable or angry feelings when these needs are met or thwarted. But the actions of the infant are not symbolically organized. The face it presents to the world is not under self-conscious control. The infant cries when it is hungry, of course, but does not *self-consciously* cry in order to persuade adults to meet its needs. Rather, adults interpret the infant's cries (sometimes correctly and sometimes not) as expressions of the infant's needs and then act in accordance with their interpretations. The symbolic interaction taking place is very much one-sided.

Children of age 5 or 6 are remarkably different creatures. First-graders are capable of speech. They can do much of the work necessary to care for themselves and meet their everyday needs—dressing themselves, feeding themselves, using the toilet, and so on. They have a far more sophisticated repertoire of conduct and a reasonable degree of control over it, so that for brief periods of time they can be left unattended by adults. How do such changes come about? What happens in the first few years of life to endow the child with a vastly expanded range of behavioral capabilities?

Clearly, physiological and psychological growth and development—what we might call maturation—are an important part of what takes place. Newborns can do very little, but during their first year, infants develop the ability to hold their heads up, to roll over from stomach to back, to sit up, to crawl, and eventually to stand erect and take their first steps. They learn to coordinate information gained through the senses and begin to distinguish between themselves and the external world. Through toddlerhood and early childhood, additional developmental processes are at work and considerable learning takes place.

Although cognitive and physical growth and development are crucially important in these early years, symbolic interactionists believe that it is the development of self that forms the most crucial aspect of this part of the child's life. Although maturation brings the capacities needed to serve as a member of the human group, it is the acquisition of self that ties the individual to the group and makes the group a part of the person being created.

Language and the Self

Developing the ability to act toward the self as an object depends on the acquisition of language, for it is in language that our symbolic capacity is imbedded and upon which self-reference depends.[1] Language is crucial to the acquisition of self in two major ways. First, language provides the system of names for self and others that makes possible the individual's participation in group life as well as the incorporation of group life within the individual. Language confronts the child with an organized society of his or her fellow human beings. Second, language provides a vast array of labels for other important objects, so that the child is brought into contact not just with the group but also with the environment in which the group lives. That is, language confronts the child with culture.[2]

Learning the Social World

The child is born into a social world, an ongoing network of interpersonal relationships among parents, siblings, other kin, and wider circles of others outside the family. This world is already in existence and confronts the new arrival as a massive, natural fact. The individuals in this world are linked to one another in a variety of role relationships, and each relationship is named. There are parents and children, brothers and sisters, husbands and wives, grandmothers and grandsons, cousins, friends, and many others. Just as the relationships among people in this network are named, so the individuals in the network are named as well. Thus, "father" is also "Daddy" and "Jared," and "cousin" is also "Maggie" or "John."

This social world confronts the child with a considerable array of objects about which the child at first knows nothing because he or she has no names for them. Gradually, the child learns to make sounds, to imitate the sounds that adults make, and to associate these sounds with particular sensations. Of paramount importance, the child learns the sounds associated with significant others—for example, "Mama" and "Daddy"—and eventually the name by which they refer to him or her.

As the child first hears and later repeats the names of people in the social world, he or she makes two momentous discoveries. The first is that *things have names*. The child learns to associate sounds with the things and people he or she regularly encounters and, crucially, that it feels good to learn and use those names. The child's first efforts to name people or things are met with positive responses by caregivers, who respond with praise or in other ways regarded as culturally appropriate. Parents enthusiastically greet the first "Mama" or "Dada," conveying through tone of voice and facial expressions that something momentous has occurred. They may write down the child's first vocabulary words and, later, sentences. Indeed, since the acquisition of language is a measure of normal development, parents also greet the child's words with a sense of relief: their child is normal.

The second discovery is perhaps even more momentous: *there is a name for me*.[3] That is, the child learns not only to associate a sound with himself or herself but also to repeat that sound and to enjoy the social response that follows. When the child learns that he or she is the object to which others refer when they use a certain name, and that he or she can also use this name, the child has made a significant leap toward the full acquisition of self. A rudimentary sense of the distinction between the child and his or her others has been replaced by a more precise way of designating self and others. Only after this crucial development occurs does the child really begin to possess a self, for only then does the child have a way of getting outside his or her own perspective and viewing self from the perspective of others.

Yet the mere knowledge of a name and the capacity to use it to refer to self yields a relatively undifferentiated self. True, the individual now has the capacity to visualize himself or herself as a separate and distinct object among many objects in the environment. And, as a result, the child's capacity to control his or her own conduct, including bodily movements, is thereby enhanced. Acquiring knowledge of one's name helps to carry forward a general process of differentiating body and self from the external world. But the self that develops initially is relatively simple, for it can be no more complex than the child's conception of the social world of which he or she is a part. Initially, this conception is rather simple.

Developing a more complex capacity for self-reference involves learning one's native language and then mastering its procedures for referring to self and others. The reality presented to the child by important others and their various names and titles is complex and must gradually be deciphered. Important social objects such as the child's mother and father have more than one name. They are "Mama" and "Daddy" to the child, but they are also addressed by other terms of reference. Thus, "Daddy" is also "Robert," "Bob," and "Mr. Jones." The child is confronted with alternative personal names as well as titles. Overlaid on these names and titles is a complicated set of personal pronouns. Thus, "Daddy" talks about himself using words like *I* and *me* and is referred to by others using words like *you, he, his,* and *him.* The child also uses these terms and has them applied to him or her by others.

It is not surprising, therefore, that children at first make mistakes in their use of pronouns. Sometimes they refer to themselves using their first name, at other times shifting to a pronoun, but often the wrong one—a child may refer to herself as "you" because she has heard herself referred to in this way. Gradually, children's usage becomes more accurate—not only in the sense that they learn to use the grammatically correct form of a pronoun (*he* or *she* as the subject of a sentence, for example, and *him* or *her* as the object) but also, and more significantly, because their usage comes to reflect the complexities of social relationships. That is, their pronoun usage comes to reflect a more sophisticated grasp of relationships between people and of the variety of perspectives from which these relationships can be viewed. Children learn a multitude of things: that *I* and *me* refer to oneself, and that anyone can use these terms to refer to self; that *he* and *him* refer to males and *she* and *her* refer to females; that older adults, if they are male, may be fathers, but that only one adult is "Father"; that just as "Sam" is a brother, so also they are brothers or sisters to Sam.

Among the earliest facts about the social world that children learn and incorporate as a basic part of their conceptions of themselves is that the social world is *gendered*. That is, they learn that there are several pairs of terms—boy and girl, male and female, man and woman—and that these terms refer to a fundamental and apparently important principle of social classification. They do not learn about the meanings of these terms immediately, but gradually as others act toward them as male or female children. Nor do children immediately grasp the basis on which others treat them as male or female; although the child is classified at birth as either male or female on the basis of external genitalia, at various points he or she may think clothing, hair length or style, or the presence or absence of a beard is the crucial determinant of this classification. The child does learn, however, that this classification is important and that it is in many ways crucial to his or her membership in society. As Spencer Cahill has pointed out, adults seem to speak and act as if babies "do not mature into 'big kids' but into 'big girls' and 'big boys.'"[4] No matter how children learn about gender and at whatever rate, the selves they develop are, from the start, gendered selves.

Along with increasing accuracy in the use of pronouns and relationship terms, as well as a grasp of sex and age as basic social categories, comes an increasingly more complex conception of self. The more the child masters these terms, the better able he or she is to represent these relationships internally, thus incorporating the social world into himself or herself. Because he or she can represent others and their perspectives symbolically ("Mommy wants me to be a good boy"), the child gains in capacity for self-control, but also becomes more susceptible to social controls. No longer simply an organism that receives care from others and is controlled directly by them, the child becomes an increasingly self-governed entity, representing to himself or herself the perspectives of others and taking them into account as he or she constructs conduct. The child becomes more adept at role taking, and as he or she does so, also becomes a more successful role maker.

Learning the Culture

Acquiring language opens up membership in the group as well as contact with the group's world—with the tangible and abstract objects that, taken together, constitute its culture. As the infant moves into and through childhood, he or she learns not only his or her own name, gender, and relationship to others, but also the names of the objects recognized by the group or society to which the child belongs. The child learns the names of tools, ideas, places, buildings, activities, plants, vehicles, and myriad other objects that constitute the surrounding culture. Children learn a common set of objects—and thus a common culture—regardless of social class or the region of the country in which they live, but they also learn about additional objects and define some objects in different ways, depending on whether their parents are wealthy or poor, farmers or urban factory workers, and so on.

The child learns about the objects of culture partly by attaching names to things, so that the visible, tangible objects within sight or reach can be talked about. Parents make an effort to teach their children the names of such objects, and children themselves are curious. Having grasped the idea that things have names, they seek to learn the names of the things they can see; indeed, they often seem driven to do so.

Learning the names of things is only one side of this aspect of socialization, however, for it is equally and perhaps even more significant that children learn the "things of names."[5] Material things within reach or view are only a small part of the vast world of objects designated by our language. Many objects have names but are not tangible or cannot be immediately apprehended. Thus, for example, children learn the meaning of words (e.g., *hot* or *no*) that are not labels for material things. They learn something of their parents' conception of the supernatural, even though for most people in our culture there are not thought to be any tangible, directly visible manifestations of a deity, by whatever name he or she is known.

The child's capacity to name and learn the meaning of intangible objects stems partially from the systematic nature of language. One of the characteristics of language is that terms can be defined in relation to other terms. In other words, we can designate and thus interpret words that are unknown to us. Parents and clergy can discuss the attributes of God, conveying the significance and nature of this unseen object through indirect means. Thus, statements such as "God will punish you if you misbehave" or "God is the good that lies in all of us" are indirect ways of conveying the meaning of an important object.

There is more to learning the meanings of objects—the things of names—than simply being able to talk about them. The meaning of a tangible thing goes beyond its name, and the meaning of a more abstract object entails far more than using other words to define it. Fundamentally, meaning lies in the actions people have taken, are prepared to take, or can imagine taking toward objects. Thus, to learn the meaning of an object is to learn not only its name but also the ways in which people are prepared to act toward it. So, for example, the child learns the meaning of *hot* not just as a label for a certain sensation but also as a term that implies certain kinds of actions. People avoid "hot" stoves, drink "hot" coffee, wear clothes of "hot" colors, say they are "hot" when they are warm but also when they are sexually aroused, and report "hot" cars to the police. The meaning of a word expands as the behavioral possibilities covered by that word are discovered. Similarly, children learn not only that *God* is the name of an unseen being, but also that this being is treated very differently from most objects—with a special sacred attitude, not the casual, matter-of-fact attitude with which most other objects are approached.

As the child learns the names of things and the things of names, he or she comes to grasp each object as presenting several behavioral possibilities. Each object can be implicated in a variety of social acts, and a major part of the socialization process entails the child's learning what these acts are and how to decide in any given instance which act is most salient. Linguistic socialization thus goes far beyond the learning of words, their definitions, and their possible grammatical relationships. It involves learning the relationships between words and deeds, between the system of labels for objects (as well as the rules for combining these labels into sentences) and the range of social acts that are possible in the world in which the child lives. In short, the child learns how to represent its own conduct and that of others linguistically, how to represent the world linguistically, and also how to link the two together.

Learning the meaning of objects applies to the self as much as to any object in the environment. The self is an object, but not one that is grasped intuitively or directly. Rather, as we suggested, it is an object grasped from and through the perspectives of others. Thus, children learn the meaning of this very crucial object, the self, on the same basis as they grasp the meaning of any other object: The meaning of the self is found in the way others act toward it. They learn the thing of this very important name by observing the way others act toward it and, gradually, by learning to act toward it themselves in the same ways as do others.

The child is, after all, an object to other people. He or she has, in their eyes, certain characteristics, abilities, limitations, and natural tendencies. The child is something toward which they act—by providing care, teaching, disciplining, loving, or even wishing the child would grow up and go away. The child thus has a meaning to parents and to other adults. This meaning consists of a set of beliefs and attitudes they hold toward the child and their readiness to act toward the child in certain ways. Thus, whether a child is felt to be strong or weak, intelligent or stupid, or wanted or unwanted will influence how parents act toward it. Such beliefs will shape what they demand of the child, the pattern of rewards and punishments they administer, and what they permit (or require) the child to do.

Beliefs about a child's attributes and characteristics stem from two major sources. First, they emerge in a particular family on the basis of a history of interaction with the child. Although widely held beliefs about children in general are a major force shaping the way adults act toward children, it is nonetheless true that each child and each family is unique in some ways. Each child has an individual history of activities, as well as a given temperament that affects the way he or she is received within the family. Moreover, the belief systems of families often include the notion that certain children take after particular kinfolk—for example, that a son is strong willed like his father or that a daughter is destined to be crazy like her Aunt Carol. These beliefs can be both positive and negative, but in either case they influence the way parents and others act toward the child and so will shape the kind of object the child becomes to itself.

The second and more important source of beliefs and attitudes toward children is culture itself. Each culture makes the child into a different kind of object at various points in the life cycle, just as each culture objectifies men and women in distinctive ways. Thus, in one culture children may be defined as special objects, having qualities and characteristics that differentiate them sharply from infants and adults. Children are viewed this way in U.S. or Canadian society, which treats children as a special and identifiable category. Other societies see children differently, viewing children very much as miniature adults and seeking not to prolong childhood as a carefree and pleasant time of life, but to move individuals toward adult responsibilities as quickly as possible.

Thus, both the pace of socialization and the kinds of human beings it produces are dependent on cultural definitions of such objects as child, childhood, adolescence, male, female, and human nature. Whether a particular individual experiences childhood as a pleasant time of play, or adolescence as a time of upheaval and stress, depends not just on the unique characteristics of individual temperament or the idiosyncrasies of his or her family but also on the more general beliefs on the basis of which his or her parents act.

Whether they originate in the general culture or in unique family experiences, definitions of the child held by important others, such as parents and siblings, affect the way people treat the child and so also affect the child's grasp of himself or herself as an object. Self-definitions are powerfully shaped by social definitions. This does not mean, however, that children come merely to mean to themselves what they mean to others, or that they simply see themselves as others see them. Children develop defense mechanisms to insulate themselves from definitions they do not like. They strive for autonomy from others. They reflect upon their experiences with others. And, crucially, in acquiring a sense of the self as a social object in a world of social objects, children acquire not just the capacity to control their conduct as others wish but also now and then to say no to social demands.

The process of role taking is central to the acquisition of self, not only a self that sees itself as others see it but also a self that is capable of resisting its definition by others. And role taking, in turn, depends on the child's acquisition of a sense of the way in which the situations in which it finds itself and of the groups to which it belongs are organized. In order to have a self, one must have some way of imagining the self from the perspective of others. And to imagine the self requires more than a name for self and others. It requires some grasp of the way social life is organized, an understanding of the role structure of situations and groups. How does the child acquire this understanding?

Stages of Socialization

Fully developing the capacity for self-reference depends on the acquisition of a sense both of the content and the organization of the family, other groups, and the community as a whole into which the child is born. That is, the child must learn who and what may be found in the world and must discover how these objects are related to one another. Mead's distinction between "play" and "the game" captures a crucial aspect of what takes place in this learning process.[6]

In what Mead called the *play stage* of socialization, the child "plays at" various roles made evident by others, their activities, and, especially as time goes by and the child learns to speak, their use of language. That is, the child imagines being and acting as someone else: At first, perhaps, the child plays at a role in rudimentary fashion by animating a toy—moving it about, giving it actions to perform. Later the child plays in a more organized way at being a mother, a police officer, or a mail carrier. Having observed the activities of such persons, the child duplicates their words and deeds in play. Imaginary floors are swept, punishments are meted out, or mail is delivered. Playing at roles, Mead wrote,

> *is the simplest form of being another to one's self. It involves a temporal situation. The child says something in one character and responds in another character, and then his responding in another character is a stimulus to himself in the first character, and so the conversation goes on.*[7]

In this form of play, the child becomes an object to self, but always by responding to and imagining himself or herself to be a particular other.

The self becomes a more complex and developed social object in what Mead called the *game stage* of socialization. The game, for Mead, epitomizes what must be done in taking the role of the generalized other. Playing catcher in a game of baseball—in contrast with playing at being a mother or a mail carrier—requires the child to take the perspective of the team as a whole toward himself or herself as a particular player. To conceive of oneself as a catcher, one must have a composite, simultaneous idea of a baseball team, the various positions involved, the object of the game, and the relationship of the catcher's position to the activity as a whole.

It is the constitution of self as object from the vantage point of the generalized other that gives the self its unity. The child playing at roles is a different self in each instance in which a role is assumed. The child in a baseball game, and later the child who is able to develop a conception of self as a member of a family and community, is able to view himself or herself as one individual who makes a variety of roles on different occasions in relation to specific others and to the community as a whole.

The acquisition of self is thus a sequential process in which each phase makes possible the one that follows. The development of language, including a name for self, makes possible the process of playing at and taking the roles of specific others. This in turn paves the way for the integration of the self in the game stage, in which the person acquires the capacity to respond to self from the standpoint of the generalized other. In this manner, as the child acquires a richer sense of the content and structure of group activities, he or she also develops a fuller sense of self.

Although many scholars have attempted to do so, it is difficult to attach any specific age levels to the development of the self through these stages. As the historian Philippe Aries reminded us, conceptions of the *child* as distinct from the infant or the adult are a historical creation.[8] It seems reasonable, given the fact that people have expected different things of children in different historical periods, to argue that the rate at which the acquisition of self will occur is dependent on such expectations rather than on developmental factors that have to do with physical maturation. Beyond the earliest stages of physical and neurological development, and except for the period of puberty, the acts of others exert more influence on the acquisition of self than internal biological changes.

Not everybody who comes into contact with the child has an equal influence on the child's acquisition of self. Because a child is exposed to its parents (or to those who take their place) from virtually the moment of birth and becomes thoroughly dependent on them for physical care and emotional nurture, they are far more significant in the child's development than are other adults. Thus, the structure of the family and of the other groups that the child comes to know later is not grasped simply in cognitive terms. Rather, some people in the social structures confronted by the child are emotionally more important to the child than are others, and role taking in relation to these *significant others* naturally has a greater impact on the self. Significant others include parents, siblings, other members of the extended kin group (such as grandparents, aunts, and uncles in North American culture), and, during later stages of socialization, teachers and peers.

The acquisition of self is not simply a process in which the child passively adopts the culture into which it is born and shapes a self that merely reflects the structure of group life.[9] Rather, in a number of ways, children are active participants in their own socialization and develop selves in tension with as well as in accord with the dominant culture. Of special significance in contemporary societies, children come under the influence of their peers from the moment they enter school. For several hours a day, in the classroom as well as on the playground and before and after school, children interact with one another in the absence of their parents. Even preschoolers spend considerable time playing together in day care and nursery school. As children move through elementary school and beyond, the influence of peers becomes even stronger as the amount of time spent with them increases.

Some degree of tension between children and their adult mentors occurs because of this development of peer cultures. Where the members of any social group interact more frequently with one another than with outsiders, they tend to develop what Gary Alan Fine has called *idiocultures*.[10] Children, for example, develop activities, beliefs, norms, knowledge, and social practices that, while derived from the adult world and ostensibly under the control of adults, are transmitted and maintained by children themselves. Whether in Little League teams or just hanging out with other kids, they develop and sustain distinctive ways of being that are transmitted directly to other kids rather than through adults. These forms of conduct—ranging from ways of defining and enforcing standards of "masculinity" or "femininity" to ideas about loyalty—serve to bond group members to one another and to separate them from others. The peer group itself becomes a generalized other with its own standards of conduct.

Moreover, children in one another's company make creative use of the role definitions and rules of the game as adults have conveyed them rather than merely replicating them. In the playgroups of nursery school as well as the friendship groups of middle school, children seem to seek a measure of control over their own lives. Kids in school develop their own status hierarchies, for example, and use what they have learned about role making and role taking creatively to include and exclude others from group activities. As William Corsaro has shown, even nursery school children resist the demands and rules of adults by engaging in "naughty" talk, playing in ways that are forbidden, or avoiding cleaning up after play. They seem moved to resist socialization by adults as much as to accept it.[11]

This is by no means a theoretical surprise to symbolic interactionists, since self-control is a key part of what the acquisition of self is about. From an interactionist perspective, the self develops as the social process is brought within the person. But socialization is not merely the internalization of social control, for individuals commonly develop interests and perspectives that conflict with those of their parents or teachers. When they resist adult rules, kids seem to be attempting to carve out selves that are to some degree independent or autonomous even while in a general sense they reflect the structure of group life.

The interactionist approach to socialization also emphasizes that children are active interpreters of their world and not merely passive sponges absorbing its lessons. If we look at the experience of growing up from the standpoint of the child, it is clear that there is a great deal that the child must puzzle out for himself or herself. Parents and other adults issue directives that are not so clearly defined or precisely formulated as to leave no room for interpretation. The rationale for parental dictates, or of the rewards or punishments they administer, is frequently not obvious to the child. There are a great many questions—about sexuality, for example—that may get answers only if the child asks those questions. Peers likewise make demands that seem unfair or whose rationale is unclear. Faced with unclear and conflicting expectations, children are forced to become active agents in their own acquisition of self.

Socialization is, in the last analysis, symbolic interaction. Once the capacity for self-reference has begun to develop, socialization occurs on each social occasion in which the child finds himself or herself. Indeed, socialization is not an experience confined to child-hood or that terminates once the adolescent has become legally an adult. Fundamentally, all of life is socialization, and the process terminates only with the individual's death.

The Everyday Experience of Self

Human beings are thinking, acting, and feeling creatures who frequently become the objects of their own attention. They think about themselves, act toward themselves, and have feelings about themselves. Thinking himself unable to do math, for example, a stu-dent pays little attention in class and does not bother to study for the exam. Doing poorly on the test, the student feels unhappy and chastises himself, but also believes that his self-image of "poor math student" has been confirmed. Believing herself destined to become a famous writer, a young woman devotes considerable effort to her English assignments. She comes to value the praise she receives for her stories and the feeling of accomplishment they give her. Success energizes her to work even harder the next time. Each of these students' thoughts, feelings, and actions has been in various ways focused on self.

This classification—thoughts, feelings, and actions—delineates the three aspects of self that we will examine in this chapter. People *act* toward themselves and others act toward them, and in doing so they jointly create various forms of *identity*. They are constantly engaged in locating themselves in relation to one another—as student to teacher, friend to friend, adver-sary to adversary, Catholic to Protestant, and in countless other ways. As they locate them-selves, they are able to interact. People *think* about themselves in their everyday lives, and in doing so they rely on (and continue to develop) their *self-images*. Derived from experience, self-images also reflect cultural ideas about human nature, about what people can and should be. And people have self-focused *feelings* that are captured in the concept of *self-esteem*. They like or dislike what they are, love or hate themselves, and feel energized or depressed by their own real or imagined actions. Although social psychologists have invented a plethora of terms for studying the person, these three—identity, self-image, and self-esteem—provide a good foundation for understanding. Each provides a lens through which one can view people and their relationships to one another and to the social world as a whole.

This trio of concepts rests on a view of the everyday experience of self that may seem to contradict many basic cultural understandings of what the self is. Western culture in particular fosters a view of the person as separate from others. This cultural tradition encourages its adherents to think of the self as an entity that really and truly exists within each person. It views self as a core structure that engages in thoughts, feelings, and actions.

The symbolic interactionist view of self emphasizes its social nature rather than its location within the individual. It casts doubt on the notion that each person has a "real" self. It looks at cultural ideas about self, soul, and person as important influences on the experience of self but not as universal truths about this phenomenon. It asserts that there is considerable variation from one culture to another in the way human beings experience themselves. At the same time, it argues that there are also great similarities across the human species. We can begin to portray this view in greater detail by examining the way people experience themselves in everyday life.

A simple experiment may be helpful as a beginning point in understanding how people experience themselves in everyday life: Recall and write down the various ways in which you have been conscious of yourself in the last few hours. I cannot perform this experiment for you, of course, but I can share with you the (slightly censored) results of my own:

> *I woke up this morning at six o'clock and looked out the window at the Sonoran desert where I am writing these words. I felt good, perhaps even a bit self-satisfied. I thought briefly about what I would do today: work more on this chapter, take a walk, do a bit of house maintenance. I remembered agreeing with my wife that we would go shopping later on. I turned on my computer and read my email messages. One was from a graduate student thanking me for the condolence message I had sent when her dog died; another was from a friend who described some of the heartache of caring for her ill and aging parents. I thought of my own sick dog and aging parents, and felt satisfied that I was being as helpful—to dogs, parents, and friends alike—as I could be. I went into the kitchen and fed the dog and made coffee; by this time, my wife had awakened and was looking for me. We sat down to breakfast and discussed our plans for the day; I briefly considered mentioning my plan to work outside an hour or so, but kept quiet because I knew she'd say that I had been spending too much time in the sun and needed a break from outside work. I went back to the computer and began to write; then I felt I needed to take a walk in order to sort out some ideas in my mind. So, I took a brief walk, putting on a hat and checking my appearance before I left the house. I waved at some visitors staying at a nearby house as I wandered down our road, feeling a bit smug because I was lucky enough to live in an area they would only visit for a few days. Then I returned home and began to write this paragraph.*

Several features of the experience of self can be teased from this mundane account. We will see these elements of self-reference again in the discussion of identity, self-concept, and self-esteem. Taken together, however, they provide an overview of the social psychological view of the self.

- Consciousness of self is intermittent.

Although it may seem otherwise, my experience of self did not involve uninterrupted self-absorption, for most of the time my attention was directed elsewhere. When I read my email, for example, I paid attention to the content of the messages and not just how they pertained to me. At breakfast with my wife, I asked how she felt (she had been ill) and what she wanted to do, and was absorbed in what she had to say and not just how it affected me. When I walked, I looked at the ironwood trees, just beginning to blossom; I felt the sun's rays, already hot at 9:30 A.M. in the desert. I looked at my neighbors' house to see if they were home and had found the newspaper that I left at their house when I got ours. I kept an eye out for interesting birds in the air and snakes on the ground. Later, sitting at the computer, I fiddled with the monitor and the screen color a bit before settling down to writing.

The experience of self is intermittent, not continuous. Human beings catch glimpses of their thoughts, feelings, and actions. When I asked my wife how she felt, I felt a momentary sense of shame because I thought briefly and selfishly that her not feeling well might prevent me from doing something I wanted to do. When I waved at the visitors,

I quickly roused myself from my deep thoughts and self-consciously put on a friendly face for them. As I began to write these paragraphs, I felt briefly self-conscious writing about me. Human beings are able to cobble together a sense of continuity and sameness—to feel that the self they experience at this moment is the same as the one they experienced a moment, or a day, or a year ago. But they do so on the basis of intermittent and often fleeting glimpses of themselves.

People experience themselves intermittently in part because their attention cannot be directed everywhere at once. Attention to self is interspersed with attention to a great many other things. I can feel the sun's warmth and feel myself feeling the sun's warmth, but not both at the same time. I can see the look of dismay on my wife's face when she finds out that I was working outside in the sun without sun block; and I can see myself crawling under a rock to escape her wrath; but I cannot do both simultaneously. For the sake of economy of effort and information processing, we attend to some things and ignore others.

The experience of self is intermittent also because thoughts, feelings, and actions are not accessible until after they have started. When a stimulus occurs, it releases a response. For example, a husband sees his wife frowning at him, and he begins to feel uncomfortable. At first this response is merely an impulse, felt by the individual, but having no definite form or obvious direction. Only as the phase of perception gets under way does the husband interpret the look on his wife's face as a frown and his own feelings as embarrassment. Only once an act has begun can it become a basis for the experience of self.

- Consciousness of self is indirect.

Such glimpses as we do have of ourselves are indirect rather than direct. When I felt briefly ashamed about being selfish, it was by imagining myself from my wife's vantage point. Shame is an individual and personal feeling, to be sure, but in order to experience it, one must imagine oneself from the perspective of another. We feel ashamed because of how we feel we will look in the other's eyes. Likewise, when I waved to a passing car, I for a moment inspected myself from their vantage point, wishing to appear as a sociable person. When I read my student's email about her dog, I was relieved that she appreciated what I wrote to her, since I had worried that she might have disapproved of my comment about her dog contentedly chewing a favorite bone in dog heaven.

The experience of self depends on the capacity for adopting the perspective—the role—of the other. I see myself as a "friendly neighbor" by momentarily adopting the perspective of "guest at a neighbor's house." I feel good about myself when I read a friend's email by putting myself into her perspective. Role taking requires knowledge of the role of the other. That is, knowledge of the roles of "guest" or "friend" enables a person to look at self from the other's point of view.

- Self-consciousness is imaginative.

The everyday experience of self is as much a product of our imaginations as of the actual words and deeds of others. The visitors I saw waved back cheerfully, but it was only in my imagination that their action could have meaning for me. I imputed to them and to myself an attitude—"friendly" or "sociable"—but my experience of both them and me was located in my imagination. They might have been saying to themselves, "There's that crazy professor our hosts warned us about!" Even reading my student's thank-you note for the condolences I had offered required me to imagine her as "sincere" rather than as "being nice to a professor."

The dependence of the self on imagining what is going on in the other's mind makes the self a more tenuous and uncertain construction than common sense tells us. Even though we participate in a social world of shared meanings with other people, ultimately we must interpret their words and deeds to know what they think of us. An experience of mine in graduate school vividly illustrates the point. During a required and much-dreaded oral examination, one of my professors listened gravely and impassively to my answers to the other examiners' questions. When it came his turn to ask me questions, he said without expression, "I have no questions." I struggled inwardly to make sense of this turn of events while outwardly keeping my cool. Was I doing so badly that he felt it better to spare me any further embarrassment? Or was I doing well enough that he felt it pointless to ask more questions? As it turned out, the latter was the case, and I passed the exam. But for a short while, my sense of self was, to say the least, uncertain, for I quite literally could not be sure what was happening to me.

- Consciousness of self requires naming.

Consciousness of self typically depends on naming oneself and others. In the illustrations I have given, I named myself in a variety of ways: friend, husband, embarrassed, neighbor, professor, and the like. These names are integral to the experience of self and to the capacity to think, feel, and act. When I pick up the morning newspaper for our neighbors and subsequently imagine (or actually experience) their gratitude, I think of myself explicitly as "neighborly." In that instance, "neighborly" is how I experience myself. When I do something that makes me want to crawl under the nearest rock, I think to myself that the feeling I feel is "embarrassment." I experience myself as "embarrassed" at that moment.

Naming of self is always tied, implicitly or explicitly, to naming others. To think of oneself as "friend" is to think of another also as "friend." To feel "embarrassed" is to feel the weight and presence of another who is the "judge" or "audience" of one's action. To see oneself as "professor" is implicitly to imagine a "student" as one's partner in interaction. To name and thus imagine the self is to name and imagine the other.

Moreover, names motivate actions. When I get to the mailbox and take out my newspaper, I see my neighbors' box and their newspaper. Identifying the newspaper as theirs leads me to think of myself—to name myself—as a helpful or good neighbor who can be counted on for a favor. Naming oneself in this way constrains subsequent actions. I can hardly keep up my image of self as a good neighbor if I selfishly return with only my own paper. I can scarcely expect that my neighbors will bring my newspaper if I never bring theirs. Naming oneself puts one into a social context of obligations and expectations, and thus exposes one to their influence.

- Consciousness of self arises from self-control.

The experience of self is particularly acute when we act purposefully. Indeed, self-consciousness essentially arises out of efforts to exert control over our behavior. It is self-consciousness, in fact, that gives human beings their generally refined and precise capacity to choose (within limits) the directions their conduct will take.

Every act begins preconsciously as an impulse whose nature and direction can become evident and governed only after it has occurred. When a friend I haven't seen in a long time greets me coldly, my response begins before I am aware of it. I feel something—a readiness to act, a sense that I must do "something"—before I know what I am doing or what I will do. Only by taking the perspective of another—of my friend, for example, or of a bystander who sees an emergent look of hurt on my face—can I assign meaning to my friend's act and decide how to respond to it. Viewing myself from the perspective of another, I may see that my initial response is one of being hurt and that it will soon be evident on my face. My response to my own forthcoming act is to check it—to put on the behavioral brakes so that I can formulate an alternative act. In place of a "hurt" response to my friend's act, I imagine myself with an "unconcerned" face. Seeing that as a more desirable act, I conduct myself in that way, not letting on to the other that a cold "hello" has hurt my feelings.

As this illustration suggests, we do not see ourselves aimlessly, but with purpose, and the purpose is usually one of self-control. We are especially conscious of ourselves in those circumstances where we seek to shape our conduct to our own purposes or to the expectations of others. The consciousness of self that arises in these circumstances is shaped by the imagination of the direction and possible future consequences of an emergent act. When I imagine myself as about to show my hurt feelings because another has slighted me, I am also apt to spin out the possible responses the other may have to my act. I may think, for example, that showing my hurt feelings may embarrass my friend, who may not have intended to hurt me. Or, I may treat the slight as confirming my suspicion that the person no longer sees me as a friend, and conceal my feelings as a way of showing I don't care.

- Self-consciousness is socially situated.

Much of the everyday experience of self involves the establishment of place or location relative to other people. Sometimes location is problematic: Is the person you thought was a friend still your friend? Will the professor who promised to write a recommendation actually do it? Will it be enthusiastic or just routine? Is the salesperson in the department store ever going to notice you and treat you as a customer? Is someone to whom you are strongly attracted also attracted to you? In these examples, what we will later in this chapter call situated identity is at issue. That is, at least one person in a situation is uncertain of how he or she stands relative to the other. Not knowing how one stands, in sociological terms, means that one does not know who one is in the eyes of the other.

In many routine situations of everyday life, of course, social location is not much of an issue. In the classroom, professor and students know who they are. The professor knows who the students are and the students know who the professor is. Their situated identities as student and professor are firmly established. To put the matter another way, each participant in the situation can name the others, at least by their roles if not by their personal names. And by naming one another, they know how to act toward one another; each knows the kind of social object the other is.

Whether problematic or not, a sense of actual, possible, feared, or hoped-for position relative to others is always a key aspect of the experience of self. We can participate in social situations only by knowing at some level how we fit with the others who are present. Sitting in an automobile dealer's waiting room, for example, a customer observes (but cannot hear) a conversation between a mechanic and the service manager. Naturally, the customer wonders if they are discussing her car and worries about how much money their discussion might cost her. When the service manager approaches, she suspects her fears are about to be realized. Even in situations where we clearly know who we are relative to others, our sense of self depends on what we take for granted. With close friends, for example, we take our relationship for granted, and in doing so feel an assured, secure sense of who we are. Should that assurance be cast into doubt, however, the sense of self is doubted right along with it. When we don't know where we stand, we don't know who we are.

- Consciousness of self relies on narrative.

Finally, human beings experience the self through narratives—that is, through stories told and retold, polished, embellished, trimmed, and refurbished.[12] People do not merely act, but tell others of their doings. They tell their life stories when they fall in love or interview for a job. They tell their teachers what they did on their summer vacations. They recount their athletic or sexual exploits to friends, reveal their innermost secrets to those they trust most, and construct more socially palatable accounts of their activities for parents and grandparents. Our symbolic species is a story-telling species.

Occasions for narrative occur almost daily, and when they do, they put the person in the spotlight and require him or her to formulate a plausible account of self. Applying for a new job, for example, one must explain why one is leaving a previous job, describe one's qualifications for the position, and state one's salary requirements. Successful job applicants tend to be those who have learned the right things to say about themselves. "I left my previous job because my boss is a jerk and fired me for no good reason" may be a truthful statement, but "I felt I couldn't do my best in an unpleasant and unpredictable working environment" may be more palatable to an interviewer.

Self-narratives are constructed in informal settings as well as formal ones. A couple falling in love, for example, exchange narratives, which become progressively more intimate as their relationship grows. The stories they tell each other about themselves are designed to portray each in a favorable light. To say this is not necessarily to dispute the authenticity or sincerity of such narratives, for people may be convinced by and come to believe sincerely in their own presentations of self. Moreover, as relationships develop, the narratives of two people become linked. "My story" and "your story" become "our story." And as narratives are linked, so are experiences of self.

The narrative quality of the self underscores an important point: The self is always in a process of becoming. The self is an emergent reality—an object brought about over time as people tell and retell stories about themselves. It is periodically revised and edited. Although many people are inclined to think of "the self" as the bedrock of being, it is a rock they constantly carve, inscribe, and polish.

Identity: The Self as a Social Object

The heart of the interactionist view of the person lies in the concept of identity. Here, we look at the self as a primarily social experience, examining in some detail how the self arises and is sustained in everyday social interaction. Later in this chapter we will more briefly examine reflexivity through cognitive and affective lenses, using the concepts of self-image and self-esteem to ask how people think and feel about themselves.

In order to explore the origins and impact of identity, we must simplify. We will do so by focusing on the typical, routine, and relatively straightforward nature of identity in everyday life, recognizing that there are many special cases and complications we must neglect here. Each of the following three illustrations of identity at work involves at least two individuals interacting in terms of named roles in a familiar and relatively short-lived social situation. They differ from one another in the kinds of roles that are represented and in the goals of their activities, but all have a similar underlying structure.

Patient and Physician

Alonso arrives at the physician's office on crutches and checks in with the receptionist, who expresses concern about his broken foot and makes sure Alonso's insurance coverage is current. At this point, Alonso becomes a patient in the hands of a variety of medical personnel: nurses, aides, x-ray technicians, and physicians. They weigh him, check his blood pressure, ask questions, probe, prod, examine, pull, push, inject, wrap, caution, instruct, and perform a variety of other tasks. Alonso is swept into an office routine, moved from place to place by others, told what to do next, and in general made the focus of a medical team who have treated hundreds of broken feet. Along the way, he answers questions ("I broke it when I fell off a ladder"), listens dutifully to instructions about how to care for the cast ("Keep it dry"), tries to ignore the pain as the broken bones are set and the cast applied, and in general acts as a patient is supposed to act.

Father and Kids

Harry has promised to take his daughter and son fishing, and on the appointed day they wake early, eat breakfast, and set off in the car, canoe on top, gear in the trunk, for the drive to the lake. They arrive, unload, launch, and begin their quest for bass and blue gill. Hooks are baited, with friendly and helpful dad showing the kids how. Lines are cast, retrieved, untangled, recast, and untangled again. Hooks get stuck on snags or clothing or in trees and have to be replaced. Kim, 8 years old, and Will, age 6, focus determinedly on the task of catching fish. Harry looks around, sees others catching fish, and thinks he might throw in a line himself. But there is another hook to be baited and a tangled line to be retrieved and fixed, and so his own fishing has to wait. Then Kim hooks a fish and follows her father's instructions on how to reel it in. Excitement prevails, although Will seems a bit upset that he hasn't caught anything, and Dad still hasn't cast a line. More fixing of tangles, baiting of hooks, casts, retrieving lines from trees, and eventually a fish for Will. After a few hours, they set out for home, tired, happy, and sunburned, the kids planning for the next trip, Dad happy with the day but also secretly thinking of when and how he might go fishing and actually catch something himself.

Just Friends

The phone rings just as we are finishing dinner; it's the neighbors, wanting to come over and see the new addition on our house. They come and admire the work (at least they say they like it) and then we all sit on the patio and chat for a while. We talk of the Harry Potter movie, happenings in the neighborhood, and tentative plans to have dinner together. The occasion is spontaneous and purely sociable: The conversation accomplishes no particular tasks, other than a dinner arrangement, and has no particular topic. We tell jokes, discuss the health and behavior of our dogs, and talk about the weather. After hanging out together for a half hour or so, it is time for the neighbors to go home to make dinner.

These are obviously simplified illustrations of everyday interactions that gloss over many details of what actually occurs in such situations. Broken feet really hurt intensely and are apt to make patients irritable, especially when nurses and physicians act like it is "no big deal" and seem to ignore your suffering. The fishing expedition has a 1950s situation comedy character, and doesn't mention the fact that Dad has finally taken the kids along and that Mom will be truly angry with him if he doesn't make it a good day for them. And it might be that the neighbors are sorry to see me put on an addition that they will have to look at from their patio.

Still, these illustrations provide a basis for exploring the topic of identity. Each illustration portrays people interacting with one another and experiencing themselves from perspectives provided by roles. That is, there are patients, physicians, fathers, sons, daughters, and friends. In each situation there is a common focus of activity—a goal or object toward which their interaction is mutually directed. Setting a broken foot, learning to fish, and enjoying friendly conversation provide a basis for experiencing the self as well as for orienting oneself toward and interacting with the other. And each situation has a more or less known duration—a beginning, middle, and end that the participants at least implicitly understand. Whatever experience of self such situations provide, the experience is finite.

Each of these illustrations reveals the presence of *situated identity*. That is, in each case we find people experiencing themselves primarily from perspectives provided by the situation and its roles. These perspectives give direction to conduct and social interaction, but they also give form to the experience of self. A patient having a broken foot set knows what to do in the social setting of a physician's office because he or she grasps the situation as a whole and the various perspectives of the others in it. But the person is also thereby provided with a way of experiencing the self in that situation—not a self with generalized attributes or characteristics, but a "patient" self, one given meaning by the experience of being a patient to the other's physician, nurse, or x-ray technician. A father teaching his children to fish likewise derives a sense of self as a "father" from the specific situation in which he instructs his children in this sport and receives their appreciation and the tacit approval of others for doing so. And a person talking with a friend earns the identity of "friend" by talking with him or her in a situation where friendly conversation is the only object.

Identity is primarily a matter of establishing and maintaining social location. Situations and their roles (and other perspectives) provide a way for people to locate themselves relative to one another. The social space within which they do so in the foregoing illustrations is that of the situation—hence the term *situated identity*. But what does it mean to possess a situated identity? We can answer this question in two ways, each of which is important to a full understanding of identity. First, we can examine how situated identities are established or produced. Second, we can ask what a situated identity "feels like"—that is, what the experience of self as situated identity means to the person in the situation.

How Situated Identities Are Produced

When people come together to interact in a situation, they generally establish situated identities without much difficulty. In fact, they ordinarily do not need to think much about doing so. Entering the men's clothing area of a department store, for example, one can readily identify the salespeople. They wear name tags with the store logo, dress in a way that seems appropriate for clerks, and occupy themselves with such tasks as straightening racks of clothing. And they act as clerks should act, approaching customers with a "May I help you?" The same is true in a variety of social situations—medical offices, fishing trips, visits from friends, classrooms, post offices, restaurants, libraries, family dinners, and so on. We readily identify other people and place them in relation to us.

The relative ease of identifying self and others in routine social situations depends on a social process that is as invisible as it is familiar. As Gregory P. Stone pointed out, people regularly make announcements of their own situated identities and placements of others in their situated identities. Indeed, Stone defined *identity* as a "coincidence of placements and announcements." A person with identity, Stone said, "is situated, that is, cast in the shape of a social object by the acknowledgment of his participation or membership in social relationships."[13] A situated identity comes into being when one person's announcements coincide with the placements of that person by others.

An identity announcement consists of anything that another can potentially interpret as an indication of the role that an individual intends or wants to enact in a situation. Merely to walk onto the showroom floor of an automobile dealership is to announce one's potential situated identity as a "customer." To wear a gold band on the third finger of the left hand is to announce to the world that one is married—and that, in certain circumstances, one should be treated as a married person and not as a potential mate. Likewise, to set up a portable electronic keyboard and begin to play on an urban street corner is to announce one's identity as a "street musician." We make announcements of identity not only through what we say and do but also through our appearance. An identity placement occurs when the other treats the individual in accordance with the announcements that person has made—when a car salesperson approaches and offers to help, or when people stop and listen to the musician and then leave some money.

People make announcements and placements with such ease that they are typically unaware that they are doing so. The department store provides an excellent illustration. The actions and appearance of the salesperson constitute announcements of the situated identity of salesperson. The name tag, mode of dress, and behavior are ways of announcing to anyone who happens to come by that "I am a salesperson." Likewise, the customer's conduct and appearance are announcements of a potential customer identity. The customer is not dressed as a clerk, but as a potential buyer of clothing. The customer wears no name tag, but does wear an expectant look when approaching the salesperson. The customer examines items on tables and racks, perhaps starting to collect things to try on for size.

The customer behavior also places the other into the situated identity of store clerk. Customers make a beeline for this individual, singling him or her out from other customers. The customer fixes a gaze purposefully on the clerk, thus indicating the intent to initiate interaction. Likewise, the clerk's friendly "May I help you?" not only announces a clerk identity but also places the customer in the identity of customer, who replies, "Yes, I'd like to try on these pants," thus confirming that placement. When announcements and placements coincide, as they do in this illustration, the situated identities of "customer" and "salesperson" are brought into existence.

Perhaps the best way to see the importance of this correspondence of announcements and placements is to examine what happens when it does not exist. Imagine approaching a store clerk who ignores you and keeps up what is evidently a personal telephone conversation instead of offering to help you. This all-too-familiar experience is irritating, to be sure, but in social psychological terms it is more. The clerk's actions not only frustrate your line of activity—you want to make a purchase and leave—but it also makes you a nonentity in the situation. You come with an announcement of a customer identity and are put into a kind of limbo. The clerk, talking excitedly with what is now obviously a friend on the other end of the line, seems to look right through you. It is as if you don't exist. And in fact, in terms of identity, you don't.

As this illustration suggests, one's capacity to act rests on the establishment of situated identity. Lacking a response from the other that acknowledges one's possession of a situated identity, one cannot act in terms of that identity or get the other to act in terms of his or her situated identity. Lacking acknowledgment from the store clerk, one can't act as a customer or get the clerk to act as a clerk. A closer look at situated identity reveals why this is so.

What makes announcements and placements coincide is not merely their correspondence with one another, but something a bit deeper. A patient and physician who are jointly focused on the patient's broken foot, for example, display mutually congruent announcements and placements. At least two other social facts underlie the correspondence: First, the two individuals have acknowledged their presence together in a social situation that demands their joint activity. They are, and they know they are, "copresent"—they are in the situation together and they have mutually recognized that the situation calls for their interaction. Second, their acknowledgment of co-presence means that each accepts the other's right to be in the situation and to make requests or even demands. The physician acknowledges the patient's presence and right to medical treatment; the patient grants the physician's right to touch his or her body and to issue commands.

The ideas of co-presence and mutual recognition of rights helps explain more deeply why it is irritating and unsettling to be ignored by a store clerk in the situation described earlier. These ideas also explain why the clerk must studiously ignore the individual in order to carry on a personal phone conversation in the presence of a customer. It is irritating to be ignored in a situation where one wants attention to be paid to one, not only because it keeps one from accomplishing a task but also because it makes one a nonentity. Acknowledgment of co-presence is a fundamental condition for the establishment of a situated identity and action in terms of it. Without this acknowledgment, there is no identity, nor is there any acknowledgment by the other of one's right to act in terms of it. As socialized human beings, we understand this fact, and we now and then make use of it. The store clerk implicitly understands that as soon as he or she recognizes the presence of the customer, the telephone conversation must end. The professor in an office earnestly talks with a student and carefully avoids noticing the student standing outside (whom the professor has in fact noticed and must therefore make a show of not noticing). To acknowledge the presence and rights of another is to begin the process of placing the other in accordance with his or her announcement.

The Experience of Situated Identity

The experience of situated identity is paradoxical.[14] On one hand, when announcements and placements coincide, a situated identity is like clothing that warms and protects even though one is scarcely aware of wearing it. Patients having their broken parts fixed, father and children spending a warm summer day together fishing, and friends hanging out together are not highly or constantly conscious of being patients, parents, children, or friends. Once these situated identities are established, they provide the framework within which people act. They are important, for the capacity to act depends on their establishment and maintenance, but they are, for the most part, invisible, and we take them for granted. On the other hand, much can and does occur in everyday life to threaten or undermine these situated identities. The patient who readily cooperates while medical personnel put a broken foot in a cast may be thinking of all the things he or she may find it difficult to do while the foot heals. Even as the loving father teaches his children to fish and basks in the approval of onlookers, he may be thinking of the next opportunity to go fishing alone. Friends passing the time sooner or later remember they have other obligations. Moreover, in any of these situations people may do things that call situated identities into question. A physician may inadvertently cause pain, the father may be unpleasant to his children because they are preventing him from fishing, and friends may criticize. In short, even as a situated identity is working to shape conduct, it is likely to be undermined. It is a powerful yet tenuous and short-lived experience.

To grasp the power and the limitations of situated identity, we must look in greater detail at what it accomplishes for individuals in their everyday lives. Two ideas—*integration* and *continuity*—help explain how situated identities function.

- A situated identity provides for the integration of the person's thoughts, feelings, and actions in a single situation.

The word *integration* refers to the "joining" or "bringing together" of something—but of what? In everyday life, it is the individual's attention, interest, feelings, skills, and energy that are brought together and focused on the situation at hand and the person's place in it. A patient in the orthopedist's office, for example, is for the duration of that encounter not interested in other things. The patient pays attention to the physician, is interested in what he or she says and does, and concentrates on listening to instructions, following directions, and enduring the unavoidable pain and discomfort. For a period of time, the individual is a patient—not more and not less—and his or her social and personal being is wrapped up in this identity.

To put this another way, a situated identity concentrates the mind, keeping distractions at bay and enabling the individual to be fully engaged with the activity at hand. Concentration is important in social life. An orthopedist performing surgery needs to keep his or her attention focused on the task at hand. A pitcher on the mound must keep distractions to a minimum in order to concentrate on delivering the ball to the plate. The situated identity of each provides the basis for this concentration. In a sense, the identity puts a set of blinders on the individual, making it possible for him or her to attend only to those stimuli that are relevant to the activity at hand.

Concentration is based on situated identity, but it is not easy to maintain. The baseball pitcher's work reminds us that much can happen to distract one from the job at hand. Fans cheer (or boo), and the opposing team's players crack wise. Although it is probably thrilling and energizing to be cheered by adoring fans, their cheers amount to a social placement of the player as "hero" or "great player." To respond to adoration by thinking of oneself as a "hero" or "baseball great" is to take leave, even if only momentarily, from one's situated identity as pitcher. Likewise, the physician must concentrate on the patient's broken foot, which presumably takes some effort if the patient is a stunningly beautiful young man or woman.

Even while people try to concentrate on their situated identities, others are doing things to undermine their efforts. Mothers interrupt children watching television or doing their homework and ask them to take out the garbage. Students knock on professors' doors and interrupt their deep thoughts. And when others are not distracting them, people distract themselves. A pitcher on the mound thinks of his family. A woman showing a property to a prospective home buyer thinks of her child in day care. A professor in the classroom remembers that later that day he or she will be chairing a difficult and contentious faculty meeting.

How do people respond to distractions? Sometimes they simply get distracted—the pitcher forgets the sign, the physician is transfixed by a shapely leg and momentarily forgets about the broken foot to which it is attached, and the real estate salesperson forgets her client's name. But whether the distraction is real or merely possible, a common response is a verbal one. The pitcher tells himself (or is told by the manager) to concentrate on the game. The physician tells himself, "It's the foot, stupid!" The real estate salesperson reminds herself that she needs a sale in order to pay for her child's day care.

These verbal responses have several things in common: First, they directly or indirectly name the situated identity that the person seeks to recover or reinvigorate (or they name the situated identity of the other): "I'm the pitcher!" "She's a patient, for heaven's sake!" "I can sell any piece of real estate!" Second, they reaffirm the person's attachment to and embracement of the role: "I am the pitcher!" The verbal self-reminder is a way to get "psyched up" for the task at hand. And third, somewhat paradoxically, these announcements also remind one that at other times and places one is firmly attached to other situated identities. The very act of reaffirming a situated identity is apt to remind us of the other situated identities we have.

- A situated identity creates a feeling of continuity. By unifying the person's thoughts, feelings, and actions for a limited period of time, it makes possible a sense of events and actions flowing logically and meaningfully from one point to another.

Situated identities organize conduct over time. The person with a firmly established situated identity knows what to do and when to do it. The pitcher plans a sequence of pitches that he thinks will outfox the batter and strike him out. The orthopedist calmly orchestrates her own and others' activities in examining the foot, setting it in a cast, reassuring the patient, and making plans for follow-up care. The real estate agent skillfully leads the client through a house, pointing out features, anticipating objections, and asking questions that will help him make the sale.

Sport provides many illustrations of the look and feel of continuity. When things are "clicking" on a basketball team, each player moves in easy coordination with the others, positioning himself or herself in just the right spot to receive a pass or attempt a shot. A golfer on her game confidently judges the lay of each hole, calculates the effects of wind and weather, and smoothly plots a strategy to achieve a winning score. A tennis player on a good day seems able to anticipate an opponent's every move and to be always in the right place at the right time. Moreover, these experiences feel good to the individual. Movement seems fluid and easy, and the individual feels in control of self and situation.

Like integration, continuity is subject to disruption. People make mistakes. They misjudge the responses of others. They sometimes don't have the ability to do exactly the right thing. The pitcher feels his arm tiring and his sense of control slipping away. The orthopedist asks for an instrument and an aide delivers the wrong one, thus interrupting the process. A jumbo jet passes low overhead, the house shakes, and the dismayed real estate agent sees the unmistakable look on her client's face: This house is not for me! The bell rings, the class ends, the game is over.

The response to such disruptions is, again, partially verbal. Just as people remind themselves who they are in a situation in an effort to regain their concentration, they do so in an attempt to restore the flow of activity. The pitcher reminds himself that he has pitched many complete games and in doing so tries to summon the energy to keep his no-hitter going. The aide who gives the physician the wrong instrument utters a brief "sorry" and shakes his head in disapproval of his mistake. Doing so is an implicit promise to self and others to redouble his efforts so that the routine won't be disrupted again. The real estate agent shrugs inwardly and reminds herself there are other houses she can show the client.

These efforts to sustain a situated identity (as well as the situation as a whole) also remind the person that he or she has a life outside this situation. An athlete may overcome tiredness or distraction and talk himself or herself back into engagement with the game. Even so, the individual may wonder whether fatigue is an indication that a career is nearing its end. To think such thoughts is to evoke an image of oneself with a life beyond a particular situated identity. When people—athletes, professors, and airline flight attendants alike—contemplate retiring and thus severing their active ties with an occupation, they think of what else they will do with their lives. And to think in such terms is to imagine a self that will continue even when one of its mainstays is no longer present.

Social and Personal Identity

Discussion of the "person beyond the immediate situation," as Sheldon Stryker[15] puts it, leads us to consider other ways in which people locate themselves and one another in social life. In addition to the *situated self* produced in each context of interaction as situated identity is created, there is an ongoing process that produces what we sometimes call a *biographical self*. Two additional forms of identity—*personal identity* and *social identity*—also provide for the integration and continuity of the person and are the main components of this biographical self. To understand why personal and social identity exist and how they function, we must examine another pair of ideas.

- Identification with others is a major driving force in human conduct. It encompasses feelings of attachment to others, common purposes in interaction with them, and likeness or similarity. Identification is associated with positive affective responses to others and to situations.

   The tendency to identify self with others is so pronounced that it seems to qualify as a basic human need. Actually, identification is better conceived as a by-product of social interaction. People must share a definition of the situation in order to interact. They must recognize that they are in the same place, that a particular range and sequence of activities are called for, and that they are linked to one another in particular ways. To purchase a new car, for example, one goes to a new car dealer, finds (or is set upon by) a salesperson, looks, tests, negotiates a price, and signs a sales agreement. These activities entail a shared definition of the situation, and to that extent, a limited perception of similarity and common purpose between seller and buyer.

   Identification is an affective as well as a cognitive experience. To identity with another person, the members of one's team, or even an abstract category of people ("the human race") is to respond with positive affect to the object of identification. The presence or even the thought of the object creates positive feelings, a hopeful and optimistic mood, a sense that life is good. A conversation with a dear friend not only enhances the sense of how much one shares experiences and attitudes with the friend but also how much the presence of the friend makes one feel good. One feels like the friend, and one likes the friend. Moreover, identification involves not only positive affect and good mood but also a variety of positive emotions: happiness, joy, excitement, and satisfaction, to name a few.

- Differentiation is also a major force. It entails an individual perspective, a feeling that the person has a particular part to play in interaction with others, that he or she is in some ways distinctive, and there are individual goals worth pursuing. Differentiation is also associated with positive affect.

   Thomas Scheff argues that although identification is an essential part of the healthy social bond, so is differentiation.[16] Identification cements people together through their mutual cognition of similarity and positive affect. In contrast, differentiation bonds people through their sense of separateness. A healthy bond, in Scheff's view, does not exist when people are joined at the hip to the extent that each cannot think, feel, or act without taking the other into account. Rather, the bond is healthy when each person is able to maintain a sense of individuality in relation to the other. People naturally seek to develop and maintain healthy bonds, Scheff says, seeking to balance the pleasures of identification and differentiation, to be attached to the other without being overwhelmed.

   Just as situated identities help individuals develop a sense of integration and continuity, they contribute to identification and differentiation. Playing in a softball game, for example, enables the person to identify with his or her team and to feel a bond with others. It feels good to win, of course, but it also feels good just to play. At the same time, the game and its situated identity of "pitcher" or "infielder" provide for a sense of difference from others. One makes a distinctive contribution to the team effort because one is a "pitcher" and one also feels a sharper sense of distinction from members of the opposing team.

But situated identity is limited as a basis for the social bond, just as it is limited in providing for integration and continuity. When the game is over, team members disperse and interact with other role partners. Likewise, when the operation is over, the surgeon sees other patients or goes home to her husband and children. In these other situations the person acquires a new situated identity and thus also new others with whom to identify or from whom to differentiate. Moreover, some situations provide much better for identification than differentiation, and vice versa. In a crowd aroused to a fevered pitch by a charismatic speaker, such as an evangelist, people strongly identify with one another but may lose some of their capacity for self-control. They are, we sometimes say, swept away by their feelings. The same may be true of people in the throes of romantic love. In contrast, situations like that of the real estate agent provide better for differentiation of self from other. The sales agent is keenly aware of the differing interest of self and other and of buyer and seller. The agent and the seller want the best price they can get for a property; the buyer wants the lowest price at which the seller will sell. Far from being merely an economic transaction, the situation fosters a keen awareness of the differing perspectives from which participants act.

Here is the point at which social and personal identity enter the picture. People develop a sense of themselves as whole beings (integration) acting purposefully and effectively in their social world (continuity) by developing forms of identity that transcend the particular situation. We call these forms of identity social and personal identity. People identify not only with particular others in immediate and short-lived situations but also with others with whom they interact over longer periods of time. They include such particular others as friends and family as well as larger groups and categories, such as communities and even abstract categories. And these kinds of others provide for a sense of individual difference as well as similarity. Table 3.1 presents a systematic comparison of situated, social, and personal identity.

Social Identity

Social identity has three identifying attributes. First, it locates the person in a social space larger and longer-lasting than any particular situation. A particular baseball game, for example, takes place within the confines of a ball park and lasts nine innings. Each player has a situated identity there—pitcher, catcher, batter, and the like—but also thinks of himself or herself as an "athlete." To claim a social identity as an athlete is to locate oneself in relation to others in the social world, specifically those who are or are not athletes. This social identity is grounded in participation in athletic events, such as being a pitcher or infielder in numerous baseball games. But the social identity of athlete goes beyond any particular game, for it places the individual as a member of a social category that differs from other categories. Membership in this category accompanies the person even when he or she is not playing baseball—hence, the social identity of athlete is larger in scope and longer in duration than the particular situated activities on which it is based.

Second, identification with a social category lies at the heart of social identity. To be an athlete—or a Jew or a born-again Christian—is to identify with others who are

TABLE 3.1 **Forms of Identity**

	Situated	Social	Personal
What is the basis of the identity?	A role is required (e.g., student, priest, friend, professor, etc.).	Membership in or identification with a community is needed (e.g., fellow students, the gay community, a neighborhood, etc.).	A life project or life story is required (e.g., becoming famous, being a nonconformist, being oneself, etc.).
How long does the identity last?	The identity lasts for the duration of the situation in which the role is located (e.g., as long as one is in class or interacting with a friend).	The identity lasts during the span of membership in or identification with the community (e.g., as long as one lives in or identifies with the neighborhood).	The identity lasts until the narrative of the life story changes (e.g., as long as one is doing things designed to achieve fame or establish differences from others).
What kinds of announcements are made?	Announcements are expressive and instrumental actions that show identification with the role and/or perform activities of the role (e.g., taking notes, wearing a priest's garb, etc.).	Announcements are about one's identifications, especially announcements made on narrative occasions (e.g., telling others about the importance of family or friends).	Announcements are about plans, projects, and individuality, especially announcements made on narrative occasions (e.g., wearing distinctive clothing, piercing bodily parts, etc.).
What kinds of placements are made?	Placements are expressive and instrumental actions by others that confirm the acceptance of the individual's appropriation of role and his or her willingness to interact in terms of the role (e.g., answering a student's questions, confessing to a priest, etc.).	Placements are expressive actions by community members and/or outsiders that confirm legitimacy of identification and willingness to accept claims of membership (e.g., treating a claimant as a friend or family member).	Placements are expressive actions that confirm legitimacy and desirability of the life story (e.g., expressing agreement or admiration).

perceived as like oneself and whose real or imagined presence evokes positive feelings. Identification with others implies that all share beliefs, values, and purposes. One person may believe that "achieving my personal best" and another that developing a "personal relationship with Jesus" is a measure of individual accomplishment. In either case, to identify is to perceive that members of one's social category share such beliefs. Likewise, members are apt to perceive that others share their goals—that fellow athletes want to compete and win or that fellow Orthodox Jews want to follow the commandments of the Torah. And identification with other members inspires positive affect. It feels good to be with them or to think about them, and doing so puts the individual in a good mood and produces positive emotions.

Third, identification converts social categories into functional (if not necessarily functioning) communities. In the classic sociological sense, a functioning community is a set of people who live in close proximity to one another over a prolonged time. The English village (such as Arkengarthdale in North Yorkshire), the American small town (Casey, Iowa), or the ethnic urban neighborhood (Boston's heavily Italian North End) are examples of such communities. In these places people know one another and lead their lives to a great extent in one another's presence. They feel a sense of shared purpose and they develop well-defined and enduring relationships with one another. Those who identify with a social category treat it as if it were a community in the classic sense. That is, they come to feel that they know other members even if their "knowledge" of others is indirect and impersonal, and that those others are "present," even if typically only in imagination.

Identification with a category as if it were a community in the classic sense does not make it so in fact, but from the individual's perspective it functions in the same way. That is, the imagined community provides an encompassing social place to which the person can attach himself or herself. It provides a set of beliefs, values, and purposes that the individual can share with others, even if only in the mind. And it thus provides not only a needed sense of identification but also an individual sense of continuity and integration. A sense of common beliefs, values, and purposes transcends the goals of a particular situation and its roles. As a result, the person can feel like a person rather than like a role, a human being rather than a title or number. Social identity provides a basis for thinking of oneself as someone who outlives the particular situation and who is not defined exclusively by its designated role.

Social identity also provides for the differentiation of self from others. Within the real or imagined community the person can carve out a distinctive place in relation to others even while identifying with them. A star quarterback in professional football is a distinguished athlete, perhaps also a model for others. A woman who identifies strongly with her company and makes it one of her communities may be viewed by others as distinctive because of her commitment, her leadership abilities, or her capacity to solve problems. Even though identification is at the core of social identity, there is an evident need for some degrees of separation and difference from others.

Identification with a particular community is also a way of differentiating oneself from people who are not members. In many instances, social identity establishes a sense of difference that looks on others with pity, condemnation, avoidance, or even violence. Evangelical Christians feel a strong need to bring others into the fold before it is too late. The old-order Amish restrict and regulate contact with outsiders, who are viewed as potential threats to the survival of the community. In other cases, outsiders are viewed as different but not necessarily to be condemned or avoided. For many gays and lesbians, identification with the gay and lesbian community provides not only the security of a social identity but also a sense of legitimate, valued difference from others.

Social identity, like situated identity, relies on the announcement/placement process. In other words, a social identity is not merely a private experience, something carried within the mind as a way of thinking about oneself in relation to others. Rather, when the individual announces a social identity, it does not fully exist until others place him or her in it. Tempting as it is to think of social identity as primarily a matter of interest to the individual, it is in fact something that other people also take into account and use as a basis for acting toward the person.

Social identity is accomplished when announcements and placements coincide. Athletes tell others of their accomplishments, get their pictures on boxes of Wheaties, endorse products, and become guests of talk shows, David Letterman or Jay Leno. These public presentations of self as athlete constitute claims about who they are and how others should treat them—as doers of great athletic deeds or role models for high school athletes. The television host who shows respect or lavishes praise on the athlete is honoring the claim and thus placing him or her in terms of this social identity. The high school audience that listens intently to what the star quarterback has to say likewise honors his or her claim. The child at the breakfast table eating the "breakfast of champions" does not directly honor the athlete's claim, but the General Mills marketing executives who decide to put the picture there clearly do so.

Placements of people into the situated identities they claim usually involve positive responses from others, but need not do so. Members of socially marginalized groups, for example, honor one another's claims for membership, but are often treated with hostility by nonmembers. The hostility of outsiders, however, probably strengthens rather than undermines the solidarity of the group and the identification of members with it.[17] Sometimes an individual whose claims of membership in and identification with a group are met with rejection or outright hostility may feel spurred to even stronger identification rather than feeling inclined to give up and go away.

Although announcements typically precede placements—someone makes a claim and then someone else honors it—the reverse may also be true. Dissatisfied with the reckless behavior of some male star athletes, a variety of people—women, sports writers, politicians—have called upon these men to clean up their act and serve as better role models for young people. These calls for better behavior are, in fact, efforts to place the athletes whose behavior is being criticized into the "role model" role and confer the situated and social identities that go with it. When the athlete bends to these demands and agrees, whether grudgingly or willingly, to be a better person, he is announcing an identity into which others want to place him.

Finally, there is an important exception to the rule that social identities depend on the coincidence of placements and announcements. Sometimes a social identity is intensely desired but the individual knows that he or she cannot reveal it without being drastically transformed and perhaps rejected by others. Gays and lesbians know that they often must remain at least partially "in the closet" because those whom they know or with whom they work would reject them if their sexual orientation became known. Indeed, the individual may be fully closeted because there is no one to whom a claim of a social identity based on sexuality may be made. Nonetheless, the social identity may form and grow stronger, absent any external confirmation, whether positive or negative.

How is this possible? The answer rests in part on the fact that individuals in contemporary society have access to a wide array of ideas, facts, opinions, and ideologies through mass media of communication. As a result, the gay or lesbian individual can learn about other gays and lesbians, and about what it means to be gay or lesbian, without much contact with other members of the category and without revealing his or her secret to friends or family. The person can read the personal narratives of gays and lesbians and vicariously participate in discourse about sexual orientation. He or she can hear homosexuality condemned as sin by preachers and respond internally with beliefs and facts gleaned from the media. And the individual can make contact with others through the Internet. In short, social identity can come into being without specific placements and announcements, for society exists in the mind and the imagination and not only in concrete interactions between people.

Personal Identity

Personal identity also locates the person in a social space larger and longer-lasting than any particular situation. It does so by differentiating one person from another and focusing on the individual's life story. Where the social identity of "athlete" entails identification and similarity, the personal identity of a particular athlete rests on the distinctive accomplishments and characteristics of a Cal Ripkin, Jr. or a Mohammed Ali. Personal identity stresses uniqueness and difference, and it is more likely to locate the individual within the society as a whole rather than any of its component communities. The work ethic of a Cal Ripkin, Jr. is of interest to other athletes or to sports fans, of course, but also to a wider audience impressed by someone who was always ready to play and never took a day off. In his 20-year career with the Baltimore Orioles from 1981 to 2001, Ripkin played in a record-setting 2632 consecutive games. And personal identity depends on the person's construction and maintenance of an autobiography—a life story that is built, told to (and by) others in various contexts, and from time to time revised to fit changing experiences or preferences. Cal Ripkin, Jr. seemed relatively modest about his accomplishments, but he was visible from time to time on television, telling his story, and sports writers and commentators often mentioned the dedication that characterized his career. Likewise, Mohammed Ali became the object of veneration, not only by fans of boxing but by many others who never saw him fight. His physical and verbal exploits are the stuff of legend, told in newspaper articles, recalled in television biographies, and dramatized on film.

The life story around which personal identity is constructed typically has one or more main themes that give meaning to the individual's actions. One person may, like Cal Ripkin, Jr., emphasize an especially strong work ethic and show up at the job day after day, ready to go to work, even at times when he or she could easily find an excuse to take a day off. Another may define himself or herself as a seeker of religious or philosophical truth, exploring first one and then another system of beliefs in an effort to discover the most plausible one. Others may seek fame, or celebrity, wishing to become a "household name," someone everybody has heard of. And some may seek full autonomy, creating a life story in which the chief goal is to be unique and to be neither dependent on or committed to others. Such themes provide a basis on which the person can interpret his or her own acts and have them interpreted by others. The steady employee who has become committed to always showing up will regard normal aches and pains from this vantage point and will likely define them as "not serious enough" to stay home from work. And if that employee doesn't show up one day, colleagues will take his or her absence as an indication that something truly awful may have happened. The person in search of full autonomy is likely to interpret any urge to connect with others as a threat to independence, and others may refrain from making overtures because they know they will be rejected.

Whatever theme is chosen, personal identity is regarded as the person's property. A social identity by definition acknowledges the importance of other members of the community with which the person identifies and views their influence as valuable. A personal identity, in contrast, is thought of as something the person creates, owns, and is entitled to modify as he or she sees fit. A dedicated worker urged by others to "take it easy" may say emphatically, "This is who I am—this is me!" A religious seeker who has settled for a time on a belief system may, when challenged by others with differing views, say, "These are my beliefs and my truth, and no one can take them away from me." The autonomy seeker will acknowledge as few obligations to others as possible, arguing that "my first obligation is to myself." In more general terms, personal identity involves a sense of ownership of "the self," a belief that one owns the rights to one's body and mind and should not cede these rights to others.

In spite of its stress on difference and distance from others, personal identity rests on shared ideas about what people can be or become, and it requires social confirmation. Every personal identity rests at some point on the individual's participation in a cultural world shared with others. A star athlete like Michael Jordan, for example, had a truly distinguished sports career; he was a unique basketball player, one whose name almost everybody knows, who inspires unusual respect. But his very distinctiveness is defined by the fact that he exceeded the typical expectations of a career in basketball. Basketball players, professors, plumbers, and police officers all orient themselves to careers typical of their fields. Professors have a six-year probationary period as assistant professors before being awarded tenure and promoted to associate professors. Police officers strive to advance through a set of defined ranks and duty assignments, and they know approximately on what schedule they might do so. The career is culturally and socially standardized, and one way in which individuals can achieve personal identity is by meeting its expectations in distinctive ways. Even the person seeking as much autonomy as possible does so against the background of cultural definitions and social arrangements. For such an individual, cultural definitions of the good life or of correct behavior are likely to be perceived as wrong, and social arrangements as overly restrictive. One can scarcely rebel without having something to rebel against.

Social confirmation of some kind is also a necessary component of personal identity, even for those seeking as much autonomy as they can get from the social world. The distinguished scientist who is keenly or even arrogantly aware of his or her unique contributions to knowledge nonetheless wants the rewards society offers. He or she would like to have the right to name species or planets, and generally welcomes the awards and the fame that come with great scientific discoveries. A rich, colorful, self-promoting business entrepreneur—Donald Trump comes to mind—craves not only the pursuit of the personal goals he or she has chosen but also the fame and recognition that come with success. And even the hermit who leaves society to live alone looks beyond the mouth of his or her cave to the horizon and not only sees a boundary that keeps self safe and secure from society but also imagines those on the other side condemning the hermit.

In other words, personal identity is dependent on announcements and placements in much the same way as situated identity and social identity. To be located in the social world in some fashion, the individual must announce that location to others, and they must in some way place him or her in terms of it. The adolescent striving for autonomy from parents announces his or her emergent personal identity as an independent being in various ways—for example, by testing or breaking rules parents have imposed, by announcing rejection of parental authority, or by breaking with the family's religious or political affiliation. Parents, in turn, place their adolescent son or daughter into this identity as they slowly modify the rules, look the other way when they are violated, or even react strongly to transgressions. Even the arguments that often occur between parent and adolescent confirm the latter's emergent independent identity. Likewise, the personal identities of star athletes, scientists, and celebrities emerge as their announcements coincide with their placements by others. Athletes grant interviews and endorse products, and people watch the interviews and buy the products. Scientists publish their discoveries and accept the awards their peers give them. Celebrities—those famous for having accomplished something noteworthy as well as those famous merely for being famous—make the round of television talk shows, grant interviews to reporters, and write autobiographies, and their audiences respond by discussing, reading, and reacting.

The three forms of identity—situated, social, and personal—are not mutually exclusive. Each person in contemporary society acquires and exercises a variety of situated identities in his or her daily life. But the individual also develops a personal identity and one or more social identities. Sometimes a personal identity is sufficiently strong that it dominates and diminishes the person's social identities. Some individuals rely on one or two mainstay social identities, whereas others manage several. Society and culture also play a major part: Some cultures make it difficult for individuals to develop any personal identities, always defining the person in relation to others. Other cultures make a virtue of strong personal identity and make attachment and commitment to others quite difficult. In all cultures and social settings, however, situated, social, and personal identities are an inevitable product of the social organization of personal life.

Self-Image: Knowing the Self

Conduct is the main focus of identity, which must be established before people can know what to do. But identity also has cognitive and affective dimensions. Identities provide a foundation for what people know about themselves, and they are the source of positive and negative affect. We will consider the cognitive aspect of the self first, and relatively briefly, since it has been more the province of psychologists than sociologists.

How is identity related to self-knowledge? Thus far we have emphasized social location. Having a situated identity means that the person knows where he or she stands in relation to other people—as father to daughter, student to professor, friend to friend. One or more social identities tell the person where he or she is placed in the social world—as a dedicated worker among less-committed colleagues, a Jew in a predominantly Christian society, a resident of an urban neighborhood, or perhaps all of these. And personal identity provides a basis for knowing oneself as a person with a life story and with goals or qualities that distinguish one from others.

Knowledge of self is not confined, however, to knowledge of identities. Human beings approach the world with a symbolic attitude, constructing useful categories, abstractions, and generalizations. This process takes place with respect to self as much as to any external object. Individuals categorize themselves as they announce identities and are placed in them by others. They use abstract ways of defining people—as introverted or extroverted, athletic or clumsy, flexible or rigid—that culture provides to characterize themselves. And people use the generalizations they learn or create as a basis for understanding themselves.

Psychologically oriented social psychologists have used the concept of the self-schema to study self-knowledge—how people know themselves, what they know, and how they use their knowledge. More formally, a self-schema is a "cognitive generalization about the self, derived from past experience, that organizes and guides the processing of self-related information contained in the individual's social experiences."[18] Individuals who see themselves as possessing a particular trait are said to be "schematic" for that trait. Thus, for example, one may be schematic for athleticism, extroversion, or unhappiness. Individuals to whom a particular domain is unimportant are said to be nonschematic.

A self-schema, like any schema, contains information about an object (in this case, the self), ideas about how the object is put together and functions, and examples of the object. So, for example, an individual's self-schema may contain information about his or her traits and characteristics (intelligent, strong-willed, compassionate toward others, ambitious, outgoing). Likewise, the same individual may have formed ideas about how these elements do or do not fit together: "I am ambitious because I want to use my intelligence and will-power to good effect." "Sometimes my ambitions get in the way of my desire to be caring and sensitive to others." And a self-schema may well contain images of an ideal self, and perhaps also images of others whom the person idealizes.

Self-schemas "theorize" the self just as schemas in general "theorize" the external world. That is, self-schemas create a theory of the self that combines categories, abstract ideas, and propositions about how things are related to one another. People create these assemblies of facts, ideas, and propositions—or adopt them from others—for practical reasons. Self-schemas reduce the incoming flow of information to manageable dimensions. They help people make sense of themselves so that they can decide how to act. They focus memory on relevant information and help the person process it. And they shape the way people see the others with whom they interact.

According to Markus and colleagues,[19] to be schematic on a particular trait is to be like an expert in a particular field. Experts are quickly able to recognize information that is relevant to their field of expertise. For example, a plumber will see evidence of a leaking pipe more readily than will a homeowner. Experts can organize incoming information readily and relate it to what they already know. A plumber will quickly observe that the leaking pipe is probably a drain pipe and remember repairing such pipes previously. Experts use contextual clues to fill in missing information and adjust their processing of information to the task at hand. A plumber will notice the location of stained wallpaper or a wet ceiling and treat these facts as clues to round out his or her picture of the situation. And he or she will be able to shift attention from the trees to the forest, for example, by seeing that although the drain pipe is leaking, a greater problem is that the floor is about to collapse because water has caused it to rot.

Likewise, the individual who is schematic on a particular dimension will develop expertise about it. A person who thinks of himself or herself as having a tendency toward depression, for example, will develop considerable expertise about depression by reading about it, talking with others, or seeking professional help. As a result, this individual may be better able to recognize the signs of an impending depressive episode than a nonschematic. He or she will be better able to remember past episodes of depression and relate this one to those experiences. Contextual clues—the perplexing behavior of others, difficulty getting going in the morning—will enable the individual to get a good picture of the impending episode before it is full-blown. And the person schematic for depression will be more likely to see that a particular detail of his or her experience doesn't fit with an episode of depression and thus shift from the smaller to the larger picture. "I'm not getting depressed, really," he or she might say, "I just forgot to take my medication last night."

What is the sociological significance of self-schemata? Part of the answer lies in the fact that the schematic information about the self influences the perception of other people. Although it is conventional—and in some degree true—to say that our conceptions of self reflect the ways others conceive us, it seems clear that the process works both ways. We see ourselves as we think others see us; but we also see others as we see ourselves, through the lens of our own self-schemata. The self as an object to itself is thus implicated in everyday social interaction because thoughts of self shape thoughts about the other. One who is schematic for introversion will pay a great deal of attention to signs of introversion in others.

Of equal importance, the concept of the self-schema enables us to portray more precisely how culture shapes the self. People in all societies are surrounded from birth by others who share and use an existing set of categories, ideas, and propositions. In contemporary societies, people are faced not only with others with whom they directly interact but also with mass media of communication that present a variety of categories, ideas, and propositions. Magazines, radio, television, movies, and the Internet make available great quantities of information about human beings and their characteristics, some of it grounded in careful science, most of it not. People are categorized as "Type A" or "Type B" personalities; "self-esteem" is said to be the primary human motivation; the idea of "addiction" is used to explain conduct ranging widely from drug dependence to gambling to excessive dependence on meeting other people's needs ("codependence").

Whether the source of categories, ideas, and propositions is one's family, teachers, *Vogue,* or the *CBS Evening News,* the result is the same. People learn what images of self are possible. Their schemas reflect what culture makes available. Sometimes they readily adopt categories and standard ideas about them, as occurs early in socialization when children learn basic categories of male and female. At other times and in other contexts, people try out ideas for a time, seeking to learn if they fit and if they aid understanding. A person with a drug problem might find that the concept of an "addictive personality" makes personal sense, and that it helps him or her avoid drug use. Such an individual will become schematic on this dimension, develop expertise, and use it for the practical purpose of staying clean. From the perspective of the individual and others who know him or her, "addictive personality" will become a "fact." From the perspective of a pragmatic social scientist, however, "addictive personality" is "true" only in the sense that it is "useful." It is not an absolute fact about human affairs, but a proposition that makes sense of experience and helps the individual in his or her daily life.

Self-Esteem

People respond to their experiences *affectively* as well as cognitively. Their relationships with others engender feelings—of love or hate, satisfaction or frustration, security or fear—and these emotional responses are crucial to an understanding of the person. These feelings are directed toward the self as much as toward others or toward the social situation. We love or hate ourselves, feel satisfied or frustrated with the kinds of persons we believe we are, and feel secure or anxious in our identities.

The affective dimension of self-objectification is *self-esteem*. Our perceptions of self are not merely cognitive efforts to decide who we are and what we are like, for we have emotional responses to what we see. One is apt to feel a sense of pride or joy when one basks in the praise of others or takes pride in a job well done, and to feel ashamed when one acts in ways that important others condemn. These are affective responses, very much like those feelings of joy, sadness, anger, dismay, and other emotions that we experience in our everyday lives. Self-esteem consists of that class of sentiments whose object is the self. These feelings are aroused in us as we attend to ourselves and see ourselves as we imagine others see us.

Conceived as the affective dimension of the self, then, self-esteem may appear to be primarily a property of the individual. It is, after all, the individual who has self-referential feelings of satisfaction or anxiety, love or shame. Yet, just as identity is a complex product of coordinated social activity, so is self-esteem. Self-esteem is a product of the situation but is also something brought to it. It is not exclusively the property of the person, but exists within a social framework of role making and role taking.

Early in this century, sociologist Charles Horton Cooley used the well-known metaphor of a looking glass to depict the nature and sources of the images of themselves people see reflected in others.

> *A self idea . . . seems to have three principal elements: the imagination of our appearance to the other person; the imagination of his judgment of that appearance; and some sort of self-feeling, such as pride or mortification.*[20]

How do feelings about ourselves arise out of this process of imagining our appearance in the eyes of the other?

> *The thing that moves us to pride or shame is . . . an imputed sentiment. . . . This is evident from the fact that the character and weight of that other, in whose mind we see ourselves, makes all the difference with our feeling. We are ashamed to seem evasive in the presence of a straightforward man, cowardly in the presence of a brave one, gross in the eyes of a refined one, and so on. We imagine, and in imagining share, the judgments of the other mind.*[21]

As people interact, guided by their respective identities, they develop images of one another. Indeed, if they have a history of interaction, it is likely that they will bring schemas for one another to the situation. As these images—of bravery, refinement, tact, competence, intelligence, kindness, cruelty, stupidity, deviousness, and the like—are established, people imagine their own appearance to others in terms of them. That is, the person forms an image of the other, then imagines his or her appearance to the other from the standpoint of that image, and feels good or bad accordingly.[22]

This approach to self-esteem emphasizes the appraisals of others as they are per-ceived by the individual in the situation.[23] In some instances, of course, others mince no words in telling us what they think of us, so that we have direct access to their opinions of us. Words of praise or condemnation from others encourage us to have specific images of ourselves. Much of the time, however, we must rely on role taking, imagining our appear-ance to the other. In either case, the result is an affective response to ourselves. Whether we are directly told how the other feels about us or we impute a sentiment to the other, the result is that we develop an attitude toward ourselves.

There is more to self-esteem, however, than our responses to the appraisals of those others with whom we happen to be interacting at a given moment. Some of the people with whom we interact are important to us and so we are apt to take their appraisals more seri-ously than those of people whose opinions we do not respect. A child, for example, is likely to give more credence to the views of parents than of teachers. An adult is likely to put more stock in the views of friends of long acquaintance than of strangers. Thus, although each situation in which we interact with others has some impact on our overall level of self-esteem, some situations have greater impact than others. The self-sentiments that arise in each situation seem to be filtered through our existing conceptions of self before they add to or subtract from our overall self-esteem.

Moreover, we add to or subtract from our level of self-esteem not just by responding to the real or imagined appraisals of others but also by comparing ourselves to them. Part of the process of self-objectification, perhaps especially in a culture that emphasizes indi-vidual achievement, entails our comparing our own activities and accomplishments with those of others. We see others of our age, for example, who have better grades, greater incomes, or more powerful positions, and these comparative facts affect our self-esteem, most likely for the worse, unless we can find some way to explain the difference. Or, in contrast, we observe others doing less well than we are and derive some feelings of self-satisfaction from our better position.

Yet it is important not to lay too much stress on the determining nature of group stan-dards and group judgments. Symbolic interactionists stress that human beings are naturally active and self-conscious creatures who acquire some degree of autonomy along with the self. We act so as to earn the approval of others; we act in ways that let us approve of our-selves because we act as others would have us act. But we also develop individual goals and aspirations. We seek not only social identities, which locate us comfortably in the bosom of community, but also personal identities, which may entail projects and goals of our own that put us in tension or opposition to others. Thus, to some extent human beings derive self-esteem to the extent that their pursuit of personal identity is successful. Viktor Gecas and Michael Schwalbe have expressed a similar idea by arguing for the importance of what they call "efficacy-based" self-esteem, which is the positive sense of self the person derives from effective action.[24] Self-esteem is achieved in part through exercise of our capacities to take effective actions—to solve problems, to create new things or ideas, or to demonstrate our autonomy from the social world.

Moreover, in their quest for the positive appraisals of others, human beings may con-sciously seek to deceive others rather than emulate them or live up to their expectations. If people sometimes genuinely and spontaneously adapt their behavior to social standards, at other times they may simply try to create the appearance of doing so. Through a variety of techniques of *impression management,* they may seek to present a self that seems to be what others wish it to be. People carefully craft their physical appearances to create the impression that they are younger than they really are. Office workers seek to appear busy with work when they are engaged in personal activities. Men and women feign sincere interest in and respect for one another when they are really looking for a one-night stand. In a variety of ways people seek to present a self that seems appropriate to the situation or that meets cultural requirements even though they are inwardly alienated from this presented self. And sometimes, it seems, they may convince themselves as well as others of the validity of their performance. As Erving Goffman pointed out, people may be "taken in" by their own performances, so that what was initially a "false" presentation of self becomes a genuine one.[25]

Self-esteem is also influenced by our own appraisals of our performances. In the classic formulation of the psychologist William James, self-esteem is influenced by the "ratio" of success to pretension. The more one aspires to a particular accomplishment or other standard of self-worth, the greater one's successes must be in order to feel worthy. How we feel about ourselves is not simply a result of what other people tell us, but of what we want to be. If you think of yourself as someone who could be a champion athlete, mere athletic prowess or modest success is not enough; you must win in order to live up to your aspirations. As James's formulation suggests, feelings we have about ourselves in particular situations are thus weighed against our aspirations. You may triumph over an opponent in a contest, but if your goal is to be world champion and you have defeated a third-rate contender, the thrill of victory may be tempered by your sense that this particular victory does not count for very much.

Self-esteem is thus not simply the product of particular situations, but also of a continual process of reflection in which the person decides what standards and what others are significant. At any given point in the person's life, we are likely to find that the person has some organized sense of what is important and what is not, of whose appraisals should be taken seriously and whose should be disregarded. Some identities, for example, are likely to be more psychologically central than others. A lawyer who has fallen short of previous aspirations to make a great deal of money may adopt a revised version of occupational identity in which the new goal is to do well enough to be respected in a community and to provide for the needs of a family. A person who succeeds at academic tasks but is uncoordinated on the athletic field emphasizes the academic identity and downplays the athletic one, thus maximizing the chances of feeling positive about self by emphasizing those activities where the most favorable appraisals and comparisons are secured.

Finally, a caveat on the nature and possible sources of self-esteem is warranted. Although much social psychological theorizing treats self-esteem as variable according to the person's social experiences, there may be limits on how much it can vary in the person from one occasion to another. It is possible that each person has a particular "set point" for self-esteem—a level of self-esteem that is customary and normal for that individual and around which level of self-esteem fluctuates. Moreover, self-esteem appears to be closely linked to mood—the person's overall sense of whether things are going positively or negatively—and may thus be affected by the same things that shape mood. These include not only positive and negative occurrences in the person's life but also internal organic and psychological factors that elevate or depress mood regardless of external events.

The Self, Motive, and Motivation

No analysis of conduct can proceed very far without encountering the question of "why" people think, feel, and act as they do. Why does one child conscientiously do what parents expect while a sibling rebels at almost every opportunity? What makes one person ambitious for wealth and power and another content with more modest ambitions? Why do some people obey the speed limit on the highway and others break it? Why do some people always feel good about themselves while others apparently never do?

In their efforts to answer the "why" question, social scientists and lay people alike frequently invoke two terms: *motivation* and *motive*. The psychologist, for example, might explain that a child's disobedience in school is *motivated* by a need to get the attention of teachers, or that a person's ambition has been shaped by the need to please demanding parents. The explanations that people routinely construct in their everyday lives often invoke the *motives* that they presume underlie their own and others' conduct. That is, people are said to have a variety of motives for their actions: love, revenge, profit, altruism, and the like. The motive for donating a healthy kidney to an ailing spouse is love, we might say, or a student's motive for giving a professor a bad rating on a course evaluation is revenge for a low grade.

Both *motivation* and *motive* have their roots in the Latin verb *movere*—to move. To explain why people do what they do, in other words, social scientists and ordinary people alike examine what "moves" conduct. If a person acts in a particular way, it must be, we think, because something pushes, impels, drives, prompts, stimulates, induces, or provokes the person to act in that way. And both terms have in common a further implication, that an important part of what moves conduct lies within the person. Social scientists and ordinary people alike recognize that behavior is shaped by external influences as well as by internal ones, but the terms motivation and motive refer specifically to the internal states. A crucial part of what moves conduct is thought to come from within the person.

Although these terms are closely related to one another—and they are doubtless necessary in the explanation of conduct—we must distinguish carefully between them (see Table 3.2). *Motivation* refers to the drives, needs, urges, and other states of the organism that shape its responses to stimuli at any given moment. In other words, to cite motivation is to point to some internal state of the individual that influences how he or she will respond to the environment at a particular time. To say that a person is "hungry," for example, is to say that he or she is particularly sensitive to food stimuli and that the impulses most likely to be released are those linked to food. A "hungry" person is more alert to the sizzle of a steak on the grill or the enticing look of a salad than, say, to other things and events that may be present and, under other circumstances, might be appealing. In other words, motivation shapes impulses and is thus most closely related to the "I" phase of conduct, in which the individual initially responds without conscious thought to a relevant stimulus. A "hungry" person smells food and begins to respond in ways appropriate to securing it: the mouth waters and the other senses become alert to the source of the smell, even before the person is conscious of doing so.

Motive, in contrast, refers to the meanings people attach to their conduct, and is thus closely linked to the "Me" phase of conduct in which the person self-consciously grasps the direction in which an impulse is taking him or her. The smell of food cooking is apt to lead the "hungry" person to announce, to self or to others, "I'm hungry." The essence of

TABLE 3.2   Motive and Motivation

	Motivation	Motives
How are people conscious of motivation or motives?	People are not conscious of motivation at all. Motivations lie beneath the surface of consciousness.	People are explicitly conscious of motives. Motives are consciously announced as people name the reasons for their conduct.
How is it related to the self?	Motivation shapes the "I" phase of conduct.	Motives shape the person's view of self in the "Me" phase.
How is it related to phase of act?	Motivation shapes impulses.	Motives are employed in the phase of perception and manipulation to direct conduct and to grasp the nature of conduct of others.
What is its relation to role making and role taking?	Motivation, by shaping impulses, provides the initial material with which the individual shapes into appropriate conduct.	Motives are invoked in the shaping process, as people interpret their own and others' conduct by imputing motives.
What are its sources?	Motivations reflect the individual's history of conditioning; his or her situated, personal, and social identities; and previously avowed motives in the situation.	Motives are socially standardized expressions of reasons (see Chapter 4) for conduct, applied in specific situations and in response to particular audiences.

motive lies in this verbalization: motives consist in what people say about their actions, as opposed to internal states (*motivations*) that shape their responses to the world around them. To announce a motive is to constitute a "Me"—a hungry, ready-to-consume-food "Me"—and to begin to organize conduct with "food" or "dinner" as its object.

Motivations and motives thus offer differing explanations of what "moves" conduct. To say that "hunger" and "sex" are motivations is only to say that at a particular moment the individual's awareness of and sensitivities to his or her surroundings are shaped by one of those particular drives or needs. Any or a great number of factors can influence the particular sensitivities of the individual at a given moment: organic states such as hunger or sexual deprivation; previous conditioning to various aspects of the environment, ranging from picking up the telephone when it rings to responding to stimuli of which one is scarcely even aware, such as others' tone of voice or "body language"; and, crucially, the *imagined* responses of others to a contemplated or completed act. Motivations such as these operate at a preconscious level, and they determine the impulse but not the whole act.

As the person experiences his or her impulsive response, it becomes a part of the "Me"—the person takes the imagined attitudes of others toward the act. At this point the determining influence of motivation temporarily ends, and the person can bring the act under voluntary control.

Motives, in contrast, exist in the things that people say about their conduct. In everyday life we frequently speak of people's motives for their actions, ask people why they behaved in a particular way, and explain to ourselves and to others the reasons for our actions and what we hope to accomplish by them. Motives are verbal phenomena; they exist because people talk about what they do. They are visible markers of the existence and the importance of self-consciousness. To claim a motive for oneself—"I'm famished!"— or to attribute a motive to others—"She hates me!"—is to experience the self.

Motivation and motive are linked to the "I" and "Me" phases of the self in another crucial respect: in the same way that the individual responds ("I") to a particular image of self ("Me"), so motives shape motivation. Verbalized motives organize the person's sensitivities to the environment and its social objects. If the internal state of hunger (as motivation) leads a man to snack between meals, he may explain (to self or others) that he is "hungry" (a statement of motive) because he didn't eat much dinner. As he says this he may respond to his own words by recalling that he also had a snack before dinner and by thinking that perhaps if he had fewer snacks he would have less need of them. Here, a motive has become a motivation—what a man has said about his act has shaped his sensitivities to his surroundings (including his own actions) and thus influenced future impulses. In Mead's terms, the "I" has responded to a "Me."

Maintaining a clear distinction between motivation and motive is important for at least two reasons. First, it is always tempting—as much for the social scientist as for the lay person—to assume that each act can be explained by linking it to a particular underlying motivation or motive. People eat, we might say, because they are hungry, or they work hard in school because they are motivated to achieve. This assumption is deeply flawed, for the conditions that move most human acts are more complex and less obvious than they appear on the surface. We eat "because" we are hungry but also for other reasons: "because" it is noon and we ordinarily eat lunch then; "because" we are restless and wander to the refrigerator to graze; "because" eating makes us gain weight and thus live up to an identity as a fat person. Few acts can be explained by a single motive or motivation, and typically even the person whose behavior is under the microscope has only a limited grasp of what has moved him or her to act in a given way.

Second, any effort to explain why people act as they do runs the risk of what C. Wright Mills called *motive mongering,* which involves substituting the observer's account of what moves conduct for the real circumstances that shape what a person does. Social scientists do this when they attempt to explain complex forms of conduct in terms of such presumably universal motivations as a "quest for self-esteem" or the "rational maximization of advantage." Such explanations typically compound their errors by blurring the distinction between motivation and motive. Even a simple explanation of a child's misconduct as the result of a need for attention or a "cry for help" attributes to the child a state of awareness that may not exist, even as it fails to distinguish between unconsciously selected impulses and consciously constructed acts. We engage in similar forms of motive mongering in everyday life when we summarize a person's action by attributing it to a particular motive, such as "love" or "revenge." It may well be that "love" is a motive for generosity, but people act generously for many "reasons" and under a variety of circumstances. A wife who donates her healthy kidney to her spouse may despise him yet fear the social disapproval that would ensue if she refused. Perhaps the student pans the professor on a course evaluation out of revenge; but perhaps the professor simply deserves the criticism.

Symbolic interactionists argue that to explain conduct we must look at the circumstances in which it is formed and at the meanings people construct as they go about their affairs. These circumstances include the internal states of individuals at various moments; and the meanings people construct are shaped crucially by what they say about their own and others' conduct. In other words, both motivations and motives are important in the explanation of conduct. In Chapter 4 we devote considerable attention to the avowal and attribution of motives in everyday life. The focus in this chapter, however, is on motivation—that is, on the way in which identity and self-esteem affect conduct at the level of impulse.

The guiding principle of the analysis is that the person's conceptions of self influence motivation. They affect the state of the person as an organism and thus influence impulsive responses to various objects and events. They shape the person's dispositions, level of anxiety, moods of depression or elation, feelings of joy or sadness, and sense of competence or incompetence. These motivations in turn affect conduct by shaping the person's sensitivities to the acts of others, to the world of objects, and to the person's own acts. How people respond to various circumstances at the level of impulse—the "I"—is affected by motivational states that are shaped by the self.

Identity and Motivation

How is identity implicated in the motivation of conduct? In general terms, *situated identity* is the master organizer of the person's sensitivities to events that transpire within the situation. Social and personal identity are more deeply rooted motivational states that shape the way we respond to situated roles and form situated identities.

Consider a patient and a physician interacting within the situation of a medical examination. Each is motivated by his or her respective identity—one person by the identity "patient" and the other by the identity "physician." To say that each is motivated by an identity is to say that of the large set of responses each could make to the situation, a subset pertaining to the identity is selected and activated. The patient, for example, has a great many wants, needs, desires, and inclinations. Only some—those pertinent to the patient identity—are activated as the patient interacts with the physician. Others—being hungry for food or affection, wanting a new car, longing for a vacation, or wishing one could understand the behavior of a rebellious child—are for the moment given a much lower standing in the person's internal hierarchy of impulses. Events within the examining room that are relevant to the patient's concern about what ails him or her will be attended to closely, but those that may be relevant to other stimuli will be noticed less quickly or perhaps not at all. Thus, the patient will be alert to the physician's facial expressions, but much less interested in the advertisement for new cars in the magazine lying on the table.

It is partly the capacity of an identity to organize the person's attention and impulsive responses in a situation that accounts for its impact on conduct. Having assumed a particular role, one has an identity that organizes relevant impulses and excludes those less important to the activity at hand. To make the role of patient, for example, one needs to attend to the physician's words and deeds. The patient identity provides the motivation to do so.

Ordinarily, the process whereby the person assumes a role and its associated identity is a swift and almost unconscious one, and the identity itself becomes taken for granted. The patient submitting to a physical examination has considerable consciousness of *self,* for he or she must interpret the physician's directions and govern his or her conduct accordingly. This consciousness of self occurs *within* a given identity—one does not have to think of the identity itself, only of the things one must do from its perspective.

People become conscious of their situated identities when they are uncertain or when they undergo change. A baseball pitcher on a losing streak wonders whether he still has what it takes—whether he can still claim the identity of major league pitcher. A young couple who see one another socially a few times may at first think of themselves as "just friends," but gradually take a romantic interest in one another. At some point they will become conscious of the change and announce it to themselves and to others.

When people consciously reorganize their situated identities—whether by expressing doubts or announcing a new identity—they also reorganize or transform motivation. The pitcher's doubts begin to undermine his confidence and weaken his concentration. The couple begin to pay attention to one another in new ways: Sexual impulses that were ignored earlier begin to be more important. Also, characteristics of the other that were formerly of little importance—such as religion or occupational plans—now become matters of intense interest as the couple begin to think of their future together. In both examples, consciously verbalized identities shape motivation in ways we are scarcely aware of.

Social identity and personal identity also have significance as motivation and motive. A person does not ordinarily make each role with equal energy or define each situated identity as equally important to the self as a whole. One may throw one's energies into parenting and do the minimum one can get away with at work. One may be an active participant in local political affairs but be content to be a bystander in the affairs of church or synagogue. Some identities, it seems, energize us much more than others, and the force with which we act seems to depend on the identity we have in a particular situation.

Situated identities are always linked to social and personal identities. If a social identity as a musician is highly salient, for example, particular situated identities will tend to engross the person to the extent to which they contribute to this social identity. Thus, one who aspires to musical fame and fortune may jump at the chance to audition for the television program *American Idol* and even forgo other opportunities to perform in order to go for the big prize. If a personal identity based on academic success in college is the dominant element of the individual's sense of self, however, he or she may regard the chance to appear on the program as far less important than preparing for the Graduate Record Examination. We tend to choose situated identities depending on the ways they contribute to our social and personal identities.

The effects of social and personal identities occur through both motivation and motives. On one hand, we carry social and personal identities with us at every moment, although well beneath the surface of consciousness. These identities organize our receptivity to various kinds of events. The ears of a community leader prick up at hearing that a political office will be vacant, not because the individual thinks of himself or herself as a "community leader" at each and every moment, but because previous designations of self in those terms have organized his or her sensitivities to the world in a certain way. The eyes of a would-be best-selling author light up when he or she hears of a particularly grue-some crime, not because of an interest in the crime but because it represents an opportunity to write a book. One does not need to think "best-selling author" at every moment in order to have this response, but at some point in the past that self-objectification was made and now shapes one's conduct at the level of impulse.

Under some circumstances, of course, people do make a point of announcing their social or personal identities to themselves and to others or of focusing inwardly on social and personal identity. A person is apt to do so, for example, when the situated identity he or she has is a socially devalued one. In a study of the homeless, David Snow and Leon Anderson discovered a number of practices whose object seemed to be to maintain a positive sense of social or personal identity in the face of the socially denigrated condition of being homeless.[26] A homeless person is not only placed in a devalued situated identity, but is in a sense stripped of any legitimate social place.

How do the homeless try to sustain a sense of dignity in the face of their predica-ment? Snow and Anderson found that some homeless people seek to do so by distancing themselves from other homeless people or institutions, in effect claiming that the situated identity does not reveal their true social or personal identity. A person might maintain that he or she is not really like other homeless people; or that homelessness is only a very tem-porary condition and the person is about to return to a normal life; or that unlike other homeless people, he or she fends for himself or herself and does not depend on shelters or other institutions for the homeless. Others among the homeless adopt an opposite tactic, making their homelessness into a virtue as best they can by embracing the situated home-less identity and claiming it as the basis of a valued social or personal identity. One might, for example, point to the way homeless people stick together and help one another, thus claiming a valued place in society by virtue of one's commitment to the important cultural value of aiding others. Finally, some of the homeless essentially retreat into fantasy or tell stories designed to create the appearance that they really once had and soon will again have better lives.

It is not only social dislocation and derogation that bring social and personal identity to the fore. The performance of every situated identity carries some implications for the person's social and personal identity. Organized sport, for example, provides opportunities for people not only to assume situated identities as athletes but also to achieve particular success or distinction and thus solidify personal and social identities and have them validated by others. The small-town high school football hero, for example, who in the last game of the season in his senior year scores the winning touchdown that upsets the favored rival, achieves not only praise at the moment but also a durable place in his community. He becomes known to others for that accomplishment, and he may make it a central feature of his social identity.

As Raymond Schmitt and Wilbert Leonard suggested, sport provides a particularly effective social context for "immortalizing" the self.[27] Those who are interested in sports—whether in a small town or the larger society—talk about sports, rate athletes and their accomplishments, and legitimize sports as an activity worthy of attention. In the small town, the accomplishments of a high school athlete may be the talk of the whole commu-nity. In the larger society, those who take a special interest in sports constitute a "social world," which is a community whose members are focused on the activity of sports and which provides a stage on which athletic feats can be accomplished and used as a basis for self-definition. In either context, individual athletic accomplishment can provide the basis for talk that locates the person within the local or wider community and thus validates the accomplishment as the basis of personal or social identity.

In these examples, personal and social identity motivate efforts to talk about situated identity and put it in the best possible light. In the face of degrading social conditions, the wish both to have a valued place and to convince others that one has such evidently remains quite strong. Exceptional performances or accomplishments, such as in the world of athletics, become a way of "immortalizing the self," which is to say, making a permanent place for oneself in some community.

We can also see personal and social identity erupting into conduct in the phenomenon that Erving Goffman called *role distance*.[28] Goffman pointed out that even in the midst of serious situated role performances, such as that of a surgeon in the operating room, people sometimes make light of their roles, act playfully, and engage in self-deprecation. Surgeons and nurses, for example, might joke about the sterility of surgical instruments, in spite of the fact that this is no laughing matter. As Goffman pointed out, such forms of conduct have the important function of easing tensions, enabling people to maintain high standards of performance without making the atmosphere oppressively heavy with sanctions. Humor is an effective means of social control, a way to remind people of their responsibilities without directly accusing them of falling short.

Role distance also arises, however, because social and personal identity lie in the background of every act. If they sometimes seem to intrude just at the point where the person is deeply engrossed with the situated role, it may be because the situated identity is threatening to "take over" the self. Taking oneself with less than full seriousness in a role is a way of reminding self and others that there is more to one than just the current situated identity. Especially where that identity is drawing a great deal of involvement from the person, role distancing may be a way of reasserting the significance of other components of the person's identity.

Social identities can also come very definitely to the surface when an event occurs that is not relevant to the situated identity, but that is very significant to a social identity. A professor delivering a lecture may be engrossed in the situated identity and role and be scarcely conscious of his or her ethnic, racial, or religious identity. But should a student make a prejudiced comment, one or more of these social identities may come very quickly to the fore. If this happens, the professor will suddenly become aware of being, say, a Jew, and will begin to approach the situation on the basis of that social identity rather than in—or in addition to—his or her identity as a professor. The professor will become alert to further such expressions and begin to make the professor role with that underlying social identity in mind.

Each time one announces a social or personal identity, one reorganizes the self at a motivational level. That is, one reorganizes one's impulses and thus alters the environment to which one will subsequently be sensitive. The parent who announces that his or her career will require the rest of the family to make sacrifices not only attempts to redefine the situation in which others act but also to transform the self. By announcing the importance of a career identity, the person is seeking to rationalize subsequent conduct as much in his or her own eyes as in the eyes of others. If one tells oneself that career comes first, one makes career impulses most important and career stimuli most significant, and at the same time makes it easier to ignore other stimuli.

Self-Esteem and Motivation[29]

Like identity, self-esteem is a motivational state that affects the person's sensitivities to the surrounding social world. Social scientists have proposed a variety of ways self-esteem shapes conduct, and the linkage proposed here represents one of several approaches a symbolic interactionist can take to this topic. Self-esteem, we will suggest, influences what the person does by shaping his or her imaginations of self and other in social interaction. In other words, self-esteem has a powerful impact upon role taking. In particular, low levels of self-esteem interfere with role taking.

The capacity to engage in successful role taking—that is, to grasp the perspective of others sufficiently well to enable one to coordinate one's conduct with theirs—rests upon three conditions. First, the role taker must have a cognitive map of the situation and its role structure, knowing what activities will take place and who will do what. To take the role of a physician, the individual must know he or she is in a medical situation and that the other is a physician. Second, the role taker must have a situated identity—the person must know not only that the other *is* a physician but also that he or she *is* a patient. As a rule, these two conditions are readily met in the situations in which people interact. People go to physicians, know who is going to perform what part, and identify with the parts they are to perform.

The third condition for adequate role taking is more elusive but no less important: The role taker must trust the definition of the situation and the identities of self and other. In other words, the person must have a reasonable degree of certainty that a given situation is what it appears to be and that the others present are who they claim to be. Ordinarily, this belief is readily created as the situation is defined and its role structure established. We go to physicians trusting that they are really who they claim to be, that they will act toward us as physicians, and that their motives are those of physicians. Indeed, one of the reasons people are able to identify with their own situated roles is that they feel assured that others are identifying suitably with theirs. There are occasions on which doubt arises— sometimes a patient thinks that his or her physician has lost interest in the case or that the physician's competence isn't what it should be—but these are exceptions rather than the rule. Trust is in large part a function of people's actions. We trust doctors because they do what they are supposed to do. Doctors trust their patients because they act as patients are supposed to act. People act in good faith, or at least they appear to do so, and trust is maintained.

But trust also depends on the attitudes that individual participants bring to situations. Sometimes people come to situations reluctant or unable to trust others. They bring anxiety or suspicion, doubting that things will go as they ought, feeling unable to rely on the good faith of others. Self-esteem is a major factor that shapes the trust—or lack of trust—that people bring to social situations.

We can begin to explore the impact of self-esteem on social interaction by examining the effects of low self-esteem, which is associated with two painful psychological conditions—anxiety and depression—that undermine the trust on which role taking depends.[30] First, low self-esteem is associated with relatively high levels of anxiety—that is, with a psychological state of apprehension or psychic tension. People with low self-esteem are more anxious than people with higher levels of self-esteem. They are more worried about their performances, more concerned that they might fail, and more keenly interested in how others are viewing them. They are more nervous, are more likely to bite their fingernails in anxious anticipation of an event, and approach the world with a kind of sweaty-palmed reluctance to engage with others. In contrast, people with higher levels of self-esteem are less apprehensive about social encounters, more likely to take things as they come, and less concerned about possible failure. They seem to exude confidence in their abilities and to take it for granted that they have a right to be where they are and do what they are doing.

Second, low self-esteem is associated with—indeed it is a clinical symptom of—depression, a disorder of mood characterized by feelings of sadness, lack of energy, hopelessness, and worthlessness that are seemingly uncaused by particular life events. Depressed people experience sadness and internal feelings of guilt or lack of self-worth even when things are going well and they have reason to feel good about themselves. Although it is typical for individuals to feel depression in the face of traumatic events—such as the death of a loved one—depression also occurs in the absence of such events. It is perhaps an especially painful experience under such circumstances, for people are unable to attribute their feelings to external events and may thus be more likely to attribute them to personal failings. People who are not depressed—and who thus also likely have higher levels of self-esteem—are more likely to feel happy and energized. They are more likely to feel worthy and hopeful, and they recover more quickly from traumatic events that do occur.

Anxiety and depression undermine the person's confidence in the social world by making it more likely that the person will imagine any given situation in negative and distrustful rather than neutral or positive terms. When we enter situations with our self-esteem more or less intact, we bring with us a trust in the others who are present as well as in ourselves. We walk confidently into the physician's office or into the classroom, and in doing so we imagine a social situation in which others can be counted on to act in good faith according to their roles and identities. But the person who enters a situation laden with anxiety and self-doubt is apt to imagine others who cannot be so readily trusted—who are perhaps hostile, or who have hidden agendas, or who are not competent, or whose motives are not as they are supposed to be. Under ordinary circumstances—that is, where self-esteem is more or less adequate—we interact with people primarily on the basis of their roles and identities. Where self-esteem is low or under some threat, we are more apt to interact with them on the basis of doubts and suspicions about their intent.

The implications for role taking are ominous. The person with low self-esteem is apt to imagine that others are making negative judgments when in fact they may not be. He or she is likely to be especially sensitive to the opinions of others, to engage in needless comparisons of self and others, and to be unable to do the very things that might earn the approval of others. As the psychiatrist Harry Stack Sullivan wrote, the person with low self-esteem finds it difficult to "manifest good feeling toward another person."[31] To put it another way, although we can think of self-esteem as a wound in need of treatment, its very existence makes it difficult to secure that treatment. People with low self-esteem are likely to react to others' efforts as if they were salt rather than salve, and they find it difficult in any case to act in ways that would make others want to give aid and comfort.

Most people, of course, do not have genuinely low self-esteem; nor do most have extremely high self-esteem. Most individuals have self-esteem that is high enough to keep anxiety from paralyzing them, but low enough to make them receptive to others' evaluations. As this formulation suggests, both exceptionally low and exceptionally high self-esteem may have important implications for the individual. Very low self-esteem is frustrating because it makes it difficult for the person to do things that would improve self-esteem. Very high self-esteem may be equally consequential because it works to insulate the person from the appraisals of others. The person who approaches every situation with customarily high self-esteem may impulsively select images of others in such a way that only favorable conclusions about self can be reached—the person may always see himself or herself as an object of admiration, regardless of how others actually feel. People with very high self-esteem may thus fall beyond the control of others' judgments.

We cannot leave the topic of self-esteem without entering an important caveat: Nothing in the preceding analysis of self-esteem, which has focused on the ways self-esteem unconsciously shapes impulses within social situations, should be taken to imply that self-esteem is a basic or primary human motivation that trumps other motivations.[32] Nor should it be supposed that human beings are everywhere engaged in a self-conscious quest to enhance self-esteem, or that there is some kind of inherent "self-esteem motive." This is not to say that affective responses—to self and to others—are unimportant in social life, for they are in fact very important. But so are the cognitive responses—the thoughts—on which role taking and the assignment of meaning to self and others depend. And so are the actions that human beings undertake. In the trinity of thoughts, feelings, and actions, no term is more important than the others.

Indeed, symbolic interactionists would say that to assign some particular significance to self-esteem as a human motive is to engage in motive mongering. Human beings are culturally diverse, and the ways in which they label, understand, and emphasize the phenomenon we have here labeled self-esteem are likewise diverse. This point is especially important for contemporary students to understand, for Western culture, and that of the United States in particular, has created a set of ideas that treat self-esteem as if its attainment were the most important human goal and the means of solving a host of personal and social problems. No such claim has been made here. Rather, we have emphasized a more modest point: the way people see themselves affects the way they see others and shapes their capacity to engage in role taking and thus also role making.

The discussion of self and motivation has largely ignored the larger social context within which social interaction occurs. We have spoken of identity and self-esteem as if the person were relatively free to go wherever he or she chooses in the social world and to present the self as he or she sees fit. Realistically, however, the others with whom the person interacts, the identities that are available, and the conduct that is possible are strongly influenced by culture and society. It is to this topic that our attention must now turn in order to complete our account of the person.

The Self and the Social Order

A variety of cultural and social factors constrain the nature and development of the self. The identities people can assume in specific situations are only partly open to their choosing, for often one has no choice about one's situated role. Likewise, one is not entirely free to choose the others with whom one will interact. In many situations of life, people must interact with specific others, regardless of their wishes or the appraisals they expect to receive from them. In addition to these fundamental constraints, people are pulled in different directions by conflicting expectations, they are subject to the influences of the communities to which they belong, and they are shaped by the special nature of modern life. In the following pages we consider the variety of ways in which culture and society constrain the self.

Limitations on the Choice of Roles

Sociologists have long distinguished between two opposite ways in which people come to enact various roles. On the one hand, many roles are *ascribed,* which means that the person is assigned a role by others on the basis of biological considerations (such as age or sex) or birth into a particular family (identified, for example, by ethnicity or religion). Gender is a clear example of ascription (leaving aside physical abnormality or surgical change of sex). The person is born with the genitals of one sex or the other, and that fact alone assigns the person to a sex category. In any situation in which people define gender as a relevant part of the role structure (and that probably includes most situations to some extent), role making and role taking are influenced by the specific ideas people have about proper, normal, and expected conduct for boys or girls, men or women. Similarly, religion, age, and sometimes even political affiliation may be matters of ascription. The person is viewed as having a set of characteristics or dispositions by virtue of having been born into a family that sees itself and is seen by others as having those characteristics.

Gender is a particularly significant basis of ascription because it is so pervasive. In most situations, making a role requires the individual not only to act from the perspective of the role but also to do so in a way others will regard as appropriate to his or her gender. Behavior that might be seen as desirable in a man—the assertive, relentless questioning of a male television reporter, for example—might be viewed as unduly aggressive or pushy in a female reporter. Gender expectations are so powerful in part because they are taken for granted as natural features of the social order. From the earliest stages of socialization, children learn to look for the differences between males and females, to enact gendered performances, and to inspect the conduct of others from a gendered perspective.[33]

On the other hand, some roles are *achieved,* which means that the right to assume a particular role does not depend on birth, but is voluntary and requires the attainment of a specific set of qualifications. In modern societies, occupational roles are largely achieved: Few individuals are regarded by their families as required to assume a particular occupation merely because they were born into that family, and no legal sanctions are available to force an individual to become what parents wish. Thus, to the extent that identity rests on such achieved roles, it lies within the person's capacity to seek out and attain it.

Even achieved roles, however, are not equally open to all. No legal restrictions prevent the child of a factory worker from aspiring to become a college professor, but social and economic circumstances make such mobility a comparatively rare occurrence. Higher education may be financially beyond the person's reach, and it may be difficult for a working-class child to imagine himself or herself as the kind of person who could have such aspirations. Where middle-class culture may confer on the child a sense of entitlement to education and a rewarding career, working-class experience may define such aspirations as unrealistic.

A person's identity, whether in a specific situation or in a larger biographical sense, is thus in many ways not within the person's control. In the United States, historically and presently, the role of an African American is often fixed by race rather than by characteristics germane to the interaction that is to take place. In many circumstances, people react differently to men and women, even though gender is unrelated to the particular activity at hand. In these situations, an ascribed characteristic that is not germane to an activity is used as the basis for establishing situated identity. An extreme example would be the hospital patient who assumes that all African American people working in the hospital are orderlies. In thus establishing the situated identity of a particular person as someone who must be an orderly because he or she is African American, the patient approaches interaction with him or her with a preconception of the role structure of the situation. Even when the patient learns that this particular individual is a physician or a nurse, the interaction that takes place is still likely to be influenced by this patient's preconceived ideas about race.

Even a role the individual has achieved the right to enact by acquiring the appropriate qualifications—such as an occupational role—subsequently constrains and shapes the self. Acquiring the training necessary to be a history professor, for example, means that one foregoes the opportunity to acquire the skills of a pharmacist, since one has invested so much time and money in preparing for the one occupation that changing occupational roles is almost precluded. Moreover, to pursue an occupation is not only to develop a conception of oneself as, say, a physician or a farmer, but also to be regarded as such by others and to be entangled in a web of social relationships with others. One is constrained by the identity one develops in the course of learning and enacting an occupational role, and by the fact that a significant part of one's self-esteem depends on the successful performance of the role. And, as Patricia Adler and Peter Adler showed in their study of college basketball players, a role performed with great success and cheered by others can overwhelm the self. Adler and Adler studied the roles and what they termed the "gloried selves" of college basketball players. Engulfed by the athletic role—facing pressures from coaches, fellow students, and boosters to define themselves almost solely as athletes—the players they studied found themselves under strong pressures to define themselves in the same terms. They concentrated mainly on the athletic role to the detriment of other present and future roles. They became almost totally defined by a role they had achieved. In a sense they were diminished as persons by their very achievements as athletes.[34]

Limitations on the Choice of Others

Just as social life constrains the development of self by providing the roles on the basis of which the self is defined, so too it limits the person's choice of others with whom to interact and his or her ability to define their appraisals as important or unimportant. These limitations stem in part from the facts of birth and ascription. One's parents are ordinarily not chosen—parents and their children are typically stuck with one another, as are siblings. Furthermore, to be born Black or White, male or female, rich or poor, is to be confined to some extent to an existing network of social relationships within the world into which one was born. In some cultural groups, the worlds of men and women may be far removed from one another in such a way that the others with whom women interact may be limited (often very rigidly) by custom, knowledge, or rules and sanctions laid down by men. Some who are born White in the United States are denied contact with African Americans, their values, outlooks, and beliefs. De facto segregation of housing and schools, patterns of hostility between groups, community sentiments, and sheer racism are among the factors that constrain or limit contact between Blacks and Whites.

Moreover, as individuals in a modern society move through a succession of age roles, from infancy through childhood and adolescence into adulthood, they encounter a series of others whom they do not choose, but who interact with one another because of their social position. Teachers, other children, members of the extended family, gang leaders, social workers, Boy Scout leaders, police officers, college professors, and employers are others with whom individuals interact, sometimes by choice, but often on the basis of chance or the decisions and actions of others over whom they have little or no influence.

The ongoing social order that confronts the individual at birth is thus in many ways an unyielding reality to which the person must adjust. Beliefs about what is normal behavior for boys and for girls, the practice of starting school at age 6, a propensity to mentally place certain ethnic groups in only menial jobs—these may be given features of the social world from the individual's standpoint. A variety of attitudes exist in the social world into which the person is born, and they shape the formation of the self. They exist only because people form their conduct on the basis of particular beliefs, ideas, and knowledge—because, for example, they have learned to act toward certain ethnic groups, girls, or 6-year-olds as particular kinds of social objects. But from the standpoint of the individual confronting it for the first time, this world of objects is real. It is there as an objective, factual set of conditions that must be taken into account in his or her conduct. That little girls are to be avoided is simply a fact for some little boys, a matter of what is "obviously" real and important.

In order to account for the development of the self, therefore, we must know the person's location in the social order. That is, we must know the world of objects and the social arrangements of the family and community into which the person is born. We must know the beliefs and values found in the family, the attitude taken toward the child in school, the kinds of peers with whom the individual associates, the sort of job attained or college attended—all of which are strongly influenced by the person's social position, by whether the person is Black or White, male or female, rich or poor, Catholic or Protestant, urban or rural, or of Italian or Norwegian descent.

How does this obdurate social world influence self-conceptions? Both consciously and unconsciously, people arrange their presentations of self in various situations so as to manifest the qualities and characteristics valued in their social world. By manifesting valued qualities, the person is able favorably to imagine his or her own appearance in the eyes of the other. The impact of the social order on this process is considerable. Desirable qualities and characteristics are personified by others with whom the person is constrained to interact, and the valued attributes of others are themselves a factual, objective part of the world so far as the child is concerned. The adjustment of conduct—which is what the presentation of self is all about—always is to a specific set of others and to particular standards of evaluation, and these are a preexisting part of the world, at least so far as much childhood experience is concerned. As one grows older, of course, one may discover that the standards by which people evaluate one another are matters of human creation, not absolutes, and that a variety of other people in the society hold different views of what is natural and proper.

Some of the most important constraints on the adjustment of conduct to valued images of others come into play at the point where the child moves out of the exclusive confines of the family and encounters a more diverse set of others. In a complex society, which divides the labor of socialization among various agents and agencies, what parents expect may well not coincide with the views of teachers. If the child imagines parents to emphasize street savvy and toughness, and teachers as wanting refinement, sensitivity, and attention to school work, the child may be able to manifest both sets of qualities only with great difficulty, if at all. If the child perceives teachers as protective or restrictive, and has already developed a self-image that emphasizes self reliance and independence, the child may rebel against their efforts to impose controls.

Such conflicts between selves fostered within the family and those encouraged in public contexts, such as schools, are not uncommon in a society as ethnically, racially, and religiously heterogeneous as the United States.[35] Ideal conceptions of the person are not the same for Christians, Moslems, and Jews, for example, nor even for all members of any of these groups, and thus contradictions between family and public expectations are inevitable. From the standpoint of the person, this may impose not only limitations on the development of the self but also a major task for impression management. It can be difficult to live up to parental images or to those of an enclosed ethnic community and at the same time manifest qualities valued by outsiders whom the person may have to please if his or her goals are to be achieved. The African American or the Jew in U.S. society may resonate best to a particular ethnic "soul" and yet find it advantageous or even necessary to strip away or conceal peculiarly ethnic qualities of manner, dialect, or belief on the job and in interaction with nonminority individuals.

Sometimes the perceived necessity of being a different person within the family or the ethnic community as opposed to the world outside leads to a bifurcation of social worlds and of the self. Inside the protective world of the ethnic family, people can interact with one another by using ethnic slang that would be misunderstood by persons who are not members of the particular group. Indeed, interaction within the group often depends on distinctions between "we" and "they" that would be offensive to outsiders. Within the ethnic context, the person can present a self that lives up to particular conceptions of what the person ought to be. Outside that context, a different self must be presented to others, one that is adjusted to conceptions of the person that are either common to all members of the society or are held and enforced by a dominant group.

The self is thus shaped by ideal conceptions of what the person ought to be, and these vary by gender, ethnic origin, religion, region, social class, and other kinds of social differentiations. It is noteworthy that many of these definitions of the ideal person are not only linked to group memberships but also depend to some extent on we-they contrasts between groups. The selves fostered among Asian Americans, Jews, White southerners, or Polish Americans are defined, not just by the beliefs and values of the group itself but also by the particular contrasts between themselves and outsiders emphasized by members of the group. To be Jewish, for example, is thus not merely to live up to a set of images of what Jews ought to be like, as defined by Jews, but also to avoid certain patterns of behavior or belief presumed to characterize gentiles.

Not all such influences on the construction of the self come from the contrast between familial and other standards. Within the family itself, the child may or may not be able to meet parental expectations. Successful parents may convey an image of competence to the child that exceeds the child's capacity to match. Sometimes parents expect more of a child at any given age than the child can deliver and, not infrequently, parental expectations are not clear—the parents present no clear image in terms of which the child can adjust his or her conduct, and so leave the child to flounder in uncertainty and anxiety.

Whether the influences come from within or outside the family, there are occasions on which the child—or the adult—is confronted with images that cannot be emulated in conduct. Sometimes no presentation of self can be arranged that will adjust to the expectations of others. Where race or class are significant bases for distinguishing among people and evaluating them invidiously, the child has a particularly vexing problem. No presentation of self can avoid the fact of race, and class can also be very difficult to overcome, since the child may be marked by patterns of speech or dress that clearly mark him or her as different. The child who is born unwanted into a family that is already defined by its members as too large can do little or nothing to alter his or her definition by others as an interloper. In such contexts as these, behavior is irrelevant to the judgments others make. The child may form an image of what is desired and present self accordingly, but to no avail, for negative appraisals occur anyway.

What strategies are available to people when self-presentation makes little or no difference? To some extent, when others base their appraisals on grounds that have nothing to do with conduct, the person is free (within limits) to define them as insignificant and their evaluations as irrelevant. The child whose teachers persist in appraising him as stupid can cease to take their judgments seriously—he may even invert their images and regard as positive whatever they see as negative. The child who has come to see herself or himself as artistically creative may withdraw from emotional attachment to parents if they see this creativity as unimportant or even undesirable.

Limits exist, however, on the person's ability to define others as significant or insignificant as he or she chooses. Parents and teachers must be endured even if their appraisals are painful to the child. Emotional attachment will not develop with teachers who act negatively toward the child, but such attachment to parents occurs to some extent regardless of what they do, since the child's earliest experience of the social world has been with them. Similarly, an employee may see his or her boss's standards as wrong and so not regard the boss as a significant other person, but it is still the boss who calls the shots at work and writes the paycheck.

Moreover, even though withdrawing recognition of others not significant to the self is a way of protecting it, such a strategy is not without cost to the person. Even when the negative appraisals of others are labeled insignificant, they may continue to have an impact on the person because they have raised doubts where none existed before. The child may define teachers as insignificant, but their appraisals may raise doubts about competence that will endure long after the child has forgotten the teachers themselves. An individual with a positive conception of self may, from time to time, encounter others who do not share that image. Even though their appraisals may thus be defined by the person as insignificant, continued interaction with them, which frequently is unavoidable, is a constant reminder of the low esteem in which he or she is held. One may encounter fellow workers who are very supportive and others who hold one's work in very low esteem. The former will be seen as more significant to self-image and self-esteem, but the latter cannot be totally ignored for they are present from day to day, and they may be in a position to affect one's advancement on the job.

Withdrawing recognition of others also is costly because it may, in time, lead to a shrinking of the circle of others with whom the person customarily associates and with respect to whose judgments the self is continually reaffirmed. As Hans Gerth and C. Wright Mills indicated, the avoidance of interaction with negative others leads to a retreat to a circle of "confirming intimate others."[36] As the person moves through successive stages in the life cycle, he or she may encounter so many negative images of self that more and more people are seen as insignificant. Eventually, the person may find only a small circle of confirming others in whose company a positive self-conception can be sustained. In the extreme, the person may retreat to a private fantasy world where no real others are encountered, only imaginary others who always give positive appraisals.

Limitations on the Choice of Stories

There is yet one more way in which the social world constrains the self, and that is by limiting the kinds of stories people can tell about themselves and the contexts in which they are permitted to tell them. As we have already suggested, the self is in part a narrative construction—an object created and modified by what people say about themselves, by the autobiographies they tell and edit in a variety of circumstances in their everyday lives. This process is deeply affected by cultural materials and social arrangements.

When people tell others about their lives, they draw not only on their own experiences but also on cultural models of self-narration. From the individual's point of view, talking to others about oneself seems mainly to be a matter of reporting biographical facts: "First I went to college, then started on this teaching career that I wanted so much, and now I feel tired and burned out and stuck in a job I despise." Or, on a more positive note, "I put myself through college and medical school, trained as a surgeon, did my residency at Massachusetts General Hospital, worked long and hard hours to perfect my trade, and I'm now Chief of Surgery at the leading hospital in our state." Such accounts report experiences, but also interpretations, and the latter are less individual inventions and more the result of culturally standard ways of giving meaning to experience. "Burnout" is a relatively recent cultural idea, a way of labeling and understanding the frustration and anger people often experience in demanding jobs they have held for a long time. It reflects not only a cultural belief that people have the right to enjoy their work (not every culture has this belief) but also a tendency to interpret individual experiences in psychological terms. Likewise, the successful surgeon's story is modeled after a cultural ideal of hard work and effort followed by success.

Cultural models for interpreting and narrating experience are varied and they change over time. The surgeon's story is a variation of an old and familiar theme in the culture of the United States: The individual overcomes obstacles, works hard, and in the end reaps the rewards of money, social standing, and professional recognition. The "self-made person" may be largely a myth, and will especially seem so to those (such as spouses) on whose efforts the success also depended, but the story nonetheless seems entirely factual to the individual who claims it as a life story.[37] Those whose hard work brought only failure or limited success also can turn to cultural models: "I would have been a success if only I had been able to get an education," for example, or "I could have become company president, too, if I had married the boss's daughter."

In the contemporary world, psychological narratives have become especially important. For example, addiction—whether to drugs, gambling, or social relationships— has become a widely available way for individuals to make sense of their lives. Individuals who seem unable to achieve a stable career, lasting relationship with another person, or a strong sense of self can interpret themselves as "codependent." That is, they can believe that they have a condition known as "codependency," a vaguely and loosely defined quasi-illness of the self and its social relationships. Although there is no "cure" for this illness, those who believe they have this condition look for aid and comfort from others who believe they have it, too. At weekly meetings of Co-Dependents Anonymous, a self-help group found throughout the United States and other countries, individuals tell one another the stories of their lives using this organization's ideas and vocabulary. Just as people can become addicted to drugs or alcohol, the organization teaches, they can become addicted to dependence on others. There is, it is said, no end to such addictions—one is always a recovering alcoholic or codependent, never a recovered one—but one can manage the addiction in cooperation with fellow addicts.[38]

Narrating the self occurs in socially structured and often obligatory occasions. Codependents tell their stories to one another in weekly group meetings. The prospective employee does so in job applications and job interviews, where the task is not only to present a competent self to a human resources interviewer but also to construct a plausible account of a job history and of aspirations for the future. The college applicant does so in the personal essay, attempting to convince an admissions committee that he or she possesses talents, skills, and virtues required for success in college. Reunions likewise provide structured occasions for people to recount their life stories to others, or to bring their life stories up-to-date. The high school reunion, for example, periodically reunites individuals who were together earlier in their lives. As individuals anticipate attending a reunion, they imagine how they will present themselves and what account they will give of their successes and failures since graduation. And they imagine how others will tell their stories, as well.[39] Even illness provides an occasion for the construction of a biography, for as individuals anticipate recovery, ongoing struggle, or death, they are forced to confront the meaning of their lives.[40]

Individuals do have choices in such narrative occasions. People attending a high school reunion can make up wild stories about their successes, as did the characters in the movie *Romy and Michelle's High School Reunion,* or, more likely, they can find ways to emphasize their accomplishments and draw attention away from their failures. The job applicant can find a variety of ways to explain a history of frequent movement from one job to another. But choices are nevertheless constrained by the terms of discourse available and the likelihood that others will accept any given narrative.

The Self in Contemporary Society

Finally, the structure of society as a whole shapes the self. People form selves not only by making and taking roles and by constructing narratives within particular situations, but also by imagining themselves as members of larger social entities. One of the ways we can portray this process is by examining the role of community in the creation and maintenance of the self. Contemporary societies, we will see, create communities in ways that differ considerably from those of the past.

A contemporary society is not only a more structurally complex entity than the societies of the past but it is a larger entity as well, one that contains multiple communities. The classic communities of the past were in many respects self-sufficient entities. The

European peasant community of the Middle Ages, for example, was in important ways a world unto itself. It produced the food and fiber on which the lives of its members depended, and a person could live a life without ever leaving the community or encountering the members of other communities. Thus, in effect, the community was also a society—a more or less self-sufficient and self-reproducing entity with little dependence on the outside world.

In contrast, a contemporary society contains a great many communities, few (if any) of which are economically self-sufficient, and most of which are dependent on other communities and on the society as a whole. The rural small town and the urban ethnic neighborhood, for example, have some of the characteristics of classic communities: They are apt to be important in the lives of their members and to be made up of individuals who spend their lives together. But such communities are not self-sufficient and generally not self-reproductive. The residents of a neighborhood live their lives together and identify with one another, but they must work outside the neighborhood and interact frequently with strangers. Small-town dwellers may have great loyalty to their town, but the town is economically dependent on other towns and on the structures of government and economy not only of the whole society but also increasingly of the whole world.

As a result, the contemporary community provides a psychological world and a place of identification for its members, but it is not the same kind of enclosing and secure world as the community of the past. The individual is keenly aware of the existence of a society whose economic and political significance transcends that of the local community. Moreover, the surrounding society is itself a tempting field of opportunities, for it offers other communities with which the person might choose to identify and it is a constant reminder that the community within which one resides is not the only option. A popular song of the World War I era wondered, "How are you going to keep them down on the farm after they've seen Paris?" This is, in fact, the common dilemma of communities in modern society—how to retain the loyalties of members who are tempted by the glamour and opportunities of the outside world.

Another major difference between the community of the past and contemporary communities has to do with the basis on which people form communities and thus identify with one another. Contemporary communities are based on a great many different grounds and not solely on the basis of territory. To be sure, urban ethnic neighborhoods and rural towns retain some of their importance as communities in the lives of their members. Life within such communities still revolves around the regular association of people who know one another well and who are bound by a sense of obligation to one another as well as by their sense of similarity. But contemporary people, because they frequently rub elbows with others who are very different from themselves, must narrow their focus in order to feel a sense of likeness and identification with others. Many people live and work near others who are very different from themselves. In order to find a sense of community, they must either overcome these differences or identify with others who, although they may not be nearby, are similar in some respect.

For each member of a contemporary, heterogeneous society, there are many possible grounds on which he or she might identify with others. For some people, a shared commitment to a set of religious beliefs provides the basis for identifying with a community. Christians who have had a "born again" experience, for example, have a strong mutual identification based on this experience. For others, membership in a social class may provide the same sense of likeness and common purpose. Modern people may find community in a social movement, identifying strongly with the women's movement, for example, or with the environmental movement; in their professions; and even, in some cases, in their nuclear or extended families. Because there are so many ways in which people are differentiated from one another, there are also many particular ways in which they can feel likeness with certain others.

The kind of community that develops from a sense of identification with similar others is a rather narrowly defined community, and it is often based on quite abstract criteria. For the person whose community consists of those who have been "born again," the sense of similarity is limited to religious conviction and experience. Persons who may be quite dissimilar in social background, ethnicity, formal religious affiliation, occupation, race, and other social characteristics can feel a sense of similarity with one another because they define these differences as irrelevant in the light of their similarity of religious outlook. They identify with one another on the basis of this one characteristic that makes them alike and downplay the significance of other matters. Theirs is, in a sense, a narrow community, one formed not out of the repeated give and take of everyday life with the same people, but out of a more self-conscious selection of others with whom to identify.

Such communities are likely to be dispersed rather than compact. The "born again" Christian may encounter few fellow community members on a day-to-day basis, for even those who are members of one's church are not really members of this community if they have not yet had the "born again" experience. The members of such experiential communities may interact infrequently with one another, relying on correspondence, revival meetings, or the programs of the "televangelists" that feature preaching or talk about the "born again" experience to confirm the existence of a community and an identity grounded in it.

Contemporary communities thus rely on the person's imagination as much as on a mundane social life. Contacts with fellow community members may be infrequent, and the sense of community must be sustained by the self-conscious imagining of the nature and scope of the community. This is less the case for communities where there is an existing organizational structure. Individuals who identify with a professional community, for example, usually have concrete social organizations to support their identification. Professional groups, boards, journals, and meetings provide opportunities for those who identify with the community to meet one another and to reinforce their sense of community membership.

Many observers argue that contemporary society has drastically transformed the nature of the self. Where classic community flourishes, the self is a stable object defined by a strong sense of social identity grounded in and certified by the community. The direction of the person's life seems fixed, the self is given continuity and integration by its place in the community, and people need not devote much energy to securing or maintaining their identities. People know who they are, and thus they know what to do. Their sense of personal identity is subordinate to their social identity as community members.

Where communities have to be constructed by finding some basis on which to identify with others, the nature of the person is transformed as much as the nature of the community. The creation and maintenance of identity requires more self-consciousness; people must decide or discover who they are in order to know what to do. They can, within certain limits, choose who they are, but they are also faced with some degree of doubt as to the choices they make. The person who chooses one community with which to identify is always aware that his or her choice could have been different. And there is also a strong temptation to identify with no community—to seek to make community and the social identity it fosters subordinate to a personal identity that places the person ahead of any community.

Ralph Turner has argued that modern people are becoming more inclined to look within themselves and to define as the "real self" those impulses and inclinations they feel are genuinely and spontaneously theirs rather than the external dictates of society.[41] Turner's view can be readily interpreted within the framework of social and personal identity. Those who identify strongly with a community tend to feel comfortable with themselves when their impulses and actions live up to the standards of the community. But those who do not have a community-based social identity, who feel confined by community or torn between the demands of several communities, may feel that the only authentic expression of themselves is in a personal identity that permits a considerable degree of autonomy. When they feel they are doing what they want to do, and thus pursuing a personal identity, they feel true to themselves.

Social identity in contemporary society is much more likely than in the past to be based on a more or less self-conscious selection of a community as its main support. Whatever the basis on which such a community is constructed or imagined, it performs some of the same functions as the organic community of the past. It provides the person with a set of similar others who can support or be perceived as supporting the person's definitions of self. Even when a community is based on rather narrow criteria of similarity, spatially dispersed, and significantly a product of the person's own imagination, it provides for a sense of continuity and integration, linking various situated identities to the social identity it provides.

People construct social identity through these contemporary forms of community in a variety of ways. Some seek to construct a community that resembles as closely as possible the community of the past. The old-order Amish, who maintain very traditional farming communities in Pennsylvania, Ohio, and Indiana, for example, attempt to enclose their members' lives in a way that is very much like the classic community. The whole of life is lived within the boundaries of the community, which rests on commitment to a traditional set of religious ideas about how people ought to live. Those who live in such communities have some contact with the surrounding contemporary world, of course, but their identities are almost exclusively grounded in the community itself, which provides a basis for identification with similar others. The outside world is important mainly for the contrast it provides—it confers distinctiveness on the person by virtue of his or her membership in this distinctive community, and it serves as a reminder of what the person should *not* be and how he or she should *not* live.

The contemporary person who seeks to ground social identity exclusively in one community need not, however, attempt to construct a classic community. Some participants in social movements, for example, have lives that are exclusively centered in the movement. For them, every act must have meaning in relation to the movement and its goals. The committed member of the women's movement, for example, may lead a life that is as centered in the movement as is that of the Amish person in that community. Yet, whereas the Amish community has many of the attributes of a classic community, the social movement does not; it is not a context within which all of life's needs can be met.

Most people have a more tenuous relationship to a community (or communities) with which they identify. The person may identify with one community—such as a profession or neighborhood—but not so exclusively that everything the person does must somehow be linked to the community. Most people, perhaps, fit this pattern, finding limited forms of community in professions, neighborhoods, religious experiences, or social movement participation, but not devoting themselves exclusively to any of them. The person may thus identify mildly with several communities rather than exclusively with one. The person may also migrate from one community to another, identifying with a number of communities over the course of a lifetime. The person may stand on the margins of two communities, unable either to identify fully with or to ignore either. And, presumably, the person may be unable to find any community with which to identify.

Where identification with a community is less than total, personal identity is a more salient component of the self. Community identification produces social identity, but the coherence and continuity of the person must also be found in the goals, ambitions, dreams, and projects that define personal identity. Thus, people must make plans, assert themselves, keep their eyes fixed on a clear image of what they want to be, and, in general, self-consciously construct themselves as autonomous persons. Some will carry a quest for autonomy to an extreme, eschewing any social identity, but most will seek some kind of balance between social and personal identity.

The contemporary person is thus in many ways a more self-conscious being than the resident of a traditional community. The self is not simply a spontaneous product of a fixed community that surrounds it from birth and that assigns it a place. It is, instead, something that must be found, constructed, or cultivated. The person must find or make a community, as well as supplement social identity with personal identity.

Keywords

Announcements An announcement is any act or gesture that serves to indicate or claim an identity in the presence of others. Everyday situations are filled with announcements, as people intentionally and unintentionally indicate their locations relative to one another. A professor's style of dress and confident manner in claiming the desk at the front of the classroom constitute announcements of the professor identity. A young woman who leans earnestly toward a young man and reaches across the table to touch his hand may be announcing her romantic interest and potential availability as a romantic partner. She may, however, merely be announcing her readiness to listen sympathetically to his sad story. As this example suggests, the nature of an announcement depends on the situation: Are the two individuals on a date or is the woman merely consoling a friend on the loss of a job?

Announcements may be verbal ("Good morning, I am Professor Hewitt") or behavioral (the professor hands out the syllabus and begins to call the roll). Frequently, announcements rely on appearance, such as the telephone repair person who wears the company uniform, gets out of a truck marked with the company's name, and knocks on your door; the judge who wears a robe and the defendant who wishes to appear respectful and middle class and so wears a suit; and the airline flight attendant who wears a smile.

Biographical Self The self is an object created in interaction with others in concrete social situations. In this sense the self is fundamentally a **situated self** (later defined). Yet the process of role taking that creates a situated self does not limit itself to the spatial and temporal boundaries of the immediate situation. Rather, people act toward themselves and one another as people who have lives that extend beyond the situation—as people who have pasts and futures, and who have other interests and responsibilities than those they are presently enacting. In other words, people engaged in everyday interaction in particular situations bring their whole selves with them, and sometimes their interaction focuses on other aspects of their lives.

Community   Community has been an important concept in the social sciences, although it is used in many different ways. Most often, the term has been used to designate small towns, villages, neighborhoods, and other territorial social aggregates where people engage in a great deal of face-to-face interaction, know one another virtually from birth, and feel a sense of loyalty to one another arising out of their common location. This usage of the word is often accompanied by a contrast between community and society, the latter designating a larger, impersonal social entity where interaction with strangers is more common and people feel little loyalty to one another. These usages are frequently highly evaluative in tone: Community is regarded as good, society as bad.

Mead used the term *community* more broadly to refer to a social entity whose members share a common framework or universe of discourse. People are members of a community if they share a common way of seeing themselves and the world, even if they do not know one another or interact on a face-to-face basis. For the individual, a community in this sense forms a generalized other—that is, a perspective shared by others from which the individual may view himself or herself and by whose standards the self is formed. Mead thought, perhaps too optimistically, that the direction of social change was toward a widening human community in which eventually all of humanity would come to share a common point of view.

This book's usage of the term *community* is closer to Mead's than to the territorial sociological conception. Even though communities based on territory (e.g., villages) have been historically important, the grounds on which communities are established have been widening. In the contemporary world, people often identify with and adopt the imagined perspectives of others whom they do not know and with whom they are not likely to have intimate contact. People identify with one another on the basis of age, generation, gender, social experiences, and similar grounds that are not linked to territory. Although communities are thus, in one sense, founded on similarity (e.g., all those who share a social characteristic such as age), they also cut across various social boundaries (e.g., those who identify with one another on the basis of age are likely to be diverse with respect to social class, ethnicity, or religion). Whatever the basis of identification and community formation, the importance of contemporary communities is their provision for and support of **social identity** (later defined).

Gender   Gender is both an easy and a difficult concept to define. Its definition is easy and straightforward in the sense that we can readily distinguish *sex* from *gender. Sex* refers to biologically defined characteristics, most notably the possession at birth of the genitalia of one biological sex or the other. *Gender,* in contrast, refers to what we learn to expect and take for granted about the behavior of males and females. The difficulty comes in deciding how to treat gender conceptually. Is it a role, so that we can speak of gender roles and gender identities, just as we speak of occupational roles and identities? Or does gender cut across the definitions of various roles, so that there are gendered performances of such roles as professor, nurse, student, and the like?

How to treat gender conceptually is not a settled matter, but the approach favored in this book is to argue that it may be *both* a way of defining how a particular role should be performed and a role in itself. Many roles open to both sexes do seem to call for different performances from males and females. Male business executives, for example, can and often must be demanding, ruthless, aggressive, and coldly rational in their calculations of business advantage. Female business executives who behave in a similar manner are frequently criticized for such behavior—they are perceived as more aggressive than their male counterparts and are accused of "acting like men." It seems clear that there is a gendered standard for the performance of the executive role, to the point that women who perform the role as men perform it seem in danger of losing their identity as women.

The interactionist approach to role sheds some useful light on this issue. For symbolic interactionists a role is a perspective in a situation. It is the place or point of view from which the individual acts in concert with others. In the foregoing example, the role in question is that of "executive." To say that there is an "executive role" is to say that there is an "executive perspective" from which people in certain situations are expected to act. We can look at gender as a limitation imposed on the perspectives from which females can act in such situations. That is, in a world where women are denied access to executive roles, they simply cannot act from this perspective. But in a society where executive roles have begun to open up to women, there can be and is still uncertainty and conflict about allowing them to act from the perspective of the executive. In other words, those who censure women for "aggression" or "acting like men" are, in effect, showing their reluctance to accept females acting from an "executive" perspective by treating them as if they should be acting from a different perspective—namely, that of "women."

Identity   Identity refers to a person's location relative to others in the situation, the community, or the society as a whole. **Situated identity** (later defined) is established generally on the basis of the person's role—that is, the perspective from which the individual is acting and on the basis of which others act toward him or her. Beyond the immediate situation, **social identity** is established on the basis of the community of others with whom the individual identifies; **personal identity** (later defined) is established on the basis of the person's efforts to establish a particular life plan or project, often involving a sense of difference from others.

All forms of identity require the cooperation and affirmation of at least some other people. In a concrete situation of interaction where the person enacts a particular role, **announcements** (previously defined) of intention to enact the role and actual enactments of the role must correspond with the **placements** (later defined) others make. That is, others must act toward the individual as he or she acts toward self in order for the situated role to constitute a situated identity. A department store customer whom a clerk refuses to recognize as a customer may wish to have the customer identity but does not fully have it until the clerk places the customer in it. Likewise, announcements of a social identity require corresponding placements by others. If the identity involves membership in a community (e.g., the "gay community" or the "Jewish community"), these placements must come at least in part from other members of the community. Even personal identities require the affirmation of at least some others, for an account of one's special abilities or difference from others requires others who will accept this account.

Because identity requires the cooperation of others, it is never merely the possession of the individual. This may be an elusive point to grasp, but it is a central one. To possess an identity fully and to be able to act with energy and conviction on the basis of it requires presence in a social world and confirmation of that identity by others. This is not to say that people do not sometimes make identity claims that are not supported by others, for they do. Transgendered individuals, for example, who have the genitalia of one sex but identify with the other sex, may feel themselves to be the other sex, but must undergo psychiatric scrutiny as well as medical and surgical procedures before they are accorded the right to act as members of the other sex. To claim an identity is to express identification with that identity; to possess an identity is to have the claim honored by others. Identity is a social and not merely an individual phenomenon.

Motivation   The word *motivation* refers to the internal springs and motors of conduct—that is, to the internal sensitivities of the person as they exist at any given moment and shape the person's receptiveness to stimuli. If I am hungry—that is, my body is in a certain physiological state because I have not ingested food for a certain period of time—then I am particularly receptive to food stimuli. I will be alert to things that I might eat, I will "graze" in the kitchen, which is an indication that I am seeking food stimuli, and the sight of food will heighten my craving for food.

Motivation operates beneath the surface of consciousness. That is, people are not conscious of being motivated in particular ways unless and until they encounter or find a stimulus that will release an impulse. A hungry person becomes conscious of his or her hunger (it would be appropriate to say "self-conscious") when a food stimulus gives rise to the impulse to eat. That is the point at which the person becomes capable of grasping the direction of his or her impending act, and may begin to think of himself or herself as acting from a hunger **motive** (later defined).

Motivation is social as much or more than it is simply physiological. That is, one may be motivated by status or a need for recognition and approval every bit as by hunger or thirst. Like physiological motivations, social ones operate beneath the threshold of consciousness. Moreover, like physiological motivations, social ones direct receptivity to and search for stimuli, and people become conscious of them only by formulating them self-consciously as plans of action. It is the hunger for recognition that tunes the individual's ears to the words of others, but it is only when he or she hears words that can be interpreted as praise that a sense of joy at earning recognition is likely to arise self-consciously.

Motive   A motive is a verbally formulated reason for conduct. A hungry person, for example, might explain scarfing down a whole bag of potato chips by asserting that "I was really hungry." A person eager for praise might respond to praise by exclaiming that "I was so anxious to learn what you thought of my work!" In these instances, people verbalize motives for their actions, and they do so usually in response either to real or anticipated questions from others. As we will see later, statements of motive are socially organized by **vocabularies of motive** (see Keywords in Chapter 4): The motives people cite are governed by the situations in which they find themselves and the audiences who judge their responses.

Stated motives do not merely reflect underlying motivations. A person who has just scarfed the bag of potato chips might be accurately reporting on a motivational state by saying, "I was hungry!" But he or she may have no idea of what precipitated the action. Some people eat in response to stress, for example, but they may not be aware that they do so. They may, in fact, honestly believe they are hungry when in fact some other motivational state has begun their action. There is no necessary connection between what we say about our conduct and the motivational sources of that conduct. Nonetheless, the statement of motives connects people and their conduct to the social world and its expectations, and makes a kind of sense of their conduct for themselves and others, even if their statements are a poor analysis of their internal states.

Personal Identity   Personal identity is based on a claim of special plans, projects, or purposes, and often entails a sense of difference from others rather than identification with them. As people proceed through the life course—acquiring and shedding roles, group memberships, and identifications—they develop a more or less autonomous sense of self. That is, they come to think of themselves as individuals with life histories and a future and not only as role players or group members. The degree to which people seek such autonomy varies within cultures as well as from one culture to another. Even in a culture such as that of the United States, where people are encouraged to develop a strong sense of individuality and difference, many are content with a minimal sense of self as an autonomous agent. Such individuals prefer to identify with the various groups to which they belong or to think of themselves as incumbents in particular roles. In other words, their social and situated identities are paramount. Others define themselves strongly in terms of personal autonomy and resist strong identification with communities or with a particular situated role.

Placements   A placement is an act or gesture that assigns a person a social location within a situation or the broader community or society. Placements may confirm the identities claimed by the person—that is, placements may coincide with announcements—or they may resist or ignore the person's announcements. For example, the airline passenger who accepts the flight attendant's smiling offer of a cup of coffee with thanks and a returning smile has confirmed the attendant's announcement of identity. The apartment dweller who invites the telephone repair person inside after looking at his or her uniform and identification card has placed the repair person in the identity he or she has claimed. On the other hand, the judge who casts a skeptical eye on a neatly attired defendant and remarks that a clean shave and tie do not change the facts of his crime has rejected the defendant's identity announcement.

Self-Esteem   Self-esteem is the affective, or emotional, dimension of the self. People become objects to themselves not only by establishing identities but also by attaching emotional significance to themselves and their actions. That is, they love or hate themselves, feel satisfied or dissatisfied, and manifest confidence or a lack of it. The concept of self-esteem summarizes the various positive or negative attitudes people may take toward themselves.

Self-esteem appears to have a great deal to do with mood (the person's position on a continuum that ranges from extreme euphoria to severe dysphoria). To be euphoric is to be energized, self-confident, positive, outgoing, and active in the extreme; to be dysphoric is to be the opposite, lacking in energy and self-confidence, negative, withdrawn, and perhaps even immobilized. Most people fall somewhere between these extremes, just as their self-esteem is neither completely assured or totally lacking. The association of self-esteem with mood is evidence in the fact that depression, one of the chief ways in which mood may be disturbed or disordered, is associated with low self-esteem. Also, medications that relieve the symptoms of depression not infrequently also raise self-esteem.

To associate self-esteem with mood and its disorders is not to say that it is a psychological or medical phenomenon rather than a social psychological one. How people feel about themselves—whether they have high self-esteem or low, elevated or depressed mood—depends on their social experiences. The normal regulation of mood in the brain (i.e., responding to success or praise with pleasure and positive self-feeling and to criticism or failure with negative feelings and depressed mood) may well become disordered or disturbed. When that happens, people cannot respond positively to positive events, and they may become depressed and think negatively about themselves for no external reason. Even then, however, it is likely that such disturbances are shaped by the person's social experiences as well as by biology.

Situated Identity   A situated identity is that location the individual has in interaction with others in a particular social situation. Situated identity is established when announcements and placements correspond—in other words, when a role and its associated identity claimed by a person are given confirmation or acceptance by the others with whom interaction is taking place. A person has the situated identity of investor, for example, when he or she indicates to a broker his or her intent to purchase stocks and the broker accepts the money and establishes an account.

What is true of all forms of identity is true of situated identity: The person has a situated identity by degrees rather than all or none. A new investor is apt to feel a bit uncertain and anxious, particularly if he or she has only a few dollars to invest. Likewise, the broker may be a little wary at first, and will carefully assess the individual's tolerance for risk and point out that it is possible to lose as well as gain money through investing. (The broker does this in order to gauge the investor's interest and commitment, but also because securities regulations require such disclosure.) At the same time, the broker may reassure the investor that even relatively small amounts of money are worth investing, and that he or she should not feel embarrassed about investing the minimum. This reassurance does not merely place the investor in the investor identity, but strengthens that identity. Likewise, new parents will have a parental identity, but that identity will grow stronger as they gain in self-confidence and as others reassure them of their competence in the role.

Situated Self   The self is always a situated social object. That is, the self is an object constituted by social interaction, and that interaction is itself always located in one or another situation, with its associated definition and role structure. To Descartes's assertion that "I think, therefore I am," the symbolic interactionist might say, "I interact, therefore I am." In other words, people have an existence as objects in situations in which they interact with others.

This assertion does not mean that people cease to exist apart from interaction, and it does not mean that

the interaction must be with real others. The brain does not stop working when the person sleeps, and there are obviously many wakeful moments when the person is alone rather than with others and when his or her attention is focused on the external world and not on the self. But even in solitary moments, the person frequently carries on imaginary conversations and other forms of social interaction with imaginary others, and these imaginings constitute a self as surely as interaction with real people. Indeed, even when the person is in the presence of real others, he or she may be imagining encounters with those not present, and so be constituting a self in interaction with them. And engrossed though the person may be with events outside the self, he or she is likely to engage in reflection from time to time. Even an all-consuming object such as a painting or a concert encourages some degree of self-consciousness, for the person occasionally tells himself or herself how much he or she is enjoying it. And, finally, one of the chief ways people occupy themselves in idle and solitary moments is by reflecting on and thus constructing a **biographical self** (previously defined).

Social Identity   Social identity refers to the person's sense of place or location in a community of some kind. Like personal identity, its referent is not the immediate situation where one has a role in relation to others, but rather a larger community to which one attaches oneself or with which one identifies. Social identity, in other words, is an aspect of the biographical self.

The link between social identity and personal and situated identities is complex. A person may identify as a Catholic or a Jew, for example, and at the same time have a distinctively personal set of career ambitions, such as to be a great writer or a famous artist. This same person enacts a variety of roles in various social situations and thus has a variety of situated identities: parent, student, customer, voter, automobile driver, court defendant, and the like. The individual does not cease to be a Catholic or Jew, nor forget about personal ambitions, in the course of doing these various roles. Likewise, the Jew in synagogue or the famous artist attending an opening reception for his or her work is the same person who on other occasions is a parent, voter, or driver.

Social and personal identities do not vanish when situated identities are claimed, though they do recede momentarily into the background. And people do not surrender their right to lay claim to various situated identities when they are momentarily engaged primarily in constructing or maintaining social and personal identities. Rather, one form of identity is put aside in favor of the other, but not abandoned. Indeed, social and personal identities make it possible to adopt situated identities, for the former provide a sense of continuity from one situation to another.

Endnotes

1. For a theoretical elaboration of the relationship between language and the self, see Michael L. Schwalbe, "Language and the Self: An Expanded View from a Symbolic Interactionist Perspective," *Symbolic Interaction* 6 (2) (1983): 291–306.

2. The term *culture,* as used here, refers to the world of objects shared by those members of a society or one of its constituent social entities. Culture is thus environmental to conduct. For elaboration of this view, see John P. Hewitt, *Dilemmas of the American Self* (Philadelphia: Temple University Press, 1989).

3. See Norman K. Denzin, "The Genesis of Self in Early Childhood," *The Sociological Quarterly* 13 (Summer 1972): 291–314.

4. Spencer E. Cahill, "Language Practices and Self Definition: The Case of Gender Identity Acquisition," *The Sociological Quarterly* 27 (Fall 1986): 302.

5. As Lindesmith, Strauss, and Denzin wrote in *Social Psychology* (New York: Holt, Rinehart, and Winston, 1977), children "discover that names have things—that is to say, that the words they learn correspond to aspects of the real world. In complex types of learning especially, the progression may be from word to things rather than the reverse" (p. 289).

6. See George Herbert Mead, *Mind, Self, and Society* (Chicago: University of Chicago Press, 1934), pp. 135–173.

7. Ibid., p. 151.

8. Philippe Aries, *Centuries of Childhood: A Social History of Family Life* (New York: Knopf, 1962).

9. For a comprehensive review of interactionist research on childhood socialization, see Spencer E. Cahill, "Childhood," in *Handbook of Symbolic Interactionism,* eds. Larry T. Reynolds and Nancy J. Herman-Kinney (Walnut Creek, CA: AltaMira Press, 2003), Chapter 35. In addition to works by Fine and Corsaro cited below (Note 10), see the following for additional research and reviews: Spencer Cahill, "Fashioning Males and Females: Appearance Management and the Social Reproduction of Gender," *Symbolic Interaction* 12 (Fall 1989): 281–299; William A. Corsaro and Donna Eder, "Development and Socialization of Children and Adolescents," in *Sociological Perspectives on Social Psychology,* eds. Karen S. Cook, Gary Alan Fine, and James S. House (Boston: Allyn & Bacon, 1995), pp. 421–451; Patricia A. Adler and Peter Adler, *Peer Power: Preadolescent Culture and Identity* (New Brunswick, NJ: Rutgers University Press, 1998); William A. Corsaro, *The Sociology of Childhood* (Thousand Oaks, CA: Pine Forge Press, 1997); Barrie Thorne, *Gender Play: Boys and Girls in School* (New Brunswick, NJ: Rutgers University Press, 1993).

10. Gary Alan Fine, *With the Boys: Little League Baseball and Preadolescent Culture* (Chicago: University of Chicago Press, 1987), pp. 191–192.

11. William A. Corsaro, *Friendship and Peer Culture in the Early Years* (Norwood, NJ: Ablex, 1985).

12. The study of the self as "narrative" is a relatively recent development but has accumulated a vast literature. For useful discussions using this approach, see Jerome Bruner, "Life as Narrative," *Social Research* 54 (1987): 11–32; Susan E. Chase, *Ambiguous Empowerment: The Work Narratives of Women School Superintendents* (Amherst, MA: University of Massachusetts Press, 1995); Arthur W. Frank, *The Wounded Storyteller: Body, Illness, and Ethics* (Chicago: University of Chicago Press, 1995); Jaber F. Gubrium and James A. Holstein, "Narrative Practices and the Coherence of Personal Stories," *The Sociological Quarterly* 39 (1998): 163–187; Holstein and Gubrium, *The Self We Live By: Narrative Identity in a Postmodern World* (New York: Oxford University Press, 2000); David R. Maines, "Narrative's Moment and Sociology's Phenomena: Toward a Narrative Sociology," *The Sociological Quarterly* 34 (1993): 17–38; Robert Zussman, "Autobiographical Occasions," *Contemporary Sociology* 25 (1996): 143–148.

13. Gregory P. Stone, "Appearance and the Self: A Slightly Revised Version," in *Social Psychology through Symbolic Interaction,* 2nd ed., eds. Gregory P. Stone and Harvey A. Farberman (New York: Wiley, 1981), p. 188.

14. This analysis of the self relies heavily upon John P. Hewitt, *Dilemmas of the American Self* (Note 2), especially Chapter 5: "A Theory of Identity."

15. For Sheldon Stryker's views on the nature of self and identity, see his *Symbolic Interactionism: A Social Structural Version* (Reading, MA: Benjamin/Cummings, 1980).

16. Thomas J. Scheff, *Microsociology: Discourse, Emotion, and Social Structure* (Chicago: University of Chicago Press, 1990), especially Chapter 1: "Human Nature and the Social Bond."

17. The classic sociological reference is to Georg Simmel, perhaps most easily accessed through *Georg Simmel,* ed. Lewis A. Coser (Englewood Cliffs, N.J., Prentice-Hall, 1965).

18. Hazel Markus, "Self-schemata and Processing Information About the Self," *Journal of Personality and Social Psychology* 35 (1977): 64.

19. Hazel Markus, Jeanne Smith, and Richard L. Morland, "Role of Self-Concept in the Perception of Others," *Journal of Personality and Social Psychology* 49: (1985) 1494–1512.

20. Charles Horton Cooley, *Human Nature and the Social Order* (New York: Scribners, 1902), p. 152.

21. Ibid.

22. Cooley did not view the individual as a passive participant in the reflected appraisals process. See David D. Franks and Viktor Gecas, "Autonomy and Conformity in Cooley's Self-Theory: The Looking Glass and Beyond," *Symbolic Interaction* 15 (Spring 1992): 49–68.

23. The classic sociological study of self-esteem is Morris Rosenberg's *Society and the Adolescent Self-Image* (Princeton, NJ: Princeton University Press, 1965); summaries of research and theories can be found in Viktor Gecas and Peter Burke, "Self and Identity," Chapter 2 in *Sociological Perspectives on Social Psychology,* eds. Karen Cook, Gary Alan Fine, and James S. House (Boston: Allyn & Bacon, 1995); *The Social Importance of Self-Esteem,* eds. Andrew M. Mecca, Neil J. Smelser, and John Vasconcellos (Berkeley, CA: University of California Press, 1989), and *Extending Self-Esteem Theory and Research: Sociological and Psychological Currents,* eds. Timothy J. Owens, Sheldon Stryker, and Norman Goodman (Cambridge: Cambridge University Press, 2001).

24. Viktor Gecas and Michael L. Schwalbe, "Beyond the Looking-Glass Self: Social Structure and Efficacy-Based Self-Esteem," *Social Psychology Quarterly* 46 (1983): 77–88.

25. Erving Goffman, *The Presentation of Self in Everyday Life* (New York: Doubleday Anchor, 1959).

26. David A. Snow and Leon Anderson, *Down on Their Luck: A Study of Homeless Street People* (Berkeley, CA: University of California Press, 1993).

27. Raymond L. Schmitt and Wilbert M. Leonard, "Immortalizing the Self through Sport," *American Journal of Sociology* 91 (March 1986): 1088–1111.

28. Erving Goffman, "Role Distance," in *Encounters,* ed. Erving Goffman (Indianapolis, IN: Bobbs-Merrill, 1961).

29. The most up-to-date and sophisticated summary of research findings on self-esteem can be found in Owens, Stryker, and Goodman, *Extending Self-Esteem Theory and Research* (Note 23).

30. See the excellent characterization of low self-esteem in Timothy J. Owens and Morris Rosenberg, "Low Self-Esteem People: A Collective Portrait," pp. 400–436, in Owens, Stryker, and Goodman, *Extending Self-Esteem Theory and Research* (Note 23).

31. Harry Stack Sullivan, *The Interpersonal Theory of Psychiatry* (New York: Norton, 1953), p. 351.

32. For critical views of the self-esteem literature see John P. Hewitt, *The Myth of Self-Esteem: Finding Happiness and Solving Problems in America* (New York: St. Martin's Press, 1998); and Hewitt, "The Social Construction of Self-Esteem," in *Handbook of Positive Psychology,* eds. C. R. Snyder and Shane J. Lopez (New York: Oxford University Press, 2001).

33. Candace West and Don H. Zimmerman, "Doing Gender," *Gender and Society* 1 (June 1987): 121–151.

34. Patricia A. Adler and Peter Adler, *Backboards and Blackboards: College Athletes and Role-Engulfment* (New York: Columbia University Press, 1991).

35. For an analysis of the problems of mixed ethnic identity, see Cookie White Stephan, "Ethnic Identity among Mixed-Heritage People in Hawaii," *Symbolic Interaction* 14 (Fall 1991): 261–277.

36. Hans Gerth and C. Wright Mills, *Character and Social Structure* (New York: Harcourt Brace, 1953).

37. See Irvin G. Wyllie, *The Self-Made Man in America: The Myth of Rags to Riches* (New York: Free Press, 1966).

38. See Leslie Irvine, *Codependent Forevermore: The Invention of Self in a Twelve Step Group* (Chicago: University of Chicago Press, 1999).

39. See Vered Vinitzky-Seroussi, *After Pomp and Circumstance: High School Reunion as an Autobiographical Occasion* (Chicago: University of Chicago Press, 1998).

40. Arthur W. Frank, *The Wounded Storyteller: Body, Illness, and Ethics* (Chicago: University of Chicago Press, 1995).

41. Ralph H. Turner, "The Real Self: From Institution to Impulse," *American Journal of Sociology* 81 (March 1976): 989–1016.

Chapter *4*

Social Interaction and the Formation of Conduct

Symbolic interactionists hold that conduct is a product of situated social interaction. We cannot explain what people do merely by pointing to social and cultural constraints. Nor can we explain why they do it by citing their motivations. Rather, conduct emerges as people act and interact in specific contexts and circumstances—going to class, having a party, making love, working on a term paper. It is in these everyday situations that people define situations, make and take roles, and form individual and social acts. This chapter examines the basic processes of situated social interaction.

The Definition of the Situation

The idea that people construct their actions based on their definitions of situations, considered briefly in Chapter 2, conceals a great deal of complexity. What is a "definition" of a situation? Where does a definition of a situation exist? How do people define situations? What happens when people cannot find or do not share a definition of the situation? To answer these and similar questions, we need to develop a more detailed analysis of situations and their definitions.

The word *situation* is used often in everyday speech in ways that only hint at the meaning of the term as symbolic interactionists use it. People speak commonly of this or that "situation," referring to some particular occasion or social context, such as a party, an argument, a predicament, or an event. "It was an embarrassing situation," someone might say, or "Here's the situation I found myself in," or "I got out of that situation as soon as I could."

141

Symbolic interactionists do not think of situations as unusual predicaments from which people try to extricate themselves, but they do employ two commonsense ideas that are conveyed in everyday speech. The first of these is:

- To refer to a situation is to locate activity temporally in relation to other activity.

Human activities occur before, during, or after one another, and when we speak of a particular situation, we mark off a particular portion of time and give it a name. A "party" may consume several hours, during which people engage in a great many particular acts—dancing, drinking, laughing, flirting, conversing, and the like. When we call a particular situation a "party," we subsume under a single label those activities that have occurred during a particular interval of time. The second idea is:

- The labels we attach to situations also locate the same events *spatially*.

The event we call the "party" presumably occurred in some well-defined place—at someone's home, for example—and is thus a fairly compact space where people get together and interact. Those assembled for a party conceive of themselves as being in the same place, and they are mutually aware of one another's presence there. Furthermore, their sense of where they are is not simply that they are in a particular physical location together, but that they are "at a party."

When people conceive or talk about the situations in which their activities occur, they do not use the same clock or yardstick a physicist might use to measure time and space. The significance of time for a "party" does not consist of the passage of a certain number of hours or minutes, nor does space refer to its location on a road map. Time and space are social and not physical dimensions. When people define a situation, they do so from their social perspectives as actual or potential participants. People locate situations temporally from the vantage point of shared ideas about the meaning of events as they occur in time. Thus, a party is something that takes place "after" an especially intense period of hard work, "regularly" on Saturday nights, or "before" someone leaves an organization or moves to another city. Place is likewise defined in social terms. A party is a place where there are "partiers," just as an argument is a place where there are "opponents." It is not geography but rather the roles, acts, and objects found in a place that make it a particular situation.

The temporal aspect of human life has a property Mead called *emergence*.[1] The meanings of a situation and of the events that take place within it are not fixed, but emerge with the passage of time. The *present*—the here and now of any particular moment—is experienced in terms of both past and future. What is happening at this moment is understood in relation to what has already occurred and what is expected (or hoped) will occur later. The "present" is specious, Mead said—we experience something we call "the present" or "now" but it does not really exist, for our consciousness is always moving through time, always focused either on what has occurred (or on the self as it has acted) or on some imagined future event or act.

Consider, for example, how people construct such events as going to a baseball game. Before taking one's seat or even leaving for the ballpark, one has anticipated the event, perhaps speculating about the lineup or who will be the starting pitcher. At this point, going to the game as a concrete, situated activity is part of the future; yet as it exists in the imagination, it shapes present acts. As the teams take the field and the first batter comes to the plate, one may recall past games when the home team beat today's opponent or snatched defeat from the jaws of victory in the ninth inning. Here, the meaning of the present is informed by the past—today's game becomes an opportunity to maintain a streak or to get revenge for past humiliation. The meaning of the situation has been progressively transformed over time in relation to expectations for the future and experience of the past.

Meaning is thus an emergent property of objects and is never absolutely fixed or established. A baseball game that was hoped would maintain a winning streak becomes a disappointment to the fans when their team loses. At no point is the meaning of "baseball game" fixed, even though the situation has the same name throughout. Rather, meaning is altered with the passage of time. The meaning of the present is shaped by what is expected for the future; as events do or do not occur as expected, a past is created and the meaning of the present is transformed.

Situations are located in social space, and they locate their participants in social space. Each human situation is located within the specific context of a collectivity, group, organization, or some other social unit. "Classes" are held in universities; "weddings" are given by families; "arguments" take place within more diverse social units but are generally linked to organized social life in some way. And just as the situation has a "place" in a larger social context, it provides a place for the individual participants within it. Their place, of course, is provided by their roles.

Both kinds of location are *relative* and not absolute. People locate themselves—that is, they maintain a cognitive grasp of "where" they are—relative to the situation and to the larger social context in which that situation exists. A cognitive map of the situation itself is given by one's sense of its arrangement of roles—of the variety of perspectives from which participants act and of their relationship to one's own perspective. One has a role in the situation relative to the roles of others. One's cognitive map of the situation as a place in the larger scheme of things depends on the fact that we routinely imagine situations as elements or fixtures of groups, organizations, and other social units. A "class" is situated within a university relative to other situations—other classes, having lunch, writing papers, going to parties, and numerous other situations of college student life.

Under some conditions, the relative social and temporal locations of participants in a situation, as well as the larger context within which the situation is itself embedded, can be drastically and swiftly transformed. In a classroom, for example, a student who directs a racist or anti-Semitic remark against another student may set in motion a wholesale transformation of the situation—a change in its definition and role structure. The offending student ceases to be merely a "student" and becomes, instead, a "bigot," just as the target of the remark becomes a "victim." The professor and some of the other students may become "defenders" or "allies" of the "victim." The situation is itself lifted from its location as a routine instance of a class in the university and becomes, instead, another skirmish in the long struggle against prejudice. It is, in other words, transported from one conceptual domain to another—from one framework of social space and time to another—even while the participants remain in one physical place.

What, then, is a "definition" of a situation? Who has it? Where is it? How do we know that it exists? The crucial fact about a definition of a situation is that it is cognitive—it is our *idea* of our location in social time and space that constrains the way we act. When we have a definition of a situation, we cognitively configure acts, objects, and others in a way that makes sense to us as a basis for acting. We have a definition of a situation, for example, when we "know" that we are at a "graduation party." We "know" there will be a graduate, as well as his or her family, friends, and well-wishers who will congratulate and celebrate in familiar ways. Our definition of a situation consists of what we "know" about what will happen and who will make it happen.

Definitions of situations thus exist in the minds of the individuals who participate in them. Definitions do not hang from invisible wires in midair, nor do they exist in a mysterious "group mind." Instead, each person acts on the basis of his or her "knowledge" of the situation, role making and role taking in terms of its sensed role structure, acting toward familiar and expected objects, cooperating in the performance of social acts. Definitions of situations are thus "shared" by participants in the sense that each person acts on the basis of a definition that more or less resembles the definition held by others. Both professor and students in the classroom, for example, share a definition of the situation in which they are together, and each person thus acts on the basis of similar "knowledge" of the situation.

There are limits, however, in the extent to which participants can fully share the definition of a situation. Professor and students, for example, may at one level have a shared definition of the situation: They are in a class together, and they share a sense of its role structure and joint activities. The professor, however, may think things are going well, whereas the students are restless and bored. At one level they share a definition of the situation, for each participant acts on the basis of knowledge, and the acts of others confirm that knowledge. Each person, by acting on the basis of a definition of the situation, constructs acts that fit with the expectations of others in the situation. Each person can employ his or her definition of the situation and its role structure to make sense of the acts of others. At another level, however, they do not share a definition. Students, acting on the "knowledge" that this is a boring class, sit through the lectures without saying anything; the professor, acting on the "knowledge" that the students understand everything being said, takes their silence as an indication that things are going well. Clearly, definitions of the situation can be somewhat incongruous and still serve as the basis for interaction.

Definitions of situations imply roles and identities. Therefore, incongruous definitions of situations imply *misidentifications* of self and others in relation to the definition of the situation. A man may invite a woman to dinner, for example, and thinking his strong feelings for her are reciprocated, begin to talk of their future together, only to discover sooner or later that she does not hold the same feelings for him. Such incongruous definitions of the situation may persist for some time before they are discovered. As we will see later in this chapter, mutual awareness of roles, identities, and purposes is not always fully open, and when it is not, there are severe constraints on social interaction. For the time being, we will concentrate the analysis on those situations where there are genuinely shared definitions.

Routine and Problematic Situations

The largest part of our everyday conduct occurs within *routine* situations with relatively congruent definitions, such as sitting down to dinner, attending class, driving a car, going to a movie, writing a paper, playing tennis, or doing our jobs. These situations are routine because they are familiar. We can easily name them, anticipate the objects they will contain, know what roles people will assume and who will assume them, and expect activities that strongly resemble activities in which we have engaged on previous such occasions.

Everyday life consists largely of a series of routine situations, and many actions in them are quite habitual. If one is accustomed to having dinner at the same hour each day, sitting down and eating seems virtually a matter of reflex. Things are in their accustomed places, the appropriate others are present, food is served on time, and much of what one does requires little self-conscious control. Many such situations are so thoroughly routine that we appear to be creatures of habit, or perhaps actors enacting a script, rather than self-conscious human beings making our roles. Definitions of situations seem to provide not only general guidelines of what to expect and what to do but also even our lines and bodily movements. Thus, for example, when two acquaintances exchange greetings, inquiring about one another's health and families, it would seem they are doing little more than behaving in a ritualistic, habitual way. Such routine situations seem completely to determine the actions of their participants.

One could take this perspective further by arguing that culture is what ultimately provides our definitions of situations. In this view, during the course of socialization we learn a large number of definitions, along with rules for applying them to the concrete situations we encounter. Thus, every circumstance is seemingly anticipated by culture and we can meet it—providing we have been appropriately socialized—by applying the correct definition of the situation.

But matters are not so simple. Although it is true that we learn in advance the definitions of many situations, we do not learn all possible definitions, nor does each episode of interaction merely require us to apply a preestablished definition. The cumulative experiences of human beings as they grow from infancy through adulthood provide them with many scripts, scenarios, and frames in terms of which they can more or less easily construct their conduct, but they are also continually confronted with unexpected and novel events. Every concrete situation is at least a little bit different from what we expected it to be. Moreover, openness to new situations and new meanings is an inherent characteristic of human conduct. We do not learn a fixed and closed set of meanings or definitions of situations but an open system in which interpretation, although it may sometimes be minimal, is always present to some degree and always potentially of great significance.

Language provides a useful analogy. In the process of learning our native language, we do not learn every possible combination of words that we will eventually use, nor do we learn explicitly the rules whereby words are to be combined. We learn a language in such a way that we can say things we have never heard before. We can create sentences that are, to us, completely novel, since we have not previously heard them spoken. It is much the same with culture and its objects and with our definitions of situations. We learn many seemingly fixed and preestablished meanings, which are roughly analogous to words, that are used to form these definitions. We also learn to create new meanings, to consider the possibility that our interpretations of a situation might be wrong, and to face the unexpected events that constantly intrude themselves into human affairs.

Thus, no situation is so routine that habit alone suffices to guide conduct. A situation may be well enough defined that there are few surprises, and habit can account for the bulk of what we do there. However, even in routine situations, people misunderstand one another, fail to get jokes, behave in selfish or unpredictable ways, disagree with one another, seek conflicting goals, compete for scarce resources, and in myriad other ways introduce novelty. When novelty is introduced, no matter how trivial or how readily we deal with it, there is at least some need to substitute the self-conscious control of conduct for habit.

Most of the unexpected events of everyday life are problematic *within* the boundaries of a defined situation. As Mead pointed out, we can see an event or circumstance as problematic only by contrasting it with something that is not problematic.[2] Suppose, for example, that a dinner guest vocally criticizes the host's cooking in front of other guests at the table. The momentary shocked silence that is likely to follow such an outburst signifies that the others find this an unusual and problematic form of behavior. Why do they find it so? Dinner guests share the unproblematic understanding that such opinions are best kept politely to oneself, no matter how bad the food might be. Even though the guest's untoward conduct in this instance will elicit a response from others—the host will be hurt and the other guests will express their strong disagreement—it will not as a rule make the definition of the situation itself untenable. That remains the unproblematic background against which the problematic event is viewed.

In contrast, some situations are themselves problematic or become so. Situations that were defined in one way can be redefined; situations that were defined can become undefined; and situations that were defined congruently can become defined less congruently. A party can degenerate into a brawl or an intimate dinner can turn into an argument. People can behave in thoroughly unexpected ways, as for example when they are under the influence of drugs, and by their baffling acts challenge the very definition of a situation. People fall into or out of love with one another at different rates, and so their definitions of social situations can be incongruous. When such disruptions occur, at least some participants will be baffled until they can reconstruct their definition of the situation and thus their place in it.

Problematic situations will be given special attention in Chapter 5. At present, it should be noted that routine and problematic situations represent two end points on a continuum. They are thus ideal types, for no situation is either fully routine or completely problematic; actual situations fall at various points between these extremes.

Role Making and Role Taking in Routine Situations

Role taking, we noted, is the process in which one person momentarily and imaginatively adopts the perspective of another in order to make a role performance that will be coordinated with that of the other. But how does one adopt the perspective of another? How does one know what that perspective is? What must one person know in order to take the role of the other?

A convenient place to begin answering these questions is with the attitudes people bring with them to situations and on the basis of which they begin to construct their conduct in them. People approach routine situations with the attitude that they *will* be routine—that objects, acts, and others will be much as they usually are and that nothing unusual will take place.[3] Basing his analysis on the work of Alfred Schutz, Peter McHugh suggested that people bring three fundamental assumptions to routine situations:[4]

1. People assume that the conceptions they have of a situation are valid—they take for granted that what they "know" as the situation is actually what is taking place. People ordinarily trust their understandings and impressions of what is going on around them.

2. People assume that others in the situation share their conceptions of it. That is, although people generally make due allowance for the acknowledged fact that no two people experience a situation in exactly the same way because they occupy different positions in it, there is still a basic assumption of shared perspectives and experiences.
3. People rarely bother to check their assumptions about a situation. So long as their definition of a situation works—so long as it allows meaningful conduct to take place—they do not need to question it.

As a student enters a classroom, for example, he or she characteristically assumes that it is the place in which a particular, announced course is meeting and that the group assembled is present for the same purpose. The student acts on the basis of this definition of the situation, assumes others are doing so, and continues to do so unless something occurs to call this assumption into question. If the course is thought to be introductory sociology but the person identified as the professor begins to teach a lesson in French grammar, the student's assumption is quickly challenged and the definition must be reformulated. But, so long as activities in the classroom can be comprehended through its definition as a routine class in introductory sociology, that definition goes unchecked.

Some care must be exercised in referring to the "assumptions" that participants make in entering and acting in routine situations. An "assumption," after all, sounds rather like a self-consciously formulated thought or announcement. But such assumptions are only occasionally formulated in so many words—the student is unlikely to say before entering a room, "I assume this is the place where Sociology 101 meets, that others are here for the same reason, and that I can act on that basis until there is some reason not to." The assumptions people make about situations exist as attitudes—as ways in which they are prepared to act in and toward those situations—and rarely as verbalizations. People do not often tell themselves (or others) what they think is going on in a situation. In fact, as a general rule of thumb, the more talk there is about the nature of a situation, the more likely it is that the situation, or something in it, is problematic for the participants.

According to McHugh, people organize meaning in a *thematic* way as they role make and role take in situations. Entering a classroom in which a sociology course is assumed to be being offered, for example, the student assigns meanings to acts, objects, and people by linking them to the central theme "sociology course." This theme provides the basis for interpreting the meanings of acts and events within the situation, each of which serves to "document" the theme. Thus, if the professor hands out a syllabus that is titled "Sociology 101" and begins to explain what sociology is, these acts serve as supporting evidence for the theme. They also reinforce the student's sense of the role arrangements of the situation— that here is a "sociology professor" talking to "sociology students."

As social interaction proceeds in a routine situation, people attempt to *fit* together the various acts and objects as they attempt to fit together their individual lines of conduct. This process, as we indicated, is a temporal one—what took place a moment ago is presumed to have a bearing on what is now occurring or is about to occur. Students assume, for example, that the outline the professor put on the board a moment ago will serve as the framework for subsequent comments and for discussion. Thus, each of the professor's statements will be interpreted as if it should fall under one of the headings in the outline. So long as this process of interpretation can occur, with each event fitted to the central theme of the situation, the definition of the situation itself remains unproblematic. Over time, the organizing theme of the situation will be *elaborated*—the course becomes not just a sociology course, but a boring one in which the professor sticks to the main point no matter how dull, or one in which the professor frequently drifts off on interesting tangents. So, too, the various objects of the situation take on a richer meaning; the professor becomes not just a representative of a role, but a good or bad lecturer, a helpful or indifferent person.

Problematic events do occur within defined situations, for people act in unexpected or seemingly nonsensical ways. Professors brag about their grandchildren, for example, and their students wonder what relevance their stories have for the subject matter of social psychology. Within limits, they will seek ways to interpret the professor's talk as relevant to the course, and one way of doing so is by waiting to see if a link between grandchildren and, for example, the self develops. If they can find a connection, then the relationship between theme and events is revealed and the definition of the situation is preserved.

The more that objects and events in a situation are problematic because they cannot be readily fitted to its theme, the more strenuously and self-consciously people search for patterns of meaning. This aspect of the definition of the situation—its *authorship* by members—cannot be stressed too much. Defining situations and maintaining meaning in situations is not merely a matter of responding to objectively present objects and events, to things that are merely there and waiting for people to understand their true meaning. Rather, defining the situation is a process in which we *create* meaning. Human beings are the authors of the meanings on the basis of which they act.

Human beings, we have said, create objects in their environment by acting toward them. Objects do not merely exist, they exist by virtue of people's defining efforts. Thus—within limits—reality is created by intentions. Clearly a proposition such as this should not be carried to absurd lengths, for a flat tire is a flat tire no matter how much one wishes it were not or acts toward it as if it were sound. But in a great many situations of everyday life, the definitions on the basis of which people act create reality.

One of the most common ways we experience this fact is in the *self-fulfilling prophecy*. When people act on the basis of their definition of the situation—even if their definition is in some respects erroneous—there is a possibility that their actions will bring about the very conditions they thought existed. If drivers believe that gasoline is likely to be in short supply because of a refinery explosion or a pipeline break, they are apt to visit gas stations more frequently in order to keep their tanked topped off. Lines at gas stations are therefore likely to be longer, and more gas will probably be carried around in individual cars rather than stored at gas stations. As a result, spot shortages may result, even though there is more than enough gas to go around. Acting on the basis of their definition of the situation, drivers helped to make it a reality.

Later in this chapter we will examine more closely problematic events that threaten the definition of the situation and show how participants cope with those events. To do so, however, we must examine the process of defining the situation in greater detail. Situations are defined, we will see, as people engage in role making and role taking, processes that are anchored in several basic forms of everyday knowledge.

The Cognitive Bases of Role Making and Role Taking

People's actions are grounded in both thoughts and feelings. To make a role performance in a way that is coordinated with the actions of others, one must have a definition of the situation—or find one—and one must have an understanding of which possible acts will work successfully and which will not. To engage in successful role taking, one must have some cognitive grasp of what might be on the other's mind—how the other defines the situation and what the other might be expecting one to do. Affect plays an important part in these processes. Typically, situations have an expected emotional tone—we expect to witness and express sadness at funerals and joy at weddings—and successful role making and role taking depend on the individual's capacity to share these feelings. Moreover, role taking is itself not only a cognitive process but also an affective one. Frequently in attempting to grasp the perspective of the other, one identifies with that perspective, coming to take it as one's own. In other words, role taking frequently generates empathy, in which one actually experiences the pain or joy of the other.

Our first task is to examine the cognitive foundations of conduct. What people do is in great part dependent on the content of individual minds as people confront and act toward one another within a given situation. There are two main reasons for stressing that what people do is dependent on what they know:

1. People must have grounds for deciding among alternative possible acts in order to control their conduct in interaction with one another. How does an individual determine, for example, if a person encountered on the street is going to be friendly or hostile, and thus whether the proper approach is wariness or trust? How do people anticipate what others are going to say next in a conversation? Clearly people do make predictions about the conduct of others in order to govern their own conduct. The problem is to determine how they do so. What do people know that enables them to grasp the perspectives of others?

2. An emphasis on the useful knowledge on which people rely carries with it the implication that even in routine situations people must be alert to the fact that there usually are alternative possibilities for others' acts and for their own. Few situations in everyday life have a script so fixed that all an actor must do is to read previously learned and rehearsed lines. To stress the importance of what people know is to stress that they often must use this knowledge to write their lines as the action progresses.

In order to specify how knowledge informs the processes of taking and making roles, we must analyze it in some detail. In this task, the phenomenological tradition has made an important contribution; the analysis on the following pages is based on that body of work.[5] The basic premise is that the members of a society share a common stock of knowledge, which is not a random assortment of facts and ideas but a very structured body of knowledge and procedures for using it. This knowledge is not "true" in a scientific sense, which is to say that it has not been produced or tested according to the accepted standards of a community of scientists. But it is "true" in a practical sense, which is to say that it serves effectively to help people decide what to do and to interpret what others are doing (see Table 4.1).

Typification
Perhaps the most crucial form of knowledge in the total stock of knowledge is what Alfred Schutz called *typifications*.[6] The idea of typifications is itself quite simple, but its implications for conduct are vast. People know what to expect of one another in particular situations

TABLE 4.1   Cognitive Frames for Role Making and Role Taking

	What Is the Key Question Asked by Role Maker/Taker?	When Is the Frame Used?	How Is the Frame Confirmed?	What Is the Role of Negotiation?
Typification	Who am I and who is the other?	Typification occurs early in situations.	Predictive or "postdictive" confirmation occurs. The typification makes past or future behavior comprehensible.	Actors try to control typification of themselves and may try to negotiate more favorable ones through aligning actions.
Probability	What is likely to happen? or Was this a likely occurrence?	Probability generally follows the establishment of a typification.	Predictive or "postdictive" confirmation occurs.	Ideas about probability are invoked in discussions.
Causality	Why is this happening or did this happen?	Causality generally follows establishment of a typification but may reflect some uncertainty about typification.	Some predictive or "postdictive" confirmation occurs.	Ideas about causality are invoked in discussions.
Means and ends	Is this an effective way to achieve a purpose?	The means and ends frame generally accompanies or follows the establishment of a positive typification.	Some predictive or "postdictive" confirmation occurs.	Ideas about effectiveness are invoked in discussions.
Normative requirements	Is this right, appropriate, moral, correct behavior?	Normative requirements generally accompany or follow the establishment of a negative typification.	Self-establishing confirmation occurs. Normative labels define conduct by fiat.	Norms are negotiable through aligning actions.
Substantive congruency	Am I defining the situation in the same way as others?	Substantive congruency occurs when typification and other frames fail.	Predictive confirmation occurs. New effort is directed to redefine the situation.	Redefinition may require open and explicit negotations.

because they "know" that various *types* of people behave in *typical* ways under particular circumstances. Students can understand and predict the conduct of a professor in the classroom, for example, because they share a typification of how professors tend to behave under various circumstances. Their typification of the professor consists of a set of expectations and assumptions about what professors usually, ordinarily, generally, or typically do. So long as the professor's conduct falls within this typification, the students can make sense of it, and so the professor's identity and the definition of the situation go unchallenged.

A typification is fundamentally an image or picture that people maintain with respect to a particular role, situation, person, or object and that organizes or catalogs their knowledge of it. On the first day of class, students ordinarily have no difficulty identifying the professor, because that person both looks and acts "like" a professor. If someone thought to be a professor takes a seat with the class, the identity of that person as the professor is undermined, and students will seek a new typification of the person. They may, for example, identify the individual as a "nontraditional student." That is, because the individual does not look "like" a typical young college student and also does not act "like" a professor, they may decide this person is someone who decided to go to college later than usual, perhaps because he or she spent a few years in military service.

As this example suggests, typification proceeds on the basis of visible and auditory *cues*. According to Gregory Stone, all interaction involves two levels.[7] We observe and respond to one another's words and deeds, to what Stone called *discourse*. These serve as bases for typification and subsequently affect the course of interaction. But we also observe and respond to *appearance*—to manners of dress, physical appearance, and demeanor—and these also shape the course of interaction by providing us with typifying cues.

Very little about people is actually visible to observers. Physical appearance (expressed in dress, posture, and facial expression) and a few overt words and deeds constitute all that is directly accessible to others. Thoughts and motives are hidden, and most situations provide an opportunity for people to display few of their talents. There are vast blank spaces in the selves people present to one another. Yet appearances, acts, and words serve effectively as cues on the basis of which others establish the identity of the person and thereby typify his or her acts. For example, it is only on the basis of such minimal physical and behavioral cues as facial recognition, manner of dress, and a few fragmentary acts that one identifies the person who is the physician in a medical office. Yet on the basis of such cues a vast array of knowledge about what physicians do, how they speak and act, and what is usual and unusual in their conduct is made available as a basis of our conduct toward them and the interpretation of theirs toward us.

Appearance is important not only because it provides us with the cues we need to typify someone initially but also because it assists us in maintaining and refining that typification as interaction proceeds. We assign identity to the physician on the basis of appearance—by dress, demeanor, and conduct in the examining room—but we continue to rely on appearance for other cues that will refine the typification. On the basis of tone of voice, body posture, and facial expression, we may typify the physician as cold or warm, self-confident or uncertain, interested or distracted, about to deliver good news or bad.

Thus, people act in given situations on the basis of typifications. They are able to predict the conduct of others because they identify them as types of people who are likely to behave in ways similar to others of their type. The very process of role taking depends on this ability to typify. People are able to grasp others' attitudes toward themselves only because they can typify their own acts from the others' point of view. For if people regard the conduct of others as typical of certain roles, groups, or categories of people, they also are aware that they are typified *by* others—that whatever they do themselves shapes their situated social identity.

Seen in this light, role taking is a process in which people are attuned to the typifications others are using to interpret their behavior. Likewise, role making is a process in which the individual seeks to devise conduct that will induce others to make desired typifications. Since some typifications are more desirable than others—better to be an interesting professor than a boring one, for example, or an upstanding citizen rather than a crook—people will seek to present themselves in ways that give others cues on the basis of which to make favorable typifications.

It is, however, only partially correct to assert that people seek favorable typifications through their presentations of self. There are many circumstances in which people contemplate acts that they know or fear will lead to their retypification in undesirable terms. Yet they perform these acts anyway, perhaps because the loss from a possible negative retypification is less than the probable gains from an act others might regard as untoward. A person may steal even though this conduct makes him or her a thief in the eyes of others. Moreover, as discussed earlier, the person's control over conduct is imperfect, so that many acts do not have the benefit of prior reflection about the possible responses of others. Often people do not control the circumstances under which they act—mistakes and accidents affect what they do—and sometimes their impulses produce acts they wish they could recall. As we will see, controlling the typifications others form of us is a common focus of our role-making efforts in everyday life.

Probability

What human beings "know" about the social world (and the natural world as well) is organized by probability. That is, people carry with them a store of knowledge about the likelihood of various events, and from time to time they refer to this knowledge as they try to make sense of the activities of others or to anticipate how others will interpret their own acts. A police officer confronted with a hostile crowd, for example, must weigh the duty to arrest those who violate the law against the likelihood of increased crowd anger if he or she does so. An officer in this situation might well conclude that arrests would probably incite the crowd to more violence and jeopardize his or her own safety.

Assessments of probability are often secondary to the establishment of typifications. That is, people first employ typifications as they define situations and establish roles and identities in them. Once a situation is defined and typifications of it and its participants have been established, there is still room for uncertainty of action or interpretation. For example, once the police officer has concluded that he or she is faced with an angry crowd and has identified its leaders, the officer still is faced with some uncertainty as to what specifically to do and how crowd members will respond. It is at this point that probability knowledge is brought into play: Given the situation and its participants, what are the alternative possible events and courses of action and what is the likelihood of each?

Causality

Our stock of knowledge also includes propositions about causality. We assume that an event has a cause and that sometimes in order to act appropriately or effectively we must first establish its cause. If an ordinarily cheerful child becomes anxious or depressed, for example, a parent will respond to such atypical or unlikely conduct by attempting to ascertain the cause. Did something happen to upset the child at school? Has the child become involved with drugs? *Why* is the child behaving in this new and unusual way?

The causal propositions brought to bear in such instances vary considerably from one society or community to another. At one time in North America, a great deal of conduct was explained and interpreted in religious terms. A child's anxiety might be interpreted as a sign of a struggle with temptation or as a consequence of sinful behavior. Gradually, people in modern societies have come to view the causes of behavior in scientific or quasi-scientific rather than theological terms. Thus, propositions that the child is anxious because of a learning disability that makes school work difficult or because of involvement with drugs are rooted in social scientific or psychological ideas about the causation of behavior. In another society, the same conduct might well be interpreted and explained as the result of witchcraft or of spirit possession.

Whatever the source of our propositions about causality—and whatever their truth as judged against some scientific standard—they serve as ways of making sense of conduct and of deciding what to do in the face of a problematic event. As with explicit assessments of typicality and probability, in the face of the problematic, people tend to assess causality. Where conduct is routine and usual, typifications function largely in the background, our assessments of probability are made rather easily, and there is not much to explain. Where conduct departs from the routine, these forms of knowledge come much more explicitly to the fore.

Means and Ends

Much of the knowledge on which people rely in everyday life takes the form of *recipe knowledge,* which consists of regular procedures people follow in order to secure their ends.[8] Knowledge of relationships between means and ends is crucial to people's capacity to negotiate their everyday affairs and to interact with one another. Knowing how to study effectively, how to take a book out of the library, how to get along with professors, and how to write a good term paper are examples of means and ends knowledge regularly employed by students.

Recipe knowledge has a double function in social life, as do all forms of knowledge. First, it is the basis for individuals' abilities to act toward various objects in their world and to secure their goals. A student who knows how to study, for example, will find passing a course easier than the student who does not know how to study. As we role make in defined situations, following typical lines of conduct as we interact with others, we make use of a great many techniques of conduct. Often we use these techniques habitually; sometimes we must more self-consciously consider what we know in order to select the appropriate technique.

Recipe knowledge is significant also because it provides a frame through which the conduct of others can be interpreted and predicted. Role taking is made possible to a great extent because people are able to treat one another's conduct as means undertaken in pursuit of ends. In a physician's office, for example, many activities are unintelligible to the patient because they depend on technical knowledge that the average person does not possess. Yet people permit physicians to engage in activities they do not understand because they can attribute purpose to what the physician does. The act makes sense as a means to something the physician wants to accomplish, even if the person does not know why it is an efficacious means.

Normative Standards

Another standard against which people measure their own and others' conduct involves their knowledge of normative requirements or preferences. As people interact with one another, taking and making roles on the basis of what they know about typicality, probability, causality, and means and ends, they make judgments from time to time of their own and others' acts in terms of what they feel to be morally appropriate or necessary. Although some of their conceptions of right and wrong are so deeply internalized that their violation leads to intense feelings of guilt or outrage, perhaps the majority are simply matters of knowing what the rules are. Thus, for example, an act of homicide may arouse very powerful feelings of outrage, whereas an act of lying or even theft might receive a far less intense reaction, even though people define both as wrong in their moral code.[9]

Norms enter into consciousness—they become objects of discourse—under problematic and unusual circumstances. They do so, for example, when conduct is questioned. When someone acts in a manner that others find strange, unexpected, or untoward, it is likely that a social norm or rule will be invoked at some point. Frequently this is done by implication rather than by explicit formulation: "Why are you upset?" is a question that implies not only a challenge to conduct but also a norm— "You should be calm"—that serves as its premise. Another circumstance in which social norms are apt to be stated (if only in a conversation with the self) is when there is some uncertainty about the course of action to be pursued or about whether a contemplated act will be regarded by others as acceptable.

This approach to social norms makes them a less significant aspect of social life than they are sometimes portrayed to be. Rather than *the* major criterion people employ to regulate their own and others' conduct, social norms are one of several forms of knowledge that people employ in their everyday conduct. The formulation of normative statements is thus a part of role making and role taking, but only a part. People take the roles of others and respond to their own conduct in normative terms, guessing whether others will formulate norms if they act in a contemplated way. It should not be thought, however, that norms are constantly implicated in acts, nor that people behave by finding the appropriate norms that govern each and every social situation.

Substantive Congruency

Finally, the definition of the situation itself is a form of "knowledge" that we routinely employ when we attempt to determine whether the acts of others seem to be based on the same definition as the one we hold. *Substantive congruency* refers to a condition in which various participants in a situation can regard one another's acts as sensible in terms of their own understanding of what is going on in the situation, what objects are present, and who the actors are. Substantive congruency thus denotes a test people apply to one another in the process of making and taking roles. One avenue of role taking is to say to oneself, "What does the situation look like from the other person's point of view?" Here the focus is on the nature of reality itself, and particularly on the question of how a view of reality imputed to another squares with one's own view.

The common situation where one individual regards a "date" as just a friendly social occasion and the other sees it as the first step down the road to romance illustrates how substantive congruency comes into play. Although the two may interact for a time with such incongruent definitions of the situation, eventually one may suspect that the other has a different definition of the situation. The romantically inclined participant may find the other too distant and cold; the friendly socializer may find the other's conversation too intimate. When this occurs, one will consider alternative possible definitions of the situation on the basis of which the other might be acting, and perhaps conclude that their definitions are not congruent. On such occasions, role taking takes the form of a reality test, and role making may well then focus on making definitions of the situation more congruent.

Each of these ways of knowing comes into play at various points as roles are taken and made in social situations. Lacking instincts of any consequence and faced with a complex social world, human beings must simply *know* a great deal in order to interact with one another. Considering the vast store of knowledge people must draw on as they act, it is in some ways surprising that human conduct is at all coordinated. The potential complexity of interaction seems enormous in view of the alternatives open to participants in many situations, the possibilities for misunderstanding and misinterpretation, and the sometimes tenuous relationship between outward appearance and inner intentions.

Symbolic interactionists have developed a number of concepts that attempt to cope with this complexity and speak to people's efforts to give some order and continuity to the apparent fluidity and precarious nature of social interaction. Taken together, these concepts all deal with various forms of *aligning actions*—that is, with the ways human beings attempt to maintain alignment or consistency among their individual and social acts, important cultural objects, and their own conceptions of themselves. These aligning actions constitute the next important topic in our analysis of social interaction and conduct formation.

Aligning Actions

The fundamental task people face as they interact is to coordinate their lines of conduct. Whether the social act they are creating is a handshake, a conversation, an argument, or a romantic encounter, each person must fit his or her conduct with the conduct of others through the processes of role taking and role making. Assuming that there is a shared definition of the situation and a shared stock of knowledge, this may seem like a relatively straightforward task. By focusing on the social act to be completed, each person can predict and interpret the conduct of others, know what they expect, and thus make an acceptable performance of his or her role.

The process is more complex than it seems, however, for three essential reasons:

- People perform acts that others do not expect.

For a great variety of reasons, people act in ways that surprise others and in doing so make the coordination of conduct problematic. People are late to meetings, they tell lies, they perform well beyond our highest expectations of them, or they fall short of the mark. Whatever the causes of such acts, they interfere with the routine flow of social interaction. When the unexpected occurs, people must deal with it in some way.

- The self is an object in every social encounter.

People do not focus only on social objects in common with others, but also act with the self in mind. Each individual act has implications not just for the coordination of conduct, but also for the person's sense of self—for identity and self-esteem—and for the person's pursuit of his or her own goals.

- Culture and its objects constrain every social encounter.

Although human beings neither internalize most social norms nor look for normative guidance at every turn as they interact with one another, they are conscious of culture and its ideal objects of conduct. "Truth," "freedom," "duty," and other key cultural objects are an important part of the environment within which human beings form their conduct. Social interaction is complicated because acts that meet the situated expectations of others, further individual goals, and enhance the self may not accord with culture. When this occurs, people endeavor to link their acts to culture in ways others will accept.

These three sources of complication in social interaction give rise to *aligning actions,*[10] which may be defined as largely verbal efforts to create an "alignment" between the substance of social interaction, the selves of those involved, and the culture they share. Aligning actions are a form of talk that pervades everyday life; they include the accounts, explanations, apologies, disclaimers, and other techniques people employ as they talk about unexpected and problematic behavior, seek to protect or defend themselves from accusations, and attempt to make their conduct appear sensible and desirable in cultural terms.

Social psychologists have identified and studied a number of forms and features of aligning actions. Among those most often employed are motive talk, accounts, disclaimers, and other aligning actions such as apologies. Each of these is a discursive technique for sustaining coordinated interaction while also maintaining the self and defining conduct in culturally acceptable, or at least meaningful, terms.

Motive Talk

Talk about motives—requested and offered explanations of *why* a person acted in a particular way—is a key organizing feature of everyday life and a major way in which potential or actual problematic occurrences are handled in social interaction. Recall the distinction between motivation and motives drawn in Chapter 3. *Motivation* refers to those internal states of the organism that govern its impulsive responses to various stimuli; *motives,* in contrast, consist of statements about conduct. Motivation is generally inaccessible to the observer; the organism's internal states, which govern its sensitivity to environing objects, are impossible to discern directly, because they operate spontaneously and immediately and because they are very quickly transformed by self-consciousness. Motives, in contrast, are very accessible, for they are the stuff of everyday conversation. People are continually avowing and imputing motives, telling themselves and others why they did what they did or why they intend to do what they intend to do.

In order to examine the significance of motive talk in social interaction, we must examine more closely the circumstances in which it occurs. C. Wright Mills, in his classic discussion of the topic, summarized the essential nature of motive talk in the following way:

> *Motives are imputed or avowed as answers to questions interrupting acts or programs. Motives are words . . . They stand for anticipated situational consequences of questioned conduct. Intention or purpose . . . is awareness of anticipated consequence; motives are names for consequential situations, and surrogates for actions leading to them. Behind questions are possible alternative actions with their terminal consequences.[11]*

In other words, the issue of motive arises when someone interrupts a line of conduct with a question, which may be raised either by the behaving person or a partner in interaction. Behind the question lies someone's view that what is taking place is "questionable"— that is, unexpected, unclear, and perhaps therefore undesired or untoward. An imputation of a motive, a call for another to avow a motive, or an unrequested announcement of a motive are ways in which people respond to such anticipated or actual questions. The goal of motive talk is to lay bare the consequences of a particular line of conduct—to make explicit the object toward which it is proceeding.

We can find an illustration in the common situation in which a parent questions a child about his or her conduct: "Why are you going to school dressed in your oldest play clothes?" In the question and the child's reply, "Because we're doing finger painting in art class today," we have a request for and an avowal of a motive. Similarly, we find the same kind of request in the parent's query years later: "Why on earth are you majoring in sociology? What will it get you?" "Because I want to become a professor and do research" or "Because I want to be a social worker" are likewise responses that avow particular motives for the act or acts in question. Questions arise because of something in the child's appearance or the college student's behavior that seems problematic to the parent, who interrupts with a question designed to reveal its consequences and remove the problematic feature.

What is taken as problematic when motive talk arises is a line of conduct that is either unexpected or, from the questioner's viewpoint, has a more desirable or more likely alternative. The parent in the foregoing example had a business career in mind for the child and so raises a question about the decision to major in sociology. Any part of the social stock of knowledge may serve as the nonproblematic background against which conduct is viewed as questionable. If a student previously enamored of the fine points of accounting suddenly takes an interest in social psychology, for example, this *atypical* behavior is the basis for raising questions. Or if the student has displayed a taste for an expensive life-style in the fast lane, a career in social work may strike the parent as a strange choice of means to this end.

Questions about motives challenge identity as well as the relationship between the act and culture. To question a child's selection of clothing, for example, is not only to express doubt about the appropriateness or good sense of the conduct but it is also about whether the child is acting from an appropriate role perspective. Has the child forgotten that today is a school day and is he or she planning to go out and play? To question the student's choice of academic major is also to question identity: Will this decision enable the child to become the kind of person he or she has wanted to become? Questions about identity raise doubts about the self, doubts that must be resolved.

The motives people offer are designed to explain an unexpected act so that it seems less problematic, to repair the person's identity in his or her own eyes or the eyes of others, and to find cultural support or justification for the conduct in question. "I'm majoring in sociology so that I can learn more about human conduct and eventually help make the world a better place" is an account that accomplishes all three goals. By attaching a positive cultural value to the decision to major in sociology ("learning" and "helping others"), the motive talker hopes to make the conduct seem sensible to his or her parents and thus also to make a positive impression on them—to induce them to identify their child as someone who wants to do socially worthwhile things.

How do people know what to say when they are asked why they are doing what they are doing? From what source do people acquire a set of reasons for their acts—reasons they can cite on appropriate occasions and that others will accept as answers to their questions? What makes the difference between an acceptable and an unacceptable motive? What determines whether an avowed motive will be accepted by others or rejected?

C. Wright Mills's concept of *vocabularies of motive* provides one way of approaching such questions. People learn to use certain words to explain their acts, but these words are neither shared by all members of the society nor used indiscriminately or at will. Rather, vocabularies of motive are differentiated along at least two dimensions. First, particular sets of motives are regarded as appropriate to specific situations or classes of situations. References to "serving God" or to the attainment of a "state of Grace" are appropriate as avowed motives in religious contexts in contemporary society, but would be regarded as out of place and unseemly in business or government, except in very carefully controlled and circumscribed usages. Thus, a president of the United States might call on "God's help" in an inaugural address, but daily justifications of conduct in terms of divine directives would be seen by most people not only as cause for concern about the separation of church and state but also perhaps as evidence of an unfit mental state. People learn that in given situations their choices of conduct *and* motives are limited by what others will treat as legitimate.

Second, particular sets of motives hold more or less sway and are treated as more or less legitimate (whatever the specific situation) by various social groups and categories. A conservative U.S. president, for example, might favor reducing or eliminating taxes on capital gains—that is, on income realized from the growing value of stocks or other investments—on the grounds that doing so will give people greater incentive to invest and will thus help the economy grow. Liberal opponents may argue that this claim is a deception, that what the president really wants to do is to give rich people a tax break at the expense of ordinary workers. Among conservatives, the avowal of motives having to do with the stimulation of investment in business is a standard and legitimate way for any given act to be justified when it is questioned. Among those not sharing this vocabulary of motives, "investment" does not evoke such an automatic and unquestioned response. From their point of view, it is an irrelevant and perhaps even an erroneous and deceptive statement designed to distract people from other, less worthy, motives.

The existence of vocabularies of motive that are specific to situations or categories of situations helps explain how people are able to compartmentalize their lives by separating motives important in one sphere from those important in another. It is often noted that gangsters (or, for that matter, corporate executives) seem to lead double lives, acting with ruthless self-interest in their occupational world but with great tenderness and selflessness toward their families. They can do so not only because each of their separate worlds has its own set of objects and acts but also because each has its own distinct vocabulary of motives, so that conduct that would be unthinkable in one context can be seen as desirable in another.

The differential distribution of vocabularies among various groups in the society—among liberals and conservatives, for example, or physicians and patients—helps explain how various groups attract and hold the loyalties of their members and also how they come into conflict with one another. The capacity of a group to attract and keep members is determined partly by its vocabulary of motives; the more it provides and supports motives that accord with a person's established or desired lines of conduct and self-conceptions, the more it is able to bind the person to it. Families, organizations, social movements, workplaces, and other social groups provide contexts in which people talk about their reasons for conduct and have their reasons confirmed by others. Thus, for example, a group of alcoholics (such as an Alcoholics Anonymous group) are bound together not just by similar experiences but also because they share a common way of talking about themselves and their activities. They share a vocabulary of motives that focuses on accepting personal responsibility and maintaining complete abstinence. Similarly, a group of conservative business people may be bound together by a shared vocabulary of motives that emphasizes the ultimate altruism of selfish capitalist acts. The "profit motive" leads to acts that benefit society as a whole, they might say. Although they might be laughed out of a working-class saloon, in their own company such motives are an important way to justify and make sense of their activities.

Motive talk is a common feature of everyday life. It arises whenever people are uncertain of the meaning of others' acts or of how others will interpret their own acts. Other forms of aligning actions—such as disclaimers, accounts, and apologies—also arise in response to problematic conduct.

Disclaimers

A *disclaimer*[12] is a verbal device people employ when they want to ward off the negative implications of an impending act—something they are about to do or say that they know or fear will be regarded as undesirable and discredit them in the eyes of others. Statements such as the following are typical of disclaimers: "I'm not prejudiced, because some of my best friends are Jews, but . . ." "This may seem strange to you, but . . ." or "I'm no expert on psychology, but . . ." Each phrase introduces an act or statement that contradicts the premise of the disclaimer. Thus, a person claiming not to be prejudiced may make a racist statement, and a self-proclaimed nonexpert may make a statement only an expert could be trusted to make.

Disclaimers are addressed to a central fact of human conduct. Any act is simultaneously imbedded in a situation, in which it either does or does not fit, and in the identity of the acting person, for which it has either positive or negative implications. A prejudicial statement, for example, typically arises during a conversation and may be quite in place as far as the definition of the situation is concerned. That is, it may fit with the theme of the conversation, be in proper sequence with the statement of a previous speaker, and be an expression of a commonly held sentiment. At the same time, those who hear the racist remark are likely to interpret it as relevant to the identity of the speaker. Because people are generally aware that their acts typify them in the eyes of others, they are frequently careful to disclaim the implications of those acts that, they feel, may get them typified in terms they do not like.

Thus, disclaimers are efforts to carry out an intended act—in this case a racist remark—while avoiding any damage to identity in the eyes of others. By acknowledging that he or she knows that an impending remark could be construed as racist, the disclaiming person hopes to avoid being considered one. The implicit theory on which the disclaimer rests thus seems to be that one who *knows* an act could be discrediting and who disclaims the identity implied by the act should not be discredited. If the disclaimer is accepted, it allows conduct to proceed and situated identities to remain unchallenged. It also aligns conduct with culture, since it establishes that those present are not acting out of prejudice, at least in their own eyes.

Disclaimers are *prospective* aligning actions. That is, they are employed when, through role taking, the individual anticipates how others will respond to a contemplated act. In effect, then, a disclaimer is an effort to control in advance a definition of a situation and the identities of those present. In contrast, another type of aligning action, accounts, is retrospective, focusing on what has already occurred.

Accounts

What happens when an untoward act occurs without an anticipatory disclaimer? Marvin Scott and Stanford Lyman argued that when the course of social interaction is disturbed by rule violations, unexpected or inconvenient activities, inconsiderate or rude behavior, and other problematic acts, a process of demanding and giving *accounts* takes place.[13] In this process, someone who commits an untoward act is asked to account for it—that is, to explain it to the satisfaction of others present. Although accounts often are demanded explicitly, they are sometimes requested indirectly or by implication, and they may be volunteered when individuals perceive that they may be called to account for what they have done.

Scott and Lyman identified two kinds of accounts, excuses and justifications, each manifesting a particular attitude toward the questioned act and the person's responsibility for it. *Excuses* acknowledge that a particular act is undesirable or wrong but deny that the individual was responsible for his or her conduct. Asked to explain why he was late for a date, a young man might explain that his car had a flat tire. This excuse admits that being late is undesirable but argues that no blame should be attached, since flat tires are accidents.

Excuses are an important social lubricant. By enabling troublesome situations to be passed over, put aside, and treated as unfortunate past history, they prevent each and every untoward act from becoming a major issue. Since much does go wrong in everyday life, excuses make it possible for definitions of situations and identities to be maintained, as well as for people to see themselves and to be seen by others in positive ways. At the same time, excuses help preserve the rules, standards, and expectations by means of which people ordinarily judge one another's acts. Excuses lay the blame for untoward conduct on someone or something other than the individual held to account, but they unmistakably preserve the definition of the conduct as undesirable. Being late is being late, even if the particular person is not blamed for this bad act.

Justifications, in contrast, are a form of account in which the person accepts responsibility for an act but denies that it should be seen as untoward or wrong. A good illustration of a justification is a *denial of injury,* which is often used by young delinquents to account for their misdeeds. A person who takes a car on a joyride and later returns it, for example, may claim that since no one was hurt by this act—the car was returned unharmed—he or she did not really steal a car and should not be so charged. A denial of injury reasons that since there was no harm done, no violation of a rule or law has occurred, even though a willful act did take place.

Justifications also lubricate social interaction and attempt to protect identity. Although social norms and laws forbid certain activities, either categorically or under certain circumstances, the status of any particular act as proscribed is never a matter of absolute certainty. As we will see in Chapter 6, when untoward conduct occurs, it is not necessarily met with an automatic allegation of rule violation or deviance. Rather, there is flexibility, both in everyday life and in the formal procedures of the law, in determining whether a particular act is or is not a violation. The existence of a vocabulary of justifications is one basis for this flexibility. Justifications provide a means by which people can decide whether particular acts constitute infractions. Equally important, the outcome of a particular effort at building a justification for an act—whether it is successful or not—bears on the kind of identity the person is able to claim. If an act is justified, then the person's identity will not be transformed; if it is not successfully justified, then a new identity, perhaps as a deviant or troublemaker, may be in store for the person.

Other Aligning Actions

Motive talk, accounts, and disclaimers do not exhaust the aligning actions people employ in everyday life.[14] Another common form is the *apology,* in which the person who has committed a challenged act admits the untoward nature of the act, accepts responsibility for it, and expresses remorse: "I'm sorry I lost my temper—it was wrong of me to act that way and I sincerely regret it; please forgive me." An apology of this sort pays homage to cultural values and attempts to maintain social interaction by assuaging the anger or irritation of those whom the violation has offended. It also attempts to restore the good identity of the offender by reminding the audience of his or her knowledge of the untoward nature of the act. Implicit in any apology is the claim that one who readily acknowledges an offense, sincerely expresses regret, and begs forgiveness should not be treated the same way—that is, retypified and given an undesirable identity—as one who neither recognizes the nature of the offense nor tries to make amends. As Nicholas Tavuchis pointed out, an apology places the fate of the offender and his or her identity in the hands of the person to whom it is offered. Only the offended person can bestow forgiveness and thus restore the offender's identity and his or her place in the social world.[15]

In his classification of aligning actions, Christopher Hunter pointed out that aligning actions can focus on unexpected desirable acts as well as on undesirable acts.[16] Human beings may sometimes fall short of what is expected of them, but occasionally they do much better. They perform heroically, do good deeds and special favors, and in other ways do more than one would expect of them in their assigned roles. Such actions "beyond the call of duty" also lead to aligning actions, for in their own way they can be as problematic as untoward acts. That is, they have consequences that were not anticipated and have to be assimilated to the situation and its definition; they alter established situated identities; and they stand in contrast to cultural objects by doing more than is ordinarily expected.

Thus, for example, someone who goes out of his or her way to aid a colleague at work, perhaps by pitching in at a time when the work load is especially heavy, creates a situation in which various alignment processes may occur. The helper may, for example, want to have the act defined by others as central to his or her identity as "someone who can be counted on when the going gets tough" or "someone who has the interests of others constantly in mind." If so, the helper may use what Barry Schlenker called an *entitling acclaimer,* which is an effort to emphasize his or her contribution. "Remember, *I* was the one who was there for you when others didn't care!" the helper may say. The helper may also use an *enhancing acclaimer,* which is an effort to stress the importance of the contribution: "You'd have been in real trouble with the boss without my help," he or she might say.[17] As with other kinds of aligning actions, acclaimers such as these are efforts to maintain the flow of interaction, to sustain or enhance identities, and to link conduct to important cultural objects.

Moreover, acclaimers illustrate another important property of aligning actions—namely, the negotiation of meanings in the situation. Those who use acclaimers typically want to put the best face on their conduct, as do those who use accounts and disclaimers. But the audience for these aligning actions may well resist such efforts to define the nature of the conduct in question or the identity of its perpetrator. A professor, for example, may refuse to accept the excuse of a student who is repeatedly late to class because of problems with transportation, arguing that the excuse is too frequently used and is therefore worn out. The professor may fear that too ready acceptance of the excuse deprives him or her of any leverage over the student's conduct. If there is no penalty for coming late—not even an altered identity—then the conduct is likely to recur. Likewise, the recipient of extraordinary help may find it in his or her interest to minimize its importance or downplay the key role of the helper. To accept the latter's claims about the crucial character of his or her help is to incur a debt that might later have to be repaid.

Emotions and Social Interaction

Although our discussion of the definition of the situation, the forms of knowledge on which role making and role taking depend, and the use of aligning actions has thus far emphasized the *cognitive* aspects of social interaction, the *affective* (emotional) dimension is equally important. Definitions of situations specify the emotional tone to be maintained, calling for light-heartedness at picnics, for example, seriousness in classes, and somberness at funerals. Roles typically have an affective component, so that, for example, nurses are expected to be "warm" and "caring," whereas physicians may display more emotional neutrality. (This difference owes in large part to the fact that nurses are predominantly female, so that emotional typifications attached to gender carry over into the occupational sphere.) Departures from emotional expectations frequently precipitate aligning actions—people have to explain why they are sad when others expect them to be happy, for example, or to apologize for losing their tempers.

Emotions are thus pervasive features of social interaction. How do the social processes that originate and regulate emotions operate? The emotion of *grief* illustrates a symbolic interactionist analysis of emotions.[18]

In North American culture, as in many others, grief is the normal emotion created when a loved one dies. The feelings associated with grief are well known: People feel sad, they are depressed, they cry, they feel sorry for themselves, and they feel alone or left behind. These feelings begin shortly after the experience of bereavement, they intensify, and they gradually diminish (or at least they are supposed to) with the passage of time.

How do we explain the emotion of grief? Since we will not be satisfied with an appeal to human nature ("That's just the natural way people feel"), how do we account for the character of this experience in our culture? One approach, a culturally deterministic one, would say that people experience grief simply because they are supposed to. That is, grief is culturally defined as a set of sensations people are supposed to have when someone close to them dies. Having been appropriately socialized, people spontaneously have these sensations and call them grief when someone close dies. This explanation has some short-comings. It does not provide an explanation of the physical sensations themselves. How can cultural expectations create bodily sensations? In addition, it does not explain why people experience different levels of grief. Some wives grieve when their husbands die, while others may be relieved or happy. And grieving for parents, while culturally expected, seems to vary according to their age and the relative social distance that has grown between them and their children. We do not have the same feelings about the death of an aged and distant parent as we do about the death of a parent whose death comes at an age younger than expected or on whom we still depend. Thus, a simply cultural explanation does not do all that we might want it to do.

Symbolic interactionism provides some of the missing details and linkages to improve a cultural explanation. Death represents the loss of a member of society. For those who have been close to the deceased, it means much more. The death of a spouse, for example, means not only the loss of a companion, lover, and friend but also the loss of a part of the self. When people who have been close to us die, we lose the supports for our own self-conceptions that those people provided. We lose part of our identity, part of what had buttressed our self-esteem.[19]

The loss of another will have a greater or lesser impact depending on the deceased's place in the individual's life. The impact will be greater, for example, on a dependent child whose parent still looms large as a figure in his or her life than for an adult faced with the death of an aging and failing parent. Lyn Lofland suggested that the level of significance of the other—and hence the impact of the other's death—is defined by seven "threads of con-nectedness" by which people are attached to one another:

> *We are linked to others by the roles we play, by the help we receive, by the wider network of others made available to us, by the selves others create and sustain, by the comforting myths they allow us, by the reality they validate for us, and by the futures they make possible.[20]*

Where these linkages are spread widely among a large number of people, the loss of any single other may have little impact on the individual's membership in the group or on everyday activities. But, where a few others command the greatest share of our attention, providing role partners, definitions of reality, and validation of ourselves, each other person is likely to be of very great significance and thus the loss of that other is likely to occasion more intense grief.

As Lofland pointed out, the extent to which people feel a sense of loss may depend on their typical definitions of the situation of death. In the past, death rates were higher in general, first experiences with death tended to occur early in life, and people more commonly experienced the death of children. Under such conditions, death itself was more routine, and so the sense of loss attendant on any individual's death may have been less. In the contemporary world, where many people experience their first significant death when their grandparents die, death may be a more shaking event simply because it is so unfamiliar. With the greater emphasis on the individual in modern life and the greater opportunity for solitude and privacy, which may encourage the elaboration of grief as well as restrict the opportunities for its expression, the emotional impact of death and the sense of loss that attends it may be greater than in the past.[21]

Whatever variations in the sense of loss there may be, loss it remains. Metaphorically, death tears a hole in the selves of those left behind. This is where the linkage between social experience and physical sensations occurs. As a general rule, physical sensations are created when human acts are blocked. That is, when some circumstance interferes with the normal course of our activities and prevents us from bringing an act to consummation, there are normal physiological results. When I experience the pangs of hunger, for example, and go to the refrigerator only to find it empty, the result is to heighten my tendency to think about food and to increase the sensation of being hungry. So it is also with grief. The loss of a significant other, by disorganizing our social worlds and conceptions of self, creates many obstacles to ordinary, routine conduct. At every turn, we are faced with habitual actions that cannot be completed as before because a significant other is not present. The sensations associated with grief—depression, frustration, anger, and so forth—are normal and spontaneous responses to the fact that the loss blocks our everyday actions.

What is made of these responses is quite another matter. All such individual experiences occur in the context of culturally preestablished meanings, and those meanings are subject to social interpretation. We must, therefore, ask what labels culture makes available for such sensations, and how social interaction makes use of these labels to influence further the sensations themselves and the meanings attributed to them.

It may seem nonsensical to say that the individual feelings associated with the loss of a loved one have to be labeled as grief before they are experienced as grief. In our culture, we take for granted that people feel grief when their loved ones die. No one has to tell us that we are grieving, and we think of grief as the natural label for the experiences we are having. This is not universally the case, however. Robert Levy, for example, reported that Tahitians discuss the feelings associated with the loss of a loved one in terms of illness rather than as grief.[22] Their cultural definitions lead them to downplay feelings of individual loss, so that while they probably have the same depressive reactions as we do, they view them in a different way.

Culture thus provides us with a vocabulary of emotions; that is, each culture accumulates a set of terms that apply to and describe the sensations that are the products of various situations. There is both variation and uniformity among cultures in this regard. The underlying physical sensations associated with emotion are real, they are important, and they are probably provoked by similar situations across many different cultures. Although cultures may differ widely in their definitions of which individuals fall into the category of important, close relationships, the death of someone in such a category will provoke feelings of sadness and depression. This is so because the underlying processes of self and the construction of acts are the same in all cultures. Yet, all cultures do not label the resulting feelings in the same way. One may treat the feelings in terms of a concept of grief, while another downplays the sense of personal loss and treats those feelings as illness.

The existence of cultural vocabularies of emotion is a clue that people have expectations about who will have what emotional experiences under what circumstances. In U.S. society, a woman whose husband dies is supposed to grieve. Not only is there a term to cover her experiences, but her friends and family act toward her on the basis of this concept. They indicate their expectations about how she should behave and feel. They treat her as someone who can be expected to grieve, and their actions are oriented toward seeing to it that this grief finds appropriate expression as well as providing social supports.

Cultural labels and social action in terms of them give rise to at least two forms of *emotion work*.[23] First, part of our emotional experience is constrained by the presentation of self and by the situation of mourning. Even in those circumstances in which individuals do not spontaneously feel the grief they are supposed to feel, they may arrange their self-presentations so as to appear as if they are grieving. Such presentations of self may range from overacted grief—dramatic displays of grief behavior that may leave no one convinced of their genuineness but do meet ritual expectations—to more carefully and artfully acted performances. Moreover, individuals are also constrained in their behavior by the actions of others and by the situation in which they find themselves. A woman who is relieved to see her philandering, good-for-nothing husband gone will be surrounded by others for whom his death is a real loss, and whose conduct will define the situation as one in which mourning is appropriate. That mood is itself constraining, for it makes behavior that departs from the mood seem drastically out of place. So the rejoicing wife may well be somber and sad not just out of concern for her appearance in the eyes of others but also so as to fit with the situation of grief and mourning.

The second form of work on emotions entails efforts to create, and not merely feign, the very emotions that are culturally prescribed when they are not spontaneously felt. In our presentations of self, it is not uncommon for us to be drawn into our performances to the extent that we begin to take them seriously. In striving to assume a mask that others will believe truly represents our feelings, we come to have the very feelings represented by the mask. We put on displays of anger to achieve a certain purpose and then find that we are indeed becoming angry. Similarly, at funerals, we may find ourselves drawn into the solemnity of the occasion and, by first assuming the demeanor of the sad, we then actually become sad.

Many social situations seem arranged as regulators of emotion. In weddings and funerals, for example, the spontaneous and genuine emotions of some are managed and kept within bounds as they interact with others. At the same time, those who bring to such occasions only the appearance of proper emotional involvement may find it necessary to "act" so as to create the appropriate actual emotions. In both cases, it appears, emotions are not individual responses to events, nor are they antithetical to organized, rational social life. Instead, emotions are integral parts of social life, and like all other forms of behavior, they are not matters of unconscious responses to stimuli, but of socially constructed meanings.

Weddings, funerals, and other dramatic events illustrate the importance of what Arlie Hochschild called *feeling rules*—that is, shared conceptions of which feelings are appropriate to a situation, and to what degree. The importance of such rules is not confined to unusual events, however. Candace Clark demonstrated that the display of the emotion of *sympathy* is likewise subject to social expectations.[24] People who have had an experience—a personal misfortune or disaster, for example—that qualifies them to receive expressions of sympathy from others generally recognize that there are limits to the claims they may make. One should not try to claim too much sympathy, or be too eager to accept sympathy, or make unwarranted claims. In other words, one should not exaggerate or misrepresent the significance of a misfortune in order to gain the sympathy of others, one should recognize that there are limits to the sympathy others will give for any particular event, and one should not appear excessively needful of the sympathy of others. Those who are asked for sympathy are likewise mindful of such rules and will sanction departures from them—claiming, for example, that some people are "always looking for sympathy" and, like "broken records," routinely exaggerate the problems that life has handed them.

The management of emotions is a task that confronts people in their occupations as well as in their associations with friends or family members. In some occupations, as Arlie Hochschild demonstrated in her study of flight attendants, a considerable amount of emotional labor is required in their day-to-day work. Airlines expect flight attendants to be cheerfully attentive to passengers, for example, as well as calm in the face of possible crises. They must maintain their emotional composure—they must work hard to avoid producing the "wrong emotions"—in the face of passengers who are frequently unpleasant or demanding. Like waiters and waitresses, sales personnel, and others who have regular contact with the public, they must learn to put on a face that often betrays their true underlying feelings. Their capacity to do so is a part of the labor they sell to their employers.[25]

Whatever the specific situation or social context, the experiencing, display, and regulation of emotions is a key aspect of social life. People are guided in their actions not merely by cognition that focuses on definitions of situations and on role making and role taking, but also by affective responses to situations, others, and themselves.

Constraint and Social Interaction

One major topic remains to be examined to complete our analysis of social interaction and the formation of conduct: the nature and consequences of *constraint* in social life. Symbolic interactionists have often been accused of painting too fluid a picture of the social world, of overemphasizing the freedom of individual actors or groups of actors to resist or overcome the influence of society and culture. By stressing the processes of role making and role taking, as well as the need to define situations, critics argue that symbolic interactionists overlook the many ways in which conduct is constrained.

Symbolic interactionists take the view that there is both freedom and constraint in social life. Human beings are not merely social and cultural automatons, but thinking, acting creatures who use the intelligence they have gained as members of society to solve the problems that confront them. Nonetheless, there are real limits to what humans can do to solve problems and to act in ways of their own choosing.

Constraint is everywhere in social life. People must form definitions of situations and interpret others' conduct in order to construct their acts, but they are typically limited in the definitions they can consider and in the interpretations they can make. They are constrained by limits to their knowledge of others and their purposes, by the power that others hold over them, by obligations to roles or to individuals who are not a part of the present situation, and by others' responses to their acts. Thus, the capacity to define a situation as one sees fit and to make a role as one chooses is far from unlimited, for the individual continually bumps into others, their definitions, and their purposes. In the remainder of this chapter, we will consider several ways in which our actions are thus constrained.

Altercasting

The aligning actions considered earlier focus our attention on what Erving Goffman called the *presentation of self*—that is, the things people do in order to enhance or protect their conceptions of themselves and their status in the eyes of others. Thus, to describe a disclaimer as an effort to avoid the possible negative typifications of a particular act is to focus mainly on the perspective of the disclaiming person as he or she seeks to pursue a line of conduct while also maintaining a desirable self in the situation.

But the presentation of self is only one side of the process of role taking and role making. The roles made by participants in any situation are reciprocal, which is to say that the role made by one person has to "fit" that made by another. In the interaction between patient and physician in the examining room, for example, the two attempt to fit their respective lines of conduct to one another. They do this by imaginatively taking one another's roles and making their own roles accordingly. In studying the presentation of self, we focus on one side of this interchange—namely, the efforts made by a particular individual to make a role and at the same time to put forth a self that the others present will regard favorably. Now we must examine the other side—the effects of one individual's acts on the other's *capacity* to make a role and preserve a valued conception of self. This process, whereby one person's acts constrain and limit what the other can do and be has been termed *altercasting,* a term that calls attention to the "casting" of the other into a particular role preferred by the altercaster.[26]

A familiar example of altercasting is found in the experience of being (or putting someone) "on the defensive." In a formal debate, for example, or in political campaigning, an effective strategy for controlling the definition of the situation is to force others to defend positions they do not want to defend or to put them in the position of having to answer charges. A candidate for president may complain vigorously about the "tax and spend mentality" of an opponent, or call his or her character into question, and in doing so force the other candidate into a defensive position, and thus indirectly confirm that the charge is worth discussing. By creating an issue, a politician forces an opponent to respond to it and thus implicitly to be associated with some of the alleged negative characteristics.[27]

In altercasting, people are constrained to act in certain ways—to make roles of a particular kind—because they are treated *as if* they were making particular roles. A politician treats an opponent as someone who *does* "tax and spend" or who *is* of dubious character and by this treatment forces the other to deny the charge and defend or explain his or her conduct. But the moment the other candidate defends or explains his or her conduct, he or she seems to accept the issue—to agree implicitly that what is charged is worth talking about and thus might actually be true.

Altercasting thus relies on a key feature of all social interaction: The imputation of roles to individuals, and action toward them on the basis of such imputation, powerfully constrains their conduct. The nature and origins of these constraints can easily be seen in another example. A common form of altercasting in everyday life occurs when one individual treats another as a more intimate friend or ally than either is accustomed to thinking of the other. Treating someone as a special friend, confidant, or intimate is a common form of interpersonal Machiavellianism. Although sometimes the intended victim of such altercasting is aware of its insincerity—recognizing, for example, that an employer is bestowing special favors and treatment only in an effort to cultivate a spy and thus find out what the employees are thinking—the victim may be unaware of what is taking place. An employer who treats a subordinate with a show of intimacy in order to elicit employee secrets may be successful in deceiving the employee, or at least successful up to a point. A child who attempts to enlist one parent as an ally in order to influence the other may well succeed in keeping one or both parents in the dark as to what is going on.

What makes altercasting work? Why should an employee be more inclined to squeal on coworkers if the boss begins to act in a friendly way? Why should a parent whom the child treats as an ally begin to take the child's part and act as an ally? One simple explanation of the employer/employee example is that the subordinate perceives an *advantage* in responding reciprocally to the boss's overtures—perhaps anticipating a raise or promotion as a possible reward and thus acting without thought to the interests of fellow workers. Another explanation might be that the employee is responding to a general *norm of reciprocity*. Alvin Gouldner defined such a norm as the belief that one ought to help those who have been helpful, or at least avoid doing them harm.[28] By reducing interpersonal distance, the employer confers something of value on the employee and the latter feels obligated to reciprocate. Similarly, by treating the parent as an ally, the child benefits from the latter's reciprocal feelings of obligation.

A more fundamental explanation of altercasting can be found at a cognitive level. The employer who acts in a more intimate, friendly fashion toward a subordinate is defining a situation in a particular way, treating it as an occasion on which formalities can be put aside and people can treat one another as equals, not as superior and subordinate. In so defining the situation, the employer influences the objects that are present and toward which conduct will occur—in particular, the boss indicates "friendly social intercourse" and "friendship" as main social objects of the occasion. Once the situation has been so defined, it requires considerable effort by the subordinate to define the situation differently and to indicate other objects—to call attention to the formal relationship between the two, for example. To change the encounter's object from "friendly social intercourse" to "boss talks to wary employee" requires self-conscious effort. The employee must actively resist the boss's preferred definition, acting in the role of wary employee rather than in the role of friend. Just as physical objects may block one's passage through a room, so, in much the same way, a social object toward which a powerful individual is acting must be taken into account by those with less power. The employee is not only induced to act in the role of friend by the very considerable press of implication in the situation, but also the employee knows that the boss controls resources and can reward or punish the desired role performance.

The effects of altercasting are not limited to the immediate situations in which people interact with one another any more than the presentation of self is so limited. Just as repeated self-presentations shape the character of self-concept, so, too, the repeated altercasting of one person by others in a particular way will affect self-concept. In many families, for instance, one individual—often, though not always, a child—is repeatedly treated as the scapegoat for everything that goes wrong. Systematically blamed and regarded as responsible for undesirable events and calamitous circumstances, the child very likely will develop a self-concept that reflects such treatment.

Altercasting and the presentation of self are two sides of the same coin. Both involve efforts to define situations by establishing identities and roles. The concept of presentation of self calls attention to people's attempts to define situations in ways they think desirable by showing themselves in a favorable light to others. The concept of altercasting reminds us that what one individual does in a situation places limits on the roles and self-presentations of others. The effects of altercasting and the presentation of self are not limited to manipulation, Machiavellian schemes, or negative consequences for self-concepts. Both may be employed for benign as well as malevolent purposes. Thus, for example, the teacher who believes that a child's performance will be improved by positive rewards and encouragement is altercasting every bit as much as the employer who seeks the confidence of an employee.

Power

Sociologists generally define *power* as the capacity of one person to achieve purposes without the consent of or against the resistance of others. Altercasting is thus a way of exercising power, since the successful altercaster is able to induce others to make a particular role without their realizing it or being able to resist doing so. Like all forms of power, altercasting involves the control of resources—in this case, control over the role of the other. Altercasting is not the sole means by which people pursue their goals, nor is the relevance of power for social interaction limited to the use of such techniques as ways of exercising control over the roles of others. Power depends on a variety of resources and is exercised in a number of ways that must be understood if our portrayal of interaction is to be complete.

The exercise of power depends, in part, on the control by one party in social interaction of resources—goods, tools, knowledge, money—that are valuable to and desired by others. When people interact, they pursue individual as well as collective ends; they cooperate in the pursuit of common goals, but they also sometimes compete for scarce resources or engage in conflict over which actions to take. Thus, for example, members of a business organization cooperate with one another in furthering the organization's goals, but they also compete for advancement within the firm, and sometimes they fight over issues they consider important, such as whether to produce a new product or enter a new market.

In such contexts, it is unlikely that all will be equal in their control of important resources. Managers, vice presidents, and department heads have more power than those whom they employ. That is, they have the power to hire or fire, make unilateral decisions, withhold information from some and share it with others, and increase the budgets for some projects and cut them for others. Superordinates also possess *authority*—that is, they claim the *right* to exercise control over the actions of others, who concede that they have this right.[29] Leaving authority aside, however, there are other inequalities of power: Some members have been around longer than others and thus know more about how the organization works; some have developed close relationships with their superiors and can more readily gain a hearing for their proposals; and some control key departments, such as data processing or personnel, and can thus make their influence strongly felt.

The exercise of power involves the same processes of defining the situation, role making, and role taking as more cooperative forms of social interaction. The more powerful person must role take, estimating what resources the other commands in order to predict how he or she will respond to an effort to use power. The more powerful person must also role make, forging a performance that will convince the other that here is someone to be reckoned with, who will not hesitate to use power ruthlessly if the need arises. Likewise, the weaker individual also must role take and role make, discerning whether the other's power is real or apparent, responding in ways that do not yield more than necessary.

Accurate role taking is, indeed, itself a resource of power. To the extent that one can accurately gauge the reaction of another to one's own contemplated act, one can calculate the act so as to secure the best advantage for oneself. If I know that an associate will abandon a course of action at the slightest hint of resistance, I can influence his or her conduct with a minimum use of my own power. If I can accurately anticipate spirited resistance, I can deploy my own resources to greatest advantage. The more accurately I can role take— imputing intentions and the definition of the situation to the other—the more leverage I have over that person.

Although role-taking ability enhances power, the possession of power—and especially authority—to some extent lessens the need to role take with accuracy. The person who exercises authority can generally get away with less accurate role taking than the person over whom it is exercised. Parents, for example, are in a position to command their children's compliance, at least within certain limits, and can thus afford to be less sensitive to their children's evaluations of them or even to their children's definitions of various situations.[30] The parent can be considerably less concerned with how the child will respond; the child, in contrast, has to learn accurate role-taking skills in order to predict the responses of powerful parents.

This link between role taking and authority should not obscure the basic fact, however, that some degree of role taking is always involved in social interaction. When a parent disciplines a child for doing what has been expressly forbidden and again forbids the child from doing it, role taking has occurred. That is, the parent has made an imputation about the child's conduct in the past and probable behavior in the future. Indeed, the very recognition by a parent that a child has done something untoward requires role taking, for the parent's interpretation of the child's act requires that the situation in which it occurred be viewed from the latter's perspective. Has a child deliberately broken a rule, or did the forbidden conduct occur by accident? The answer to this question—even the act of raising it—rests on parental role taking, on the imputation of motives to the child, and on the perception of the situation as the child saw it.

One of the less obvious ways people exercise power in everyday life is through their control of the physical setting in which interaction occurs. Role making and role taking do not occur in a vacuum, but in the midst of props, physical objects, machines, locations, buildings, and habitats that have human meaning and usually are human creations. People do not merely interact in social spaces provided by roles, but in banks, stores, homes, physicians' offices, schools, parks, automobiles, beaches, factories, halls, and myriad of other places, each with its objects, colors, sounds, and other physical attributes.

People act in and toward such physical settings to some extent on the basis of habit. That is, they react both to specific places they have been before and to certain colors, sounds, or other aspects of their physical surroundings on the basis of conditioned responses rather than self-consciously. Some people are put at ease by soothing colors and canned music in a dentist's office, made to feel a sense of awe as they sit amidst the grandeur and ritual of a large cathedral, or impelled to feel somber by furnishings, casket, dress, and the serious demeanor of attendants at a funeral home. Even the route by which a person customarily drives to and from work generally is a setting in which many habitual responses occur—stopping at a particular traffic light, for example, or being especially alert at a dangerous intersection.

To the extent that people do respond habitually to certain settings and physical conditions, it follows that whoever has the power to control the physical elements of a situation also has considerable power to control how people in that situation will act. Indeed, this is the rationale that underlies the widespread use of canned music, controlled lighting in factories and offices, and similar practices. To influence conduct, in this view, one must control the stimuli to which people habitually respond.

Although habitual responses doubtless figure to some extent in shaping people's definitions of situations, *interpretations* are of greater importance. The dental patient knows that he or she will soon face discomfort in the dentist's chair, and that no matter how soothing the music might be, it is no substitute for an anesthetic. The congregant participating in a Mass at the Notre Dame Cathedral in Paris sees the same architectural grandeur as the casual tourist, but the former is apt to feel a sense of mystical connection with the deity while the latter keeps quiet out of respect rather than religious devotion. Indeed, social settings of a variety of kinds—medical offices, churches, funeral homes, banks, executive offices—are designed to foster interpretations, and not merely unthinking responses, by those who enter them. The rituals of donning rubber gloves and masks or breaking open packages of sterile instruments in a medical setting have an obvious practical justification—protection of the patient and physician from the transmission of disease. But they also have symbolic import, as means of conveying to patients the *impression* that everything possible is being done to safeguard the patient's health.

Awareness Contexts

Our discussion of social interaction has so far assumed that people present themselves genuinely and role take with reasonable accuracy. For numerous routine situations, it is quite valid to assume that there is no deception and that role taking is generally accurate. Parents and children, doctors and patients, teachers and students—most of these people, most of the time, interact in a context where roles are mutually and accurately understood and taken for granted. People trust others to be who they appear to be, and they act genuinely from the perspectives of their own roles.

Many situations in everyday life, however, are characterized by ignorance, suspicion, or pretense, and not by openness. People deceive one another about their true intentions. Spouses are unfaithful. Seemingly dedicated government employees turn out to be spies. How does social interaction work under such conditions? Do the same fundamental processes of defining the situation, role taking, and role making operate in such contexts?

Barney Glaser and Anselm Strauss approached this topic through the concept of the *awareness context,* which they developed in a study of the interaction between dying patients and their families, physicians, and hospital staff. They defined an awareness context as "the total combination of what each interactant knows about the identity of the other and his own identity in the eyes of the other."[31] In an *open* awareness context, each participant knows the others' true identities—that is, the roles others intend to make in the situation—and his or her own identity in their eyes. In a *closed* awareness context, one interactant is ignorant of either the others' identities or his or her own situated social identity. In *pretense* contexts, interactants are aware of one another's identities but pretend not to be; in *suspicion* contexts, participants suspect that one another's identities are not what they appear to be.

Examples of these awareness contexts in the real world are numerous. When friends suspect one another's loyalty, for example, they are in a suspicion awareness context. A married couple, each of whom is carrying on an affair and knows the other is also doing so, but who pretend that everything is normal, are sustaining a pretense awareness context. The dying patient who does not know about his or her impending death and is not told by family or physician is a part of a closed awareness context.

Description and analysis of awareness context are essential to a full understanding of how people interact and of the outcomes of their interaction. The operations of a confidence scheme, for example, depend on a particular kind of awareness context. From the standpoint of the con artist, the task is to keep the mark unaware of the deception being perpetrated—but also to ensure that the mark is not really a police officer in disguise. Awareness—knowing who knows what about whom—is an object of prime importance to the success of the scheme, whether it involves bilking a widow out of her life savings or persuading a business executive to buy worthless or stolen securities.

In general, when the awareness context is not open, considerable energies are devoted either to opening it up or keeping it closed. Thus, in the hospital context described by Glaser and Strauss, considerable effort goes into the engineering of a closed context by the staff. Physicians and nurses talk to dying patients *as if* they were going to live; they control their outward manner in order to keep from giving away the show; and often they minimize their contacts with the patient so as to reduce the risks of discovery. Moreover, patients who suspect the worst about their true condition may become devoted to the task of discovering their actual prognosis.

Suspicion and pretense awareness contexts represent occasions in which a great deal of interaction is focused on the definition of the situation. Although such situations are marked by doubt or pretense as to whether others are actually who they seem to be, it is more basically the definition of the situation itself that is at issue. If one's partner is a con artist and not a helpful new friend, then one is a victim of a con, not a beneficiary of friendship, and the situation is a con operation, not an exchange of benefits. If one is being conned, one acts toward the object of getting back one's money, or of going to the police while enduring the embarrassment of having been successfully deceived. If one is being helped by a friend, the object is to think of a way to reciprocate. It is the situation, as well as objects and identities, that is being defined.

Awareness contexts constrain interaction. That is, what people know, do not know, suspect, or pretend with respect to one another constrains how they will interact. Wives who suspect their husbands of philandering will concentrate their efforts on discovery and proof. Nurses seeking to deceive a dying patient will guard every word lest they disclose information that would reveal the patient's true condition. Con artists who think the mark may be an undercover police officer will be careful about what they promise. Ignorance, suspicion, and pretense shape definitions of situations and set the conditions within which role making and role taking occur.

Conventional and Interpersonal Roles

A final consideration in our analysis of constraint and social interaction requires a distinction between two fundamentally different kinds of roles. As Tamotsu Shibutani pointed out, people interact with one another in two capacities.[32] On the one hand, they interact on the basis of standardized, known, and labeled positions in various situations. People are mothers, physicians, store clerks, assembly line operators, police officers, men, women, and so on. In the myriad of situations in which people act, they have a grasp of the situations as wholes and of the positions of various participants expressed in terms of such *conventional roles*. Much of our sense of the structure of routine situations in everyday life stems from our capacity to identify one another as acting from the standpoint of such roles.[33]

On the other hand, people do not interact with one another merely as makers of conventional roles, but also as unique human beings. A child does not relate merely to a "mother," but to "my mother"—a specific and in some ways unique human being with whom the child has had sustained contact. When people engage in repeated interaction with one another, networks of interpersonal relationships develop in which people have a sense of mutual position that reflects individual peculiarities and their history of contact with one another. That is, they come to define and make *interpersonal roles*. When two friends meet, each is responsive to a set of expectations, claims, and obligations with respect to the other. Each has a sense of position—and of the structure of the encounter as a whole—that is informed by the interpersonal role of friendship rather than by a particular conventional role.

In some situations, people simultaneously make conventional and interpersonal roles. Parents and children respond to one another on the basis of fairly standardized expectations of how parents and children typically behave. This is especially true of the parents, whose wider experiences have exposed them to general typifications of parental conduct. At the same time, children and parents make and take roles on the basis of a unique set of relationships that build up over time and are a central part of their interaction. Similarly, coworkers in an office make conventional roles assigned to them in the hierarchy of office life; at the same time, they are friends, enemies, rivals, colleagues, lovers, shirkers, stooges, partners, and the like.

The overlay of conventional and interpersonal roles is responsible for some of the complexity of social life. People simultaneously typify one another's acts on the basis of the two sets of roles, and they must decide in any given situation which should be the controlling typification. Is my partner in interaction acting as my enemy? Or as my subordinate? Even though sociologists frequently describe such situations in terms of role conflict or role strain, which presumably people seek to avoid, it should not be supposed that they always attempt to do so. Quite the contrary, such situations provide the basis for office intrigue, warring factions, academic politics, love triangles, and a great many other forms of interaction that, although often painful and embarrassing for people, also add spice to their lives.

Each type of role is constraining, but in a different way. Conventional roles constrain us not only because they pose a set of obligations we must meet but also because they shape our view of social reality. They are the source of our most basic images of social structure and of our location within it. In some instances (e.g., gender roles) conventional roles generally seem to be natural and inevitable features of the social world. Moreover, they are also so deeply merged with the self that they seem to be the essence of the person, as well.[34] Indeed, gender roles can be so constraining that they override other roles in a situation, as, for example, when a male cannot see past gender roles in order to interact appropriately with a female physician or boss.

Interpersonal roles also constrain. Like conventional roles, they present us with duties and obligations—but to individuals rather than to abstract conceptions of what we should or must do. They are likewise sources of our images of social structure. They point to our sense of structure as composed not just of the formally labeled roles of a group or society, but also of the unique way in which, over time, we come to see ourselves in relation to others in that structure.

Keywords

Aligning Actions   Aligning actions are primarily verbal expressions given during interaction to align the substance of the interaction, the selves of the participants, and their shared culture. They include accounts, disclaimers, motive talk, apologies, acclaimers—indeed, any expression that functions to create such an alignment. Although aligning actions are inherently verbal, they are often supported by a rich, nonverbal body language of shrugs, smiles, grimaces, mock cringing, sincere facial expressions, and the like.

Alignment is a metaphor intended to convey something of the complexity of social interaction and of the multiple and sometimes conflicting objects that people confront as they go about their affairs. People sometimes want to do things that would make them ashamed of themselves or cause them to be censured by others. They may desire to cheat on their income taxes or their partners, for example, and dislike their own inclinations even while feeling them intensely. They have such desires or inclinations in part because their culture makes them available to them. The culture of the United States may encourage people to value honesty and fidelity, for example, but it also, in both subtle and obvious ways, rewards those who get away with a well-placed lie or have an extramarital affair. People are also capable of wanting things that defy social expectations simply because they are creatures with selves who are capable of formulating lines of conduct that will accomplish goals on which others would frown. In other words, people are inclined sometimes to break the rules merely because they can.

The result is that people are faced with the dilemma of pursuing their ends, of which they are sometimes ashamed or which may be censured by others, while at the same time maintaining good relations with those others, keeping their self-esteem and identities intact, and making their activities seem sensible and reasonable in cultural terms. Aligning actions are efforts to deal with this kind of dilemma by excusing, redefining, explaining, evading, justifying, and apologizing for one's actions. The philanderer can blame his errant ways on stress or alcohol, apologize to his wife, and promise never to do it again. The tax evader can claim the mistakes were made in the preparation of the return, and the liar can argue that she lied only to protect loved ones from an unpleasant truth or to ensure national security. Culture and the self are satisfied, and life goes on!

Altercasting   Altercasting is the social process in which one person's acts constrain and shape the acts of another by "casting" the other into a role of the altercaster's choosing. Putting others "on the defensive," extracting cooperation and secrets from employees by treating them as special friends or confidants of the boss, and creating the role of the "family scapegoat" are examples of altercasting. In each case, the actions of one or more persons assign a role to the other, and in assigning that role call forth actions commensurate with it. The other feels compelled to defend a position he or she may not really want to defend, the employee feels some obligation to cooperate with a nosy boss, and the scapegoat comes to accept a disproportionate share of the blame for things that go wrong in the family.

Altercasting is a more pervasive feature of social life than its formal definition or these examples may make clear. In part this is because the sociological image of situations and their roles often emphasizes the stability and institutional fixity of roles rather than their sometimes volatile and interpersonally created nature. Parent and child may interact in terms of these formally named **conventional roles** (later defined), but they also form **interpersonal roles** (later defined) that are less the product of standardized expectations and more their own creation. That is, for example, mother and son also may become allies, enemies, or friends, and when they do so it is often because of the efforts of one member of the pair to altercast the other into a new role relationship. Mother may be seeking an ally against an abusive father or a companion in an otherwise lonely life. Indeed, in most situations of social life, people perceive that they can influence the conduct of others by reshaping their role relationships with them, supplementing conventional roles with interpersonal ones.

Awareness Context   The awareness context is the total combination of what participants in a situation know about one another's identities—of what each knows about the identities of others and his or her own identity in the eyes of others. Keep in mind that situated identities are based on the perspectives (roles) on the basis of which people interact. To know, to suspect, to pretend, or not to know who the other is or who one is from the perspective of the other is thus crucial to the interaction that takes place. It not only makes a difference whether the other is a real friend who can be counted on for help or a deceitful individual who tells stories behind one's back but also whether one knows the truth about the other, and for that matter, whether the other knows whether one knows the truth.

Awareness is a property of a situation as a whole rather than of its individual members. In a confidence scheme, for example, where unscrupulous securities dealers strive to rob an elderly widow of her life savings, it is the situation as a whole that is a closed awareness context. The widow does not know she is being cheated—she does not know the securities salesperson is a crook and she does not know she is a victim in the eyes of the salesperson. The latter does know exactly who the victim is, of course, but does not know for sure that the victim is being deceived. The unequal and incomplete distribution of knowledge makes the situation a closed awareness context, and the context as a whole constrains the interaction of all participants. The widow cannot act in her own best interest precisely because she is being

deceived; and the perpetrators of the scheme must exercise caution because they cannot be sure the widow does not know and is not leading them into a trap.

Conventional Roles   Conventional roles are standardized, widely known, and labeled perspectives from which people act in a wide range of situations. These roles are standardized because they have a commonly understood definition and set of associated behaviors and expectations. Most members of the society are aware of the roles and can employ their knowledge of them in role taking, even if they may not enact the roles themselves. These roles have names that are widely recognized. Thus, for example, father, mother, physician, professor, president, lawyer, student, and similar roles are conventional roles.

To say that a **role** (see Keywords in Chapter 2) is conventional is not to say that all who enact the role do so in exactly the same way or that there is universal agreement on how they ought to do so. People's grasp of any role is general enough to encompass considerable variation in its enactment, and even a great deal of disagreement about how it should be enacted. This is because roles provide people with general perspectives from which to act, rather than a specific list of activities or duties. Moreover, roles are known in relation to one another—by definition, a perspective does not stand by itself but is one among several related perspectives from which action can occur. Thus, people understand roles such as parent, child, father, mother, brother, and sister not independently of one another but in relation to one another. There may be wide variation in how people enact these roles, with some siblings expressing and feeling strong obligations to one another and others having more distant relationships. Yet both kinds of siblings would recognize their relationships as brother and sister and agree in many respects on what this relationship entails. Even people who disagree strongly and politically on the mother's role in contemporary society nonetheless recognize the name and the general perspective from which mothers act.

Emergence   Emergence refers to the peculiar yet crucial nature of meaning as something never final or finished but always in the process of being created. Even in defined situations where roles and objects are clearly understood and laid out in advance, meanings are constantly being created, refreshed, and transformed. The work of meaning is never done!

The emergent nature of meaning is crucially important to the symbolic interactionist view of how the social world works, and especially how ongoing interaction works. If social meanings were fixed and final there would be little or no room for variation, change, or novelty in social behavior. People would dutifully do what their roles tell them to do, they would always and invariably do it, and they would not think of changing or even want to do so. But, of course, things do change. People have impulses that make them want to act contrary to the ways their roles encourage them to act. They make mistakes in role taking and so embark on lines of action that others find undesirable, or at least unexpected. They think of new ways of accomplishing familiar tasks.

People are able to behave selfishly, unpredictably, creatively, or mistakenly in part because their conduct is dependent on meaning, rather than being determined by slavish cultural programming. And their selfish, unpredictable, creative, and mistaken conduct makes them even more dependent on meaning, for it gets them into predicaments from which only reconsideration or reformulation of meaning will allow them to escape and opens up opportunities they can only take advantage of by grasping new meanings.

Interpersonal Roles   Interpersonal roles are those perspectives that are created by people who interact repeatedly over a period of time and who come to develop a set of mutual definitions and expectations that depend more on their history of interactions than on conventional expectations. Friends, lovers, allies, and enemies are examples of interpersonal roles. There are some standard ideas about these relationships, for participants in a culture will share some basic ideas about friendship, the conduct of lovers, the nature of alliances, and how to deal with enemies. Such roles differ from **conventional roles** (previously defined), however, because the actual interaction in terms of them depends greatly on the actual pair of individuals involved and the specific relationship they have created. The relationship between, say, student and teacher is conventionalized enough that strangers who have never encountered one another before can interact in terms of these roles. A professor knows how to interact with a new crop of students he or she has never met, and students can deal with a substitute teacher they have never seen.

In contrast, interpersonal roles depend on the unique pair of interactants, and participants are not so interchangeable. If a teacher is absent, the school principal can find a substitute teacher. If a friend is gone, a new friend may be found, but there is no agency that

will find a temporary substitute. Likewise, there are no substitutes for enemies and allies—their relationships of enmity or alliance are based on a specific history of doing one another harm or good.

Norms   Norms are expectations of what ought to be—of how people ought to conduct themselves and what they ought to do or ought not to do. Symbolic interactionists approach norms in an unconventional way, and there are several features of their approach to keep in mind. First, symbolic interactionists tend to take a somewhat ethnomethodological view of norms, regarding them as sense-making devices rather than as guides to behavior. In other words, norms are more likely to be invoked after the fact of behavior in order to make sense of it than before the fact in order to decide what to do. Second, the fit between norms and conduct is a rather loose one. In any given situation, it is possible to invoke a variety of norms to warrant or justify a particular act. Third, symbolic interactionists generally reject the idea that orderly social behavior is maintained because people learn to conform to norms. Orderly behavior depends on the maintenance of meaning in general, and norms are a component of meaning but not its only source nor the sole guarantee of the social order. One of the orientations people can take toward the social world is to live up to the norms it imposes, but this is only one orientation. More commonly, people act on habitual and practical grounds, making sense of the situations they are in and attempting to solve the problems they encounter.

Power   Power is the capacity of one or more people to achieve purposes without the consent of or against the resistance of others. This definition is broad enough that it covers a great variety of forms of power and contexts in which it is exercised. It is also sufficiently broad that it encompasses the specifically symbolic interactionist approach to power as well as the approach of other perspectives.

Virtually every interactionist concept lends itself to inspection in relation to the exercise of power. Control over the definition of the situation and facility in role taking, for example, are sources of power in everyday social interaction. Likewise, awareness context, aligning actions, and emotions provide contexts in which to examine the exercise of power: Manipulating awareness context is a way of controlling others without their assent or even their knowledge. The rhetorical capacity to engage in effective motive talk is a way of gaining legitimacy for actions that would otherwise seem to be unwarranted exercises of power and thus rendering them authoritative. And the capacity to arouse particular emotional states likewise is a resource of power.

Power is a useful concept but a slippery one. The concept is used best when it leads to a careful examination and detailed exposition of the means people employ in various situations to exert control over the behavior of others. The power of professors over students, for example, is analyzed by showing how professors control the selection of reading materials, shape the emotional tone of the classroom, define the situation of interaction with students, establish certain awareness contexts, and engage in altercasting. To explain complex social behavior merely by asserting that one party had the "power" to compel the other to behave in certain ways is to gloss over the actual processes of social interaction and thus to engage in mystification rather than explanation.

Situation   A situation is a container of social interaction, a particular intersection in social time and space of people, objects, and acts, with a name and a shared definition that specifies an expected set and duration of activities. Situations have duration—that is to say, they have beginnings, a timetable of activities, and endings. They have social location, since they exist relative to other situations, and they are generally located within the walls of organizations or the boundaries of groups or other human aggregates. They contain actors and their individual and social acts and objects. They are also defined, which means that people share ideas about what is going on, who is doing it, why they are doing it, when they will stop doing it, and where they are doing it.

Symbolic interactionists often focus on the definition of the situation, since it is the definition that encompasses and predicts the other aspects of the situation from the standpoint of participants. If people define a situation as a cocktail party, it will have cocktail party consequences: They will see other participants as partygoers, perform acts that are performed at cocktail parties, and do so for the two or three hours that cocktail parties generally last.

This emphasis on the definition of the situation should not, however, be allowed to obscure the fundamental importance of the concept of the situation itself. Symbolic interactionists take the position that all

human conduct is situated—that is, anchored in and attached to a situation of some kind. The "situatedness" of conduct is a crucial feature of the interactionist outlook, and one that makes them critical of other sociological and social psychological approaches that gloss over the situation in favor of abstract social forces of one kind or another. Thus, for example, interactionists do not talk vaguely of "power" or "conformity," for the exercise of power or the workings of conformity are themselves situated.

Vocabularies of Motive   A vocabulary of motives is a set of situationally specific terms that may be invoked by people (or imputed to them) in an effort to answer actual or anticipated questions about conduct. The symbolic interactionist view of **motivation** and **motive** (see Keywords in Chapter 3) emphasizes the gap between these terms: Motivation is internal and unconscious; motive is public and verbal. Motives are avowed or imputed, both by self and others, and so a crucial question about motives is how they are chosen or selected. Without denying that motives can occasionally be formulated in a way that approximates internal motivation, symbolic interactionists argue that the choice of motives reflects the available vocabulary of motives. That is, what people say about their own conduct or impute to the conduct of others depends on their social location and on the situation in which the conduct occurs. Different institutional contexts and types of situations make available different vocabularies of motive.

The concept of vocabulary of motives calls attention to the fact that what we say, as well as what we do, has a situated character. From the viewpoint of symbolic interactionists, we cannot explain what people do by appealing to particular or general motives—such as profit or altruism—because their acts are situated and thus explainable on the basis of the meanings available and used in the situation. Likewise, we cannot explain what people say about their conduct merely by assuming that their avowed motives correspond with their real ones, or that their avowed motives are efforts to conceal their real ones. Their motives are as situated as their acts and must be explained on a situated basis. Part of the explanation thus depends on the vocabulary of motives that has come to be accepted in particular situations—religious motives in religious contexts, sexual motives in sexual ones, and altruistic motives in contexts where an altruistic vocabulary of motives is acceptable and expected.

Endnotes

1. The approach to the definition of the situation taken here is influenced by the work of Peter McHugh, *Defining the Situation* (Indianapolis, IN: Bobbs-Merrill, 1968), which in turn depends on George H. Mead, *The Philosophy of the Present* (Chicago: Open Court, 1932) for its emphasis on emergence and relativity.

2. George H. Mead, *The Philosophy of the Act* (Chicago: University of Chicago Press, 1938), pp. 6ff.

3. See Joan P. Emerson, "Nothing Unusual Is Happening" in *Human Nature and Collective Behavior: Papers in Honor of Herbert Blumer*, ed. Tamotsu Shibutani (Englewood Cliffs, NJ: Prentice-Hall, 1970).

4. McHugh, *Defining the Situation* (Note 1).

5. See McHugh, *Defining the Situation* (Note 1); Harold Garfinkel, *Studies in Ethnomethodology* (Englewood Cliffs, NJ: Prentice-Hall, 1867); and Alfred Schutz, *On Phenomenology and Social Relations*, ed. Helmut Wagner (Chicago: University of Chicago Press, 1970).

6. See Schutz, *On Phenomenology and Social Relations*, pp. 111–122 (Note 5).

7. See Gregory P. Stone, "Appearance and the Self: A Slightly Revised Version," in *Social Psychology through Symbolic Interaction*, 2nd ed., eds. Gregory P. Stone and Harvey A. Farberman (New York: Wiley, 1981), pp. 187–202.

8. See Peter Berger and Thomas Luckmann, *The Social Construction of Reality* (Garden City, NY: Doubleday Anchor, 1967), pp. 42ff.

9. See Randall Stokes and John P. Hewitt, "Aligning Actions," *The American Sociological Review* 46 (October 1976): 838–849.

10. Stokes and Hewitt, "Aligning Actions" (Note 9).

11. C. Wright Mills, "Situated Actions and Vocabularies of Motive," in Stone and Farberman, *Social Psychology*, p. 326 (Note 7).

12. John P. Hewitt and Randall G. Stokes, "Disclaimers," *The American Sociological Review* 40 (February 1975): 1–11.

13. Marvin Scott and Stanford M. Lyman, "Accounts," *The American Sociological Review* 33 (December 1968): 46–62.

14. Christopher H. Hunter has extended the concept and classified the forms of aligning actions. See his "Aligning Actions: Types and Social Distribution," *Symbolic Interaction* 7 (Fall 1984): 155–174.

15. See Nicholas Tavuchis, *Mea Culpa: A Sociology of Apology and Reconciliation* (Stanford, CA: Stanford University Press, 1991).

16. Hunter, "Aligning Actions: Types and Social Distribution," pp 157–158 (Note 14).

17. See Barry Schlenker, "Impression Management," *The Self Concept, Social Identity, and Interpersonal Relations* (Monterey, CA: Brooks-Cole, 1980).

18. See Kathy Charmaz, *The Social Reality of Death* (Reading, MA: Addison-Wesley, 1980).

19. See Dale A. Lund, Michael S. Caserta, Margaret F. Dimond, and Robert M. Gray, "Impact of Bereavement on the Self-Conceptions of Older Surviving Spouses," *Symbolic Interaction* 9 (Fall 1986): 235–244.

20. Lyn H. Lofland, "The Social Shaping of Emotion: The Case of Grief," *Symbolic Interaction* 8 (Fall 1985): 175.

21. Ibid.

22. See Robert I. Levy, *The Tahitians* (Chicago: University of Chicago Press, 1973).

23. The phrase and elements of this analysis are drawn from Arlie R. Hochschild, "Emotion Work, Feeling Rules, and Social Structure," *American Journal of Sociology* 85 (November 1979): 551–575.

24. See Candace Clark, "Sympathy Biography and Sympathy Margin," *American Journal of Sociology* 93 (September 1987): 290–321; and Clark, *Misery and Company: Sympathy in Everyday Life* (Chicago: University of Chicago Press, 1997).

25. See Arlie R. Hochschild, *The Managed Heart: Commercialization of Human Feeling* (Berkeley: University of California Press, 1983). See also Hochschild, *The Second Shift: Working Parents and the Revolution at Home* (New York: Viking-Penguin, 1989), and Hochschild, "Ideology and Emotion Management: A Perspective and Path for Future Research," in *Research Agendas in the Sociology of Emotions,* ed. Theodore D. Kemper (Albany: State University of New York Press, 1990), pp. 117–142. For a discussion of ways the concept of emotions contributes to sociological explanation, see J. M. Barbalet, *Emotion, Social Theory, and Social Structure: A Macrosociological Approach* (Cambridge: Cambridge University Press, 1998). For a historical analysis of changing standards of emotional expression in the United States, see Peter N. Stearns,

American Cool: Constructing a Twentieth Century Emotional Style (New York: New York University Press, 1994).

26. See Eugene Weinstein and Paul Deutschberger, "Some Dimensions of Altercasting," *Sociometry* 26 (December 1963): 545–566.

27. Peter M. Hall, "A Symbolic Interactionist Analysis of Politics," *Sociological Inquiry* 42 (1–2)(1972): 35–75.

28. See Alvin W. Gouldner, "The Norm of Reciprocity: A Preliminary Statement," *The American Sociological Review* 25 (February 1960): 161–178.

29. For an analysis of various processes of power, see Peter M. Hall, "Asymmetric Relationships and Processes of Power," in *Foundations of Interpretive Sociology: Original Essays in Symbolic Interaction. Studies in Symbolic Interaction,* Supplement 1, eds.

Harvey A. Farberman and R. S. Perinbanayagam (New Haven, CT: JAI Press, 1985), pp. 309–344.

30. See Darwin L. Thomas, David Franks, and J. Calonico, "Role-taking and Power in Social Psychology," *The American Sociological Review* 7 (October 1972): 605–614.

31. Barney G. Glaser and Anselm L. Strauss, "Awareness Contexts and Social Interaction," in Stone and Farberman, *Social Psychology,* pp. 53–63 (Note 7).

32. See Tamotsu Shibutani, *Society and Personality* (Englewood Cliffs, NJ: Prentice-Hall, 1961), pp. 324–331.

33. Ralph H. Turner, "The Role and the Person," *American Journal of Sociology* 84 (July 1978): 1–23.

34. For empirical studies, see Louis Zurcher, *Social Roles: Conformity and Creativity* (Beverly Hills, CA: Sage, 1983).

Chapter 5

Social Psychology and Social Order

The preceding chapters developed a symbolic interactionist theory of conduct that emphasizes both self and the situated nature of social interaction. But the situations in which selves are created and in which conduct is formed are embedded in a larger framework of people, groups, organizations, social classes, institutions, and society as a whole. These larger units, many of which are removed in time and distance from the immediate situation, nevertheless have a significant influence on what people do. Our task in this chapter is to link situated conduct to the social order that lies beyond the immediate situation.

In our everyday lives we take the existence of a more or less orderly social world for granted. We belong to social groups, identify with various communities, and engage in a variety of familiar activities. Groups may welcome or reject us, communities provide solid or fragile supports for the self, and the activities in which we participate seem rewarding or punishing. The social order itself may seem just or unjust, and it may be peaceful or conflict laden. Nonetheless, it is something external to us, a seemingly natural feature of the way things are. It is just there.

Sociologists seek to explain what we in our everyday lives take for granted. How is organized social life possible? What is the nature of social order? How do groups, communities, and society itself come into existence? How do the activities of interacting individuals produce these larger social units? How do these larger realities, in turn, constrain the conduct of interacting individuals?

Symbolic interactionists have proposed two complementary answers to such questions:

- *Social order is a constructed reality.* A more or less orderly and predictable social world arises out of the naming, classifying, and discursive activities of participants.
- *Social order is the result of social coordination.* Social order arises from the self-conscious efforts of people to coordinate their activities.

To characterize these answers as complementary is to say that both social construction and social coordination are involved in the creation and maintenance of social order. On one hand, social order is a social object—that is, something indicated and talked about as people go about their everyday lives. On the other hand, it is at the same time a product of their interaction, a result of the fact that they take one another into account as they pursue their individual and joint goals.

Social Order as a Constructed Reality

From the standpoint of its individual members, a society is a thing with an existence independent of themselves, even though its continued being depends very much on them and their behavior. The society has a name—the United States, Canada, India—that established its corporate existence, and it is thought by its members to possess a more or less distinctive way of life expressed in its values, practices, beliefs, and political institutions. For the most part, the society to which any of us belongs appears as a massive, durable, and given part of the world, a reality taken for granted as we go about everyday life. It is there when we are born, it affects our life chances for better or worse, and it will continue to exist after we are dead.

A society, in short, is an *object* toward which its members act, and to a great extent, the fact of social order is simply the fact that people act toward and so constitute this object in a stable, orderly fashion. Thus, for example, Americans act toward the United States in a variety of ways that serve to constitute it as a stable, persisting object. Reciting the Pledge of Allegiance, arguing about the role of the United States in the Middle East, talking about what is wrong with this country, or extolling "the American way of life" in political speeches—all are ways in which people constitute and act toward a particular kind of object, a nation-state. It is, in large part, their acting toward it that defines it, constitutes it, and causes it to persist.

What is true of a society as a whole also is true of the smaller groups, organizations, communities, institutions, and other units that make it up. The orderly and stable existence and persistence of these units depends in part on the fact that people act toward them as objects. General Motors, the city of New York, the American Medical Association, the institution of the family as well as any particular family group, the friends of Joe Smith who lives in Peoria—all are more or less stable and orderly social units within the larger society. To be sure, their existence depends on people coordinating their conduct in particular situations. Five days a week Joe Smith goes to work in a factory that produces parts for automobiles manufactured by General Motors (GM). That he does so is one key basis of GM's continued existence, but the corporate giant also continues to exist because Joe Smith and others like him act toward it as an object. They talk about what GM will do in the upcoming contract negotiations or how many workers it will lay off if sales do not improve. They conceive of it sometimes as very much a threat or as an omnipresent force controlling their lives, and they hate it or feel loyal to it. So, too, Joe Smith's family and circle of friends persist because he and they act toward one another in certain ways at particular times—but also because they are conscious of being a family or a group of friends and so constitute themselves as social objects.

Talking

One of the key ways the members of a society constitute and uphold the social order is by talking about it. Everyday life is filled with occasions when people simply talk to one another, situations in which the chief social object is conversation. Chance encounters, coffee breaks, cocktail parties, formal conferences and seminars, speeches, religious gatherings, radio and television talk shows and interviews, informal get-togethers, and numerous other contexts are marked by the fact that talking is the central and most observable form of behavior.

These encounters may seem sociologically unimportant, for they sometimes appear to their participants merely as devices for passing time and thus as unrelated to the real work of society. We are prone to think that what really matters sociologically are actual transactions between buyers and sellers in the marketplace and not what people say to one another about the high cost of housing or health care. Talk is so commonplace that we tend to regard it as nothing more than a reflection of more important processes and developments. After all, we might say, what counts is not what people say about a candidate or about the electoral process but whether and how they actually vote on election day.

Talk may be cheap, but it is nonetheless sociologically important. Its very ubiquity makes it an important part of the cement that binds the social order. Whatever the situations in which it occurs, talk is a primary means by which people sustain the world of objects in which they live. This is especially true of abstract objects—such as institutions, groups, values, principles, organizations, and the society as a whole—for we do not experience these abstract objects in quite the same way we do more tangible things. One can touch a chair and act toward it by sitting in it or using it as a footrest. But people experience and act toward abstract objects, such as institutions, groups, and values, primarily by talking about them.

Talk thrives on problems. One of the most common forms of talk, for example, takes the form of complaints, griping, and expressions of disaffection. The state of the economy, terrorism, the presumed decline of the family, the corruption of politics, the faults of ethnic groups other than one's own, the disloyalties of supposed friends, the difficulties people have with their cars and appliances, the high cost of medical care—such complaints about life constitute a major topic of conversation, debate, and disagreement. People may occasionally say that the world is a delightful and perfect place, but they spend much of their conversational time talking about problems, troubles, difficulties, and disasters.

Talk shapes our view of social order, but people obviously do not discuss problems for the sake of social order. People gripe, gossip, criticize one another, worry about conspiracies, argue, and in other ways confront the problems they face, not in order to construct social reality, but simply because they face real or imaginary problems. Other people do nasty things, ambition and effort go unrewarded, children misbehave, and employers and teachers treat us unfairly. In dealing with and especially talking about these matters, we give shape and substance to our ideals, our values, and our conceptions of how things work in the society and how we think they should work.

The way people talk about problematic events and situations is culturally and historically variable. One culture, for example, may encourage people to keep a stoic silence about personal problems, while another may encourage discourse about them. And a single culture may present different faces at different times. In the 1950s, for example, a number of books and articles appeared that expressed concern about a growing tendency in the United States toward conformity. Scholars such as David Riesman wrote books about the decline of *inner-direction* and the rise of *other-direction.* By the 1970s and 1980s, the attention of social critics shifted to *narcissism,* and they worried that Americans were becoming too wrapped up in themselves, too selfish, too inattentive to the needs and interests of others. Although there is no evidence that the culture itself changed dramatically over the intervening years, the way in which some social critics perceived problems did change. The focus of their discourse, however, remained on the problematic relationship between the person and the social order.[1]

Although variable from one era to another and from one society to another, the propensity to talk about the problematic is itself inherently human. It is when a line of conduct is blocked that the distinctively human capacity for its conscious, deliberate control comes to the fore. People tend to take their activities for granted until something interferes with their capacity to attain their goals. They are apt to talk about the high cost of medical care when they experience it or see others whose savings have been eaten away by a major illness. They are apt to talk about the state of the economy when their aspirations for a better standard of living seem thwarted. Under such circumstances, talk is a major way by which people attempt to restore their lines of conduct or redefine their goals.

People do not talk only about problems, of course, nor merely about the present. Often they talk about the past—about important events, fond memories, places they used to live or work, their travels, and other matters in the recent or distant past. Such talk is also significant in constructing the social order and linking the person to it.[2]

A common way Americans talk about the past is by labeling decades and generations. Decade labeling entails naming calendar decades and assigning dominant or significant characteristics to them.[3] The "Roaring Twenties," the "Turbulent 60s," and the "Me Decade" of the 1970s are examples of this practice of decade labeling from the twentieth century. The first decade of the twenty-first century has yet to earn such a label. Generally led by the mass media, people attribute distinctive qualities and characteristics to calendar decades. Thus, the 1950s are portrayed as a decade of boring conformity, the 1960s as a decade of social turbulence and upheaval, and the 1970s as a decade of excessive self-preoccupation. Likewise, generations acquire names and characteristics: The "selfish" and "self-centered" *Baby Boomers* were born during the considerable rise in birth rates that started in 1946, just after the end of World War II, and lasted until the beginning of the 1960s. The supposedly "aimless" and "bored" members of *Generation X* are said to have been born anywhere from the late 1960s to the 1980s, for there is no widely agreed definition of this generation. And there is a more recently minted *Generation Y,* with as yet undetermined psychological characteristics, said to be the children of *Baby Boomers.*

The significance of these categories lies in the characteristics *imputed* to them. Labels for decades and generations provide what sociologist Fred Davis has called a "moral narrative." Thus, the "boring" and "conformist" decade of the 1950s is held in popular discourse to have been followed by the social protests of the 1960s, when people are thought to have rejected the materialism and conformity of the previous decade for serious efforts to make the society better. Later decades were constructed as those in which people withdrew from social concerns and turned exclusively to the pursuit of their own well-being or that of their families. Whatever the reality of these decades—and it is far more complex than the labels imply—discourse about them emphasizes important values, beliefs, and aspirations of members of the society.

Explaining Disorder

In addition to talking about problems or about the past, people also talk about social order itself, largely by trying to *explain* disorder. In a common type of everyday conversation, people try to explain to their own satisfaction the causes of a problematic situation, whether it is one in which they are participants or one they observe from a distance. Such situations take many forms, but they have in common the fact that people see them as problematic. A married couple who quarrel repeatedly; a riot or some other disturbance; the delinquency of one's own or a neighbor's child; seemingly inexplicable, bizarre conduct by a public official—each of these situations may be viewed as problematic by somebody, and each may be the topic of a conversation in which people seek to explain the nature and causes of the problematic occurrence or situation.

What makes a situation as a whole problematic? One mark of a problematic situation is that people see it as *disorderly,* as somehow falling outside the usual bounds of social experience. In nonproblematic situations, social order is taken for granted—the situation is defined well enough that people are able to interact more or less routinely, even when some untoward event occurs that merits an account or a disclaimer. Problematic situations, in contrast, are those in which social order no longer is taken for granted. The definition of the situation as a whole is called into question and viewed as requiring special effort to comprehend and define what is taking place.

Not all problematic situations elicit efforts to explain what has gone wrong. A crowd that gathers on a street corner, for example, represents a problematic situation to a police officer, who must define the situation in order to decide what action to take. A sudden disturbance and rush toward the exits of a large auditorium likewise is a problematic situation to those present, who must define it in order to know whether to call the police or fire department or whether to leave the building or merely return quietly to their seats. In situations such as these, people define the situation in order to act in it, and explanations are of secondary importance.

People construct explanations when their chief focus is on disorder itself, which they perceive exists when they cannot make sense of a situation in terms of their customary stock of knowledge. In making sense of one another's acts, people ordinarily rely on their conceptions of typicality, probability, causality, means–ends relationships, normative requirements, and substantive congruency. In role making, for example, the stock of knowledge enables people to know what is expected of them and how others will respond to their conduct; in the giving of accounts and disclaimers, the stock of knowledge guides the selection of a disclaimer or the framing of an account. Social disorder exists when the usual processes of motive talk, accounting, and disclaiming do not sufficiently restore routine—when people persist in behaving in an undesirable way, for example, despite the fact that they have repeatedly been called to account for their conduct, or when they persist in behaving in ways that seem unlikely to lead to the goals they say they have.

So defined, social disorder is a construction of reality, a belief that things are, for some reason, not working the way they usually are thought to work, or a perception that something is amiss in social relations. A married couple, for example, may find themselves quarreling so frequently that the arguments themselves become a matter of concern to others as well as to themselves. The frequent quarrels may be viewed as strange in several different ways—as atypical of this couple, for example, considering their past history of marital adjustment; as harmful to their children; or as improbable in light of their recent accomplishments and successes. On whatever grounds the perception of disorder is based, the effect is to impel a search for an explanation—for some convincing statement of how this problem has been produced and what is likely to remedy the situation.

Quasi theorizing is a name for one process in which people construct such explanations.[4] It is a peculiar kind of explanatory process, however, for it runs counter to our commonsense notions about how we should find explanations. Ordinarily, people begin with something to be explained and then seek a plausible account of its causes. In quasi theorizing, however, people tend to identify the cause *before* the effect and to construct the reality of the latter in terms of the former. In other words, they perceive a set of conditions that match the cause they have settled on, rather than finding a cause that can account for an observed set of conditions.

Consider the case of our quarreling couple. At a certain point in their relationship, they may have come to the realization that they argue too much, that they do not very much like this state of affairs, and that something ought to be done. Having arrived at the point where they view their arguments as problematic, they seek to construct an explanation, a process that occurs in a series of steps. First, they agree on a *solution* to their problem. "We have to learn to communicate better," one may say. This statement is a tentative basis on which to construct the reality of their problem. If the other agrees, perhaps saying, "You're right, because sometimes I don't think you understand what I'm talking about," we have the beginnings of a quasi theory of communication as an explanation of their discord. In the next phase of the process, the reality of their problem is perceived in terms that mirror the solution on which they have agreed. In developing a quasi theory of communication, people will say that most of their disagreements *really* are problems of communication and understanding, that the issues about which they have quarreled—money, sex, life-style, and so on—really are superficial, and that when the problem of learning to understand one another's views is solved, the things on which they agree will outweigh the few matters on which they still disagree. At some point in their discussion, they will invoke generalizations about the importance of communications in human affairs: "Most disagreements are caused by failures of communication," they may say, thus effectively subsuming their particular case under a more general rule.

At this point, the participants are likely to buttress their explanation in two additional ways. First, the couple may begin to rewrite their past history of quarrels, reinterpreting them in the light of the new insight about communication. They will look to the past and find examples of other quarrels in which they thought they understood one another's points of view, but in fact did not. Second, they will introduce other values and beliefs in support of the explanation. They may agree, for example, that since they have remained together despite their quarreling, it must mean that they are really alike and in agreement, that they really belong together, and that their communication problem is only temporary.

Quasi theorizing thus produces an explanation of social disorder. It is a hopeful explanation (from the perspective of its creators) since it holds out the possibility that the disorder will yield to order if the solution is applied. It is not merely an explanation, of course, for in the process of explaining social disorder the quasi theory also *creates* its reality. The situation of the married couple is transformed from an undesirable and disorderly condition of too many quarrels into one of unnecessary quarrels caused by failure to communicate.

Paradoxically, the focus on explaining social disorder found in such forms of talk as quasi theorizing plays a role in sustaining a sense of social order, for it is in such problematic situations that important parts of the social stock of knowledge are given new life and sustained in memory. Such talk affords an opportunity for the standards of social order to be exercised, for familiar aphorisms to be used and once again proven "correct," and for important beliefs and values to be affirmed. Distinctions between right and wrong, the typical and the atypical, the desirable and the undesirable are preserved by *use,* and so it might be argued that occasional failures in social order play a positive role in its maintenance by affording such opportunities.[5]

Quasi theories, along with disclaimers, accounts, and other aligning actions discussed in the previous chapter, are also an important means whereby the members of a society reaffirm and preserve their culture—that is, the world of objects in which they live and with which they must contend. When people explain disorder, give accounts, or use disclaimers, they attend to and thus also reaffirm important cultural objects. For example, the value placed on honesty is reaffirmed by an attempt to explain why a child is persistently dishonest; likewise, an excuse or apology for dishonesty calls attention to honesty and asserts its significance. When people verbalize their values through aligning actions, they act toward them as objects and thus bring them to life even in circumstances where conduct has violated them. As a result, these objects continue to form part of the landscape—part of what people notice, attend to, feel they must respect, and take into account in their conduct.

The social construction of social order depends on this continual reaffirmation of culture. A sense of social order depends on people's capacity to coordinate their conduct or on their ability to understand and remedy the occasional problematic situation. It also ultimately relies on the conviction that there is a reasonably stable reality that they can take for granted. Humans seem to want not only the sense that they can predict one another's conduct but also the sense that the world is a more or less familiar and stable place. To construct social reality, therefore, they must continually reaffirm culture.

Social Problems

Talk about disorder and problems is not limited to day-to-day occurrences in which people construct explanations of problematic situations. There is a larger, more macroscopic way in which social reality is constructed through discourse about *social problems.* A social problem may be defined as a collective object of concern, a condition felt to pertain to society as a whole or to important parts of it and believed to be both undesirable and changeable. Such a collective construction of reality defines some condition—such as divorce, crime, homelessness, or child abuse—as a serious problem worthy of attention by officials, the media, and the public. Definitions of specific conditions as social problems are advanced from time to time by various social groups, and they tend to demand and get a great deal of attention for a period of time before the public focus shifts to some other problem.[6]

Collective definitions of social problems do not arise simply in response to objective social conditions. There have long been poor and homeless people in the United

States, for example, as well as child abusers and governmental officials who accept bribes to influence their decisions. Conditions such as these are "discovered" from time to time—or not, as is often the case—and as attention to one problem diminishes, another is discovered to take its place. Thus, for example, poverty was rediscovered as a social problem during the 1960s, the environment came to be a focus of attention during the 1970s, and various forms of drug abuse have clamored for priority during and since the 1980s.

To point to this parade of social problems is not to deny their reality, nor to be callous to the pain and suffering of the afflicted. Poverty, environmental decay, homelessness, and child abuse are by no means figments of the collective imagination. But social conditions are subject to many layers of definition and interpretation. Problem definitions thus tend to undergo change as well as to be matters of intense social controversy. Poverty was once widely viewed as a moral failing of the poor, a condition resulting from sloth and indolence. Later, the poor were seen as culturally deprived, unable to take advantage of opportunities because they lacked knowledge or cultural skills. More recently, barriers to opportunity such as racism, social class discrimination, or limited access to education, jobs, and housing have been emphasized. These contrasting views still contend for priority in the public arena.

Social problems are the focus of attention and action in several ways. Intellectuals and scientists theorize about them and conduct research. Government agencies are legislated into existence in order to deal with them. They become important political symbols, usually lending themselves to diverse uses in the arena of political debate. At times, social problems take on a nearly universal symbolic value, appearing almost everywhere in society. Whether the object is the environment, child abuse, or homelessness, it is a ubiquitous social presence. The nightly news is filled with talk about the problem of drugs and proposals to wage war on it. Governmental units such as the Environmental Protection Agency become the focus for the discussion of environmental issues. Political debate focuses on the urgent need for action to deal with problems, such as poverty or homelessness, and charges of inaction or overreaction fly back and forth. Advertisers promote "natural foods" and put pictures of missing children on milk cartons.

Social problems come into existence when claims makers are successful in promoting their view that a particular social condition is a problem. A claims maker is anyone who acts to focus public attention on a condition by publicizing it through books, speeches, or television appearances, promoting legislation to deal with it, raising funds to support organizations that emphasize the importance of solving the problem or do research to find solutions, or engaging in collective actions, such as "take back the night" marches by women's groups. Claims makers rely heavily on the mass media of communication, seeking out sympathetic reporters who can be expected to write supportive stories, staging events that will be reported on television news, or appearing on television morning news programs or talk shows. It may not be an exaggeration to suggest that a social problem does not have legitimacy in U.S. society until the media have granted it their seal of approval.[7] The War on Drugs waged by several U.S. presidents relies heavily on media coverage of the drug menace, of efforts to rid neighborhoods of "crack houses" or meth labs, and of the activities of the federal "drug czar." Television news reports help make drug use a bona fide social problem deserving of serious public and official attention.

Sometimes collective efforts to define social problems focus on the basic institutions of a society—alleging, for example, that poverty exists because it is in the interest of an exploitative capitalist class to perpetuate poverty and thus keep wages low, or that resource depletion and environmental degradation are caused by a wasteful system of production that must continually expand if it is not to collapse. More typically, however, people reject social problems claims that attribute causality to basic social institutions, preferring to focus on relatively superficial aspects of underlying conditions and to ignore the possibility that inherent faults of the social order are responsible for the problem. Thus, poverty is seen as society's failure to include everybody in its opportunity structure rather than as a basic feature of the operation of the social system.

Although social problems seem to focus on social failings and to generate considerable controversy, they also and somewhat paradoxically offer a basis for consensus on what society should ideally be. To agree that child abuse is an evil that ought to be eliminated is, of course, to admit that society is not all that it could be, but it is also to specify what a good society should be. However it is defined in relation to a specific social problem, the good society is an idealization of social order, a collective vision of the kind of society to be sought. Social problems thus provide at least the potential for unifying diverse interests, ideas, and aspirations.

Social problems reflect more consensus on ends, however, than on means. It is easier to achieve agreement that the environment should be protected or that homelessness should be ended than on how to achieve such goals. But the lack of consensus on means is partly what gives the problem its unifying effect. If people disagree on what will solve the problem, then each person can identify his or her conduct as a potential solution. Toyota can point to its hybrid gas-electric automobile, while the average citizen takes pride in efforts to recycle.

Widespread discourse about social problems contributes in one additional way to a conception of society as an orderly and predictable place. The conditions around which conceptions of social problems are built—drugs, crime, violence, urban decay, pollution, homelessness, and the like—are reminders that the world is an uncertain and sometimes hostile place, and that the human capacity to mold the physical and social environment is limited. Such conditions threaten to undermine the human sense of purpose, control, and meaning. The inherent optimism of social problems definitions—the belief that solutions can be found—is a means of reaffirming faith in human control. We treat crime and pollution as problems, organizing actions against them, not only because they are objectively harmful but also because our strategies of control and solution help to preserve a belief in human mastery over the world.

A social problems conception of environmental problems, for example, helps to preserve faith in the power of technology. It is because of human technological prowess that some environmental problems, such as air pollution and resource depletion, exist. At the same time, such environmental problems lend themselves to the belief that they are amenable to technological solutions. Resource depletion? Pollution? Invent processes that will use abundant resources (e.g., cheap energy from the sun) and that will control and render harmless (or, better, recycle) wastes now dumped into rivers. Such technological fixes to environmental problems may or may not succeed. They clearly do, however, help to sustain a conception of human beings as masters of their world, so technologically competent as to be able to endanger the environment, but also powerful enough to repair the damage they have done.

Social Order as Coordinated Activity

Social order is created as people talk about it and act toward it, but it is also achieved as they strive to coordinate their conduct and produce the great variety of joint activities that make up the society. We can describe several ways in which people coordinate their social activities and thus produce the social world in which they live.[8] The countless situations in people's everyday lives, even of those who do not know one another and are separated by time and space, are nevertheless sewn together into a complex social fabric. We cannot fully describe it here, but we can examine some of the ways in which this social coordination is achieved. The overall image on which we will rely is derived from the work of Herbert Blumer.

Consider such varied activities as banking transactions, religious services, lectures, wars, and congressional debates. Each of these is what Herbert Blumer has called a *joint action*—an organization of several different acts of many participants into a single whole. A joint action,

> *while made up of diverse component acts that enter into its formation, is different from any of them and from their mere aggregation. The joint action has a distinctive character in its own right, a character that lies in the articulation or linkage as apart from what may be articulated or linked. Thus the joint action may be identified as such and may be spoken of and handled without having to break it down into the separate acts that comprise it.*[9]

A lecture to a university class, for example, consists of many articulated acts of a professor and several students—speaking, listening, taking notes, asking questions, answering questions, and the like. The identifying mark of the joint action we call a "lecture" is not any one of the specific acts in which individuals engage, but their articulation with one another in a particular defined situation.

Just as we (both as social scientists and as participants in social activities) can speak of various joint actions and thus constitute them as objects in our experience, we similarly can speak of and constitute the collectivities that engage in such joint actions. We speak of bankers and their customers, priests and congregants, professors and students, the Iranian Army, the United States Congress, workers at Microsoft, or John Jones's family, each of which is a named collectivity comprised of, but also more than, the individuals that make it up. Just as the interlinkage of individual acts is what constitutes a joint action, so the interlinkage of individuals, rather than the specific persons themselves, is what constitutes a collectivity.

From the perspective of symbolic interactionists, society consists of extended interlinkages of joint actions and collectivities in which diverse people and activities are interconnected over space and time. If we examine a society as a whole, we find that banking transactions, religious services, university lectures, wars, congressional debates, and other joint actions, along with the collectivities in which they take place, are linked with one another in complex and highly systematic ways, whether viewed at a particular point in the history of a society or over the course of its development from one time to another. Economic, religious, educational, military, and political institutions—each of which is itself a complex network of joint actions—are related to one another in a variety of ways. Religious beliefs justify economic activities, for example, and political affairs are influenced by military activity.

How is this complex of joint actions, collectivities, and institutions held together? How are the activities of one sector coordinated with those of another? What makes for the seeming persistence of patterned and stable joint actions, collectivities, and institutions over time? The coordination of a whole society and its component parts and activities is a topic that lies well beyond the scope of social psychology. We can approach these questions by considering the basic social processes through which social coordination is accomplished. From a social psychological point of view, the social bond, problem solving, negotiated order, horizontal and vertical linkages, careers, boundaries, and social movements are particularly useful concepts with which to study social coordination.

Creating Social Bonds

A fundamental way social activities are coordinated is through the establishment of stable interpersonal attachments, or *social bonds*. Thomas Scheff argued that the main quest that underlies human actions is the maintenance of intact, healthy social bonds. In Scheff's view, the need for social bonds is never completely filled and may be uniquely frustrated in contemporary society.[10] Although symbolic interactionists refuse to assign priority to any single motive or motivation, it is nonetheless clear that social bonds are crucial to the coordination of social life. Human beings seem to develop a web of social bonds—to feel a sense of attachment and belonging to several other people who are themselves interconnected.

A healthy social bond, Scheff says, is one that balances the needs of the individual and those of the group. On the one hand, social bonds involve closeness as well as knowledge of the point of view of the other. Bonds of friendship or those between siblings, for example, entail a sense of intimacy between people and mindfulness of the other's values and beliefs. On the other hand, social bonds also require differentiation, which is the capacity to recognize the other as a separate being, different from one while at the same time connected to one. A healthy bond between parent and child, for example, requires that each respect the other's differences and separate being even while feeling a sense of closeness.

The balance between closeness and distance is crucial to Scheff's theory of the social bond. If there is too much closeness, the individual suffers at the expense of the group. In a family whose members define loyalty to the family in terms of conformity to its opinions and practices, the child who believes or acts differently is seen as betraying the family. In such a family, members feel "engulfed," lacking space to breathe or to be in the slightest way different. If, however, there is too little closeness, then the group suffers because there is nothing to hold it together. Individuals suffer, as well, for there is nothing to bind the individual member to others. Parents and siblings are apt to feel isolated and unable to communicate across the spaces that separate them.

Human social bonds must be constantly tested and renewed, for they do not endure merely through inertia or because of built-in genetic mechanisms. Each encounter with another provides an opportunity for the bond to be strengthened, repaired, or undermined. A married couple, for example, does not form a bond that subsequently maintains itself without help. Rather, each occasion of interaction between them—at the dinner table, working side by side in the yard, at a party with friends, or in the bedroom—is an occasion in which the bond is weakened or strengthened.

The basis for a social bond is each member's recognition of the other as a legitimate participant—as someone who belongs and has the right to be interacting with the other. This mutual granting (or withholding) of legitimacy involves both actions and feelings. The members of a bond coordinate their actions, often harmoniously, but sometimes in conflict. Adult children cooperate in caring for their aging and infirm parents, for example, although sometimes they disagree about what should be done. Their actions, cooperative or not, legitimate the presence and participation of the other. Participants in a social bond also demonstrate feelings toward one another—respect for one another's contributions, admiration of the other's special abilities, and, sometimes, disapproval of the other's actions. A social bond and the activities that take place within it thus constantly generate feelings of pride and shame. A feeling that one is a legitimate member of a bond generates feelings of pride; a sense that one has let the other down creates shame.

Social bonds provide not only motivation but also some of the most important contexts within which human social activities are coordinated. Much of what people do they do with friends, family, coworkers, and others with whom they develop attachments. Over time, these attachments produce interpersonal roles that shape people's conduct toward one another as well as their identities. Nonetheless, contemporary people also live in a more impersonal social world in which they interact with others whom they scarcely know and with whom they feel no direct bonds. As we will see, then, the establishment of social bonds is only a part of the story of social coordination.

Solving Problems

Sociologists generally emphasize the patterned and repetitive nature of social life, stressing that the vast majority of problems that arise in everyday social life have predetermined solutions, which have been found by previous generations and codified in the social stock of knowledge. In this view, the typifications, causal propositions, and other forms of knowledge we discussed in Chapter 4 are more or less routinely applied, and nothing much is new or different in day-to-day life.

If any activity could be accurately so characterized, it would occur in the small and isolated societies of the past in which there was a relatively stable relationship between people and their environment, few options for individuals to depart from routine patterns of behavior, and few events that might disrupt everyday routine. There is considerable doubt that any society has ever been quite so stable; certainly modern societies are not. It is clearly more accurate to portray contemporary U.S. society, for example, as one in which people confront a series of problematic situations in which they must be inventive than as one dominated by numbing routine. Much of modern life is not clearly and routinely prescribed, but is, instead, left open and negotiable. As Blumer argued, these areas of "unprescribed conduct are just as natural, indigenous, and recurrent in human group life as are those areas covered by pre-established and faithfully followed prescriptions of joint action."[11]

Symbolic interactionists see a problem-solving orientation as inherent in the symbolic organization of human conduct. Because people are not tied to a limited set of responses to an environment, but must instead interpret their world in order to respond creatively to it, the world is inherently open rather than closed and susceptible to definition in terms of the problematic rather than fixed and immutable. A moment's reflection will suggest the extent to which attention to problems is a constant feature of everyday life. Those occasions on which activities are utterly routine are few and far between. More commonly, problems of diverse kinds arise and are solved in everyday activities. Cars do not start, people fail to show up for meetings, tasks seem difficult to understand, others' feelings are hurt, parties have to be organized, ball games are canceled and rescheduled, unexpected deaths occur, marriages dissolve, people disappoint us, employers are unfair, babies get sick, and so the list could be extended into a catalog of the problems of everyday life.

To take this perspective is to argue that social coordination is accomplished in part by means of the joint orientation of people to the solution of everyday, practical problems. A great deal of joint action, in this view, consists of the articulation of individuals' lines of conduct around problems that confront them. Some institutions and organizations, of course, are particularly concerned with organizing responses to problems; science, medicine, the other helping and teaching professions, and safety and security forces are noticeably problem centered. Their everyday work routines regularly call on them to respond to conditions that others define as problematic. But even in the most routine activities and occupations, difficulties must frequently be overcome and problems solved.

People's efforts to *solve* their problems in a practical way are just as important to social order as is their routine conduct in culturally established and predictable lines. What, after all, is a family, which is a social unit we might well consider fundamental to social order? To characterize it as a set of roles, rules, and social relationships focusing on the bearing and raising of children is sociologically appropriate. To treat it as an object constituted by people's talk about it is also accurate. Yet people in their everyday lives experience and conceive of their families to a great extent as a series of situations in which they confront and solve practical problems. In this sense, a family (depending on one's age, religion, ethnicity, social class, and the like) is changing diapers on a child who ought to be toilet trained, managing to feed a family on a limited budget, achieving some kind of mutually satisfactory sexual adjustment with another person, coping with the occasional rebelliousness of children (or of oneself or one's spouse), deciding whether to buy a new television set or how to pay for expensive medical care for a chronically ill child, and responding to a host of other problems. A family is a set of situations to be confronted and problems to be solved.

The propensity to organize in the face of the problematic is fundamental to the coordination of conduct, not any particular organized solution. As Blumer reminded us, the standard solutions to commonly experienced human problems, as well as those solutions invented in response to situations in which there are few prescriptions for conduct, depend on the processes of indicating and interpreting objects in the environment. A food server taking the last of many orders during a busy day, cleaning tables, serving food, and making change is engaged in a process of social interaction that depends on meaning, objects, and interpretation, however routine it may seem, every bit as much as a family organizing to cope with the death of its breadwinner. It is a crucial fact that

> *the meanings that underlie established and recurrent joint action are themselves subject to pressure as well as to reinforcement, to incipient dissatisfaction as well as to indifference; they may be challenged as well as affirmed, allowed to slip along without concern as well as subjected to infusions of new vigor. . . . It is the social process in group life that creates and upholds the rules, not the rules that create and uphold group life.*[12]

Negotiating Order

Sociologists often portray social order as if it flowed spontaneously from the fact that people obey rules, enact their roles appropriately, and use standard procedures for dealing with the problems of everyday life. Coordination is seen as a consequence of adequate socialization, for if people have mastered their roles and the relevant stock of knowledge, their activities will mesh smoothly—men will know how and when to be fathers, breadwinners, or husbands, and their conduct will be coordinated with that of women as well as of other men. When, for one reason or another, conduct fails to be appropriate to a role, mechanisms of social control will come into play: People will be sanctioned for their departures from the norms and efforts will be made to resocialize them.

Such an account scarcely does justice to what actually happens in everyday life. Coordination and social order are as much the results of people's self-conscious efforts to produce them as they are the spontaneous, unconscious products of their activities. Everywhere in social life we see bargaining, negotiation, deliberation, agreements, temporary arrangements, suspensions of the rules, and a variety of other procedures in which the accomplishment of social order and coordinated activity is a deliberate undertaking. The life of a middle-class family in U.S. society, for example, seems well described as an effort to negotiate an orderly set of relationships among people who sometimes have conflicting interests, competing demands on their time, and divided loyalties. Keeping peace among the children, finding time to do things around the house as well as earn a living, securing agreement on where the family will take a vacation or whether the husband's or wife's job will take precedence in determining where the family will live—organizational tasks such as these are the stuff of everyday life.

If much of human group life is oriented toward the solution of practical problems, the coordination of individual and group activities undoubtedly is among the major problems to be faced in any society or organization. Negotiation is one of the most characteristic human responses to such problems. The concept of the *negotiated order* was developed by Anselm Strauss and his associates to account for how the ongoing activities of a complex organization such as a hospital are coordinated so as to pursue its paramount goal, helping sick people to get better.[13] Although the concept pertains explicitly to organizational life—hospitals, schools, corporations, government agencies, universities, and the like—it can, as Peter Hall suggested, be extended to the societal level, where it provides one useful model of what social order is like and how it is attained.[14]

Theoretically, organizations such as hospitals coordinate the activities of their members by inventing rules and formal procedures. These specify the activities of various personnel so that they can coordinate their efforts on behalf of their patients. They describe duties, obligations, rights, limitations, and other requirements pertaining to the various roles that are played in the organization. They specify who has what kind of authority over whom, and presumably give members a fairly comprehensive picture of the work that is to be done.

Actually, the situation is considerably more complicated. Even though all members may agree in theory on the abstract value of making sick people well, they conduct their everyday organizational lives amidst a myriad of details that often seem remote from this lofty objective. The goal is a sort of organizational cement, symbolically useful but of little concrete guidance in the day-to-day activity of nurses, physicians, dietitians, orderlies, and others who must coordinate their efforts on the patients' behalf. In addition, individuals and subunits may hold a number of additional values or goals that from time to time take precedence over the chief goal of the organization. Nurses and physicians are interested in their pay and social status as well as in curing the sick; department heads are apt to think of their domain as more beneficial or important than others, and so compete with one another for a larger budget; physicians are private practitioners and researchers as well as hospital affiliates, and so must divide their time; some support personnel, such as orderlies and aides, often are overworked, asked to do jobs that go beyond their training, and are badly underpaid; and so the list of complicating conditions could be extended.

The important point is that in the ongoing operation of an organization, no simple, easily achieved coordination of activities can be found. There are too many competing aims, individual interpretations of organizational goals, divided loyalties, internal disagreements over resources, and other complexities. Although organizations formulate rules and procedures to cope with such matters, no set of rules will be absolutely clear about lines of authority, responsibilities, or rights. Constitutions, bylaws, procedural rules, "the book"—these apparently unambiguous devices for the coordination and regulation of activity usually are far from definitive. No set of rules can cover all possible contingencies that may arise, and so, by common consent, rules are broken from time to time, even by people pledged to uphold them. Because organizations experience turnover in personnel, no one will likely know all the rules that are theoretically in force. Sometimes rules are made to deal with situations and then forgotten as new personnel and new problems arrive on the scene.

How, then, is social order accomplished? Strauss's answer is that an ongoing process of negotiation takes place, one in which agreements, contracts, and understandings among various members of the organization, made from time to time and occasionally renewed or allowed to lapse, serve as the basis for coordinating activities. Since rules may be ambiguous or even lacking, members agree on certain interpretations, exceptions, or new rules. If jurisdictions seem to overlap, as between physicians and nurses, participants will seek to develop understandings about who is entitled to do what and when they are supposed to do it. If the responsibilities of several categories of personnel directly responsible for patient care—registered nurses, licensed practical nurses, nurses' aides, and orderlies, for example—are ambiguous, working agreements will be created to specify approximate lines of responsibility.

Negotiation does not, of course, occur in the same ways in all contexts, nor is its importance equal in different kinds of organizations. On the basis of research in public schools and a review of other studies of negotiation, Hall and Spencer-Hall suggested a number of circumstances that influence how much negotiation occurs and how important it will be.[15] First, they argued, where teamwork and coordination are required and where activities are public and involve some novelty, there will be more negotiation than under circumstances where people do their work alone and where it is very routinized. Special education teachers, for example, who move from classroom to classroom or who must coordinate their work with that of regular classroom teachers find they must engage in more negotiation than regular teachers, whose work is isolated in one classroom and tends to be quite routine. The propensity for negotiation is also fostered by organizational size and complexity (the larger and more complex the organization, the more likely there will be competing subunits that must negotiate); by the broader dispersion of power and feelings of equality or efficacy (teachers are more likely to negotiate with one another than with superiors); by the delegation of authority by the organization's leadership; by actual or planned changes in the organization that require existing arrangements to be renegotiated; and by the presence of professionals (such as physicians or psychologists) who think of themselves as autonomous and therefore as entitled to negotiate the terms and conditions of their work.

Negotiation is ubiquitous, not only *within* the many organizations that make up the society as a whole, but at the societal level as well. Given that a complex society such as the United States or Canada is made up of regions, ethnic and religious groups, social classes, organizations, groups, social movements, and many other units with like, common, and competing interests, social order depends on the ongoing negotiation of orderly relationships among them. Two elements of this societal level of negotiation are especially noteworthy:

- *Self-interest.* Given the multitude of units and individuals that make up a society, the interests of particular units or individuals are rarely felt (by them) to coincide with one another, and often not with those of the society as a whole.
- *Power.* Individuals and collectivities are not equal in their capacity to influence one another or to pursue their interests successfully.

The pursuit of self-interest, along with the need to negotiate between competing interests, is inherent in the problem of maintaining social order. Self-interest manifests itself in a variety of ways and contexts. In the hospital organization, for example, physicians may feel greater loyalty to their profession than to the particular hospital in which they have privileges. In the larger society, Roman Catholics may find it in their interest to support state aid to private schools, while Protestants oppose such assistance, perhaps on constitutional grounds or perhaps only because it will aid Catholics. City politicians may oppose changes in the distribution of state or federal assistance to cities if such changes will reduce their control over how the money is spent or eliminate its value as political patronage. In each of these cases, various processes of negotiation are employed to reach agreement among contending parties.

In the course of their negotiations, individuals and groups attempt to exercise power over one another—that is, to bring to the negotiations whatever resources they can in order to achieve their goals at least cost or without the consent of others. The resources of power are varied, ranging from naked force to the control of information and knowledge, the dispensation of rewards by controlling jobs and financial resources, and the manipulation of symbols. However power is exercised and no matter by whom, it is an important determinant of social order. It influences who will be able to bargain successfully, whose definitions of the rules will prevail, and how individuals and collectivities will define and pursue their self-interest.

To provide a full analysis of the negotiation of social order in the political process, or of the nature of the groups that form any given society as well as their interests and the distribution of power, is beyond the scope of this book. What must be stressed here is that power, negotiations, and self-interest are central to interactionist conceptions of social order and that such phenomena are important concerns of social psychology. When we examine the situations people define, the roles they make and take, the objects toward which they act, and the routine and problematic circumstances they confront, we discover that these elements of social life are inextricably bound up with inequalities of power, the pursuit of individual and collective interests, and the ongoing negotiation of social order, whether in any of the numerous units that make up a society or at the societal level itself.

One cannot, for example, understand either the dynamics of U.S. society as a whole or the lives and selves of individual members without grasping the patterns of competition, conflict, and cooperation that have developed among various ethnic and religious groups. In ethnically and religiously diverse societies such as the United States and Canada, a negotiated order among such groups is a crucial aspect of the structure of the society that shapes individual lives.

Americans, for example, have historically taken three differing approaches to the negotiation of relationships among ethnic groups and to their status in the society as a whole. One, which was perhaps the dominant view during the nineteenth century, assumed that the United States was fundamentally an Anglo-Saxon culture, and that newly arriving immigrants should adopt this culture as quickly as possible. A second approach, which came into favor later, argued that the United States was a "melting pot" that would, through a mixture of citizens of diverse origins, produce a new, hybrid culture. And the third view, which also emerged as the tides of immigration swelled in the late nineteenth and early twentieth centuries, was based on a belief in a pluralistic society in which no group would be forced to abandon its culture and in which all would be free to live as they saw fit.

Each of these views of ethnicity constitutes a different negotiating position on the basis of which groups relate to one another and to the society as a whole. If, for example, those who are White, Anglo-Saxon, and Protestant believe that their culture is the "true" U.S. culture and that other groups ought to assimilate it, they are likely to act to persuade or coerce others into doing so. They will seek to "Americanize" immigrants, by which they mean that immigrants should learn and subscribe to their definitions of what constitutes U.S. culture. Such efforts occur, for example, when groups try to have English declared as the nation's "official" language. Often efforts of this kind are stimulated by large-scale immigration into a particular area, which arouses in existing groups a sense that their position is being threatened. This occurred dramatically in South Florida, which experienced significant immigration of Spanish-speaking people from Cuba beginning in the 1960s.

In recent decades, the vigorous and self-conscious pursuit of civil, economic, and political rights by African Americans has helped to reinforce consciousness of ethnic affiliation and identity in the United States. During the same period, pluralism—which we now speak of as "diversity" or "multiculturalism"—has also gained a wider measure of support. In place of an emphasis on assimilation or on the melting pot has come a greater emphasis on the positive aspects of ethnic heritage, the contributions of each ethnic group to the society as a whole, and the right to maintain ethnic differences. It is likely that the growth of ethnic pluralism improved the negotiating position of other groups, such as gays and lesbians, in their quest for social redefinition by making the existence of diversity seem more normal.

The position of the individual in the society or any of its constituent units cannot be grasped apart from the negotiated order of ethnic, religious, and other groups that exists at any given time. For African Americans, for example, the growth of ethnic pride probably has been of considerable aid in buttressing individual self-esteem and bolstering individual and social energies. For Jews, a greater acceptance of pluralism in the society has meant an increasing willingness to be openly Jewish and therefore different from the putative cultural "mainstream" in the United States. To take a different example, White males currently construct their conceptions of self under circumstances very different from what they once were. White Protestant men once could assume that they were and had the right to be the central, dominant figures in the society. Now they have lost the sure sense of ownership and entitlement they once possessed, and they often regard themselves as under attack from African Americans, women, and minority groups of all kinds.

Establishing Horizontal and Vertical Linkages

Negotiation does not occur only *within* particular organizations as people with formally specified responsibilities and particular interests negotiate the actual day-to-day operation of a factory, university, or hospital. In a complex society, there are many linkages or interconnections *between* organizations, groups, social classes, and institutions. Professionals and their associations are linked to clients on one side and to the organizations in which they work on the other side. Organizations that manufacture basic products such as steel are connected to other organizations that utilize these materials to manufacture washing machines, automobiles, and other consumer goods. Companies producing goods are linked to those that wholesale or retail them. Small groups such as families, as well as large entities such as political parties, are linked to a variety of other units: workplaces, communities, governments, churches, schools, and the like.

These linkages are both horizontal and vertical. Social units are linked *horizontally* both because individuals are simultaneously members of different units and because the units themselves are interdependent. I am at the same time a professor in a university and a husband and father within my family. It is likely that what I do in one context will have a bearing on what I do in the other. The amount of time I devote to my family, for example, sets some limits on the amount of time I can devote to my job. Moreover, people are linked one to another in personal networks of friendship or acquaintance that often fall outside organizational or group boundaries. These ties provide channels of communication and thus part of the coordination of activity in everyday life.[16]

Sociologists have treated this kind of linkage in terms of such concepts as role conflict and role strain, and the chief question of social psychological interest is how individuals manage their personal economies of time and energy to cope with the competing demands of different social units in which they participate. Groups and organizations make demands on individuals, who must decide how to respond—how much time to allocate to particular organizations or activities, for example, or to which activity to give priority. Frequently the individual's response is worked out in various negotiations. The employee who wants to put family first will have to negotiate or renegotiate a place in the work organization, finding some way to retain a job while putting in less vigorous effort (and probably also settling for fewer rewards from the job). The spouse who wants to devote more time to work will have to secure the cooperation of his or her family.

Horizontal linkages between social units also exist because such units participate in various exchange relationships. Thus, companies sell one another products and raw materials. Charitable organizations, such as the United Way, contract with employers to run charity campaigns and to have deductions made from their employees' paychecks. In these and countless other linkages between organizations, negotiations take place *between* one organization and another. More precisely, the representatives of such organizations negotiate and reach agreements about how their organizations will interact.

The study of the patterned interconnections among larger social units in a society is not the main concern of social psychologists. Even so, such matters are not beyond the scope of interests of social psychologists. This is because when we think of large organizations interacting with one another, the actual negotiation that takes place is between individuals and groups of people, not between organizations as such. A company, a state legislature, and a political party are not acting entities. Organizations do not act; people do. And although one often need not study the actual points of contact between organizations to see how they are linked to one another in general terms, frequently the study of how real people in differing organizations actually deal with one another is very revealing about how negotiation between organizations takes place.

Social units are also linked *vertically*—or hierarchically—because the activities of some control or strongly influence the activities of others. Harvey Farberman provided a fascinating illustration of such vertical linkages, as well as of the way organizations interact with one another, in his study of the automobile industry.[17] This study examines linkages among automobile manufacturers, new car dealers, and used car dealers. It is a study of a context of organizational negotiation where relationships among social units are very unequal, with the manufacturers dictating a set of conditions within which others in the industry must operate.

Farberman examined how certain illegal operations in the retail and wholesale automobile business are linked to the operating policies of automobile manufacturers. According to Farberman, the auto manufacturers force their dealers to earn profits on new car sales in a high-volume, low-margin operation. The manufacturers want to sell a large number of cars in order to realize their own economies of scale, and they force their dealers to maintain large inventories of cars and pressure them to sell them at a slim margin of profit. This is costly to dealers, not only because the per-car profit is low but also because they incur large interest costs in maintaining large inventories of expensive cars. Thus the dealer has to keep the cars and the cash moving in order to stay afloat.

These conditions, Farberman showed, foster a number of illegal practices. Faced with limited profits on new car sales, dealers cheat on repairs—charging for repairs not done, submitting false warranty claims, overcharging the customer—as a way of increasing profits. Moreover, they must also quickly turn over their inventory of used cars taken in trade on new cars in order to generate the flow of cash they need to maintain their new car inventories. To manage this turnover, dealers hire used car managers whose job is to retail the good used cars taken in trade and to sell the remainder at wholesale. The latter cars are sold to used car operations, which themselves will sell some cars at retail and wholesale the rest.

The process of disposing of used cars sets the stage for additional illegal activities. First, used car dealers find that they must pay kickbacks to the new car dealers' used car managers in order to be sure of an adequate flow of used cars to their operations. This practice is overlooked by new car dealership owners, even though it costs them profits, because they desperately need the cash. Second, the used car dealer needs a ready source of cash with which to pay the kickbacks—since one cannot pay an illegal kickback by check. This cash is generated in part through the practice of the "short sale." The customer is charged a certain amount for a car, but only part of that amount is written on the bill of sale. The customer pays the difference in cash "under the table." This practice gives the used car dealer the cash needed to pay kickbacks (tax-free cash), and it also saves the customer some money, since the sales tax on the car is based on the price of the car listed on the bill of sale.

The system is complex, involving linkages between several different organizational units—manufacturers, new car dealers, used car dealers, and customers. These organizational linkages are not abstract, of course, but are established by real people, each with self-interests as well as the interests of their organization in mind. Each negotiates on behalf of self or organization, and in the process forges linkages—in this case involving criminal acts—between them. It is worth noting that the definitions of the situation on the basis of which people act at one level may have little connection with the definitions that exist at other levels. The customer who sees an opportunity to save a few dollars on the sales tax through a short sale probably has no idea of the place this act has in the larger, vertical linkages of various levels of the automobile industry.

Making Careers

A fourth way in which joint actions are coordinated and organized at various levels involves the temporal dimension of human activity. Herbert Blumer pointed out that "any instance of joint action, whether newly formed or long established, has necessarily arisen out of a background of previous actions of the participants."[18] Just as an orientation toward the solution of everyday problems and the ongoing negotiation of social order link people horizontally and vertically, joint actions are temporally linked. The concept of *career* captures the nature of this linkage.

In the simplest sense, the background of earlier experience out of which any joint action arises consists of previous instances of such joint action. Today's transaction with a banker is much like yesterday's; managing a religious service is pretty much the same from one week to the next; the routines of dealing with one patient are similar to those for dealing with another for a physician and office staff. This temporal character of social activity is important to social order, for the recognition of various activities as typical of similar activities carried on at other times is essential to preserving a sense of orderly joint action.

The concept of career points to the fact that the temporal organization of activity runs deeper than merely the recognition of similarity between past and present joint actions. We usually think of a career in relation to an occupation or profession, where it denotes the course of an individual's expected and actual occupational activities from one stage to another, often involving increasing responsibility and pay. Careers have timetables—that is, members are expected to spend a certain amount of time in each stage and then to advance to the next stage within a limited period of time. A new member of a university faculty, for example, typically spends six years as an assistant professor, at which point he or she is either given tenure and promoted to the rank of associate professor or let go.

Sociologists have come to use the term *career* somewhat more broadly to denote the temporal sequencing of joint actions in any sphere of life and not merely in reference to occupations. Thus, while we can talk about the careers of teachers, automobile workers, or musicians, we can also discuss the shorter-term careers of people in such institutions as mental hospitals, universities, and military service, in deviant activities such as theft or prostitution, in political affairs or public life, in love affairs and friendships, and in a great variety of other activities. In essence, this broadened concept of career points to the fact that people organize their own participation in joint actions, as well as organizing their interpretations of others' actions, with an eye on various points in the past and future.

The joint action of a patient and physician in the latter's office provides a good illustration of the concept and its import for social order. For the patient, a particular encounter with a physician is not simply an isolated, single situation in which the task is to make an appropriate patient role. This particular encounter is embedded in a temporal sequence of joint actions in at least two ways. First, this office visit occurs between past and future visits, for each medical problem itself has a career around which treatment is organized. The patient interprets what is done today within the framework of what has already happened and what is thought will take place next. Second, this visit, as the others, constitutes a joint action that is temporally connected with joint actions involving people other than the physician. Before seeking medical help, one is likely to discuss the matter with family or friends, considering the potential impact of the news one might receive from the physician. Will the prognosis be favorable or unfavorable? Will an illness interfere with plans already made? Will the patient be alive a year from now? And after the visit, the patient considers the implications of the news for his or her future.[19]

The physician also views the illness in terms of its career, or "course," and sees a particular visit in that context—as part of an effort to diagnose what is wrong, or as an occasion to deliver effective treatment or assess the efficacy of treatment. The physician also views this patient in relation to patients seen earlier and later in the day, for each day has its temporal flow. An encounter or a series of encounters with a particular patient also is an event in the professional career of the physician. Perhaps this patient has a rare disease that will offer the physician an opportunity not only to treat the patient but also to do research that will further a promising career. Or perhaps this patient is one more routine case in a career filled with uninteresting and unchallenging cases and thus a source of confirmation for the physician's growing feeling that medicine has not turned out to be as exciting as hoped or anticipated.

One reason for the importance of careers to social order is that people regularly develop expectations about what they will be doing at various points in their lives. Patients expect that they will recover over a course of treatment. Physicians expect that their incomes will grow as their reputations increase. Professors expect that they will be promoted to higher ranks, and they have a fairly precise idea of when that should occur. Psychiatrists expect that mental patients will exhibit a predictable sequence of reactions to the course of therapy they are offered. People involved in love affairs expect increasing degrees of intimacy with the passage of time.

Career expectations are not necessarily fulfilled. A sociologist in his or her twenties who looks forward to promotion to professor by age 35 may not be able to achieve this goal. The aspiring actress may never get the break that propels her into a series of increasingly successful roles. The young baseball catcher who starred in the minor leagues may never perform as well when he reaches the majors, and even if he does, there may be no spot open for him.

Career expectations run up against a variety of objective realities: inadequate performance, aging, limited opportunities, injury, economic changes, wars, and the like. When this happens and an individual encounters circumstances that make it impossible to realize career expectations, he or she must make adjustments. The individual who has embarked on an occupational career with certain mobility aspirations and who has built a self-conception around them must now remake the self in accord with new realities. The position actually attained must be reinterpreted, viewed no longer as a stepping stone on the way to the top but as a satisfactory accomplishment in its own right.

In a study of professional hockey players and orchestra musicians, Robert Faulkner detected a number of themes that people invoke as they come to terms with immobility.[20] Seemingly locked into a particular position, the individual can emphasize its benefits as against the costs that would have to be paid for moving on and up. "I like it here, and going somewhere else for a better job would involve too much politics and too much scrambling," one might say. One may redefine one's expectations for esteem on the job, expressing satisfaction at doing a good job and giving up the quest for the peak of one's profession. One may redefine the job so that it looms less large in one's life, giving more importance to family. "I could do better," one might say, "but my spouse and children would suffer if I tried."

The individual is not the only one who must adjust to the realities of limited opportunity within the organization, for it is a problem for the organization itself. Just as individuals become oriented toward progression through a career, organizations rely on those expectations to motivate individuals' efforts. But as individuals find their horizons closing in and learn to make their adjustments, their reduced aspirations and commitments become organizational problems. The university, for example, must find a way to maintain the loyalty and effort of faculty members whose high aspirations have been thwarted, just as baseball teams must win the efforts of all their players, not just the stars. Thus, the resocialization of individuals to confront new circumstances is not only an individual problem but one that also affects organizational success.

Just as important, these examples suggest that socialization is associated with orderly *participation* in social life just as much as with *preparation* for it. The adult confronts many circumstances that demand new learning. From the individual perspective, resocialization—by adjusting to limited success or by learning new skills—is a matter of adjustment to life circumstances. From an organizational perspective, successful resocialization is just as crucial to the organization's efforts to maintain itself. Indeed, from the perspective of social order, socialization in adulthood is as crucial to the coordination of social activities as is the learning of basic knowledge and social skills in childhood.

The social order thus is supported in part by a framework of expectations geared to the passing of time. Individuals are tied to the social order because they organize their efforts in relation to such expectations. Social order thus rests, in part, on individuals' biographies—on their ordering of joint actions in a variety of contexts in relation to their own careers. To see a society as a set of interlocked joint actions is thus to portray a set of conditions across time as well as among people at any given time.

Forming Boundaries

The coordination of social activity is also accomplished by the creation and maintenance of a variety of social boundaries that divide various categories, groups, and communities from one another.[21] Gender is one such boundary; using the minimal biological facts of sex differences, culture classifies people as male and female and constructs gender differences. The ethnic and religious divisions to which we referred earlier in this chapter form important boundaries, as do race and social class. Gender, race, ethnicity, religion, and social class constitute fundamental lines of division in modern society; we might call the boundaries they create "structural," since they are integral to the very organization of the society itself. Other boundaries are more ephemeral. Social controversies over capital punishment or abortion, for example, also create criteria of classification that separate one category of person from another. Such boundaries are typically the product of social movements, a topic to be considered later in this chapter. And even such media creations as the "Yuppie" or "Generation X" provide a basis for classifying people according to character or life style and thus creating boundaries between them.

A social boundary resembles a fence or border that governs relationships between those on opposite sides. The gender boundary, for example, regulates the times and places in which men and women may interact with one another and how they may do so. It influences who may work with whom and who may be friends with whom. Thus, female police officers have encountered resistance to their becoming partners with male officers out of concern that intimate relationships would develop and undermine their marriages as well as interfere with their work. Likewise, on the same grounds, many people question whether men and women can be "just friends." Gender is not an absolute barrier, of course, since the worlds of men and women connect at numerous points in the family, in school, on the job, and in the community. But the existence of the boundary establishes the fact that there are two worlds and regulates the contact between them. Likewise, boundaries of race, religion, or ethnicity shape interaction across such lines and establish the existence of separate social worlds. Even the boundaries established between those on opposite sides of an issue govern their interaction. Previously existing social relationships, such as friendship, may be undermined when an issue such as abortion comes into play. Those who oppose abortion regard with suspicion those who favor it, are wary of interacting with them, and find that when they do interact, they do so as representatives of their causes rather than on some other basis.

Boundaries such as these frequently arise out of the processes of conflict and negotiation within and between organizations, which we discussed earlier. Once in existence, they come to be seen, at least for a time, as natural features of the social landscape. It thus seems obvious to those who have come to accept and even count on these boundaries that men and women are "different" or that those whose opposition to abortion is absolute are "extremists," who constitute a danger to society. Boundaries provide points of reference in social life. They enclose those who live on one side of the boundary and exclude those on the other side. And they make it possible to distinguish between friend and foe, the virtuous and the evil, the like and the different.

Boundaries have four main characteristics that help us grasp how they operate and how they are involved in the coordination of social activity. First, boundaries rest on the application of a principle of social classification—some relatively clear-cut criterion on the basis of which people can be divided into categories. Such principles of classification frequently oversimplify the complex nature of human beings and exaggerate the importance or the consequences of their differences. We are assigned to a sex category at birth when the genitals are inspected and someone announces "It's a boy!" or "It's a girl!" From the minimal facts of sex differences, enormous differences between the genders—most of which have no biological foundation—are inferred. Likewise, people are classified as "heterosexual" or "homosexual" in their sexual orientations and assigned conclusively to one category or another, despite evidence that sexual orientations are probably not quite so rigidly fixed in biological terms.

Racial classification in the United States frequently divides people into categories of "Black" and "White," thus not only ignoring other possible categories (e.g., "Asian" or "American Indian") but also converting a continuum of skin color and other physical attributes into rigid categories. Moreover, the categorization is often absurd or illogical in ways not apparent to those who apply it, particularly to those in a position to enforce it: A single "Black" ancestor will make a person Black in the prevailing scheme of racial classification, but a single "White" ancestor does not make a person White! Although racial categories have no scientific validity, they are nevertheless treated as real in the social world, and they have real consequences. Social class boundaries in the United States are more difficult to pinpoint, since a majority of people find a way to label or regard themselves as "middle class." Nonetheless, people make distinctions between "blue-collar" and "white-collar" workers, or between "lower class" and "middle class," or between the college-educated and those who graduated only from high school. For the duration of such issues as the cultural battle over abortion, people are classified as "pro-choice" or "pro-life" even though this simple categorization overlooks the complexity and frequent ambivalence of individual attitudes.

Second, boundaries count. Gender, race, and social class pervade almost every aspect of social life. Social interaction almost invariably requires participants to establish and enact gender, for example. As we have already seen, role performances are inspected for their conformity not only with gendered typifications of roles but also with a more general typification of "male" and "female." Perhaps the clearest indication of just how central gender is to our perception and reproduction of social arrangements is the discomfort and awkwardness that people feel when they must interact with someone whose gender they cannot conclusively determine, or their embarrassment when they misidentify someone's gender. Moreover, gender classification establishes an individual's credentials for entry into a variety of social situations, organizations, and roles—ranging from toilets to clubs to occupations. Likewise, race and social class are consequential bases of classification and treatment. An African American male jogger in a predominantly White neighborhood will be very conscious of the fact that his "race" may be not only a barrier between him and others but also a cue that residents or the police may use in order to typify him as a criminal rather than as an upstanding citizen. Likewise, membership in the working class, as evidenced by patterns of speech or dress, may affect an individual's life chances because "middle-class" people—potential employers, college admissions interviewers, or prospective mates—take class into account in their perceptions of skills and qualities and in their decisions to employ, admit, or marry.

Boundaries matter not only because they affect how the powerful or privileged treat the less powerful or less privileged but also because membership in a category often entails loyalty to and acceptance of control by other members. Indeed, the third characteristic of boundaries is that they tend to promote *identification.* If a boundary is important in social life, those on each side of the boundary will either take it for granted that others regard it as an important basis for the construction of self or explicitly encourage them to do so. So pervasive a boundary as gender, for example, naturally becomes a main component of biographical identity, for gender is situated in almost every social encounter. It becomes "second nature," a part of our habitual attitudes toward ourselves and others. But people are also more explicitly and self-consciously encouraged or required to identify with a gender category. For example, when members of the women's movement urge all women to feel obliged to support the movement and to be conscious of their gender, they are encouraging gender identification. Filling out an application form that requires checking a gender category or having a "boys'" or "girls' night out" constitute gender identity announcements that contribute in a small way to identification with gender. Even when men and women joke about the "battle of the sexes," they invoke the underlying idea that men and women owe loyalty to their respective genders.

Racial classification also prompts demands for identification. The existence of racial categories thought to be significant prompts the members of each group to demand that others of their group be loyal to the group and its standards. Because "Blacks" and "Whites" hold negative typifications—stereotypes—of one another, members of each group are likely to regard the other as a threat. Prejudiced White Americans may regard every Black person they meet as a probable criminal or welfare mother; Black Americans will be alert for signs of racism when they interact with Whites. As a result, members of each group are apt to insist on racial solidarity—to demand that people define themselves as Black or White and classify and treat one another on this basis.

In other words, boundaries encourage the development of strong feelings of the differences between "we" and "they." "We" are virtuous—our culture is better, our values more correct, and our morals superior. "They" are evil, and what is more, "they" are against us. Group solidarity and individual identification tend to thrive on the creation of such boundaries and their resulting encouragement of a sense of difference between oneself and "the other." Indeed, often it is the portrayal of the dangerous "other" upon which the depiction and maintenance of the virtues of the in-group depend. Some contemporary women, for example, define female virtues in contrast with an image of male flaws. Whereas men are portrayed as prone to violence, excessively individualistic, and unable to experience or communicate feelings, women are depicted as peacemakers, community and relationship builders, and capable of acknowledging their emotions. This is not surprising, considering that males have often defined their virtues by making invidious comparisons with women. By contrasting in-group virtues and out-group flaws, category members provide an explicit rationale and vocabulary for identification with the group.

Finally, boundaries entail social controls that help maintain the boundaries, as well as sanctions for departure from them or efforts to cross them. Members of a religious group who fear that their children will marry someone of another faith may go to some lengths to prevent this from happening. Parents may demand that their children date only coreligionists, send them to parochial schools, or lecture them on the dangers of leaving the fold. And if the child does marry an outsider, sanctions may be imposed. Orthodox Jews, for example, may observe mourning rituals for a child who marries a non-Jew, regarding the child as if he or she were dead. Members of the in-group may publicly criticize those who seem not to respect boundaries. Prepubescent boys sometimes taunt their friends who play with girls with cries of "sissy!" Working-class Americans are often quick to notice and censure their fellows who attain middle-class jobs or incomes or who adopt middle-class life-styles. Some African Americans criticize others for "acting White" when they do not display appropriate loyalty to the group.

Techniques of social control and the application of sanctions are only part of the explanation of how boundaries are maintained, for the bulk of the work is done in everyday life and without a great deal of explicit attention to the boundary. Wherever people recognize and use a principle of classification, or wherever they take classification for granted, they create and sustain boundaries. Thus, to search for the men's room in a restaurant is to lend support to categorization by gender, as is a tendency to talk about cars or sports and thus exclude women who may not be interested in these topics. (Indeed, even to write the preceding sentence is to reproduce the boundary!) To ask a Chinese American where to find the best Chinese restaurant is likewise to act to maintain a boundary (and to impose an identity on the other), for in the posing of the question lies the assumption that this individual will naturally know such things. Boundaries exist because people voluntarily recognize and take them for granted as well as because they are enforced.

Boundaries provide significant reference points in the coordination of conduct and the construction of social order. Those committed to a particular boundary, such as gender, find in it a stable way of imagining and talking about the social order as well as a standard for conduct. Boundaries, artificial though they may be, provide guidance in everyday life, specifying what is permissible and what is off limits. But those who regard a particular boundary oppressive or evil also find in it a way of imagining what social life could be and a reference point for conduct that transgresses and thus challenges the boundary. Indeed, a good part of what goes on in contemporary society consists of *struggles* over boundaries as well as between those on opposite sides. Strife, argument, contention, disagreement, cultural conflict, and other signs of such struggles seem in many ways to be among the most stable and recurring features of life in contemporary United States, and thus main features in its social order. The "politics of identity," as it is sometimes called, has become a prominent feature of social life.[22]

Creating and Joining Social Movements

We come now to the final topic in our examination of the coordination of social activity: the *social movement*.[23] A social movement is a collective effort to bring about some change in society or a part of society (or to resist such a change sought by others). The change may involve a return to earlier ways of doing things or to values that, in the eyes of movement participants, have been abandoned or neglected. The ideologies of conservative political movements or religious revival movements often have this quality. The movement may seek to prohibit some form of activity that has gained widespread acceptance. The temperance movement in the nineteenth century and the antiabortion movement of today are examples of this kind of movement. Social movements may have very particular goals, such as racial equality or environmental protection, or more general ones, such as moral revitalization.

Whatever their goals, ideologies, forms of organization, and methods, social movements are oriented toward social change. They seek to restructure the society, to alter its values, beliefs, practices, and modes of organization. Thus, it would seem, there is a simple relationship of opposition between the social order the movement would like to create and the social order that exists and against which it struggles. In the United States of the 1950s and 1960s, a social system existed in which African Americans were *legally* excluded from jobs, educational opportunities, and public accommodations. At the same time, there was a civil rights movement opposed to that social system and dedicated to reforming it so that people would enjoy equal opportunity and equal social treatment.

Although adequate in general terms, this view of social movements as forms of collective behavior standing in opposition to social structure is also potentially misleading. For, indeed, social movements are in some ways very intimately tied to the social order they seek to change, and under some circumstances social movements can even be said to form a part of social order.

The values of social movements, for example, are often closer to the dominant values of the society than they seem. The women's movement, for example, seeks (among other goals) to overcome discrimination against women in employment, opening for them the same kinds of careers that are open for men. The goal runs counter to prevailing discriminatory practices, but it also accepts the widespread belief that occupational success, which often plays a dominant and oppressive role of its own in the lives of men, is what really counts. In opposing one aspect of the social order, the movement implicitly lends its support to another.

Moreover, social movements, although they seek to change dominant modes of social organization, themselves use organizational means to attain their ends. A movement is not just a set of ideas or a program of objectives, but also a set of organizations, each with members, leaders, and resources to be secured and allocated, and methods of internal and external negotiation. In short, social movement life is organizational life. Movements find they must organize their activities, and in so doing they provide structure for the lives of their members. They are the source of opportunities, careers, rewards, and disappointments. Even movement organizations committed to maintaining their flexibility and to resisting ordinary hierarchical forms of organization find they confront the same problems as any organization. Things have to get done, procedures have to be adopted for getting them done, and people have to be motivated to do them.

Movements are also linked to existing social arrangements because they negotiate with existing social groups and organizations. The image of a movement as the opposition can obscure the fact that movement leaders are in frequent contact with those whose politics they oppose, developing close professional and sometimes also personal relationships. Leaders of various movements at the local level are often as integral to local government as elected officials and appointed boards and committees. Such leaders attend meetings, make presentations, are addressed on a first-name basis by officials, and often seem to feel entitled to and are accorded the right of special attention when they testify at hearings or otherwise participate. This is not to say that such groups get what they want, or that such victories as they win are well received by the establishment. It is only to suggest that they are an important part of the local landscape—they are as visible and sometimes as permanent as more formal political institutions.

The same is true at the national level. Congressional hearings on environmental legislation, for example, will frequently include invited testimony from various social movement organizations, such as the Sierra Club, the National Wildlife Federation, or the National Parks and Conservation Association. Such organizations are invited because they have gained status as legitimate political actors and are thus accorded the right to speak on behalf of the environmental movement.

In this sense, it sometimes seems that social movements are an integral part of social structure. Particularly in recent decades in the United States, social movements have become so plentiful that their very existence on the social landscape is taken for granted. Moreover, they are an important part of the process whereby decisions are made. They are yet movements, for they define themselves as such and see their objectives as being substantially at variance with contemporary social practices. Their presence not only influences decisions but also seems to be a necessary part of the process whereby decisions are made. Thus, for example, it is hard to envision policy decisions about environmental matters being made without the participation of environmental movement organizations. Not only do social movements thus participate in the coordination of social activities, but also by their visible presence they shape the social construction of reality.

An understanding of the process in which people become attached to social movements is helpful in explicating the link between the social order that movements construct and the people who participate in them. Sociologists have examined this process in a variety of ways, including studies of those who become members of fringe religious movements.

Periodically, newspapers and television report the bizarre beliefs or behavior of the latest religious group to become the object of public alarm. This became true especially following the Jonestown tragedy in 1978, when 913 followers of the "People's Temple" led by Reverend Jim Jones committed mass suicide at their utopian agricultural community in Guyana. After a visit by U.S. Congressman Leo Ryan, journalists, and relatives of cult members, Ryan and four others were ambushed and killed before they could leave. Soon afterward, followers of Jones committed suicide en masse. Following Jonestown there was widespread public concern about cults and their alleged capacity to "brainwash" their members to make them susceptible to the most extreme demands of their leaders. Years later, in 1993, the Branch Davidian group in Waco, Texas, raised the same kind of fears when its members stood their ground against the Federal Bureau of Alcohol, Firearms, and Tobacco over the issue of illegal weapons kept at their compound. The Davidians met a tragic end in a violent confrontation with the Bureau and the FBI that led to a fire and the deaths of many of the compound's occupants. Even more recently, in 1997, 39 members of the Heavensgate group in California took their own lives, believing that the appearance of the Hale-Bopp comet was a sign that they would be taken up into a "higher dimension" by a spacecraft.

Why do people develop beliefs and engage in behavior that others regard as bizarre, foolish, insane, or just plain tragic? What attracts people to groups whose ideas are so at odds with what most people think? How are people able to maintain such beliefs? How can people go to the extreme of suicide in defense of the group or in pursuit of its goals?

A classic approach to such questions was offered by John Lofland and Rodney Stark, who studied in its earliest form a religious group we now know as the Unification Church, the so-called "Moonies," named after their leader, the Reverend Sun Yung Moon. Based on their participant observation of what they called the "Doomsday Cult," Lofland and Stark proposed a general explanation of how conversion to such religious movements occurs:

> *For conversion a person must experience, within a religious problem-solving perspective, enduring, acutely-felt tensions that lead to defining her/himself as a religious seeker; the person must encounter the cult at a turning point in life; within the cult an affective bond must be formed (or preexist) and any extracult attachments, neutralized; and he/she must be exposed to intensive interaction to become a "deployable agent."*[24]

The conditions outlined by Lofland and Stark are said to be individually necessary for such a conversion and, taken together, sufficient to produce it. In other words, people are motivated to join religious cults by enduring problems or tensions in their personal lives. But it is not sufficient to feel lost, anxious, or unhappy, for the person must also define these tensions in a religious context and come to regard himself or herself as a religious seeker, someone who might find solace by joining a religious group. Further, the person must encounter the group at a turning point—that is, at some point of extreme tension or "hitting bottom" such that the person feels something must be done. If these conditions are met, then the formation of a social bond within the movement, the neutralization of ties to family and friends who might oppose the person's membership, and intensive interaction within the group will convert the person to full membership. The individual will believe and act as a member of the group.

Lofland and Stark's analysis of the process of becoming a "Moonie" provides a highly plausible explanation of conversion to cult membership. It suggests that when an individual cannot find a sense of meaning and a feeling of "belonging" in more mundane and widely accepted religious groups, the resulting "tensions" will motivate him or her to look elsewhere. If the person encounters a cult at a period of extreme tension and forms bonds with its members, then the stage is set for conversion to the cult and its perspective.

Despite its plausibility, critics have pointed to limitations of the Lofland and Stark model. David Snow and Cynthia Phillips studied conversion to a Buddhist movement, imported to the United States from Japan, in order to test the model.[25] The *Nichiren Shoshu* movement, like the Unification Church, seeks to transform society by transforming its individual members, enabling them to experience personal rebirth and happiness. But where the Unification Church regards the acceptance of Christ as the way to personal change, the Nichiren Shoshu movement focuses on the repetition of a chant, the Nam-Moyho-Renge-Kyo.

Converts to Nichiren Shoshu, Snow and Phillips found, did not invariably experience tensions or define themselves as religious seekers prior to joining. Some did, but most did not. They contend that explaining attraction to a movement in terms of prior motives is a questionable approach. When people join religious movements, the researchers point out, they tend to reinterpret their past, to find new meanings in experiences they used to define in different ways. In other words, people who convert to a cult may "discover" that they had problems and learn to define membership in the cult as a solution to those problems. Defining oneself as someone who has experienced tensions and must seek a solution in religious terms may thus be an effect rather than a cause of conversion.

Snow and Phillips also questioned the importance of severing ties to others who are not members of the cult. Indeed, they argued that conversion to the Nichiren Shoshu Buddhist movement actually may have strengthened ties to others outside the movement. One reason, they propose, for the difference between their findings and those of Lofland and Stark is that the Unification Church is a communal movement that works hard to absorb all of the time and loyalty of adherents. Nichiren Shoshu is not communal and does not seek total loyalty. As a result, ties to nonmovement members are a threat to the Unification Church, but not to Nichiren Shoshu.

These authors do offer empirical support for two of the elements in the Lofland and Stark explanation. They argue that affective bonds and intensive interaction are necessary for conversion. An affective bond—essentially what Scheff calls a social bond—serves to make a group's message more credible to a prospective believer. Because the messages of such religious or quasi-religious groups are often at odds with beliefs in the surrounding culture, it may take some doing to overcome the skepticism of the potential convert. The formation of a bond seems essential to overcoming this skepticism, perhaps because the bond strengthens the social pressure on the prospective convert to believe. The bond itself may become the important thing to the convert, with belief and practice following gradually over time.

Intensive interaction provides the context within which the potential convert comes to participate in a group's universe of discourse. The Nichiren Shoshu, as other groups seeking converts, attempt to structure the time of prospective converts, providing numerous occasions for them to participate in the group's activities and see others doing so. Where affective bonds enhance credibility and increase social pressure to believe, intensive social interaction "normalizes" the group's ideas and practices. Spending several nights a week with other members, receiving one's own ritual scroll (to which the chant is directed), and hearing others talk about the movement and its goals all make the movement and its ideology seem quite normal or matter-of-fact.

Keywords

Boundaries   A boundary is a social line dividing the members of one social category from those of another, such as men from women, working-class people from middle-class people, members of one ethnic or religious group from those of another, and so on. In some instances, boundaries are clearly drawn and people are acutely aware of the differences between one category and another. This is still the case with gender in the United States, for example, in spite of improvements in the economic condition of women. People still know who is a woman and who is a man and what that difference entails. Other boundaries are less clear, and people may find it difficult to spell out exactly what the differences mean. In the case of social class they may even sometimes deny that such boundaries exist.

The concept of a boundary is important because it calls attention to the part social divisions play in the organization of social life. Concepts such as community or role call attention to the ways in which people identify themselves with social units or activities and with one another. Thus, to speak of the "gay community" is to emphasize the ways in which a set of people are bound together by identification with one another and by a common sexual orientation. To grasp fully how such communities function in the social world and in the identities of their members, however, we need to recognize that differences from others are as important as similarity to other community members.

Distinctions between "gay" and "straight" guide the identities of both, as well as interactions between them. Such boundaries define the way people visualize and talk about the social world, and they influence their coordination of everyday conduct.

Careers   In everyday language, *career* refers to an individual's movement through various stages or levels of an occupation or profession, as in a "medical career" or "business career." Although the "career" is thought of informally as the property of an individual, occupations have typical career patterns, which specify periods of training, income expectations at various ages, the pace at which people are promoted from one level to the next, and the like. Individuals commonly measure their careers against these norms.

Symbolic interactionists use the term *career* more broadly as a metaphor to convey the idea that temporal patterns and expectations are not only widespread but essential to social order. Thus, for example, physicians have occupational careers, and they expect certain patterns of income, professional recognition, and influence over time. But from the perspective of physicians, illnesses also have careers or "trajectories," for treatment of a patient involves not only a diagnosis of the problem but also a prognosis—a prediction of the rate at which the patient will either recover or decline. Likewise, even a simple social act such as a conversation has a "career" in the sense that people share and communicate expectations about how long it will last and how to signal its impending end. Shared ideas about temporal progress or stages of development of illnesses, conversations, occupations, and a host of joint actions enable people to participate in the actions in an orderly way.

Horizontal and Vertical Linkages   Symbolic interactionists argue that conduct is situated, but these situations themselves are located within larger and more encompassing contexts—within groups, organizations, social classes, and other such social entities. Moreover, these social entities are themselves linked to one another both horizontally and vertically. These concepts are meant to sensitize us to two key facts.

First, social entities have *vertical linkages,* for some groups, organizations, or social classes are in a position to exert control over others or must depend on others. Large, increasingly global corporations, for example, are able to shift their manufacturing operations to countries with lower labor costs in order to keep their profits at desired levels. The implications for workers are clear: Their livelihoods, as well as the communities in which they live, exist and cease to exist at the whim of corporate executives in other parts of the globe. To take another example, the poor in the United States are dependent in various ways on the social policies of the federal and state governments with respect to welfare rules, as well as on the generosity of private charities. And smaller, supplier companies are tied in relations of unequal power and dependency to larger companies who buy their products and services.

Social psychologists do not attempt to explain why such vertical linkages exist, but their work can scarcely ignore them. The power of large corporations over workers, of men over women, or of the welfare bureaucracy over the poor makes a great deal of difference to workers, women, and the poor. It shapes their identities, their capacity to make roles, and their need to be accurate and perceptive role takers. In other words, the processes of identification, role making, and role taking do not occur in a vacuum but often in contexts of unequal power.

Horizontal linkages refer to a second key fact: The individuals whose actions constitute the society are simultaneously members of several social entities, which are themselves interdependent. For example, people are simultaneously breadwinners and parents, voters and consumers. Companies sell products to one another, governmental agencies interact with one another and with the public, and charities cooperate in such fund-raising enterprises as the United Way. Although these relationships—between people and organizations—often involve power and control, they do not always do so. Thus, linkages are horizontal in the sense that individuals and groups at roughly similar levels of power negotiate with one another. Again, even though it is not the social psychologist's task to explain the nature of these linkages, the basic processes of self, social interaction, and conduct formation are situated in these complex horizontal linkages.

Negotiated Order   The negotiated order is that social order that emerges from negotiations. A union contract, for example, is a negotiated order that emerges from a formal process of contract negotiation, is signed by the parties who have bargained, and governs relationships between labor and management for a specified period of time. Negotiation produces socially coordinated conduct—that is, labor agrees to work under certain conditions and management agrees to those conditions, such as pay, raises, and job conditions. Negotiation also produces a constructed sense of social order. That is, people who have negotiated a social order have a shared sense of how their activities are and should be coordinated.

Negotiation   Negotiation is a social process in which participants strike various kinds of bargains or agreements, of limited scope and duration, that define the nature of their relationships to one another, as well as their mutual responsibilities. Negotiation occurs not only between individuals as individuals but also between individuals as members and representatives of groups and organizations. Negotiation may be highly formalized, such as contract negotiations between unions and corporations, which are governed by complex state and federal labor laws. Negotiation may be quite informal, as when various trades—such as carpenters, electricians, and plumbers—at a construction site informally agree on how they will coordinate their work schedules.

Problem Solving   Problem solving refers to those human activities whose focus, or object, is the solution of the practical problems that arise in the course of everyday life. Problem solving is important for social order in two respects. First, a great deal of the everyday coordination of social activities occurs in the context of solving prob-lems—getting flat tires fixed, arranging for the care of children, resolving problems in interpersonal relation-ships, and so forth. Second, a great deal of the everyday experience of **social order** (later defined) depends on the sense that problems have been or are capable of solution. People achieve real social order by solving problems, and they achieve a sense of social order either by solving them or by talking about their solutions.

Social Order and Disorder   The concepts of social order and disorder developed in this book rest on the basic idea that social life involves both the coordination of social conduct and the construction of images of that conduct. People are engaged in their everyday lives in coordinating their activities with those of others. Employees punch time clocks and try to keep their bosses happy, or at least at bay. Purchasing agents try to find the goods and services their companies need at the best possible price and quality. Children try to decipher their parents' expectations, and parents try to keep their children fed and clothed and out of trouble. These same people are also engaged in talk about their experiences: Employees and employers gripe about one another, pur-chasing agents try to predict future trends in their indus-tries, and parents and children talk about one another.

Social order depends on both coordinated activity and the social construction of social order, and in this sense it is hard to say that it either exists or does not exist. From the vantage point of an outside, disinter-ested observer, parents and children may be acting in highly regular and predictable ways, doing what countless other parents have done, are doing, and will

do. In this sense, we could say that a social order exists, for it seems apparent that their activities are coordinated in predictable ways. From the vantage point of the par-ents and children themselves, however, things may seem different. First-time parents of adolescent children may be unnerved by their children's rebelliousness and feel that their world is falling apart when they are really just living the experience of other parents. Can we say that a social order exists in this situation? The answer really depends on whose perspective we adopt. From the parents' vantage point, the world is falling apart and they must do something to repair it. From the stand-point of others, they are experiencing what other par-ents have experienced before them, and they will probably live through the experience.

Social Problems   Symbolic interactionists have devel-oped a distinctive approach to social problems, one that emphasizes the socially created and transformed nature of their definitions rather than the objective conditions that may or may not underlie them. The interactionist approach to environmental problems, for example, emphasizes the ways in which these problems are defined over time rather than any objective conditions that are claimed to exist by those engaged in the defining. Thus, a social problem is a condition defined as problematic and needing solution, regardless of the status of any "objec-tive" conditions that may underlie the problem. Interac-tionists take this approach not to deny that there may well be objective conditions that create human unhappiness or misery, but because problem solving seems to be such an important part of the coordination of social conduct and the construction of **social order** (previously defined).

Endnotes

1. For analysis of this form of talk about the self, see John P. Hewitt, *Dilemmas of the American Self* (Philadelphia: Temple University Press, 1989).

2. For an analysis of the process of memorializ-ing, see Stanford W. Gregory, Jr. and Jerry M. Lewis, "Symbols of Collective Memory: The Social Process of Memorializing May 4, 1970, at Kent State Univer-sity," *Symbolic Interaction* 11 (1988): 213–233. For an analysis of the creation of a major political charac-ter, see Barry Schwartz, *George Washington: The Making of an American Symbol* (New York: Free Press, 1987).

3. Fred Davis, "Decade Labeling: The Play of Col-lective Memory and the Narrative Plot," *Symbolic Interaction* 7 (1984): 15–24.

4. See John P. Hewitt and Peter M. Hall, "Social Problems, Problematic Situations, and Quasi-Theories," *The American Sociological Review* 38 (June 1973): 67–74; and Hall and Hewitt, "The Quasi-Theory of Communication and the Management of Dissent," *Social Problems* 18 (Summer 1970): 17–27.

5. This discussion bears a family resemblance to the classic position of Emile Durkheim that crime and its punishment arouse collective sentiments and thereby

contribute to social order. See Emile Durkheim, *The Rules of Sociological Method,* 8th ed., eds. and trans. G. Catlin, S. Solovay, and J. Mueller (New York: Free Press, 1964).

6. For a useful collection of studies of the construction of social problems, see *Images of Issues: Typifying Contemporary Social Problems,* 2nd ed., ed. Joel Best (New York: Aldine de Gruyter, 1995).

7. For the classic formulation of social problems theory, see Malcolm Spector and John I. Kitsuse, *Constructing Social Problems,* rev. ed. (New York: Aldine de Gruyter, 1987). For an excellent review of social problems theory and research, see Joel Best, "Social Problems," in *Handbook of Symbolic Interaction,* eds. Larry T. Reynolds and Nancy J. Herman-Kinney (Walnut Creek, CA: AltaMira, 2003), pp. 981–996.

8. For an overview of the issues surrounding symbolic interactionism and social structure, see David R. Maines, "Social Structure and Social Organization in Symbolic Interactionist Thought," *Annual Review of Sociology* 3 (1977): 235–259. Also see Maines, *The Faultline of Consciousness: A View of Interactionism in Sociology* (New York: Aldine de Gruyter, 2001).

9. Herbert Blumer, *Symbolic Interactionism: Perspective and Method* (Englewood Cliffs, NJ: Prentice-Hall, 1969), p. 17.

10. Thomas J. Scheff, *Microsociology: Discourse, Emotion, and Social Structure* (Chicago: University of Chicago Press, 1990).

11. Blumer, *Symbolic Interactionism,* p. 18 (Note 9).

12. Ibid, pp. 18–19.

13. Anselm L. Strauss, D. Erlich, R. Bucher, and M. Sabshin, "The Hospital as a Negotiated Order," in *The Hospital in Modern Society,* ed. Eliot Friedson (New York: Free Press, 1963), pp. 147–169. Strauss, *Negotiations* (San Francisco: Jossey Bass, 1978) provides a major extension of the concept of negotiation.

14. See Peter M. Hall, "A Symbolic Interactionist Analysis of Politics," *Sociological Inquiry* 42 (1–2) (1972): 35–75.

15. Peter M. Hall and Dee Spencer-Hall, "The Social Conditions of the Negotiated Order," *Urban Life* 11 (October 1982): 328–349.

16. See Gary Alan Fine and Sheryl Kleinman, "Network and Meaning: An Interactionist Approach to Structure," *Symbolic Interaction* 6 (Spring 1983): 97–110.

17. Harvey A. Farberman, "A Criminogenic Market Structure: The Automobile Industry," *Sociological Quarterly* 16 (Autumn 1975): 438–457.

18. Blumer, *Symbolic Interactionism,* p. 20 (Note 9).

19. See Kathy Charmaz, *Good Days, Bad Days: The Self in Chronic Illness and Time* (New Brunswick, NJ: Rutgers University Press, 1991).

20. Robert R. Faulkner, "Coming of Age in Organizations: A Comparative Study of Career Contingencies and Adult Socialization," *Sociology of Work and Occupations* 1 (May 1974): 131–173.

21. For essays dealing with the creation and maintenance of boundaries in several areas of social life, see *Cultivating Differences: Symbolic Boundaries and the Making of Inequality,* eds. Michele Lamont and Marcel Fournier (Chicago: University of Chicago Press, 1992). For approaches to inequality from a symbolic interactionist perspective, see "Symbolic Interaction and Inequality," ed. Leon Anderson, a special issue of *Symbolic Interaction* 24 (4): 2001.

22. For essays dealing with this topic, see *Social Theory and the Politics of Identity,* ed. Craig Calhoun (Oxford: Blackwell, 1994). See also John P. Hewitt, "Self, Role, and Discourse," in *Self, Collective Behavior and Society: Essays Honoring the Contributions of Ralph H. Turner,* eds. Gerald Platt and Chad Gordon (New Haven, CT: Jai Press, 1994), pp. 155–173.

23. For an analysis of social movements, see Ralph H. Turner and Lewis M. Killian, *Collective Behavior,* 3rd ed. (Englewood Cliffs, NJ: Prentice-Hall, 1987), Part 4.

24. John Lofland and Rodney Stark, "Becoming a World-Saver: A Theory of Religious Conversion," *American Sociological Review* 30 (1965): 862.

25. David A. Snow and Cynthia L. Phillips, "The Lofland-Stark Conversion Model: A Critical Assessment," *Social Problems* 27 (1980): 430–447.

Chapter *6*

*Deviance and
the Social Order*

In Chapter five we examined a variety of boundaries that people create as they seek to coordinate their conduct. One additional boundary demands special attention, for it seems almost invariably to develop when people associate with one another. On one side of this boundary lie people who view their own conduct as acceptable, normal, or reasonable; on the other side lie those whose conduct is condemned, viewed as abnormal, or thought to be inexplicable. Put in other words, this boundary distinguishes between conduct that is thought to uphold social order and conduct that is held to undermine it. Sociologists have customarily described this boundary by using such terms as "deviance" and "deviant behavior." The terms are slippery, but they provide a useful starting point for analyzing this boundary and showing its importance to a symbolic interactionist analysis of conduct.

The sociological category of *deviance* encompasses an astonishing variety of conduct. At one time or another, murder, rape, assault, robbery, drug use, juvenile delinquency, homosexuality, securities fraud, price fixing, labor racketeering, prostitution, and mental illness have all been lumped into this category. It is so broad and diverse, in fact, that one can question whether it has any utility at all. Armed robbers and fraudulent securities dealers both break the law and both seize other people's valuables for their own use. But their social origins are probably different, and whereas one relies on force or the threat of force, the other uses deception. Both the prostitute and the schizophrenic have careers, but contemporary people in the United States tend to interpret the former in moral terms and the latter in medical terms. Some people condemn homosexuality as immoral or sinful, whereas others regard it as an alternative sexual orientation, neither better nor worse than heterosexuality or bisexuality. What possible warrant can there be for lumping such diverse forms of behavior together?

The essence of deviance as a sociological category does not lie either in the particular characteristics of behavior itself or in similarities among those who engage in it. Instead, deviance is a category of behavior and of persons who are classified and treated as such by the members of society itself. What makes the prostitute and the schizophrenic alike is not their behavior or motivations, but rather the social treatment they receive at the hands of ordinary people, police, courts, social workers, psychiatrists, and other agents of social control. Deviance, we will see, represents a real or imagined threat to social order, and the deviant is accorded a special and discredited position in relation to it. Accordingly, the focus of this chapter is on how deviance is socially constructed and perceived, and how it is linked to the construction of social order and the coordination of social conduct.

An Interactionist Conception of Deviance

The approach to deviance we will develop originated in the *labeling perspective,* a body of research and theory created (in part by symbolic interactionists) beginning in the 1960s. Criticizing existing theories of deviant behavior, labeling theorists sought to emphasize the socially constructed nature of deviance. Howard S. Becker, a leading proponent of this approach, succinctly summarized its central tenets:

> *Social groups create deviance by making the rules whose infraction constitutes deviance, and by applying those rules to particular people and labeling them as outsiders. From this point of view, deviance is not a quality of the act a person commits, but rather a consequence of the application by others of rules and sanctions to an "offender." The deviant is one to whom that label has successfully been applied; deviant behavior is behavior that people so label.[1]*

Becker's approach sought to remedy some of the defects of then-dominant theories of deviance. Existing theories tended to treat deviance as a distinctive quality of the deviant person or of his or her acts. Becker's definition proposed that deviance is a quality or qualities *imputed* to the person and to conduct by a process of social classification. Diverse forms of conduct are alike because they are defined as alike, not because of some shared inherent characteristics. Becker's approach also recognized that the creation of boundaries between deviant acts and persons—*outsiders*—and others is not automatic but results from conflict, negotiation, and the use of power. It is the *successful* application of labels that creates deviance, not simply either the attempt to do so or the act that provokes the attempt.

Becker's definition of deviance is a useful starting point, but it is not wholly satisfactory. It well captured the socially constructed nature of deviance: social groups create deviance by applying rules and sanctions to offenses and offenders, and in doing so they choose from virtually the whole range of human activities. Sexual orientation, in this view, is just as available as a basis for classification as deviant as is taking the life of another. At the same time, as Edwin Schur pointed out in criticizing Becker, the definition of deviance as "behavior that people so label" does not specify the grounds on which they do so.[2] What kinds of conduct do they so label? Any kind? Or are there limits on what may be called deviant? It can be argued that whereas homicide is widely considered a form of deviance, there is considerably more variation in the treatment of sexual behavior with members of one's own sex. If so, we need to examine the question of why some activities are more often chosen than others for classification as deviant.

Kai Erikson approached the thorny issue of what may or may not be called deviant by regarding deviance "as conduct which is generally thought to require the attention of social control agencies—that is, conduct about which 'something should be done.'"[3] Although this definition does not fully solve the problem of what *kinds* of conduct are likely to fall within the category of deviance, it does offer at least the beginnings of a standard: a sense that "somebody" ought to do "something" about the conduct in question. Conduct that in some or all cultures or under some or all circumstances is susceptible to classification as deviant is conduct that somehow arouses a sense of concern, a belief that something is amiss with the conduct or the person engaging in it.

Exactly what this "something amiss" may be is more difficult to specify. One approach—the approach often taken by those whom the labeling theorists criticized—would be to argue that people think that "something must be done" when laws or widely held social norms are violated. Alas, people witness (or themselves engage in) many such violations without arousing the feeling that something ought to be done. They break speed laws, cheat on their income taxes or on their spouses, steal office supplies, lie, and in other ways break the rules without outrage, remorse, or guilt. Moreover, whatever the "something amiss" might be, we can be fairly certain that it is highly variable from one culture to another and from one historical era to the next. Even though some acts, such as physical assault, theft, or taking human life may more universally arouse this sense of concern, variability is the rule rather than the exception. Particular acts do not always arouse this sense of concern, they do not do so in every culture, and not all members of a particular society exhibit the same degree of concern that something ought to be done in response to particular behavior. Family violence—both child and spouse abuse—is a matter of public concern, but acts (such as the corporal punishment of children or wife beating) that nowadays elicit widespread condemnation were once rather widely tolerated and even supported. Clearly there is a "something" of variable and changeable character.

We can specify our definition of deviance more precisely by suggesting that the belief that "something must be done" is aroused when a *breach of social order* is perceived and/or claimed by those with the capacity to apply deviant labels or to enlist those who have that capacity. A breach of social order entails a perception that the normal, usual, typical, and routine round of activities in the society or some part of it is being threatened or undermined. Whether the threat is "real" or "imaginary" is not at issue: It is as difficult for some people to think that homosexual relations between consenting adults are a "threat" to the social order as it is for others to think that they are not a threat. The issue is not the "reality" of a threat, but rather the fact that one is alleged, whether on the basis of a violation of norms, laws, or the self-interest or power of a particular social group.

Defining deviance as a category of behavior socially constructed as a threat to social order permits a variety of conduct to be seen as *possibly* subject to such classification, yet gives conceptual unity to the category. Any conduct targeted as a breach of order may be placed in the deviance category, provided there is someone who is ready to do so and able to mobilize support for doing so. The mobilization of support is crucial, for the classification of conduct as deviant is not automatic. People do not always find themselves in harmonious agreement with any particular label or its application under given circumstances. Many Americans readily agree that anti-war protest during a war is unpatriotic, an attack on the very foundations of the society; others feel as vehemently that even violent protest is moral in the context of what they see as immoral activity. Those who supply cocaine and other illegal drugs say that they see nothing wrong with their activities and that those who use legal drugs such as alcohol or tobacco are being hypocritical in making other drugs illegal; those who oppose the use of illegal drugs see the very future of the society endangered unless those drugs are eradicated. Social groups may find agreement easier in relation to some activities—homicide comes readily to mind—although even in such cases, they may more readily agree that something ought to be done than on what precisely should be done. The ongoing controversy over capital punishment in the United States suggests that responses to conduct defined as deviant are as variable as the classification itself.

Whether a particular form of conduct is viewed as deviant, therefore, is an outcome of negotiation and social definition. The distinction between legal and illegal protest is not fixed; it changes from time to time, depending on court decisions, the political views of local police and district attorneys, and the arguments that defense attorneys make and that judges and juries accept. It is not the inherent character of substances, but rather social processes that determine at any given time which drugs are legal and which are not. Whether capital punishment is practiced or outlawed depends on the political process in the states and in Congress as well as on the disposition of cases brought before the Supreme Court of the United States.

The perception of social disorder is only one element of deviance, for just as various acts come to be regarded as threats and classified as deviant, so those who commit them are seen as threatening and called deviants. As Jack Katz suggested, the attribution of a particular kind of status to the deviant is fundamental to the phenomenon of deviance. Katz argued that

> *the sociological existence of deviant phenomena is constituted by the imputation of deviant ontological status to human beings. The ontological status imputed to deviants is a negative essence, which is analytically the mirror-image of imputing to human beings a positive essence, or charisma. The one is an imputation of subhuman nature, the other of superhuman nature.*[4]

This idea carries us to the heart of the phenomenon of deviance: Not merely a category of *behavior* defined as a breach of social order, deviance also establishes a category of persons, viewed as somehow not fully normal, not in possession of normal human capabilities or dispositions, and perhaps not even fully human.

Deviance, Katz emphasized, is in many respects the opposite of charisma.[5] Some members of any society come to be defined as better than average, possessing superior capabilities, dispositions, or motives, whereas others become defined as worse than average, filled with undesirable motives or socially destructive capabilities, or perhaps simply lacking the capacity to act in appropriate ways. That people become so viewed is, of course, a function of socially imputed qualities and characteristics. Even though the concrete accomplishments of the charismatic figure may be the grounds on which he or she gains charisma, its maintenance rests equally on the *belief* in its existence. Similarly, deviants acquire negative essence because of their acts and the way they are defined. Belief in their badness, ill will, corruption, uncontrollability, and danger, however, are sustained as much by public imputation as by anything they subsequently do. Even the reformed criminal or recovered mentally ill person is feared in many quarters, just as the retired charismatic military hero or social movement leader retains the luster of charisma even after the glory days are past. Both negative and positive essences, once attached, tend to stick.

Deviance is thus sociologically identified by the perception of threat to social order and by the attribution of negative being to individuals. If an automobile suddenly veers onto a crowded sidewalk and kills several people, for example, we do not consider this an instance of deviance if we later discover that the car's brakes failed through no fault of the owner or the manufacturer. We see the event as tragic, but not as deviant. If we learn that the driver was drunk, however, then the act becomes deviant: We attribute a negative essence to an individual who, in disregard of the safety of others, operates an automobile that he or she is unable to control because of a decision to drink too much alcohol. In addition, we perceive this event as threatening in a broader sense, for we are apt to see the public safety as threatened by a more widespread problem of drunk driving, of which this is but one instance. Likewise, if the cause of an airplane crash in which hundreds die is found to be faulty maintenance by the airline or poor design by the manufacturer, the definition of the event as involving deviance comes into play.

A crucial element of this approach to deviance is the insight that neither the perception of threat nor the attribution of negative essence simply reflects the *discovery* of reality, although it often seems that we are uncovering the truth rather than socially constructing it. Clearly, there are many instances where it seems that there is little leeway for the "discovery" of any but the obvious "truth." If we observe someone who has previously threatened another take out a gun and shoot and kill that person, it seems fairly obvious to all concerned that this is a premeditated killing, that it represents a threat to the social order, and that a person who commits such an act is different from the rest of us. Even here, however, the act is judged deviant because there is widespread social agreement that such acts are criminal and that something needs to be done about those who commit them. One can imagine other circumstances—such as the late nineteenth-century American western frontier community, or perhaps even the contemporary urban scene—where at least some people are far more tolerant of such individual acts of violence and more inclined to see the perpetrator as acting from legitimate motives. The issue of what is threatening and what is not cannot be settled by appeal to the objective meaning of the act itself; here, as in social life generally, the meaning of an act lies in the response it elicits from others who have the capacity to do something about it.

One benefit of this approach to deviance, then, is that it makes somewhat easier the understanding of why a variety of forms of conduct can fall under the sociological rubric of deviance. The way we deal with the mentally ill (that is, those whose behavior earns them the modern label of mental illness) so closely resembles the way we treat other forms of deviance precisely because mental illness seems to elicit both a perception of threat to social order and the attribution of negative essence. Those classified as insane or deranged are quite often perceived (in the majority of cases, wrongly so) as a threat to community order. Their behavior arouses fear, distaste, or simply a desire to keep one's distance. People who are mentally ill are viewed as strange, dangerous, behaving in unpredictable ways for unfathomable reasons, and therefore as different from the rest of us. Despite the redefinition of insanity as illness, a movement founded on a concern to treat persons afflicted with mental illness more humanely, the mentally ill are often still perceived as a danger and an inconvenience. Perhaps this is because their definition as ill does not substantially alter the negative quality of the essences imputed to them. As earlier experience with such diseases as tuberculosis and cancer, and more recently with AIDS, has shown, medical conditions can easily arouse fear of contamination and loathing of the potential contaminator, even when people rationally understand that the problem is medical and not moral.

The *perception* of behavior as deviant relies on the perception of threat and the attribution of responsibility to the deviant. *Discourse* about deviance often—but by no means always—incorporates an additional element: normative conceptions. That is, the vocabularies with which we discuss deviance rely heavily on conceptions of right and wrong, even though the underlying reality is formed by perceptions of disorder and the attribution of individual cause. People do not merely talk about the threat that violent crime poses to upstanding citizens and decry the evil motives of criminals, for they also organize their conceptions of and their talk about crime in terms of right and wrong. "It is wrong to steal," we say; "it is sinful to have sexual relations with another of the same sex," some assert; "drugs are dangerous and lead us to do things we should not do," many people feel.

From the interactionist perspective, normative talk about deviance is an expectable but by no means inevitable practice, and it does not define the essence of the phenomenon. Social norms frequently are violated without any allegations of deviance. The mark of deviance is that a breach of social order is perceived and then attributed to the act of a specific individual. The act may be real or imaginary, and even the deviance may be, for a time, hypothetical, as when a murder has obviously been committed but there is not yet a suspect. Even though most acts are subsequently classified by people in reference to the norms, not all acts are so treated. Mental illness, for example, is marked by the perception of individually attributed acts that breach social order, yet it is not usually seen in normative terms. Indeed, the very classification of certain kinds of behavior as the result of illness suggests an effort to avoid defining them in normative terms. Defining conduct as a violation of norms usually implies that the violator's act will be seen as willful and knowledgeable unless shown to be otherwise. When we say that someone has broken a rule, we usually imply that he or she did so with knowledge of the rule and also with full intent to break it. To describe conduct as the result of mental illness, however, is to imply the lack of voluntary, knowledgeable violation. Yet, it should be noted, the person said to be mentally ill is judged no less a threat to social order, nor is that person's ontological status thereby made less negative.

One final note is in order. In many cases, deviance is a matter of degree, not an all-or-none classification. As Edwin Schur pointed out in his definition of deviance, behavior is deviant

> *to the extent that it comes to be viewed as involving a* personally discreditable *departure from a group's normative expectations, and it* elicits *interpersonal or collective reactions that serve to "isolate," "treat," "correct," or "punish"* individuals *engaged in such behavior.*[6]

Schur's definition recognizes that deviance is a variable phenomenon, not an absolute one—that any given act is more or less deviant, depending on whether it is noticed; and if noticed, taken seriously as a departure from group standards and attributed to the individual; and, if so taken, elicits a social reaction, whether an informal sanction in everyday life or the formal sanctions of police and courts.

Why Deviance Exists

The definition of deviance as personally discreditable threats to social order leaves a major question unasked: Why are boundaries created between deviant and nondeviant conduct and between upstanding members of a society and "outsiders"? The same question might be asked about any kind of boundary-making activity in social life: Why do people use principles of social classification that result in the creation of boundaries between types of people—boundaries that have consequences for people's lives, encourage identification with "us" and alienation from "others," and are enforced by social sanctions? The answer in the case of deviance is much the same as for other types: Boundaries arise out of people's practical efforts to organize their lives, secure their ends, and solve problems.

It is not difficult to see how this answer applies to the construction of "murder" or "burglary" as discreditable threats to social order. The circumstances in which people kill other members of their family or community are highly varied, of course, but taking another's life does raise practical problems: How will the deceased person's economically dependent family members survive? How should they be compensated? Is the murderer likely to kill someone else? Under such circumstances, it is useful to have regular and organized ways of dealing with an event that, however uncommon it may be, occurs often enough to be problematic. Ideas about forms of homicide (justifiable or not, premeditated or not) and about what to do when a life is taken (punish the offender or demand restitution) thus arise as ways of organizing social responses to a particular kind of event. The same might be said of theft, embezzlement, vandalism, and other forms of deviance involving property. In societies where individuals have exclusive rights over various forms of property (such as land, money, goods, or ideas), the appropriation of property without the consent of the owner or without compensation will arouse similar concerns: Will the rights of others to their property be safe in the future? How should the victim of theft be compensated? What is the community's interest in the individual's loss? And the ideas created over time—about the community's interest in protecting rights in property and the way to treat those who violate those rights—become standardized ways of defining and solving a problem.

When people classify acts and actors by calling them "deviance" and "deviant," they are doing what people must do in order to act successfully in their world. They are interpreting the meanings of acts and assigning motives to actors in order to decide what to do in response. What is true of conforming or unproblematic acts is also true of those acts that end up being classified as deviant: Any act lends itself to a great variety of interpretations, depending on the context of the act and the imputations others make about it. Did a woman kill her husband because he regularly beat her and she couldn't take it anymore or because she had a lover and wanted her husband out of the picture? Is a man taking a computer home from work in order to do work or to steal it? Is a youngster driving a car on his way home in the family automobile or is he taking a ride in a stolen vehicle? The interpretation and classification of a particular instance of conduct determines the way others will respond to it.

It is easier to see the utility of deviance boundaries with respect to some forms of conduct than others. The taking of human life, for example, may be perceived as a potential threat to social order in any society. We could say that a sense of concern about homicide is a natural, existential response and that the development of norms or rules against it is thus very likely. This approach has something to recommend it, for despite the fact that every society has systematic rules for excluding certain categories of people (e.g., enemies, strangers, those not considered fully human) from the general rule that murder is wrong, the act itself seems inherently a threat to social order. It is, in a sense, difficult for human beings not to interpret murder as a problematic act. Likewise, where private property exists, it is difficult not to define interference with property rights as a problem to be dealt with.

Mental Illness

Mental illness provides another illustration of conduct where we can readily grasp why a sense of concern about social order is aroused. Indeed, as Morris Rosenberg persuasively argued, symbolic interactionism enables us to pinpoint precisely what it is that people find unusual about at least one particular form of mental illness, psychosis.[7] We call certain behavior "insane," Rosenberg said, because we are unable to grasp the perspective from which the person exhibiting this behavior has acted—our efforts at role taking are unsuccessful—and we attribute this failure to the other's conduct and not to our own inability or unwillingness to try to understand it.

Rosenberg argued that the criteria psychiatrists use to identify psychosis, although sound and useful from a medical point of view, do not really tell us much about why we find psychotic behavior disturbing. Psychiatrists rely on such criteria as "subjective distress" and "impairment of functioning" to diagnose this and other forms of mental illness. People in many circumstances, however, experience subjective distress or impaired functioning but are not considered mentally ill. The loss of a job or the death of a child are occasions on which people are upset and do not function as they normally would, for example, but we do not therefore consider them psychotic. Indeed, we find these reactions quite typical and would be surprised if they did not occur.

Yet, mentally ill people clearly do exhibit distress and impaired functioning. The psychiatric view tends to treat their behavior, thought, and affect as objective indicators—or symptoms—of illness. The problem, however, is that behavior that under some circumstances is treated as evidence of psychosis is viewed entirely differently under other conditions. Rosenberg used the example of a wealthy movie star who was arrested for shoplifting and whose behavior was later psychiatrically diagnosed as kleptomania. The same behavior from a poor youth living in a slum would probably be regarded as sane and not as evidence of illness. If conduct under the former circumstance is considered symptomatic of insanity, but not under the latter condition, then what makes the act sane or insane is not the act itself but rather the way others interpret it. Similarly, whether a belief in ghosts indicates insanity depends on one's cultural surroundings; to believe seriously in ghosts or leprechauns in a culture where these beings are assumed to exist is to be sane; to believe seriously in such beings in contemporary North America might well raise questions about one's sanity. To be depressed when a spouse has died is considered normal in U.S. culture, whereas to be depressed for no apparent reason is taken as a sign of illness.

Whether behavior, thought, or affect is regarded as "sane" or "insane" depends on whether and how an observer makes sense of it. Observers cannot understand why a wealthy person would shoplift from a store, whereas they can grasp a poor individual's reasons for stealing. In the former case, they cannot successfully role take—that is, observers cannot impute any perspective or motives to the other that would enable them to see the conduct as an expression of the person's role. In the latter case, they can do so—observers can grasp the perspective of a poor person as one from which theft is a possible act and perhaps even a necessary one. Likewise, they can successfully put themselves in the shoes of the grieving survivor and understand why he or she is depressed—depression seems to be a likely and reasonable reaction to a loss. But under some conditions people seem depressed even though observers can find no good reason for them to be. When role taking thus fails, they are inclined to take depression as an indication of mental illness.

Role-taking failure does not invariably lead people to view others' conduct as indicative of insanity, but only when they believe that the failure is not their own fault. As Rosenberg pointed out, people do not consider babies insane, even though their behavior is often difficult to fathom. Rather, people assume that they just have not been able to figure out why the child behaves in a particular way. By the same token, patients do not consider physicians insane, even though they do things—shining lights, using unintelligible terms, poking and prodding in strange ways—they cannot fathom. Patients assume, instead, that physicians know what they are doing even if they, due to ignorance of medical procedure, do not.

But under some conditions, observers attribute failure of role taking to the behavior of the other rather than to themselves. Where people think they should observe conduct that is typical of an individual or a role incumbent, and where observed behavior seems atypical, improbable, and inexplicable, people are likely to say that the fault lies with the acting person. If a friend begins to act depressed and one cannot interpret his or her mood as typical of this person, as a likely response to experiences he or she has had, or as a rational response to the situation in which we find the person, then one is apt to think something is wrong with the individual. One may not immediately jump to the conclusion that the individual is mentally ill—people seem to avoid applying this label as long as they can—but one is at the very least suspicious that something may be amiss and that the problem lies with the friend.

Rosenberg's approach to mental illness fits well with the general approach to deviance developed here. That is, social suspicions or judgments of insanity or mental illness seem to focus on the individual whose behavior is in question, and they seem to attribute to that person a special and not very positive status. Although it is the puzzling behavior of others that strikes us as noteworthy, once we have begun to think of the behavior as insane, we also consider the person to be insane. Mental illness, much like other forms of deviance, is a label that, once applied because of our inability otherwise to understand a person's behavior, comes to apply to the whole person and not just to the behavior. Once this happens, all of the negative stereotypes—such as unpredictability or violence—attached to mental illness become attached to the person.

Moreover, not only do we attribute a deviant ontological status to the person as a way of accounting for his or her conduct, but also a sense of threat to social order is mobilized. It is difficult and uncomfortable to deal with people when we cannot successfully role take. Our normal expectations about how people will behave are not met, and so there is a sense of discomfort, at the very least, and often a sense of more serious threat. People who address us in a babble of incoherent words or who seem depressed when there is no reason to be depressed disrupt our usual assumption that we are living in a world where people understand one another and interact in an orderly fashion. Furthermore, because stereotypes have grown up about the conduct of the mentally ill—that they are dangerous and prone to violence, for example—there is also a deeper sense that we might be harmed if they are not isolated and controlled.

Moral Enterprise

It is more difficult to take an "existential" view of deviance when we move much beyond murder (and other violent acts against persons), property crimes, and mental illness. The amount of time and money devoted since the 1960s (without any apparent success) to stamping out the use of marijuana seems to many people far out of proportion to the threat posed by this drug. This is particularly the case if one compares the health consequences of marijuana with those of tobacco, a legal and by all accounts far more deadly drug. The same can be said of sexual and reproductive conduct: The existence of laws against fornication, sodomy, the sale of contraceptive devices, and abortion at various times in the United States requires that we ask how and why such deviance categories are created.

A fundamental insight of symbolic interactionists has been that the creation of deviance categories as well as the making and enforcing of rules against various forms of conduct results from both individual and collective enterprise. Categories and rules do not emanate automatically from the culture; they do not spontaneously appear. Rather, rules are the result of collective efforts of definition and redefinition. Howard Becker stated the point forcefully:

> *Wherever rules are created and applied, we should be alive to the possible presence of an enterprising individual or group. Their activities can properly be called moral enterprise, for what they are enterprising about is the creation of a new fragment of the moral constitution of society, its code of right and wrong.*[8]

Becker illustrated this view by showing the use of such moral enterprise by the Federal Bureau of Narcotics in seeking passage of the Marijuana Tax Act of 1937, which rigidly controlled marijuana by heavy taxation. Officials of the bureau sought to bring marijuana within their official jurisdiction and waged a sustained public relations campaign in order to gain congressional support. Their campaign was ultimately effective not only in securing legislation but also in widely publicizing the alleged dangers of the drug.

Before the bureau's campaign, law enforcement officials had expressed little concern about marijuana, and few states had laws prohibiting it. There was, in other words, no widely perceived breach of social order in the use of this drug until a group of moral entrepreneurs—perhaps motivated as much as anything by a desire to see the powers and budget of their bureau expanded—succeeded in creating such a public perception. The evils of the drug were dramatized, rules against its sale and possession formulated, and the perversities of its users highlighted, not by the spontaneous responses of people to an obvious breach of order, but because of moral enterprise.

Analyzing the American Temperance Movement, Joseph Gusfield showed that such moral campaigns are closely related to how the constituent groups of a society view one another.[9] Rural Protestants, who had traditionally dominated U.S. culture and had upheld temperance norms, began to feel more and more threatened by urban, Catholic, and working-class immigrants as the nineteenth century wore on. Increasingly, temperance-oriented Protestants turned their attention away from a humanitarian concern for the victims of alcoholism and toward a more combative, coercive effort on behalf of the prohibition of alcohol. The use of alcohol became seen as a violation of the Protestant conception of moral conduct and a practice with unfortunate consequences, as well as a potent symbol of the decline in status and influence of the older Protestant groups relative to those of newcomers. The successful passage of the prohibition amendment provided a way for Protestants to assert what they felt was their legitimate "moral ownership" of U.S. society in the face of their declining actual status and power.

Useful as these explanations are to an understanding of how and why categories of deviance are created, an important caveat is in order: Moral enterprises, like all other human activities, arise out of diverse motives, as do societal responses to those efforts. Thus, to claim that the anti-marijuana campaign was moved by the desire of a federal agency to expand its scope is not to claim that as the only motive. Likewise, to argue that Protestants favored prohibition because of their social status anxieties is not to claim that was the only reason for the ultimate success of the Temperance Movement. To argue for simple motivational explanations would be to engage in the very motive mongering we condemned in Chapter 4. Doubtless there were and are public officials, clergy, teachers, physicians, and parents genuinely concerned about the effects of drugs on their children. The effects of excessive drinking on family life and public order are not figments of the imagination, nor were they at the time of the Temperance Movement, and many people were and are opposed to drink because they perceive it as a real social problem. By the same token, contemporary people who oppose abortion or support an amendment to the U.S. Constitution that would forbid marriage between two people of the same sex may very well hold these beliefs sincerely because of their religious convictions.

Yet the same caveat applies to explanations anchored in the "sincere" beliefs of people as to those anchored in sociological investigations like those of Becker or Gusfield. Those firmly opposed to abortion under any circumstances often claim religious motives for their beliefs and actions. Symbolic interactionists would hold that such claims, like all motive claims and imputations, have to be subject to some scrutiny, and for the same reasons: Acts arise out of diverse motivations and can be attributed to a variety of motives, both by those who engage in them and those who witness them. When people cite motives for their actions, they are apt to come to believe in and claim sincerity for those motives, even if the circumstances that originally prompted their actions were quite different. Thus, the claim by anti-abortion activists that they oppose abortion for religious reasons may be true enough, but not necessarily constitute the "whole truth" as a social scientist might view it. One has only to point to a variety of religious beliefs that do not seem to prompt such heated action and social controversy to grasp that the explanation of an activity requires us to look further than the motives cited by participants.

Moral enterprise provides an explanation of *how* deviance categories are created, and only indirectly addresses the question of *why*. Social research can show how a particular social movement comes into being and, over time, creates a deviance category such as alcoholism, drug abuse, or abortion. It can ferret out the complex motivational underpinnings of involvement in and support for such a social movement. But in the last analysis, there is no definitive answer to the question of why, other than the answer to the question how. Social boundaries are created out of human actions; they arise out of the practical activities of people in their worlds; they have consequences for people on either side of the boundary, some of those consequences intended and some not. Boundaries exist because people create them, but there is no single explanation of why they do so.

The Causes of Deviance

An approach that finds the reality of deviance in a combination of perceived threats to social order and attributions of personal essence clearly complicates the problem of identifying the "causes" of deviance. Rather than being an objective reality, a fixed and given part of the social world, deviance is to a great extent a product of human definitions of what the world is like. This is not to say that there are no causes of deviance apart from social definitions. People kill and steal from one another for a variety of reasons and in many different circumstances; they use drugs sometimes because they are taught to do so and sometimes because the drugs allow an escape from painful realities; they develop homosexual or bisexual rather than exclusively heterosexual orientations for reasons that are scarcely understood; and so a list of "deviant" forms of behavior might be elaborated and the potentially diverse causes of each specified.

The symbolic interactionist approach eschews any effort to find any simple set of causes of deviance or to view deviance as a form of conduct sharply differentiated from the ordinary. The same processes of defining the situation, role taking, and role making that are found in everyday life also underlie deviant conduct. Those who engage in deviance have goals and purposes, just as do those who avoid deviance. And the self is as crucial an object in the experience of one who engages in deviant forms of conduct as it is in the life of one who does not. Moreover, if deviance arises from the same processes and circumstances as ordinary conduct, there are no simple keys to its explanation and control. It is an unavoidably diverse phenomenon, which resists simple explanations.

The applicability of standard symbolic interactionist concepts to the study of deviance is illustrated in Lonnie Athens's intensive study of violent criminal acts and actors, which relies primarily on in-depth interviews with violent offenders convicted of such crimes as homicide, rape, and robbery.[10] Athens found that, contrary to conventional assumptions that depict violence as the result of unconscious motivations or emotional outbursts, people "commit violent criminal acts *only after* they form violent interpretations of the situations which confront them." The violent criminal actors in Athens's study assessed the situations in which they found themselves and self-consciously came to the conclusion that violence was an appropriate or required course of action. Athens also found that each actor's self-image affected his or her assessment of the situation. Those with nonviolent self-images committed violent acts only in situations in which their interpretations called for physical self-defense; those with violent self-images interpreted a wider range of situations as calling for violent actions.

Athens's study points to the necessity of taking actors' definitions of situations into account in explaining their deviant conduct. It also underscores the *decisional* nature of much deviance. The origins of many forms of deviance seem to lie in the assessments and interpretations of people as they act in their social worlds rather than in some more uniform, hidden causes that, if discovered, might make control of deviance easier. If such clear-cut acts of deviance as rape or assault are the result of conscious (and, from the standpoint of perpetrators, even "rational") decisions to act in given ways, then it is especially difficult to grasp the causality of deviance. If people define situations in novel, unexpected, and *mistaken* ways, then any given situation may provoke a variety of definitions and acts, some of which may be deviant.

In a similar vein, Jack Katz also argued that in order to understand crime, we must see it as the criminal sees it. Katz described how many forms of criminal activities seduce the criminal through their own rewards and excitements. Various crimes—from the thrill-seeking crimes of adolescents who vandalize, joyride in stolen cars, or shoplift to cold-blooded and seemingly senseless killings by adult, hardened criminals—hold positive attractions for those who perpetrate them. Although criminals may recognize what they do as wrong and even be ashamed of their crimes, the actual doing of a particular crime may be interesting, exciting, gripping, and ultimately compelling. In addition to its particular emotional rewards, each crime entails a particular set of joint actions that must be completed and each fosters a distinctive understanding of oneself in relation to others. Thus, Katz wrote that often for adolescents,

> *shoplifting and vandalism offer the attractions of a thrilling melodrama about the self as seen from within and without. Quite apart from what is taken, they may regard "getting away with it" as a thrilling demonstration of personal competence, especially if it is accomplished under the eyes of adults.*[11]

For these and other crimes, the perpetrator sees himself or herself faced with a particular challenge, and the crime is a way of meeting it.

The hypothesis that deviant conduct has multiple causes—and that it may, for some people, become an inherently attractive way of life—seems at least as plausible as any of the current theories of particular forms of deviance that see them in singular terms. Indeed, it is this hypothesis that partly accounts for the appeal of the symbolic interactionist perspective, which permits the apparent diversity of causes of given forms of deviance to be accommodated with the fact that each form often seems to us in commonsense terms to be uniform—that is, to have certain identifiable and inescapable characteristics. The social construction of deviance as a category of act and person is what accounts for the apparent uniformity of deviance, not its underlying causes.

This point holds more generally about all human conduct. An exceedingly complex set of situations, biographical experiences, individual motivations, and combinations of persons interacting with one another can be assumed to lie behind each observable act or sequence of acts. As I sit at the computer, composing this paragraph, for example, a multitude of factors impinge on and help shape my act. While I am acting within my definition of the situation—writing a book—I also am subject to other kinds of influences. The telephone may ring, a student may knock on my door to ask a question or just to chat with me, or my mind may wander away from my situated role and into other aspects of my life. Thus, how I actually write this paragraph—what I end up typing into the computer—results from a great number of influences, many of which really have little or nothing to do with the act of writing.

An observer would have little difficulty seeing my conduct as typical of someone in my position. No one else can fully penetrate my mind and predict what I am going to do, where I will get my examples for a point I am trying to make, or what I will end up saying. I cannot even fully predict these things myself. Yet, somehow the end product of my conduct appears meaningful and expectable. It can be seen as sensibly related to the definition of the situation I am in, as living up to the expectations associated with my role, and as typical of me as an individual. Put simply, no matter how complex the actual causes of my conduct, it often seems very simple and straightforward when viewed from the perspective of someone who shares my definition of the situation.

Thus we should underscore the fact that putting people and their acts into categories is not only a phenomenon related to deviance but also to all human conduct. In our efforts to make sense of the world we inhabit, including our own conduct in it, we sort people into categories—such as insane, criminal, homosexual, exceptional, or abnormal—and then treat the boundaries we have created as real and significant. The fact that the causes of conduct that lead people to become categorized in such terms are diverse should give us a clue that perhaps the causes of any conduct are multiple. Even though the extraordinary character of the kinds of conduct we call deviance and of the persons we call deviants tends to make us pay attention to them and look for underlying causes, we should not lose sight of the fact that all conduct has exceedingly complex antecedents and situational influences. We label good guys, the average person, and heroes just as much as we label the so-called nuts and crooks. In either case, the categories we use and the assumptions that lie behind them exert a powerful influence on what we see and how we explain it, not only as ordinary people but as sociologists looking for the causes of given forms of behavior.

Deviance and Identity

The social categories of deviance also affect the lives and future conduct of those to whom they are applied. Because they prompt the attribution of negative essence, deviant acts reflect negatively on the situated, social, and personal identities of those who engage in them. It is individuals who are held responsible for their acts and who are targeted for correction, rehabilitation, punishment, isolation from society, and other such responses intended to root out the causes of the behavior from the individual and to protect the society from him or her. This social treatment establishes and sometimes controls the identities of those who are labeled as deviant.

Most people make a variety of roles in their day-to-day affairs and thus have a variety of situated identities. They are, for example, office workers and fathers and husbands and volunteer firefighters and many other things. Their social and personal identities are constructed out of these situated identities. Although some roles are much more important than others as bases for viewing and defining individuals—and for their defining themselves—few roles prevent us from making other roles. For women, for example, certain roles are more difficult to make; to the extent that some people think that women cannot be competent engineers or truck drivers, women will have difficulty entering such roles and building them into their identities. Gender is thus a very powerful identity—that is, an identity that strongly affects the way others view the person and the way the person views himself or herself. Still, both men and women make a variety of roles and thus have a variety of situated identities.

Deviance often confers not only a powerful identity but also a controlling identity. If an individual is identified as deviant in some respect—such as a bank robber, a juvenile delinquent, or a psychotic—that identification tends to become the main or even the sole basis on which others define and relate to the person. The establishment of a deviant identity in the eyes of others tends to negate all or most other possible identities, especially so in the eyes of those others who regard the deviance category in question as particularly grave. That other identities are negated means that the individual is seen as incapable of assuming them. In spite of whatever identities the person *announces,* others *place* him or her in the deviant identity.

Thus, for example, someone who is accused and convicted of murder becomes—at least in the eyes of the public—a "murderer," someone whose very essence is defined by this label and whose other possible roles and identities thereby become inoperative. Likewise, even today, if an individual is publicly labeled as homosexual, the result may be that at least some people will be unwilling to regard that person in any other capacity except as homosexual. That is, their attitudes toward the person would be profoundly shaped by the knowledge of his or her homosexuality, they might tend to see homosexual motives underlying most of the person's conduct, and they might in some cases try to prevent the person from assuming other identities, such as being a neighbor in an apartment building or a coworker on the job.

In many forms of deviance, formally constituted agencies of social control—police, courts, probation officers, attorneys, and the like—attach deviant identities to individuals. Thieves and murderers are apprehended, indicted, tried, convicted, and incarcerated; and each step in this process is not only a part of the application (or misapplication) of justice but also the attachment of an identity to a person. The "due process" to which the Fifth Amendment to the Constitution entitles Americans is a matter of law as well as the attachment and certification of identity.

Deviant identities are not only attached by official agencies but also in less formal ways. The thief or murderer comes to have a criminal identity as much through the efforts of the mass media as through the operation of the criminal justice system. This is perhaps especially true of "leading" criminal figures—those who acquire a substantial local or national reputation, such as Al Capone and other gangsters of the 1930s or Mafia leaders in later years—as well as serial killers whose activities are sensationalized by the media. Moreover, even when particular forms of deviance go unattended by the police, their discovery in informal social circles is sufficient to attach and sustain a deviant label. Except for those involved in "tearoom sex" (the making of impersonal homosexual contacts by men in public places), most homosexuals are not formally charged or processed by the police or courts for sex offenses, even though laws against sodomy remain on the books in many states. Yet, the discovery of an individual's homosexuality by friends or associates is sufficient to give that person a new identity in their eyes, particularly if they disapprove of homosexuality. Where attitudes are rigidly homophobic, redefinition of the individual concerned is likely to be substantial and to entail considerable imputing of negative essence. Even where attitudes are relatively tolerant, some redefinition is likely, if only to the extent that the individual now becomes someone whose homosexuality is understood and accepted because *otherwise* this person is "normal."

If the individual acquires membership in a deviant category—and is assigned a situated identity as deviant—as a result of legal processing, public labeling by others, or retrospective reinterpretation, how does this fact shape the person's social and personal identity? Are deviant labels applied only by others, or are they also self-applied? Does the person build a deviant label into his or her social or personal identity? If so, how does this affect subsequent conduct? Does labeling itself become one of the causes of deviance? Can the person under some circumstances resist a deviant label?

Labeling an individual as deviant implies several *possible,* but not inevitable, developments. To grasp them, we must first grasp the distinction between primary and secondary deviance. *Primary deviance,* Edwin Lemert argued, arises out of a variety of factors—"social, cultural, psychological, and physiological"—and it has little to do with the person's sense of self.[12] For various reasons, individuals perform acts that are considered deviant: adolescents get in fights, for example, or people drink too much or use other powerful drugs. *Secondary deviance,* in contrast, consists of "deviant behavior or social roles based upon it which becomes a means of social defense, attack or adaptation to the overt and covert problems created by the societal reaction to primary deviance."[13] Primary deviance arises out of diverse causes; secondary deviance arises because of the way others react to this primary deviance. What processes might be at work?

First, because the person to whom a deviant label is attached is thereby placed in a category of people who are similarly labeled, there is at least implicitly some pressure to identify with others who are so labeled. To impute a negative essence—whether "criminal" or "homosexual" or "insane"—is to create a boundary between the person and those who are not so labeled. Others may tend to avoid this person, to exclude him or her from their social circles, and to refuse to give the person a job or to sell or rent housing. Labeling also encourages a sense of "membership" in the deviance category and thus some degree of identification—a sense of likeness and common purpose—with others who are deviant. The labeled deviant is pushed out of conventional situations and associations and pulled toward deviant ones.

Those who are labeled may perceive some advantage in such identification. Lumped in with other adolescents who are called "delinquents," the young person may feel that he or she can be fully accepted only among such others. Despised or rejected by those who hold strongly homophobic attitudes, the gay or lesbian individual may conclude that only by socially identifying with a gay or lesbian community will he or she truly feel at ease, be accepted by others, and thus have any sort of normal opportunity for maintaining self-esteem and constructing a personal identity.

Second, because categorization as deviant frequently offers the person only one role to perform and one situated identity to claim, the person may also feel some pressures to learn to think, feel, and act in fairly standardized ways implied by the label itself. To be labeled "deviant" is to experience the pressures of altercasting—that is, to be handed a role and to be subtly (and sometimes not so subtly) pressured to accept it. In part, these pressures are effective because they encourage the individual to think of himself or herself solely in terms of the proffered role and identity. The labeled delinquent, in this view, comes to think of himself or herself as delinquent, and this concept of self then prompts the individual to enact a delinquent role.

By the same token, the person who is able to maintain a self-definition as "normal" is likely to be the one who can resist this altercasting. It is important to grasp that individuals do not necessarily or automatically accept the identities that are handed them through deviant labeling. They do not necessarily thus identify with other deviants, learn to make deviant roles, or think of themselves as deviant. Delinquents assert that they are not really bad; homosexuals maintain that the only thing that differentiates them from others is sexual orientation. Relying on a combination of inner resources, in the form of previously established personal and social identities, and support from others, labeled deviants are able to resist accepting some or all of the implications of the new identity that others try to attach to them. Their success in doing so also depends on their capacity to engage in successful aligning actions—to excuse, justify, and otherwise account for their actions in ways that leave their identities relatively unharmed.

Any labeling of an individual, however, will have at least the effect of generating doubt where previously there was an unproblematic concept of self.[14] A young boy who gets into trouble with the police may be treated as an ordinary delinquent—as typical of the hundreds of juveniles with whom they have dealt. Even though the police may act toward the youth *as if* he has the usual delinquent propensities—lying, being disrespectful, being ready to go out and get into trouble again—this one episode of labeling probably will not lead to a substantial change in self-concept, but it will probably raise some doubts and anxieties. Subsequent episodes are sure to do so. The boy who has never before encountered any official sanctions and then, through bad luck or circumstances, has one or two run-ins with the police, may experience a subtle change in self-concept. Where previously no question had ever been raised, he may now ask, Is there something wrong with me? Told by police that "all you kids are alike," he may begin to wonder if, in fact, this is not so.

There is some evidence that whether labeling affects the self depends on where the individual is located in the social structure. Gary F. Jensen's studies of delinquency, for example, seem to indicate that being labeled as a delinquent has more effect on Whites than on Blacks.[15] Given the systematic exclusion of many African Americans from educational and occupational opportunities and their frequent devaluation and denigration by Whites, they may be less inclined to doubt themselves on the basis of labels commonly applied by Whites. The more an individual is integrated in a given social order, the more its labels have significance for the self; the less a part of that world the individual feels, the less compelled he or she feels to regard its judgments as significant.

Self-labeling may be as significant or more significant than labeling by others. The delinquent whose primary offense goes undetected by police may nevertheless be aware that he or she has broken the law and even consider himself or herself a delinquent because of this fact. To be sure, the act would have a different meaning had it been detected by others—an act is, in the terms of Schur's definition quoted earlier, "more deviant" if others see it and label it than if the person alone thinks he or she is a delinquent. In some cases, the application of labels to the self is *the* crucial basis for establishing a deviant identity. This is true of homosexuality: People very early learn to avoid displaying what at first seems to themselves a very unusual sexual orientation and then later come to think of themselves as gay or lesbian, often seeking to conceal this fact from audiences who might publicly label them in a negative manner.

Others' formal and informal responses to deviance may thus contribute to the elaboration of deviant conduct and thereby become one of its causes. Although we should not ignore this aspect of the deviance process, neither should we overemphasize it. Labeling contributes to deviance, but it is not its only cause. As we have argued, there is no more sense in asserting that deviance has a single cause than in asserting that any other form of conduct has a single cause. The human social world is complex, and the forces that influence what we do are likewise complex.

Keywords

Charisma Charisma is usually defined as the possession by an individual of unique, unusually positive abilities or characteristics—strength, personality, character, wisdom, virtue, and the like—that induce others to pay special attention to this individual and to accept his or her influence. Charismatic leaders seem capable of holding an audience spellbound and getting their followers to obey commands they would resist if issued by someone else. Charismatic leaders appear to have a special "presence"—to inspire a level of attention and awe in others that ordinary people cannot command.

Two things are particularly important about charisma from a symbolic interactionist point of view. First, charisma arises from imputations people make about a leader and not only, or even mainly, from the special qualities of the leader. In other words, charisma, like beauty, lies in the eye of the beholder. President John F. Kennedy had a great deal of charisma, and it is easy to suppose that it arose from his height and bearing, his rugged good looks, or his manner of speaking. But, in fact, one can just as well argue that the United States was ready for such a leader after the 1950s, and that Kennedy was an ideal person to be imbued with charisma. Moreover, he had more charisma after his assassination than before, when he was a controversial political figure.

Second, charisma reveals an important feature of social order: People's hopes and aspirations for their society and their wish for an orderly and predictable social world sometimes become embodied in particular individuals. Sociologists think of social order as resting on social structure and culture, which provide for the coordination of social activity. But as a constructed reality, social order is also embodied or personified by charismatic persons. The reverse is also true: Social *disorder* is represented by those persons to whom a negative ontological status is imputed—most notably criminals and the insane, who personify threats to established conceptions of normality.

Deviance   Deviance is a category of persons and their conduct thought to present a threat to social order, to whom negative essence is attributed and about whom it is thought something should be done. The reality of deviance, therefore, does not lie in the essence or even in the conduct of those considered deviant, but rather in the system of classification that makes them deviant. Deviance is a product of social classification.

This approach to defining deviance does not represent a judgment on the part of the sociologist that undesirable conduct is merely an artifact of classification. Like others, sociologists would rather not be mugged and would readily agree that frequent muggings are a threat to social order about which something ought to be done. Rather, viewing deviance as a social classification rather than an objective reality reminds us that it is as important to explain the creation of social rules and the circumstances under which social control is brought into play as it is to explain the conduct that is scrutinized.

Labeling   Labeling is the result of a process of social classification. A deviant label, for example, arises out of a process in which persons are classified as deviant. Labels are important, in the interactionist view, for the same reason *naming* more generally is important. Names define situations and their members, specifying how we are to act toward others and what kinds of treatment they are to be given. *Friend* and *enemy* are thus as much labels in this sense as *murderer* or *rapist*. It is sometimes argued rather simplistically that deviant labels tend to encourage the persistence of deviant behavior, on the theory that labels create a deviant identity that the person then enacts. Labels may have such effects, but no more in the case of deviance than in the case of other kinds of labels. People are socially classified in various ways, but they do not necessarily accept their classifications or come to believe in the labels others attach to them.

Mental Illness   Mental illness is a social classification that results in the attachment of labels to the individual—for instance, insane, depressed, psychotic, or schizophrenic—and his or her treatment as a real or potential threat to the social order. This classification is rooted in the inability of those who apply the classification to grasp the perspective of those to whom they apply it. In other words, we call people insane when we cannot understand the perspective from which they are acting and do not believe it is our fault that we cannot understand.

To define mental illness in this way is to say nothing about the causes of the various mental and medical phenomena that may lead to this classification. Depression and schizophrenia, for example, are legitimately viewed as medical conditions. The depressed person is not depressed because he or she is classified as depressed, but because of one or more specific neurological conditions that may be identified and treated. The social classification, as opposed to the medical classification, of persons as mentally ill takes place without a keen regard for precise medical categories or explanations. The social psychologist may be interested in the way a medical condition, such as depression, is linked to the person's social experiences, but the social psychologist is also interested in the way ordinary people define depression, how they classify people as depressed, and why depression is bothersome from the standpoint of others.

Moral Enterprise   Moral enterprise is Howard Becker's phrase for the active pursuit of definitions of various forms of behavior as deviant and usually also for the resources and authority to combat these forms of conduct. The concept helps in specifying why certain kinds of behavior are singled out for scrutiny and for classification as deviant. That is, some rules arise not because people spontaneously experience fear or revulsion at the behavior they are created to prohibit, but because specific individuals and groups campaign to create such fear and revulsion. Drug laws in the United States are a good example of moral enterprise, not only in the original campaign against narcotics and marijuana but also at present. There now exists a substantial antidrug industry whose economic and career interests depend on the maintenance of antidrug hysteria.

Social Control The concept of social control refers to a variety of social arrangements that are brought into play in order to regulate and sanction the behavior of individuals and groups. The most obvious mechanism of social control is the formal mechanism of the legal system—that is, the laws, police, courts, and prisons that define, detect, adjudicate, and punish criminal behavior. Social control, however, exists in every sphere of social life, and may be informal as well as formal. Within friendship circles, for example, people exert informal social controls by criticizing, ostracizing, or gossiping about one another. Parents exert social control by "grounding" their children or by enforcing "time outs." Social control may also be positive as well as negative. Friends, for example, praise one another and thereby reinforce desired behavior; and parents point to the accomplishments of other people's children and thus set standards for their own.

The relationship between social control and the conduct it is intended to prohibit or foster is complex. Undesired forms of conduct stimulate social controls. Parents respond to a misbehaving child by calling for a "time out," and police respond to a robbery in progress by pursuing suspects, making arrests, and pressing charges in court. But social control also has a life of its own, sometimes creating deviance or even eliciting the behavior it is intended to regulate. Thus, for example, agents of social control, such as drug enforcement agents, look for violations of the law in order to justify their employment. Parents may strive to regulate their children's lives for the sake of doing so (because they can) and not because their children's behavior is especially problematic. Indeed, in many circumstances the existence of social control provokes rebellion, as when children consciously or unconsciously provoke their parents' ire by doing what they know is prohibited, or try to get away with undetected rule violations to assure themselves they are not completely ruled by parental expectations.

Endnotes

1. Howard S. Becker, *Outsiders* (New York: Free Press, 1963), p. 9. For a review of sociological approaches to deviance and the symbolic interactionist response, including labeling theory, see Nancy J. Herman-Kinney, "Deviance," in *Handbook of Symbolic Interaction* (Walnut Creek, CA: AltaMira, 2003), pp. 695–720.

2. See Edwin Schur, *Labeling Deviant Behavior: Its Sociological Implications* (New York: Harper & Row, 1971), p. 23ff.

3. Kai Erikson, "Notes on the Sociology of Deviance," in *The Other Side*, ed. Howard S. Becker (New York: Free Press, 1964), pp. 9–21.

4. Jack Katz, "Deviance, Charisma, and Rule-Defined Behavior," *Social Problems* 20 (1972): 192.

5. Charisma, in Max Weber's words, is "a certain quality of an individual personality by virtue of which he is set apart from ordinary men and treated as endowed with supernatural, superhuman, or at least specifically exceptional qualities." See Max Weber, *The Theory of Social and Economic Organization*, trans. R. A. Henderson and Talcott Parsons, ed. Talcott Parsons (New York: Oxford University Press, 1947).

6. Schur, *Labeling Deviant Behavior*, p. 24 (Note 2).

7. This discussion of mental illness relies on Morris Rosenberg's "A Symbolic Interactionist View of Psychosis," *Journal of Health and Social Behavior* 25 (September 1984): 289–302.

8. Becker, *Outsiders*, p. 145 (Note 1).

9. Joseph Gusfield, *Symbolic Crusade* (Urbana: University of Illinois Press, 1963).

10. Lonnie H. Athens, *Violent Criminal Acts and Actors: A Symbolic Interactionist Study* (London: Routledge and Kegan Paul, 1980); and Athens, *Violent*

Criminal Acts and Actors Revisited (Urbana: University of Illinois Press, 1997).

11. Jack Katz, *Seductions of Crime: Moral and Sensual Attractions in Doing Evil* (New York: Basic Books, 1988), p. 9.

12. Edwin M. Lemert, *Human Deviance, Social Problems, and Social Control* (Englewood Cliffs, NJ: Prentice-Hall, 1967), p. 40.

13. Ibid, p. 17.

14. See the classic analysis of this point by David Matza, *Becoming Deviant* (Englewood Cliffs, NJ: Prentice Hall, 1969).

15. Gary F. Jensen, "Delinquency and Adolescent Self-Conceptions: A Study of the Personal Relevance of Infraction," *Social Problems* 20 (1972): 84–102.

Chapter 7

The Value of
Symbolic Interactionism

The time has come to ask questions that perhaps many readers have been asking throughout this book: What is the value of symbolic interactionism as an approach to the study of social life? Does it offer anything that the ordinary person can use to help make the human condition better—or even to make his or her own life better? What is the point of all this theorizing and research?

These questions have no easy answers. Social science does not enjoy a particularly good reputation in the contemporary world, either among students or the public at large. It often seems to express murky ideas in turgid, jargon-laden prose or to tell us only what everybody already knows. Sometimes it seems bent on reducing the complexity of human experience to crude formulas, or on stripping away any sense of mystery about life and portraying human beings as naked economic creatures. Moreover, the very idea of scientific knowledge itself is under attack from various quarters. Some argue that science—particularly social science—does nothing more than legitimize existing social inequalities and power arrangements. Others think that any quest for empirical generalizations or for explanations of human behavior is foolish and that any scientific effort to describe social reality distorts it.

I work from a symbolic interactionist perspective because I think it offers the best hope of a humane science—one that avoids distorting our diverse human natures into particular and narrow caricatures, but also one that respects and emphasizes the value of theoretically guided empirical inquiry as one of the best hopes of humankind for creating a better world. In these concluding pages, I try to explain why I hold this conviction.

The Significance of Symbols

Symbolic interactionists seldom tire of pointing out that it is the capacity for symbolic communication that endows human beings with their distinctively human capabilities. Symbols enable us to name the objects and situations that we confront and then take useful, adaptive action in or toward them. Our symbols name a complex social and physical world, one that is as much abstract and therefore "unseen" as it is material. Moreover, they expand the framework of space and time within which humans live, enabling us to remember the past and anticipate the future and to respond to real or imagined events at a considerable distance as well as those close at hand. Symbols also increase both the capacity and the necessity for social cooperation. In the course of human evolution, they fostered more precise communication and at the same time sped us on a course in which the social world became the necessary source of both individual learning and the satisfaction of individual needs. Most dramatically of all, symbols give rise to the consciousness of self by making it possible for human beings to become objects of their own experience and action. These consequences of using symbols shape our human natures, both as participants in everyday life and in that particular contemporary way of being we call "social science."

Human beings share with all other living creatures the propensity to survive in the world in which they find themselves. Their "prime directive" (to borrow a phrase from the contemporary version of *Star Trek*) seems to be to engage their environment actively, to struggle with it, and to achieve such mastery over it as they can in order to stay alive. The world with which they struggle is a complex one, however. It is a world that is, in some ways, far more challenging than that faced by other creatures. It is one that encompasses not only immediately present situations and stimuli to which people must respond but also distant and imaginary ones. We are stimulated to act not only by problems or opportunities we can see but also by those we cannot see and can only imagine. Thus, a real threat or insult from another human being prompts us to respond, but so does an imagined slight. The smell of a fresh-baked loaf of bread on a winter day stimulates our hunger, but so also may the imagined applause of one's peers for an accomplishment that still lies in the future. We throw ourselves into such concrete tasks as baking bread or writing books, as well as into more abstract and elusive ones such as "loving" or "doing our duty."

To be a symbol-using creature who is free to range in fact and imagination across wide expanses of space and time, and to respond to the imagined as if it were real, is to gain considerable freedom from determination by the surrounding world. Faced with immediate problems or challenges, human beings do not need to respond only in terms of the objects that are at hand (nor need they always respond immediately) but can instead think of alternative courses of action and the tools with which to accomplish them. We can choose to bide our time and respond to a real or imagined insult at some later time; we can even choose to disregard an insult by thinking of it as unintended. We can have fantasies of future success or anxieties about whether we will ever achieve it, but we can also channel fantasy and anxiety into constructive actions that will help us get what we imagine we want. We can transform the merely biological act of eating bread into an act of cooperation or emotional solidarity with others.

Symbol-using creatures can do these things because they act toward *objects* rather than merely in response to stimuli. Before we human beings can act toward the world, we must name it; that is, we must attach significance to the stimuli that confront us at any given time and we must formulate objects toward which we subsequently act. "I don't get mad, I get even," we may tell someone who has injured us. We transform images of success and applause into plans of action, and then we undertake these plans as a way of finding success or fulfillment or whatever object we have named as our goal. We say to others, "Let's share this meal and celebrate being together." The very fact that we can name the world toward which we act opens myriad possibilities of action toward it.

Yet, naming the world in order to act toward it is not merely something we human beings *can* do, it is something we *must* do, for much of the time we have little or no choice in the matter. Human beings are not mere biological creatures with a fixed set of behavioral capabilities, a limited number of instincts, and the comfort of learning a relatively fixed repertoire of conduct that will enable us to cope with a relatively stable environment. We live in a cultural world that is itself a human creation. We live in a world of names we have created and used. We live amidst complexities of meaning and of social organization that both rest on our capacity to use symbols and that are the result of hundreds of centuries of our actual use of them. Although we surely rely on habit for a great many of our everyday responses—how could we ever act at all if we had to deliberate about everything?—we nonetheless must frequently interpret and name events that confront us if we are to act successfully toward them. We must recognize an insult as such if we are to decide how best to answer it; we pursue an ambition by naming our goal and continually reminding ourselves of it. Human beings are, in short, *required* to interpret the world in order to act in it. Life confronts human beings with problems and opportunities, and in order to solve the former and take advantage of the latter, they must give them meaning. Moreover, a creature who must find meaning in events in order to act is, in a sense, *driven* to find meaning. We construct meaning in order to solve problems, but we also sometimes look for meaning, even where it does not exist, because it is in our symbolic nature to look for it. The quest for meaning enables us to adapt, but sometimes it also makes us crazy.

What we know—as individuals and as participants in social life—arises out of our individual and collective efforts to find meaning as we try to solve the problems and to utilize the opportunities that the environment presents to us. For our individual and collective capacity to discover useful meaning—that is, to interpret or name problems and opportunities and the objects we will use to confront them—depends on what we *know*. The members of any given society share a considerable body of socially created knowledge that has proven useful in solving the problems and meeting the opportunities they have repeatedly faced. Each individual masters a portion of this knowledge and applies it in the particular circumstances with which he or she is confronted. In either case, knowledge of all kinds—theoretical as well as applied, general as well as particular—has a highly practical character. Human beings are problem-solving creatures driven to create practical knowledge.

We are also intensely social creatures. Having created a complex symbolic world, we human beings inhabit it together. We depend on one another to learn what we must know in order to adapt to the world and solve the problems it throws at us. We can survive infancy and the extended period during which we have little or no capacity to take care of ourselves only because we live in the company of and are cared for by others of our kind. Although many other animals are social and their offspring must learn a great deal from them in order to survive in their world, we humans have magnified and intensified our social natures through our dependence on symbols. We not only must learn how to respond to and act successfully or adaptively in the world in which we live, but we must also learn a great deal about that complex, abstract, and often distant or invisible world. We must learn a host of names for material and abstract objects; we must learn a cognitive map of the social relations in which we ourselves are implicated and on which we depend; and we must learn both the names of the things we can see and the invisible things associated with names we hear but for which there are no concrete referents.

Our intensive sociality has two consequences that bear particularly on our understanding of the nature of knowledge. First, the stock of knowledge accumulated by a society constrains the way its individual members know their world. The individual's knowledge depends on the social stock of knowledge and its distribution in any given society. Second, our human sociality and our socially created knowledge open up the possibility—though they certainly do not make inevitable—that we can discover the ways in which our participation in human life constrains what we know and can be.

Little question exists that the knowledge we human beings acquire as members of a society constrains the ways we can imagine the world and respond to its problems and opportunities. This is so, first, because our ways of knowing the world inevitably incline us to notice some things and fail to see others. If we collectively "know" that people either succeed or fail in life according to their abilities and their willingness to work hard, then we will view those who succeed as industrious and those who fail as lazy, and we will probably not even recognize the existence of obstacles that make success difficult for some people. If we "know" that people commit crimes because they have been denied legitimate opportunities for success, then we may not see that some individuals may find the opportunities and excitements of crime to be greater than those of more legitimate forms of activity could ever be. Our everyday, socially shared knowledge of the social world is a basis for blindness as well as for insight into its operation.

This is essentially what George H. Mead meant when he argued that we grasp what is problematic in social life over and against the background of that which is not problematic. Our grasp of problems—of others' actions that may be insulting or threatening or of their apparent failure to work as hard as we think they should—is always formulated relative to ideas, beliefs, and other forms of knowledge that we think are secure. When we attempt to create new knowledge in an effort to deal with some problem, we do it by relying on what we already know and understand. There is really no escape from this fact, for we cannot question everything at once or make everything problematic at once. Human beings need some secure place to stand when they try to solve the problems that confront them, and that place is provided by the knowledge they feel they can take securely for granted.

Moreover, much of what we know and understand is effectively hidden from us because it is embedded in the language we speak and therefore in the names we are prepared to attach to objects in our world. Contemporary Americans, for example, respond to some problematic forms of behavior by calling them "alcoholism," by which they mean a kind of disease in which the victim finds it impossible to control his or her consumption of alcoholic beverages, with frequently destructive consequences for the individual and for those around him or her. Embedded in the word *alcoholism* is a more complex set of attitudes toward the "alcoholic," attitudes of which we are scarcely aware when we use the term, even though they dispose us to act toward that person in specific ways. That is, the term inclines us to look for "treatment" and to apply to this "disease" the same assumptions we might apply to any disease—namely, that steps can be taken to control it, if not to cure it. Once we learn and routinely use a set of terms to describe the world, the actions we can take are in many ways constrained by the words, the objects they denote, and the forms of action these objects invite.

Moreover, the words we use to designate the objects in our environment did not necessarily arise out of a collective and democratic process in which everybody participated equally. We speak of "alcoholism" not because the term more or less spontaneously arose out of various human efforts to cope with a perceived problem by giving it a name and an interpretation. Rather, we think of the excessive consumption of alcoholic beverages as a "disease" essentially because a variety of people, including physicians, have convinced us that it is a disease. Medicine, with its conceptions of disease and cure, is a general way of "knowing" the world, and, in the course of the last century or so, its practitioners and their allies have employed it to think about a wider variety of phenomena than merely the illnesses and infirmities of the body. A variety of individual and social problems have been medicalized, including alcoholism, drug use, and many other behavioral difficulties and problems of adjustment. Mental illness is one of the more obvious illustrations of how the medical model of human conduct and problems has been extended.

As these illustrations suggest, what people "know" is subject to influence by those who have an interest in having people "know" the world in a particular way. The medical establishment has power over us because we have come to share their ways of knowing the body and its various problems. Likewise, psychologists and psychiatrists exercise power over us because we have been persuaded to think of our behavior in the language they provide. Contemporary people worry about their self-esteem or pursue self-actualization because they have "learned" from psychologists that these are real and important phenomena. In a similar vein—but with far deeper penetration of our consciousness and more serious consequences for our behavior—our "knowledge" of what is natural or possible for men as compared with women, or black-skinned people as opposed to white- or yellow- or brown-skinned people, or those who are poor versus those who are middle class, reflects a variety of ways in which we have been taught to regard, understand, and speak about the social world and our own place in it.

No one should underestimate the extent to which our "knowledge" of the social world is also "ignorance" of it, or the degree to which particular social classes, professions, or organizations exert unseen power by shaping the very language with which we grasp ourselves and the social world in which we live. Such forms of "power" are far more subtle than the exercise of naked force. One ordinarily has no difficulty knowing when one is being forcefully conscripted into military service, or when one lacks the wherewithal to purchase a decent place to live or food for one's family, or when one is denied opportunities solely because of one's color or gender. But when we "know" that women are "emotional" or that the care of children is their sole "natural" vocation, we are powerfully constrained in our actions, but in a way that is more diffuse and far less obvious.

Another side to this coin provides a basis for at least some optimism about the capacity of human beings to avoid being duped. Human beings are capable of "knowing" their world as one in which they may be deceived; they can make their secure knowledge itself problematic and ask whether what they take for granted ought not to be. To put this another way, we human beings seem to be capable of thinking about ourselves as the potential victims of our own assumptions as well as of the "knowledge" that various others would have us possess in order to foster their interests. If we are susceptible to influence by professionals bent on extending their influence and prestige by shaping the way we solve problems and the kind of help we seek in doing so, we are also capable of seeing and talking about that very susceptibility.

Human beings have the capacity to make our own "knowledge" of the world problematic partly because the flow of problems that confronts us is never ending. Although it may be true that in the distant past, culture and society changed at a glacial pace, in the contemporary world, things seem to happen more quickly. We seem no sooner to recognize and formulate a social problem than another comes along; actions we take to solve one problem have unanticipated consequences, and today's solution thus becomes tomorrow's problem. No human society on the face of the earth has ever been in sufficient stable equilibrium with its human and material environment that it achieved a stable and finite body of "knowledge" that could definitively solve all its problems. The contemporary human condition especially seems to be one of ceaseless change with an unending parade of problems. Thus, perhaps more now than at any other time in history, everything we "know" can be in question, subject to revision, open to doubt.

There is another, more fundamental reason why human beings have the capacity not only to develop new knowledge about the world but also to become conscious of the limits of knowledge. Human beings are creatures with *selves*. Thoroughly social creatures, permeated by socially created and controlled knowledge, we are nonetheless creatures with individual self-consciousness. This fact has enormous implications for both knowing and acting.

The concept of the individual human being developed by George Herbert Mead, and to a large extent shared by his friend and mentor John Dewey, is distinctive in its ability to portray both the tension and the fine balance between the individual and the social world. On the one hand, this view of the person makes the self a product of the social order. Mead explains the emergence of individual self-consciousness as a product of membership and participation in the social world. We have consciousness of self because we are born into the stream of social life and come to share its names and knowledge and apply them to ourselves. We learn to see ourselves as others see us, and we do so by adopting the language and the organized social perspectives made available in the social world around us. We seem to be thoroughly social creatures.

On the other hand, symbolic interactionism also views the self as a social force in its own right. Socialization endows the individual with the capacity to cooperate in social acts with others, but it does not create an automaton who unfailingly reproduces the meanings and actions he or she has been taught. Joint actions—handshakes, cocktail parties, social movements, wars, and so on—exist because individual actors who share a conception of what they are doing come together and assemble their individual contributions into a social whole. But it is the *individual* who acts, who does the interpreting, naming, and coordinating that permits joint actions to proceed or that disrupts and derails them. To have a self, therefore, is not merely to be a thoroughly programmed agent of society, but also, just as importantly, to be one who chooses, who decides, who exerts control over his or her own conduct and that of others.

One important consequence of the existence of a self, then, is that it endows the individual actor with the capacity to recognize and act in the pursuit of his or her self-interest and to conceive of himself or herself in opposition to the social world and not just as dependent on it. When symbolic interactionists say that the self is a social object, they imply not only that we constitute this object by seeing it and acting toward it from the imagined perspectives of others but also that we come to value this object and to feel that we own it and must protect it. The self is something we create and sustain jointly with others, and in that sense its "locus" is not strictly speaking within the body or brain but in the social world that surrounds us, nourishes us, and often challenges us. Still, it is the particular living and breathing organism who lies at the center of this social world, who experiences impulses, and who exerts control over his or her conduct. Indeed, the influence of the surrounding social world on us depends on our *imagination* of it; when we engage in role taking in an effort to form our conduct, we respond to our imaginations of others and our interpretations of their words and deeds. There is, in short, a sentient being who is as much responsible for the creation of the self as is the surrounding social world.

Moreover, it is the individual who experiences the problematic situation and who initiates the knowing and problem solving. The sense that a situation is problematic, that there is something that needs to be done, that there is some gap in knowledge or understanding that needs to be filled arises first in the *individual* mind. Human conduct, including efforts to confront and overcome problematic situations, is thoroughly a social affair because it is based on shared assumptions and perspectives, shared knowledge, and some form of social coordination (whether cooperative, competitive, or conflictful). Yet, this intensely social and problem-solving conduct ultimately rests on what transpires within the single individual as much as on what transpires between individuals. Through their capacity to rebel, to innovate, to resist social influences, and to apply social knowledge creatively in an effort to solve problems, individuals make felt their influence on the social world.

Although this reading of Mead is often slighted in favor of one that merely emphasizes the social nature of human beings, I believe his social theory encourages us to see the individual and the society as always in a potential state of tension and the individual as the potential innovator, inventor, and creator of new forms of conduct. In the last analysis, every human act begins with an impulse over which the person has no control and that often takes the person by surprise. To be capable of self-consciousness is to have the ability to subjugate this impulse to social demands, and that is perhaps what we most typically do. A creature with a self can also see the possible value of this impulse, however, both to self and to others, and allow it to be completed in behavior.

The Uses of Knowledge

The interactionist conception of human beings and of the way they know themselves and their social world implies a way of viewing the knowledge of social science. Although a full account of how symbolic interactionists study the social world, what they feel they may learn about it, and what they think they and others ought to do with this knowledge would fill more than this chapter, I can outline a few principles that offer useful guidelines.

First, human beings seek knowledge in order to solve problems, and the test of knowledge—of its truth—lies in its practical consequences for our lives. The quest for knowledge of any kind is no mere idle pastime that we undertake because we have nothing else to occupy our time. The effort to know arises in those situations where for one reason or another something interferes with our effort to do something. This statement is as true of scientific knowledge as it is of everyday affairs, and it is as true of our quest for religious or philosophical knowledge as of the search for practical understanding. We seek to know in order to act successfully in our world, and we believe we have achieved truth when we are able to do so.

This pragmatic conception of truth seems obvious when we apply it to the knowledge we seek and use in our everyday lives, but perhaps not so obvious when we apply it to such spheres as religion or literature. One wants to learn about how an automobile works, for example, so that one can drive it well enough to get a driver's license and then put the car to use. If the car fails to start, one wants to learn what is wrong with it so that one can start it again as quickly as possible. But in what sense does religious doctrine constitute practical knowledge? Those who are committed to a particular version of religious truth probably prefer to think of religion as a matter of faith or of revelation from a supernatural being, not as something that exists to solve practical problems. In addition, many who write novels would perhaps say that their stories express truths about the human condition but would deny that they write them to solve particular problems.

Yet, religion and literature—and, for that matter, music and art—are ways of "knowing" the world, and people act on the basis of the knowledge these disciplines produce. Religious faith usually dictates that people act in certain ways. It may do so through an explicit set of commandments, whether the Ten Commandments of the Jewish and Christian Bibles or the larger set of specific directives contained in the Book of Leviticus and still followed scrupulously by observant Orthodox Jews. Those who believe such "truths" attempt to act on the basis of them. Religious beliefs may also indirectly influence conduct. Early followers of the Swiss theologian John Calvin (whose contemporary religious descendants include Baptists) believed that God had preordained that some people would find salvation in the hereafter, whereas others were doomed to eternal damnation and could do nothing to be saved. Such beliefs make people anxious about their eventual fate—each person wonders whether he or she is among the elect who are predestined for salvation or those unfortunates who will burn in Hell. The Calvinists also believed that even though there was nothing one could do in order to earn salvation, one's success in earthly pursuits nevertheless could be interpreted as a sign that one was among the elect. The result was indirectly to encourage efforts to succeed in worldly pursuits, for in doing so one could find reassurance that God had decided that one would spend eternity in heaven. Religious forms of "knowledge" thus form grounds for action just as much as more practical forms; their "truth" likewise depends on their capacity to promote action.

What about science itself? Does it also represent a quest for practical knowledge? Clearly, the birth of contemporary scientific inquiry during the seventeenth century in England and Europe was stimulated in part by considerations associated with the rise of industry, warfare, and other practical concerns. In the contemporary world, the practical consequences of scientific knowledge are visible everywhere. Modern technologies are grounded in scientific discoveries. Although much science is conducted without any particular interest in or concern for the immediate practical uses of the knowledge that might be gained, even theoretical inquiries are "practical" in the sense that they attempt to organize and make sense of accumulated scientific discoveries. Even such theoretical endeavors as the effort by physicists to create a general theory of the universe are motivated by an effort to solve a problem. The problem is a highly abstract one—how to make sense of complex and often contradictory data about the universe—but it is a problem, nonetheless, and the practical value of a theory is precisely that it makes sense of those data. A theory is true to the extent that and so long as it continues to make sense of the data.

Social science likewise arose as a response to problems. As industrialization transformed human societies in the eighteenth and especially the nineteenth centuries, old patterns of human life were disrupted and new ones were created. Sociology, in particular, evolved in the late nineteenth and early twentieth centuries in the United States in an effort to understand and cope with the social problems associated with industrialization, the growth of cities, and large-scale immigration from other countries. Throughout this century, sociologists have pursued their discipline not only in an effort to answer questions raised by their own research and theories but also in an effort to contribute in a practical way to the solution of social problems.

The question, then, is how a symbolic interactionist social psychology seeks to make a practical contribution to human affairs. What does this approach offer to those who study it and grasp its view of the social world?

Although in principle I think symbolic interactionism can contribute to the solution of problems in a variety of ways, here I want to advance the idea that an important component of its contribution involves the teaching and learning that goes on (or should) in colleges and universities. Symbolic interactionism proposes a method for the empirical study of social life; it provides a perspective on the social world. Its method and perspective are valuable not merely because of any specific solutions to social problems they may produce but also, more importantly, because they offer a different platform from which each of us can understand our own lives and those of others.

The special method that symbolic interactionism recommends is participant observation, so named because the social scientist is both an observer of some sphere of social life and, in some way, a participant in it. Symbolic interactionists believe that we cannot study the social world from a distance, and that if we want to examine and understand it, we must do so at close hand. The reason, of course, lies in the interactionist view of conduct as dependent on meanings. If people form their conduct on the basis of meaning as they interact with one another, then one must grasp their meanings in order to explain why they act as they act. We must discover what lies on the minds of those whose conduct we would scrutinize. Doing so requires us to interact with them, to live cheek by jowl in their worlds, at least for a time, in order to see how and why they define situations, make and take roles, and interpret their worlds as they do. Symbolic interactionism encourages its practitioners and their readers alike to enter into the worlds of those whose lives they would understand.

The special perspective of symbolic interactionism I have in mind here is its capacity to help people understand not only the lives and perspectives of others but also the ways in which their own individual lives are linked to the surrounding social world. Symbolic interactionism tries to reveal the social origins of the self, the nature of social constraints, and, crucially, the ways in which the social order depends on the actions of individuals with selves. It seeks to show how society forms individuals, how it limits individuals, and how it makes individuals what they are. At the same time it portrays human actors who are capable of changing the very social order that has formed them.

Both the method and the perspective of symbolic interactionism, in my view, foster the capacity to appreciate the diversity of the world we live in and the common humanity that unites all of us. To study the worlds of others by entering them and constructing, as best we can, an account of their members' lives and problems is to help convey a sense of what it means to be human in the many ways it is possible to be human. We study the lives of others—of various minorities and majorities, of women and men, of children and adults, of the oppressed and their oppressors—so that we may grasp the diversity of human life and, in grasping it, perhaps learn to take a somewhat more humble and less chauvinistic stance toward our own lives. To study the worlds of others is to learn something of our own humanity as well as that of others. It is to learn that the world forms and shapes everyone, that problems that seem unique and private may also be the concerns of others, and that we have much in common as well as much that divides us.

No one can fully penetrate the social worlds that others have constructed and communicate a completely accurate or totally undistorted view to those who live outside. No one can fully grasp his or her own life experience in relation to the surrounding social world or communicate that experience fully to others. Neither are the worlds of others intellectually or emotionally accessible only to those who live there. To argue that no outsider can depict, or has any right to depict, the lives of any particular group of human beings—it seems to me—is to abandon any hope that human beings can live in both diversity and harmony. To argue, for example, that no man can possibly understand the world as a woman understands and lives it, or that Whites should never try to speak or write about the experiences of Blacks, is to say, in effect, that the barriers that divide one group from another are too great for understanding to pass between them.

Symbolic interactionism asserts that human beings share a social psychology—our dependence on symbols and our distinctive capacity for selfhood—and that we can transcend those social and cultural barriers. One way of transcending them is to understand that they exist, to attempt to depict life behind those barriers, and to show how each of us, no matter where or how we live, participates in a common humanity. The practical value of social psychology, then, lies partly in its capacity to reveal this common humanity through research and analysis. To act on the basis of this knowledge is to increase our individual capacity to appreciate diversity and to grasp our own dependence on and responsibility for the social world in which we live.

The second principle is that any form of knowledge—everyday knowledge, religious knowledge, scientific knowledge—is partial and tentative. In our everyday lives, we act on the basis of what we know about driving cars or raising children and tend to believe that we can generally regard such knowledge as sure and certain. To one degree or another, however, we are prepared to question that knowledge and learn new ways of behaving. In matters of religious beliefs, we are perhaps more likely to cling to a faith once we have arrived at it; certainly those whose whole lives are invested in a particular religious faith will cling to that faith with particular conviction. Even religious faith can wear thin for some people—the precepts of their religion seem to lead them astray, they find their faith unsatisfying, or another faith becomes more appealing—and so they seek a new faith or perhaps discard the idea of religion entirely. Furthermore, we approach scientific knowledge particularly with the idea that it is always tentative and subject to revision. Scientific knowledge is based on the belief that the ultimate test of truth is a process of empirical inquiry in which hypotheses and theories are tested against the real world. Indeed, the ideal of scientific procedure is to look for instances in the world that will contradict a hypothesis. In that sense, it differs from other forms of human knowledge, since it intentionally questions its own validity and always looks for evidence that it might be in error.

Clearly, the rigor and care with which human beings scrutinize their knowledge and the standards they apply in evaluating it vary among different forms of knowledge. In everyday life, we are concerned with the immediate practical results of what we do. We are not interested in assembling the various bits and pieces of our practical understanding of the world into a coherent, meaningful system. We are content to use a more fragmented approach, relying on bits and pieces of knowledge about how to drive cars, discipline children, bake cakes, conduct weddings, and perform the countless important tasks of everyday life. We are very empirical in our approach—we want knowledge that works—but not very theoretical. In matters of religious faith or philosophical belief, we may be considerably more theoretical—we want our various beliefs to fit together in some coherent way, to make sense as a general way of looking at the world. We are not very empirical, however, in matters of religion—we do not make systematic observations of the world to test our religious beliefs, but rely more or less on faith that what we believe will ultimately turn out to be true. In matters of science, we tend to be both theoretical and empirical; we want to generalize about reality, to create theories that will explain the world, to form hypotheses about the world, and to test these hypotheses against our empirical observations.

Symbolic interactionists believe that the tentative and problem-centered character of human knowledge means that a final or complete body of knowledge will never exist. We do not believe that it is possible to assemble a picture of the natural or the social world that is in every way so complete, final, and total that no additional knowledge can be sought or gained. Rather, because new problems continue to confront us, we must continue to grapple with the world and seek new knowledge of it. As a result, the body of knowledge we possess is always changing; old "truths" are continually being shed as they cease to work and new "truths" are discovered as we confront new problems. No symbolic interactionist would argue that scientific knowledge progressively assembles a more complete picture of the world and that doing science of any kind is therefore like putting together the pieces of a jigsaw puzzle. Rather, the shape of the puzzle keeps changing as we approach it from first one angle and then another; it is never complete.

Still, interactionists believe that some knowledge is better than none, especially if that knowledge is a result of the empirical study of the social world based on verifiable, public methods of inquiry that can be understood by and checked by others. Symbolic interactionism yields knowledge of social worlds and social processes that is open to empirical verification and revision. This knowledge—of how others conspire to hide their identities from us or to manipulate us, of the social sources of self-esteem, or of the way individual transactions in the automobile business are shaped by industrywide practices— holds no panaceas for the solution of social problems. The knowledge is short term and may have to be revised. Still, it is knowledge and does provide us with some basis for acting in the world in which we find ourselves and for solving the problems that arise within it.

Symbolic interactionists believe that empirical knowledge is a good thing. They believe that empirical knowledge is valuable to have despite the fact that such knowledge

is never complete or perfect and never can be. They hold no illusion that the mere possession of knowledge can compel others to yield to its truths. Knowing that the course of the
transaction in which an individual buys a used car has been influenced by a chain of connections at one end of which lies a powerful industry and at the other end of which, a weak
consumer will not necessarily get that individual a better price for the car. Nor will that
knowledge by itself bring about a change in the way the industry acts. Nonetheless, it
seems worth betting that knowing is better than not knowing in this situation, and that with
such knowledge the individual is more likely to be able to take effective actions. A little
knowledge is potentially a very useful thing—not necessarily, or even typically, a dangerous thing.

A third principle is that our knowledge of reality shapes that reality. We human
beings seek knowledge in order to solve problems and then act on the basis of what we
learn. Our actions, in turn, shape or influence the conditions under which we live. Symbolic interactionists believe that the relationship between human beings and their world is
one of mutual determination—the environment, social or material, influences and constrains us, but our actions toward it also influence or shape it. If this is so, then in a general
sense what we "know" about the world influences the "reality" of that world.

Perhaps an example will clarify this idea and show why it is important. Contemporary Americans are faced with the apparent fact that their schools do not do as good
a job as they would like in educating many children. Standardized test scores have
declined, many students do not read at grade level, and competence in science and math
seems lower than educators and parents feel it should be. A variety of explanations of
this state of affairs—and ways of changing it—have been proposed and debated. Much
emphasis has been placed, for example, on establishing national curriculum standards
and on holding schools accountable by periodically testing students. If schools are failing, the argument runs, it is because expectations of students are neither clear nor high
enough and because teachers and principals are not held to account for their schools'
failures.

Whatever the validity of this point of view, it has become established "knowledge"
and enshrined in legislation. Curricular standards have been created and periodic testing
regimes established. What effect does such "knowledge" have? Critics of these educational
reforms point out that where laws specify what must be taught to students at various grade
levels and in various subjects, considerable time and effort will be spent not only in revis-
ing lesson plans but also in documenting how they meet the standards. Teachers in some
states, for example, must justify in writing the connection between any given day's lesson
plan and the curricular standard it meets. This is a very time-consuming activity, but it produces at least the illusion that standards are being implemented. Likewise, critics argue
that periodic testing makes it likely that teachers will orient their lessons to the tests their
students will take rather than to developing a deep understanding of the subject matter. In
other words, they will teach students to do well on standardized tests, but not necessarily
do a better job teaching them to understand or use ideas. If teachers are successful in this
effort, test scores will likely rise, and the "knowledge" that testing promotes accountability
will be "confirmed."

Knowledge, then, has consequences, not only for the actions we take on the basis of
it but also for the nature of the world in which we live. Even as we create explanations of

problems, we provide people with a basis for acting to solve them as well as a way of perceiving their social world. Even as we seek to understand the motives on the basis of which people act, we provide them with motives for acting and with ways of understanding their own actions. When we seek to "know" the social world, therefore, we are not learning about a reality that is simply "out there," fixed and final. Rather, we are engaged in creating that reality even as we seek to know and understand it.

If scientific knowledge is tentative and at the same time so consequential, should we ever act on the basis of it? If we can never know anything with certainty, since what we know today is likely to be untrue or irrelevant tomorrow, then perhaps we ought to abandon any pretense at objective empirical inquiry. If the actions we take on the basis of what we think we know are likely to have consequences, many of which we cannot anticipate and may be quite different from what we intended, then perhaps we ought to do nothing out of fear of doing something wrong.

I can imagine no conclusions more inimical to what symbolic interactionism stands for. We do influence the social world when we study it and produce knowledge on the basis of which we and others act. Sometimes we are wrong or think we know more than we do. Yet, what alternative is there but to act as intelligently as we can on the basis of what we think we know? The symbolic interactionist approach to knowledge is a humble one. It recognizes that there may be many ways to truth and that each is prone to error. It grants that behind particular versions of truth there always lurk particular interests and unequal power to pursue them. Still, it believes empirical truth is worth pursuing, that we are worse off without it, and that the pursuit of such truth in the long run may offer the best hope of reconstructing a human world in which all can live in dignity and peace.

Much has occurred in the world since 1976, when I wrote these concluding words of the first edition of this book. Notwithstanding those changes, the rise and fall of various versions of utopia, and what seems to be an unrelenting attack on the values of Western enlightenment and the worth of social science both from within the academic world and without, I believe these ideas still hold true. Thus I close this chapter in much the same words as I have in each of the nine previous editions of this book.

Sociology promises, stated C. Wright Mills, "an understanding of the intimate realities of ourselves in connection with larger social realities."[1] What the sociological imagination promises, however, it does not easily deliver. If sociology and social psychology represent potential contributions to the advancement of human intelligence—and to the betterment of the human condition—they do so only if exercised. They are not storehouses of facts and formulas to be applied mechanically to human problems, but ways of looking at the reality of the human condition. As such, they are everyone's property and responsibility. They are a set of tools not only for those with power but also for those over whom it is exercised.

It is thus in the things individuals might do on the basis of its insights that I think the greatest value of social psychology lies. The only final advice an author can give is to urge readers to struggle with these ideas and to use them to good ends. That is not revolutionary advice; indeed, both revolutionaries and reformers will find it wanting, since it appears to hope that a better society can come about through the struggles of informed and educated people. In a world brimming with ideological movements whose leaders seek to impose their own utopias on the rest of us and with professional reformers who underestimate the magnitude of their task and think the world will easily yield to goodness, this is not popular advice. Still, the democratic ideal of informed people struggling with their world and its problems seems to me a good one, and this book has sought in a small way to contribute to it.

Endnote

1. C. Wright Mills, *The Sociological Imagination* (New York: Oxford University Press, 1959), p. 15.

Index